LIVING-ROOM

LIVING-ROOM MATSUNAGA-SAN

Keiko Iwashita

1

MATSUNAGA
SAN

LIVING-ROOM

Contents

room 1
– 3 –

room 2
– 53 –

room 3
– 95 –

room 4
– 133 –

MATSUNAGA

SAN

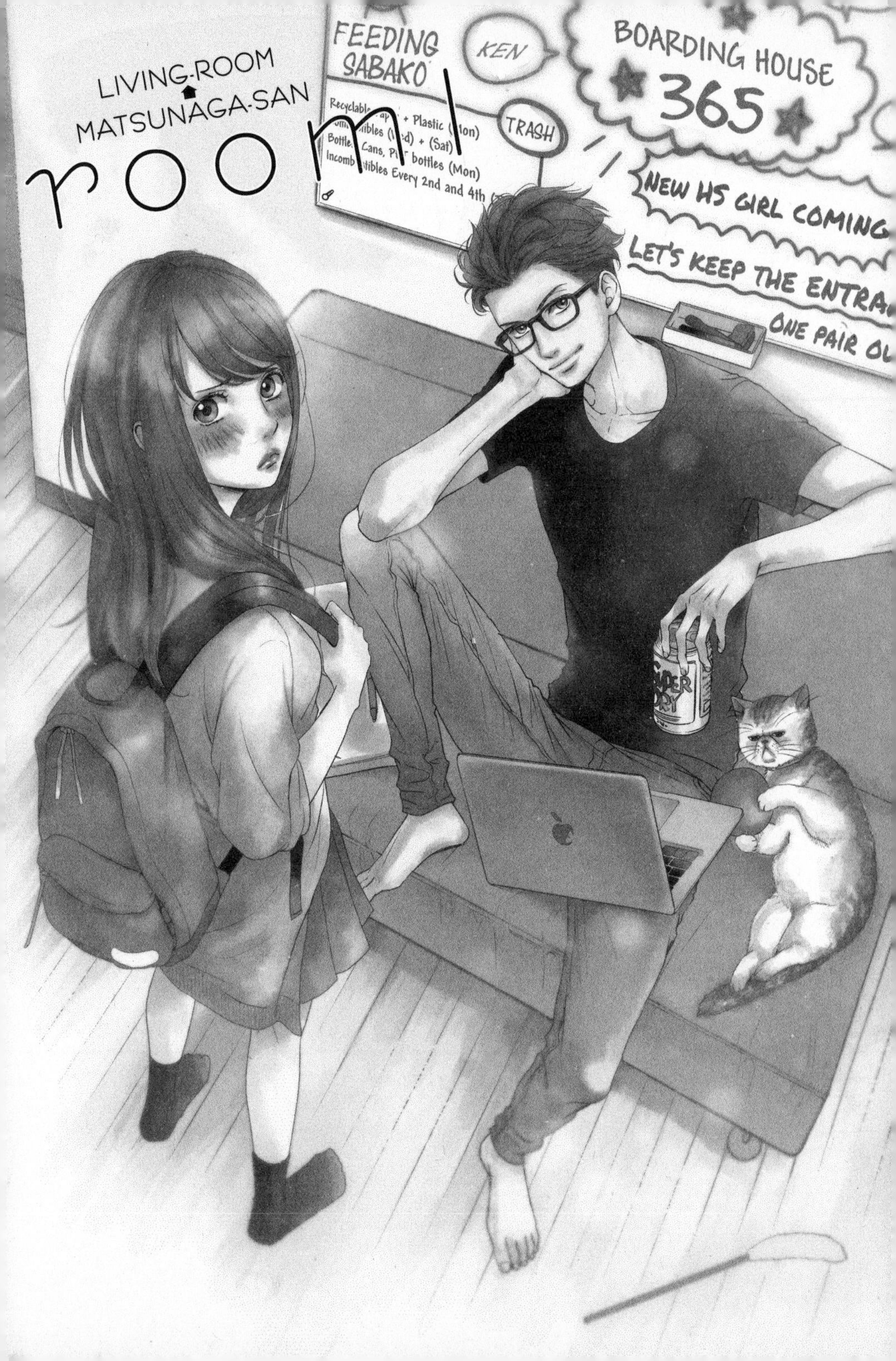
LIVING-ROOM MATSUNAGA-SAN
room
FEEDING SABAKO
KEN
TRASH
BOARDING HOUSE 365
NEW HS GIRL COMING
LET'S KEEP THE ENTRA
ONE PAIR O

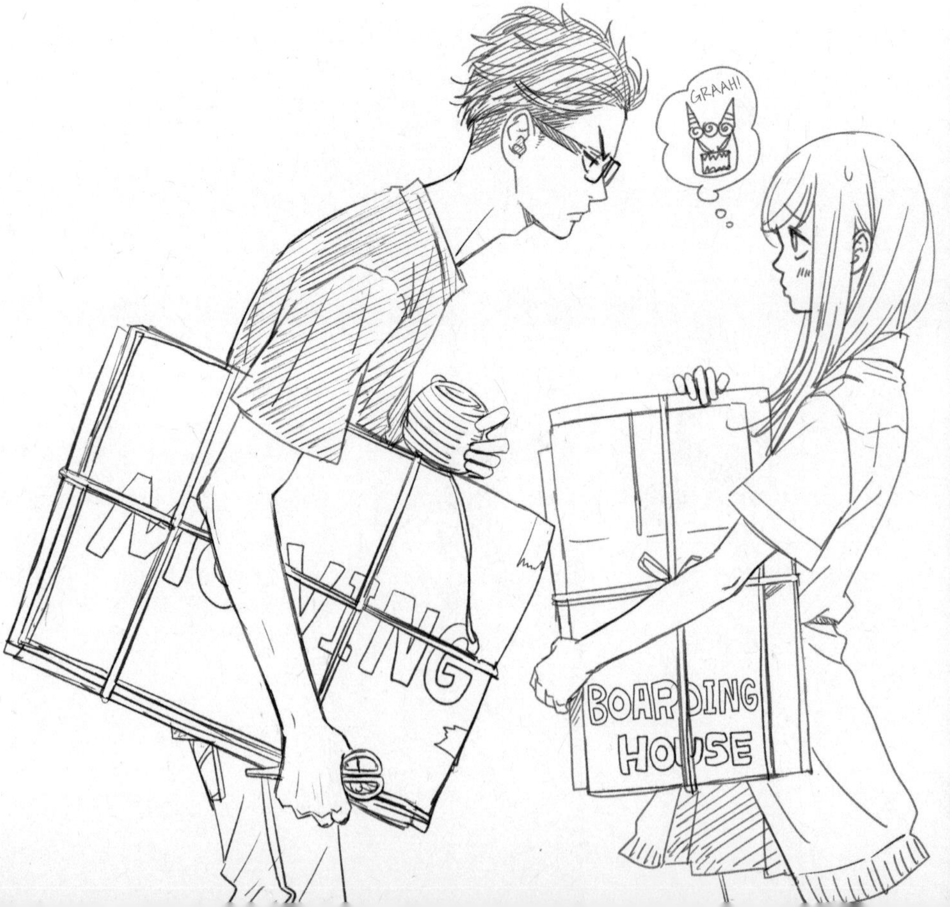
GRAAH!
BOARDING HOUSE

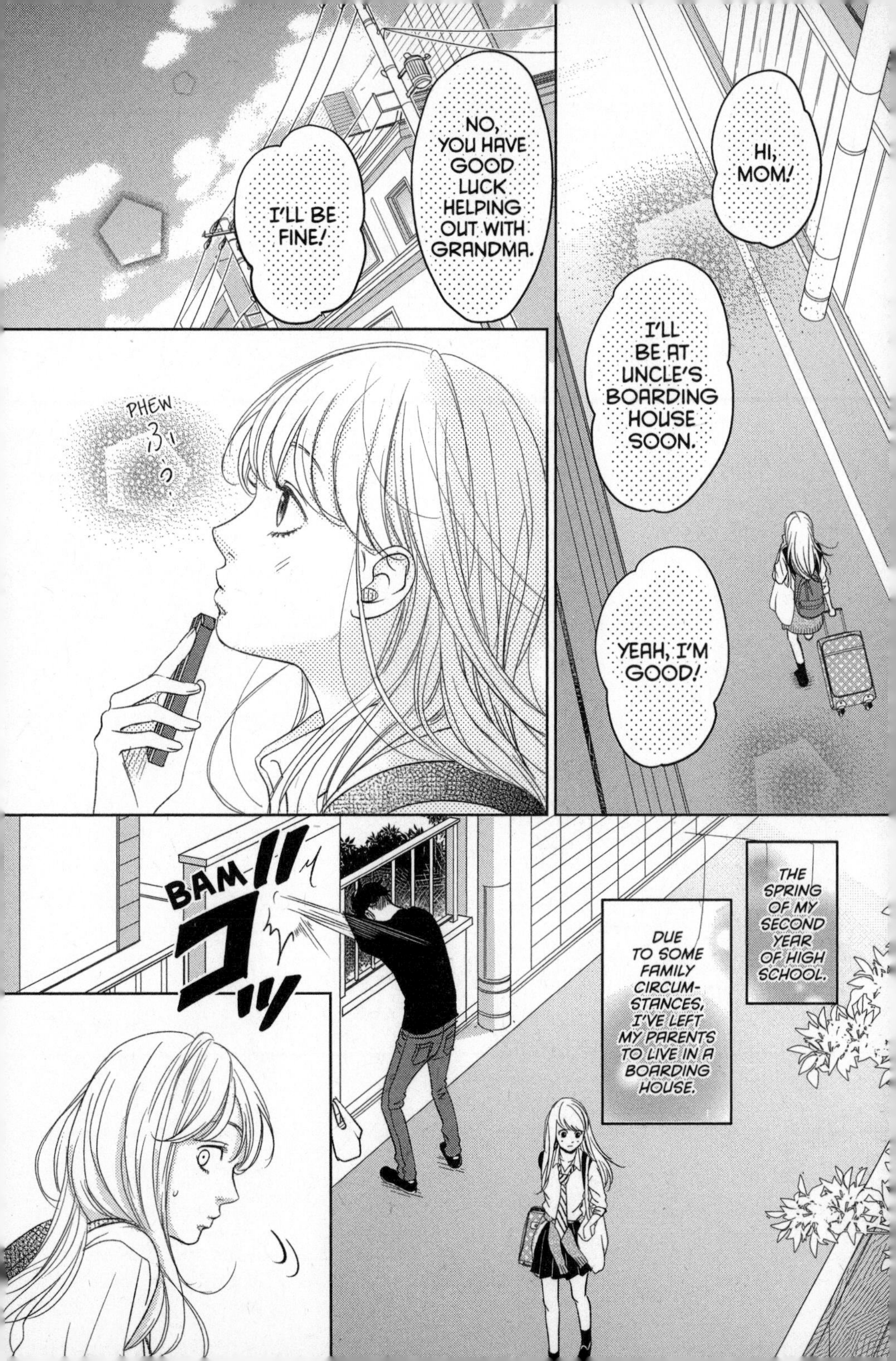
HI, MOM!
I'LL BE AT UNCLE'S BOARDING HOUSE SOON.
YEAH, I'M GOOD!
NO, YOU HAVE GOOD LUCK HELPING OUT WITH GRANDMA.
I'LL BE FINE!
PHEW
THE SPRING OF MY SECOND YEAR OF HIGH SCHOOL.
DUE TO SOME FAMILY CIRCUMSTANCES, I'VE LEFT MY PARENTS TO LIVE IN A BOARDING HOUSE.
BAM

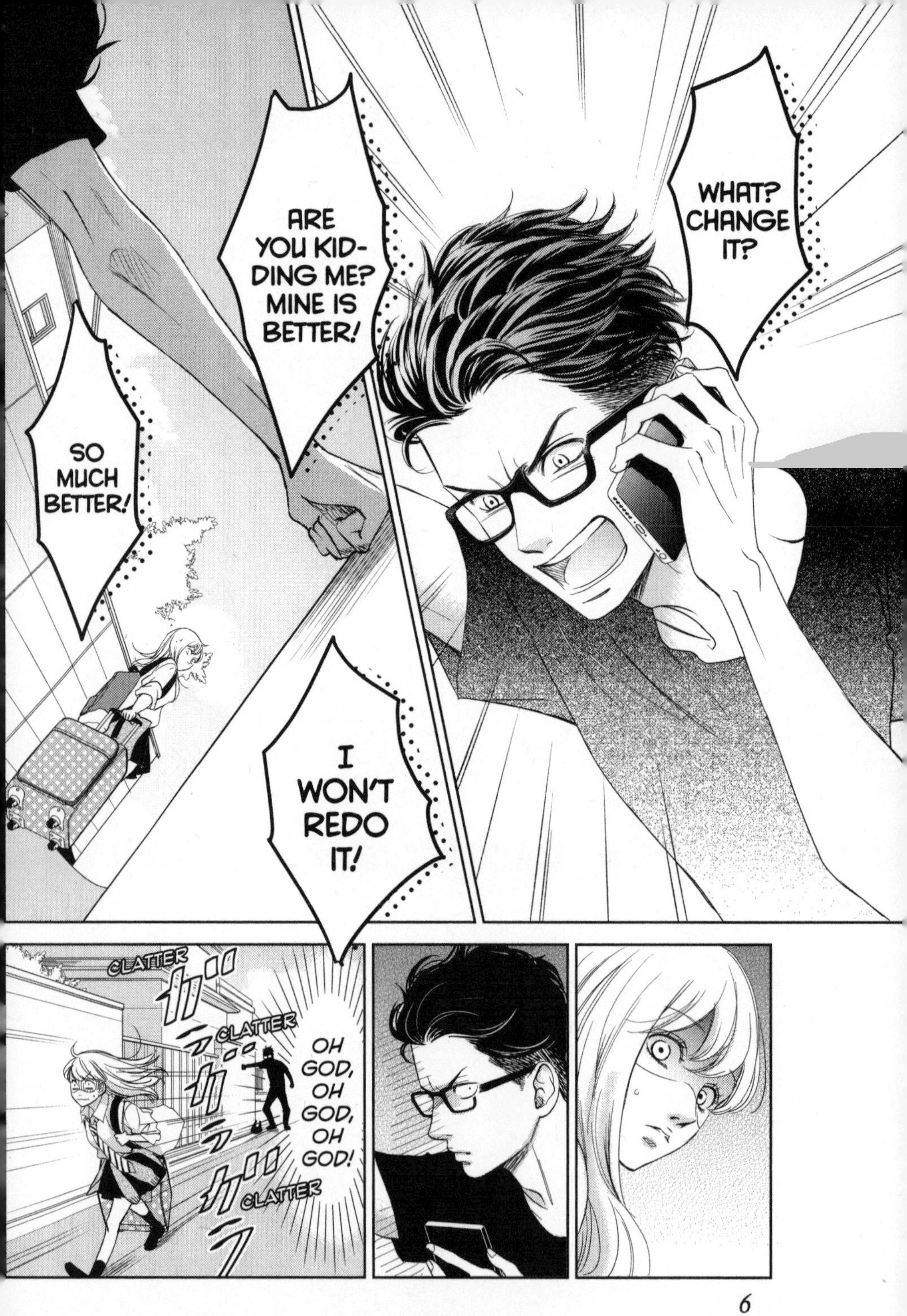
WHAT? CHANGE IT?
ARE YOU KID-DING ME? MINE IS BETTER!
SO MUCH BETTER!
I WON'T REDO IT!
CLATTER
CLATTER
OH GOD, OH GOD, OH GOD!
CLATTER

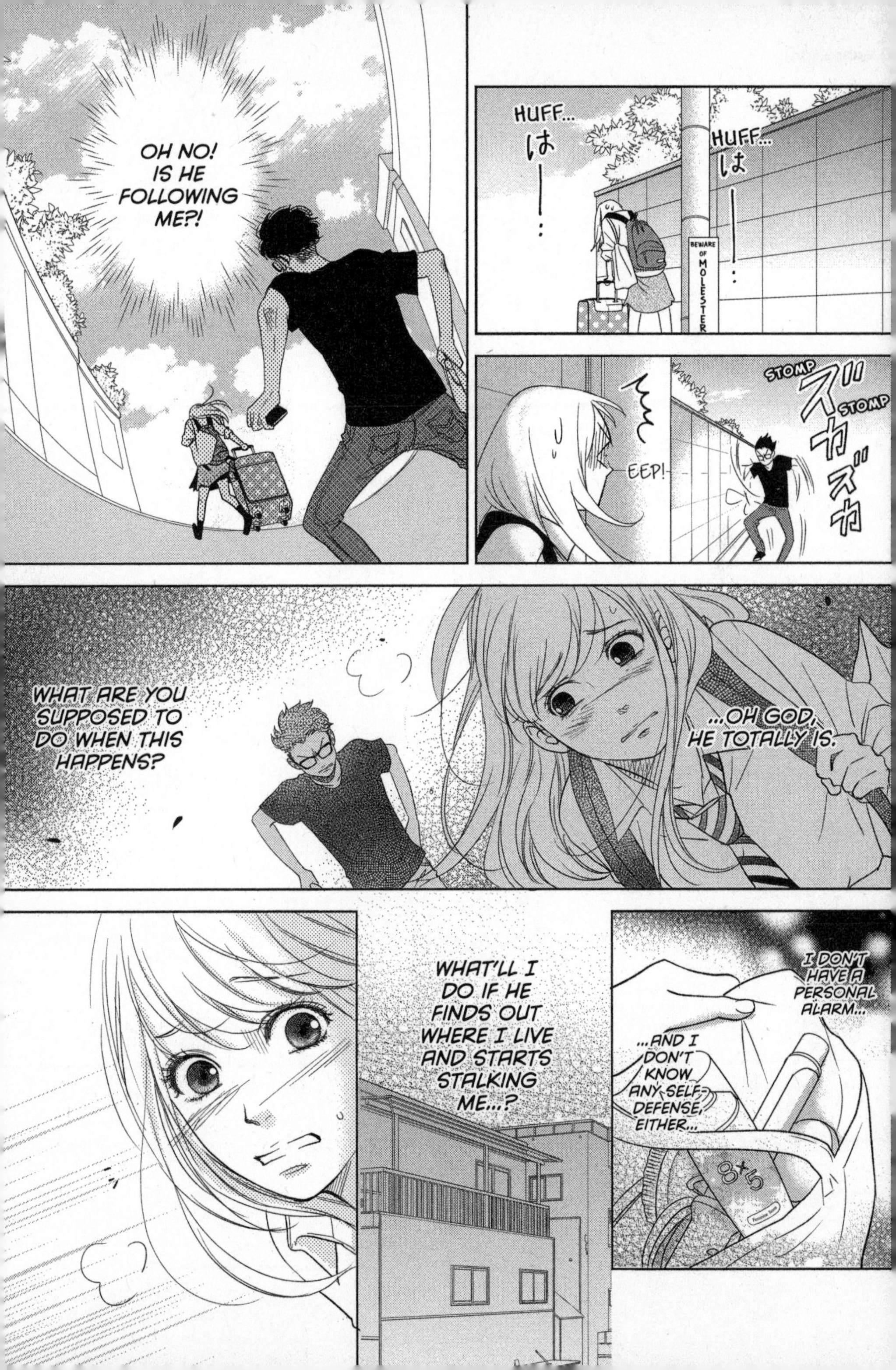

HUFF...
はー…
HUFF...
はー…
BEWARE OF MOLESTER
STOMP
ズカズカ
STOMP
EEP!
OH NO! IS HE FOLLOWING ME?!
...OH GOD, HE TOTALLY IS.
WHAT ARE YOU SUPPOSED TO DO WHEN THIS HAPPENS?
I DON'T HAVE A PERSONAL ALARM...
...AND I DON'T KNOW ANY SELF-DEFENSE, EITHER...
WHAT'LL I DO IF HE FINDS OUT WHERE I LIVE AND STARTS STALKING ME...?

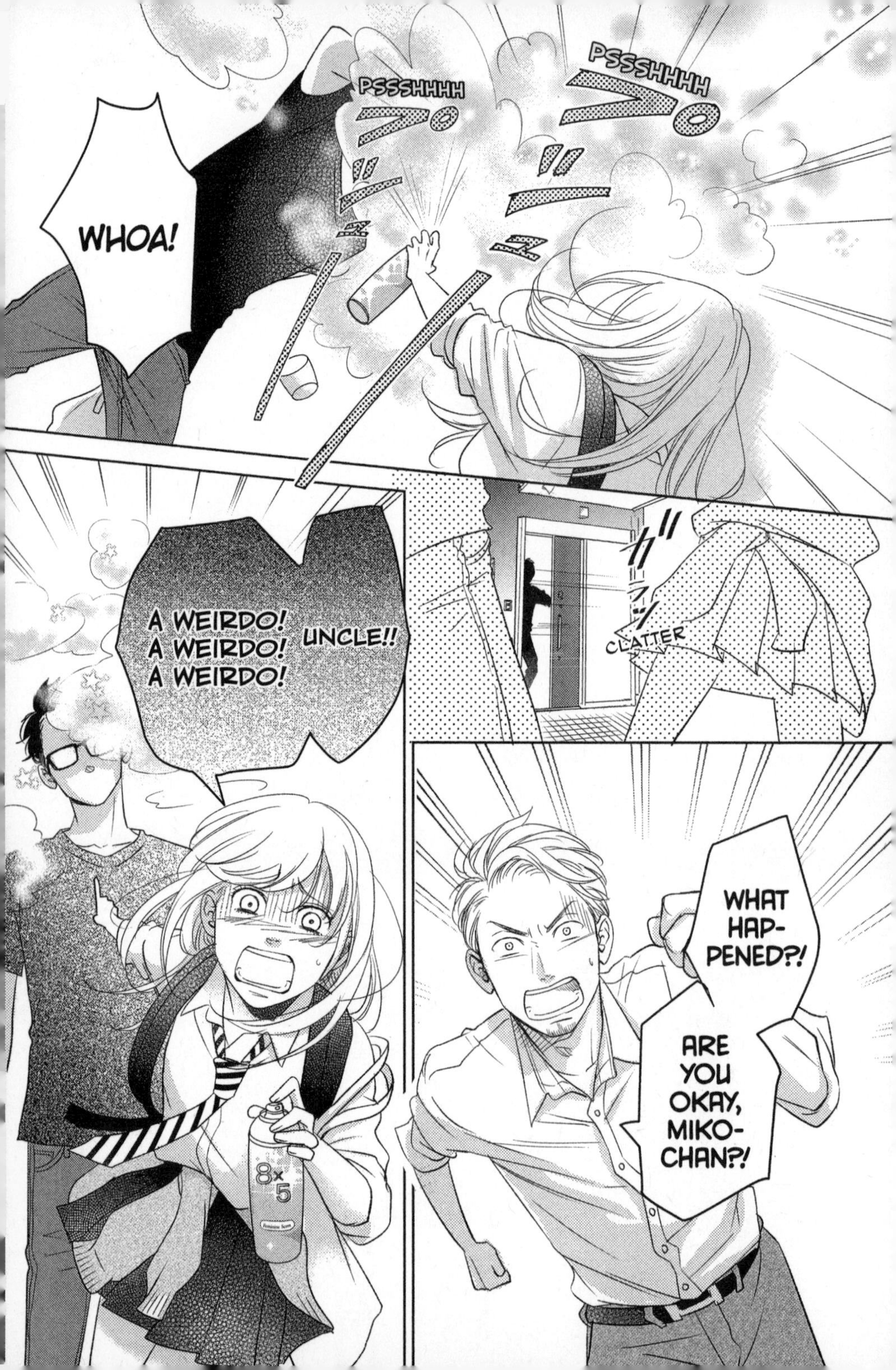
PSSSHHHH
PSSSHHHH
WHOA!
CLATTER
UNCLE!!
A WEIRDO! A WEIRDO! A WEIRDO!
WHAT HAP-PENED?!
ARE YOU OKAY, MIKO-CHAN?!

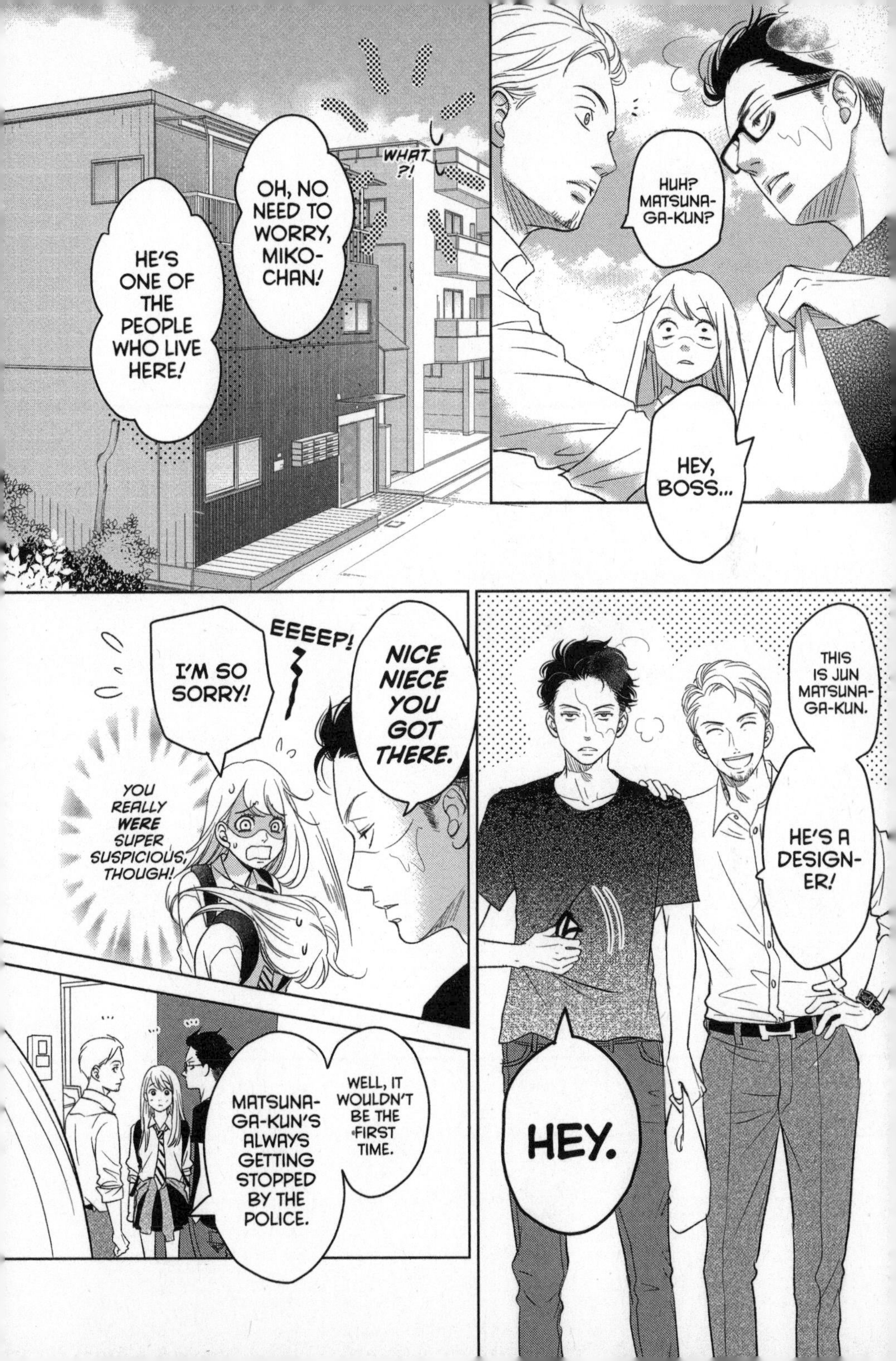
HUH? MATSUNAGA-KUN?
HEY, BOSS...
WHAT ?!
OH, NO NEED TO WORRY, MIKO-CHAN!
HE'S ONE OF THE PEOPLE WHO LIVE HERE!
THIS IS JUN MATSUNAGA-KUN.
HE'S A DESIGNER!
HEY.
NICE NIECE YOU GOT THERE.
EEEEP!
I'M SO SORRY!
YOU REALLY WERE SUPER SUSPICIOUS, THOUGH!
WELL, IT WOULDN'T BE THE FIRST TIME.
MATSUNAGA-KUN'S ALWAYS GETTING STOPPED BY THE POLICE.

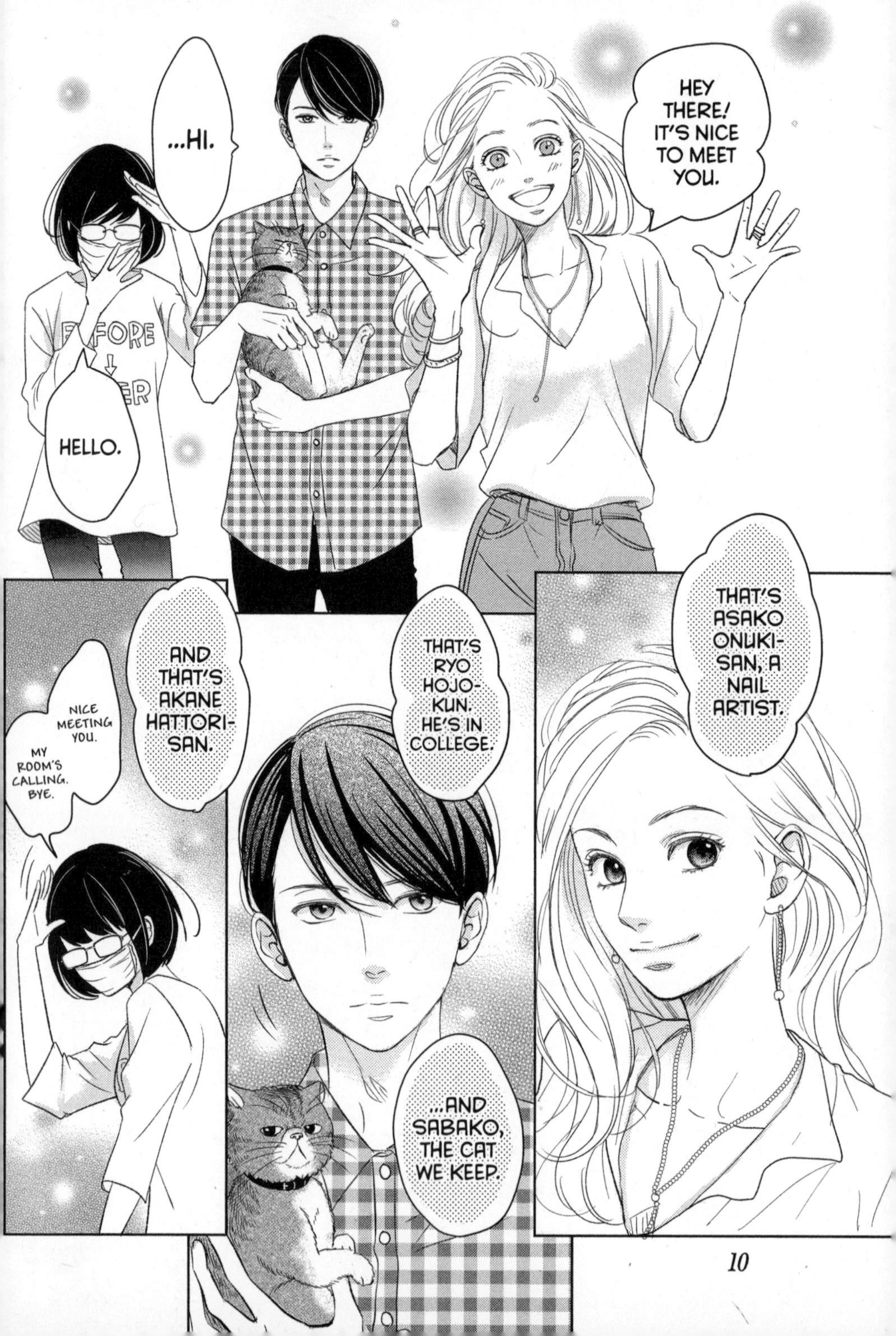
HEY THERE! IT'S NICE TO MEET YOU.
...HI.
HELLO.
THAT'S ASAKO ONUKI-SAN, A NAIL ARTIST.
THAT'S RYO HOJO-KUN. HE'S IN COLLEGE.
...AND SABAKO, THE CAT WE KEEP.
AND THAT'S AKANE HATTORI-SAN.
NICE MEETING YOU.
MY ROOM'S CALLING. BYE.

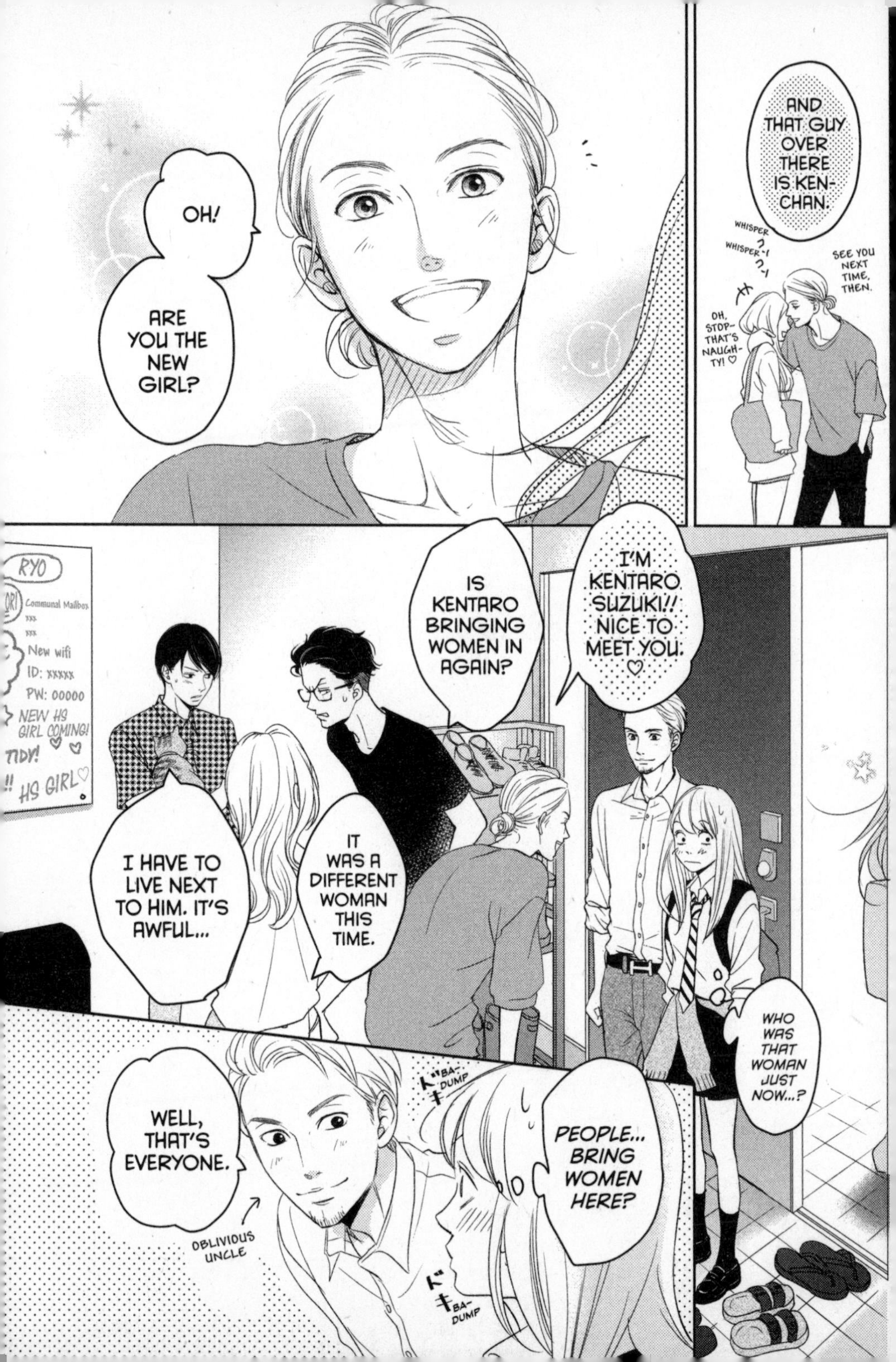

AND THAT GUY OVER THERE IS KEN-CHAN.
WHISPER WHISPER
SEE YOU NEXT TIME, THEN.
OH, STOP—THAT'S NAUGHTY! ♡
OH!
ARE YOU THE NEW GIRL?
I'M KENTARO SUZUKI!! NICE TO MEET YOU. ♡
IS KENTARO BRINGING WOMEN IN AGAIN?
IT WAS A DIFFERENT WOMAN THIS TIME.
I HAVE TO LIVE NEXT TO HIM. IT'S AWFUL...
RYO
Communal Mailbox
New wifi
ID: XXXXX
PW: 00000
NEW HS GIRL COMING!
TIDY!
HS GIRL
WHO WAS THAT WOMAN JUST NOW...?
PEOPLE... BRING WOMEN HERE?
BA-DUMP
WELL, THAT'S EVERYONE.
OBLIVIOUS UNCLE
BA-DUMP

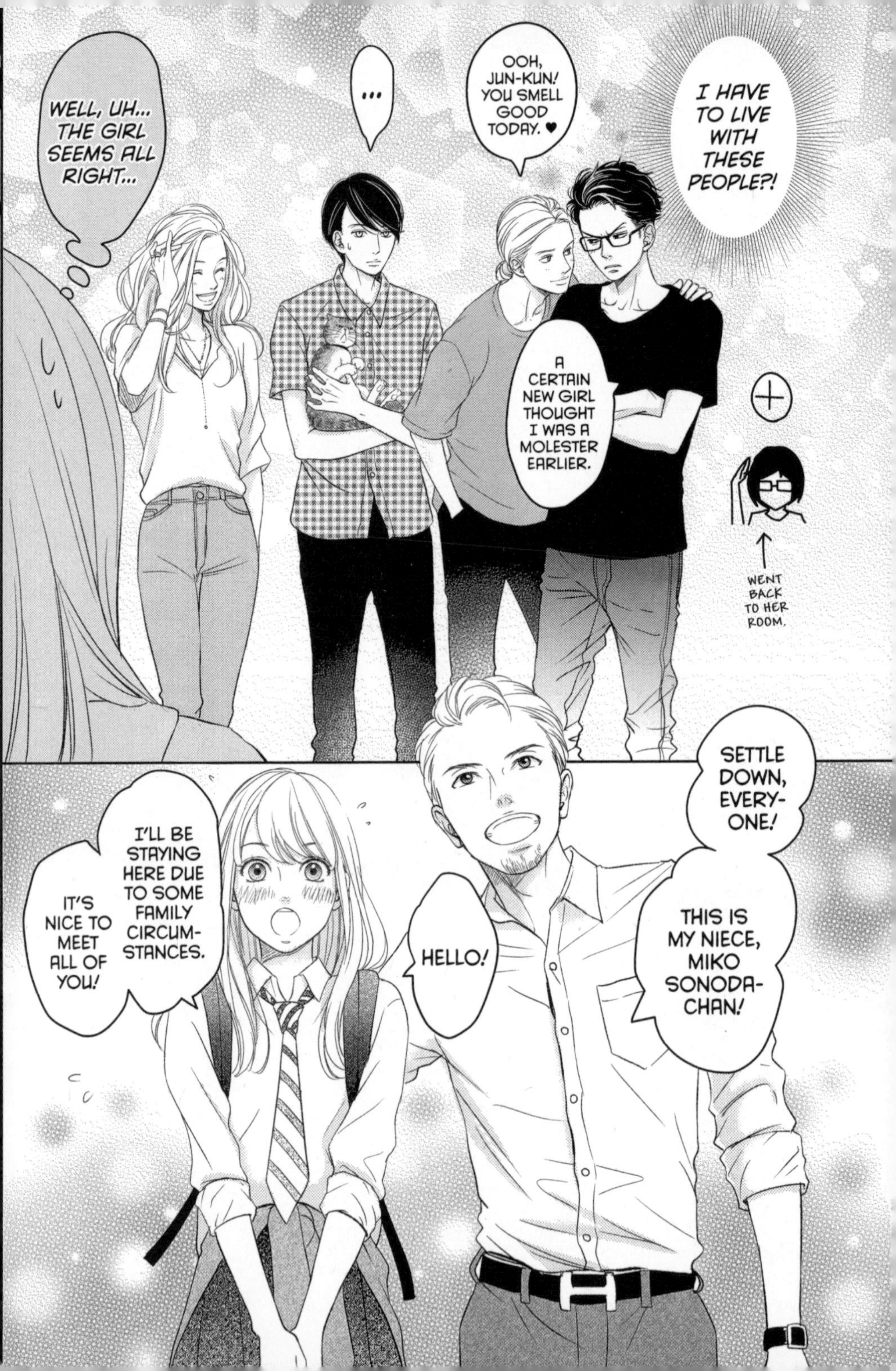
I HAVE TO LIVE WITH THESE PEOPLE?!
OOH, JUN-KUN! YOU SMELL GOOD TODAY. ♥
...
WELL, UH... THE GIRL SEEMS ALL RIGHT...
A CERTAIN NEW GIRL THOUGHT I WAS A MOLESTER EARLIER.
WENT BACK TO HER ROOM.
SETTLE DOWN, EVERY-ONE!
THIS IS MY NIECE, MIKO SONODA-CHAN!
HELLO!
I'LL BE STAYING HERE DUE TO SOME FAMILY CIRCUM-STANCES.
IT'S NICE TO MEET ALL OF YOU!

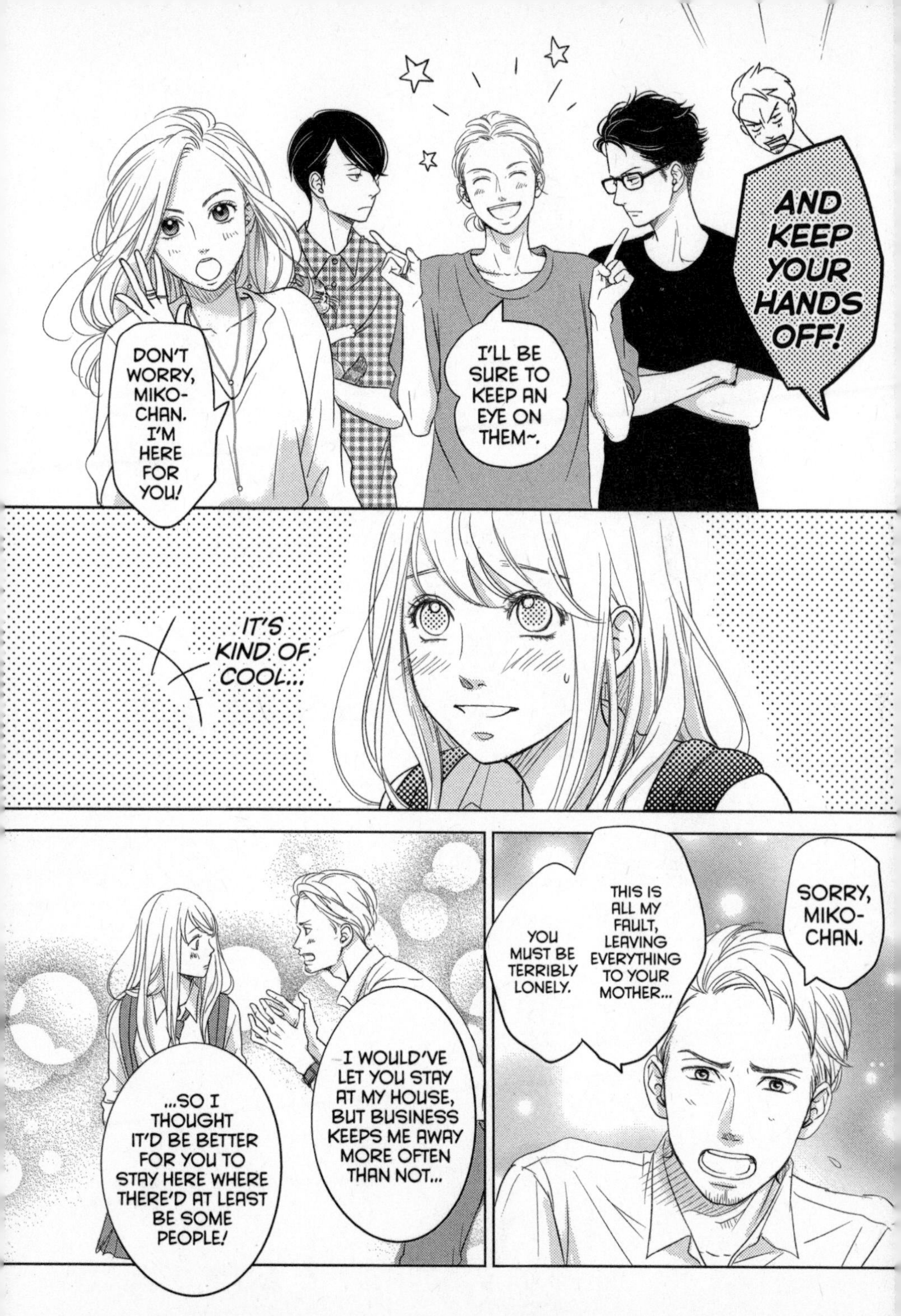
AND KEEP YOUR HANDS OFF!
I'LL BE SURE TO KEEP AN EYE ON THEM~.
DON'T WORRY, MIKO-CHAN. I'M HERE FOR YOU!
IT'S KIND OF COOL...
SORRY, MIKO-CHAN.
THIS IS ALL MY FAULT, LEAVING EVERYTHING TO YOUR MOTHER...
YOU MUST BE TERRIBLY LONELY.
I WOULD'VE LET YOU STAY AT MY HOUSE, BUT BUSINESS KEEPS ME AWAY MORE OFTEN THAN NOT...
...SO I THOUGHT IT'D BE BETTER FOR YOU TO STAY HERE WHERE THERE'D AT LEAST BE SOME PEOPLE!

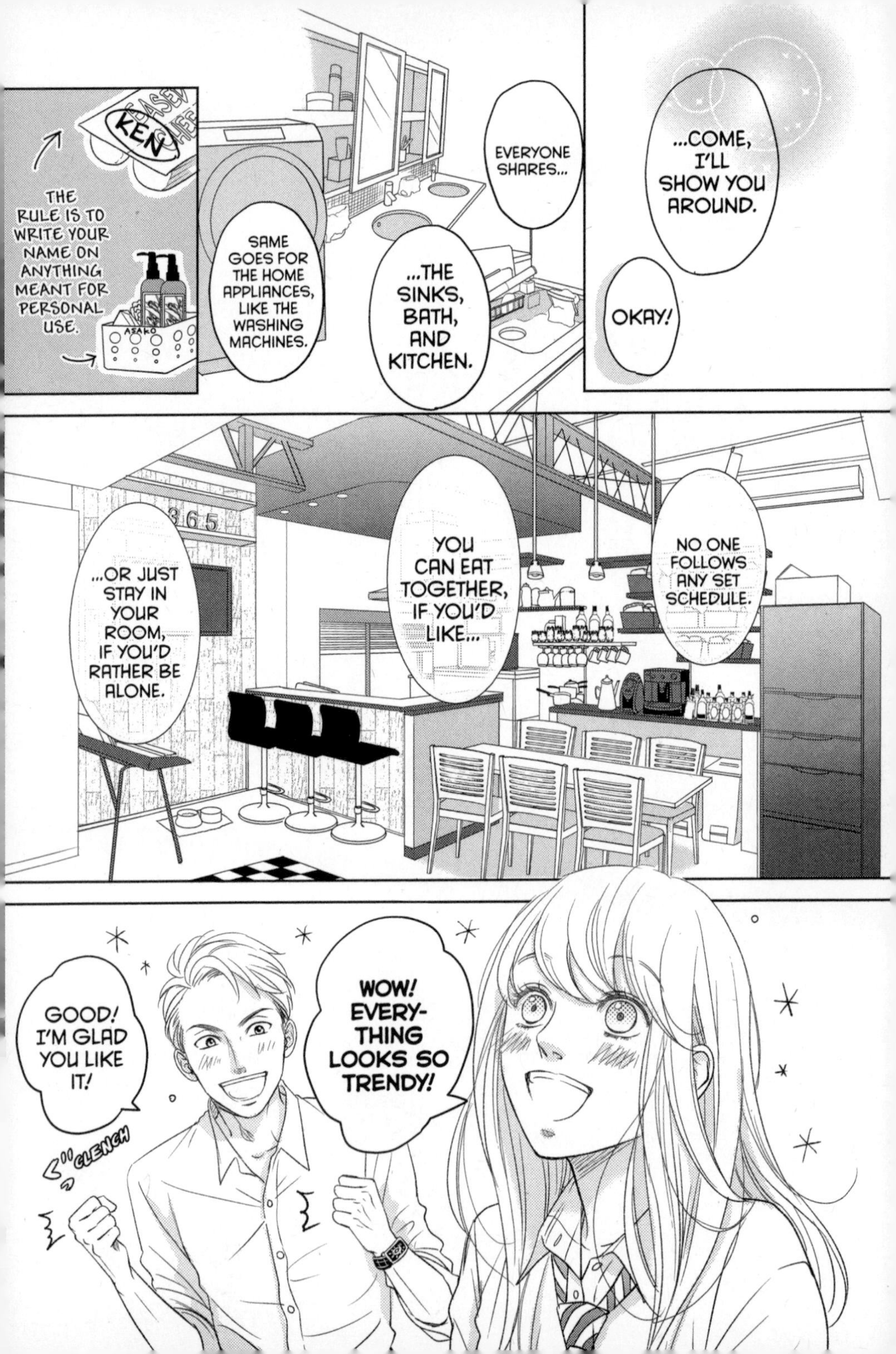
...COME, I'LL SHOW YOU AROUND.
OKAY!
EVERYONE SHARES...
...THE SINKS, BATH, AND KITCHEN.
SAME GOES FOR THE HOME APPLIANCES, LIKE THE WASHING MACHINES.
KEN
ASAKO
THE RULE IS TO WRITE YOUR NAME ON ANYTHING MEANT FOR PERSONAL USE.
NO ONE FOLLOWS ANY SET SCHEDULE.
YOU CAN EAT TOGETHER, IF YOU'D LIKE...
...OR JUST STAY IN YOUR ROOM, IF YOU'D RATHER BE ALONE.
365
WOW! EVERYTHING LOOKS SO TRENDY!
GOOD! I'M GLAD YOU LIKE IT!
CLENCH

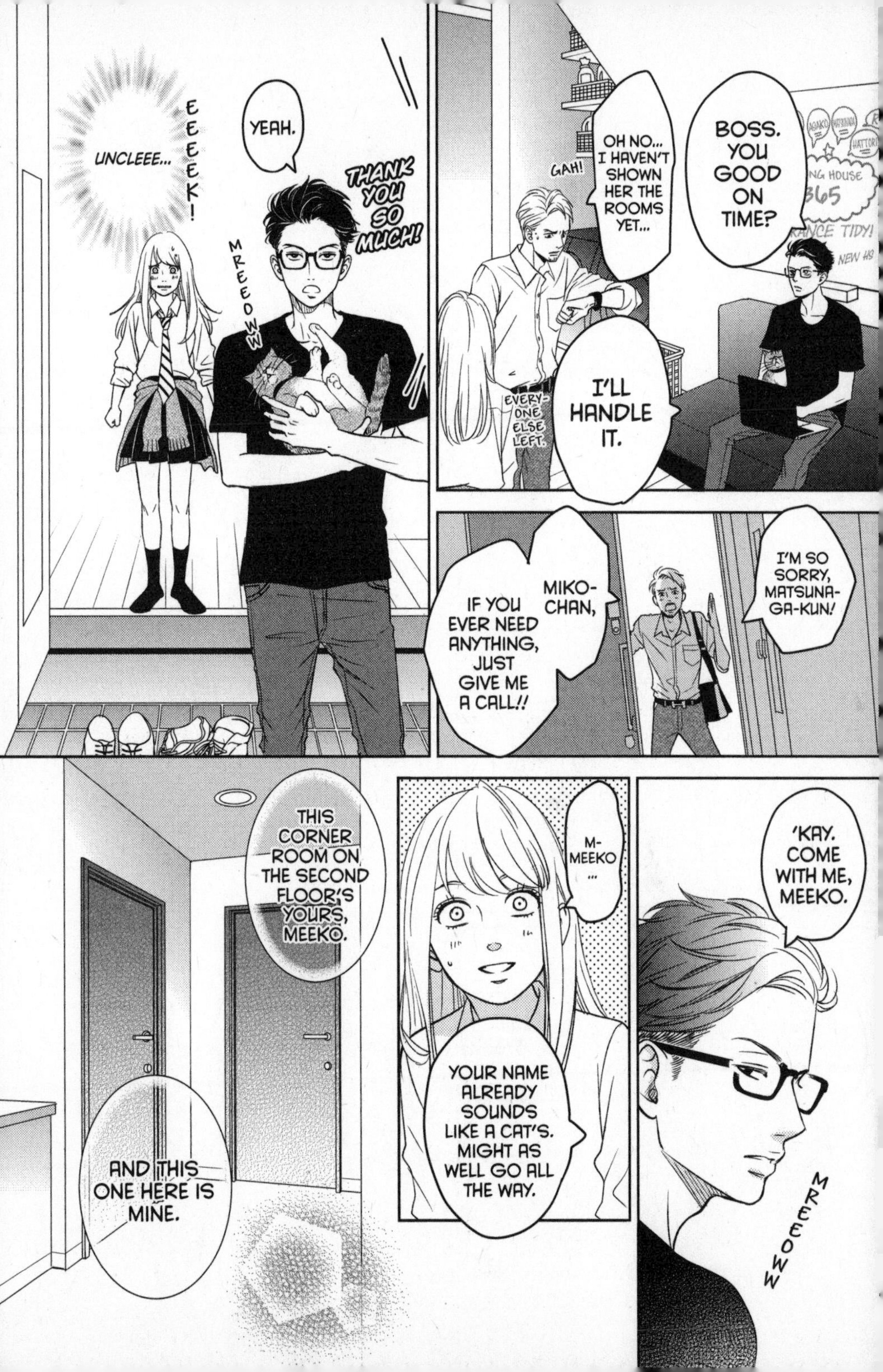
BOSS. YOU GOOD ON TIME?
OH NO... I HAVEN'T SHOWN HER THE ROOMS YET...
GAH!
I'LL HANDLE IT.
EVERY-ONE ELSE LEFT.
I'M SO SORRY, MATSUNAGA-KUN!
MIKO-CHAN,
IF YOU EVER NEED ANYTHING, JUST GIVE ME A CALL!!
THANK YOU SO MUCH!
YEAH.
UNCLEEE...
EEEEEK!
MREEEOWW
'KAY. COME WITH ME, MEEKO.
MREEEOWW
M-MEEKO ...
YOUR NAME ALREADY SOUNDS LIKE A CAT'S. MIGHT AS WELL GO ALL THE WAY.
THIS CORNER ROOM ON THE SECOND FLOOR'S YOURS, MEEKO.
AND THIS ONE HERE IS MINE.

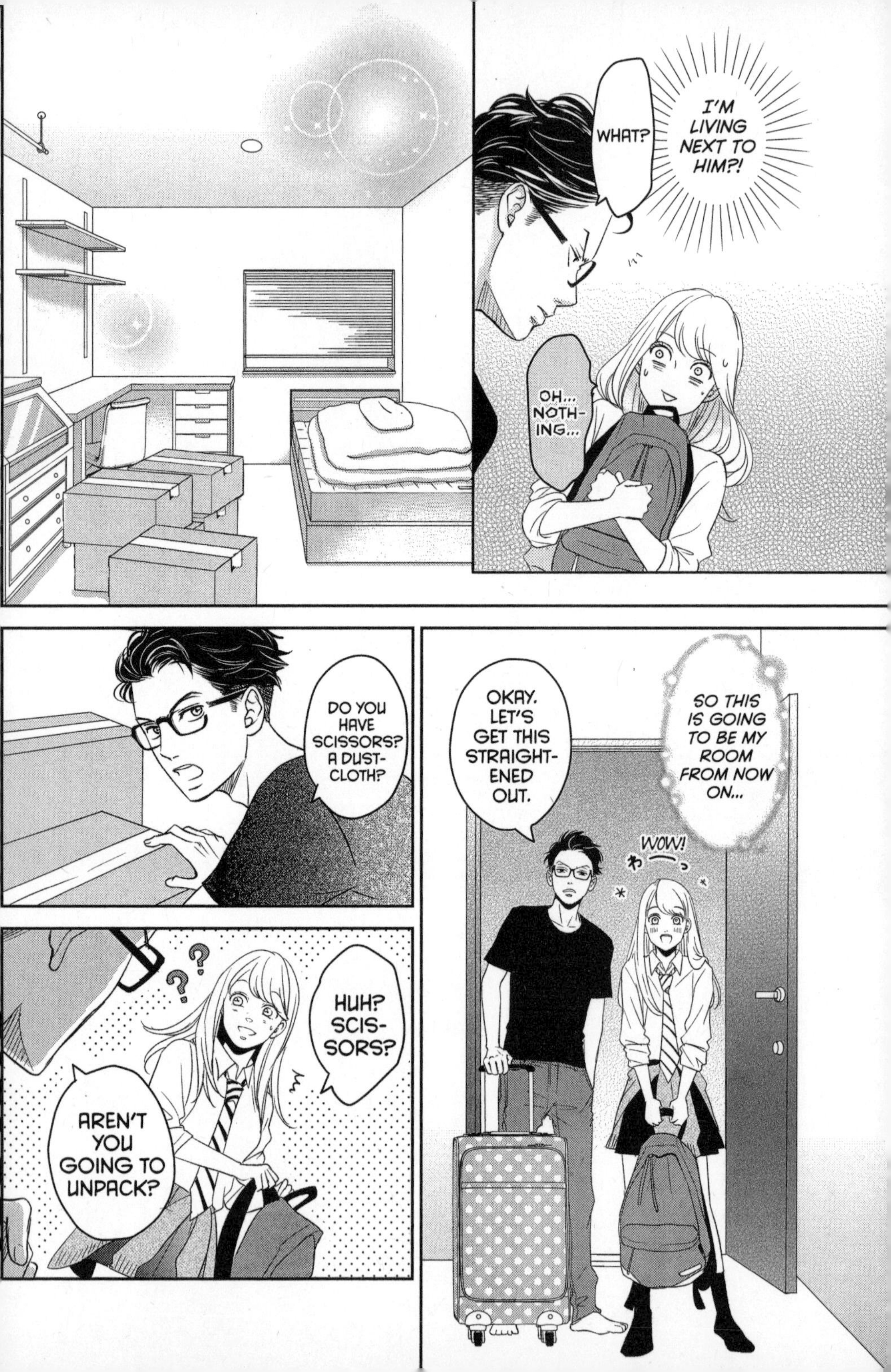
WHAT?
I'M LIVING NEXT TO HIM?!
OH... NOTHING...
OKAY. LET'S GET THIS STRAIGHTENED OUT.
SO THIS IS GOING TO BE MY ROOM FROM NOW ON...
WOW!
DO YOU HAVE SCISSORS? A DUST-CLOTH?
HUH? SCISSORS?
AREN'T YOU GOING TO UNPACK?

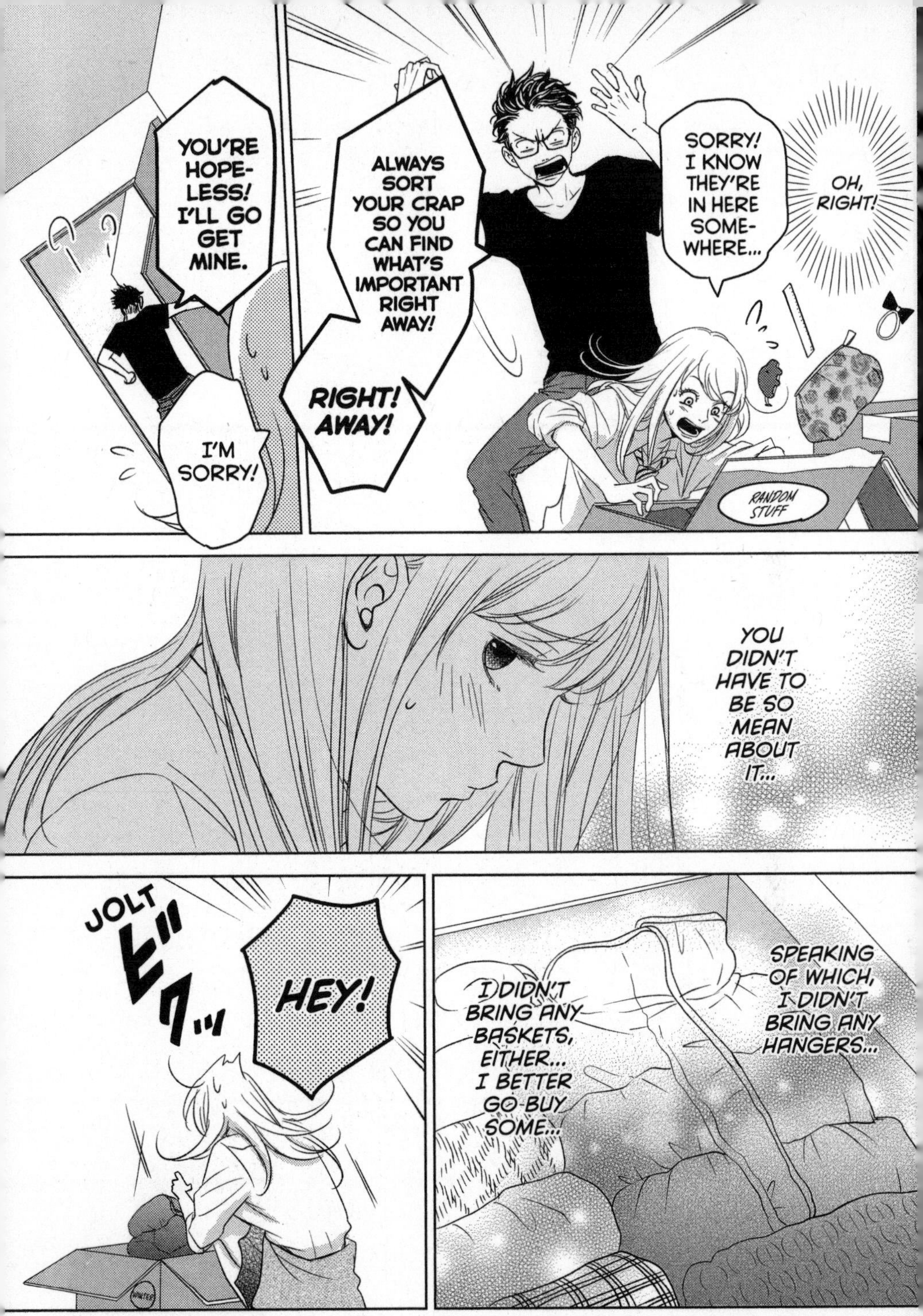
OH, RIGHT!
SORRY! I KNOW THEY'RE IN HERE SOME-WHERE...
ALWAYS SORT YOUR CRAP SO YOU CAN FIND WHAT'S IMPORTANT RIGHT AWAY!
RIGHT! AWAY!
RANDOM STUFF
YOU'RE HOPE-LESS! I'LL GO GET MINE.
I'M SORRY!
YOU DIDN'T HAVE TO BE SO MEAN ABOUT IT...
SPEAKING OF WHICH, I DIDN'T BRING ANY HANGERS...
I DIDN'T BRING ANY BASKETS, EITHER... I BETTER GO BUY SOME...
HEY!
JOLT
ビクッ

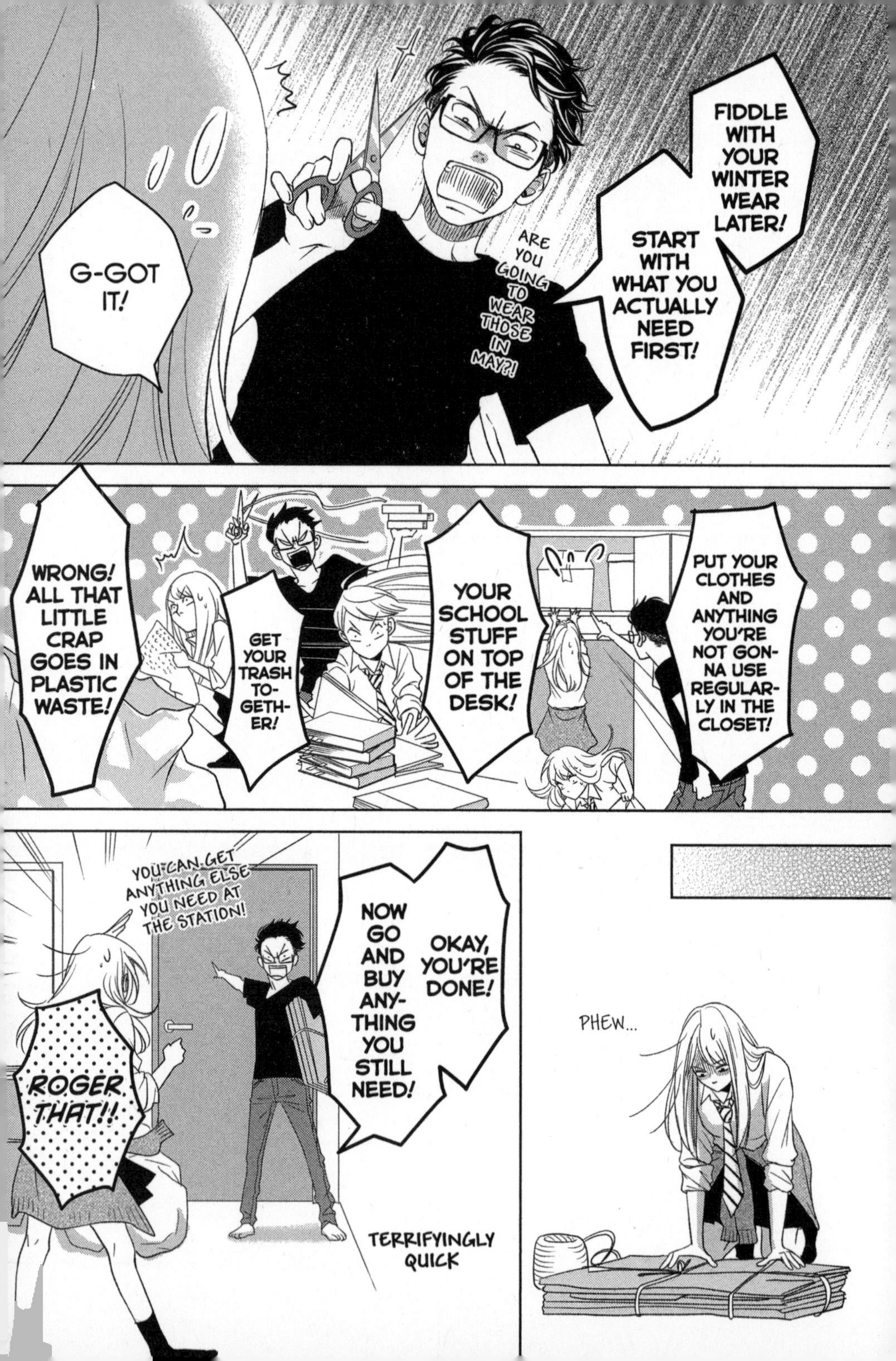
FIDDLE WITH YOUR WINTER WEAR LATER!
START WITH WHAT YOU ACTUALLY NEED FIRST!
ARE YOU GOING TO WEAR THOSE IN MAY?!
G-GOT IT!
PUT YOUR CLOTHES AND ANYTHING YOU'RE NOT GON-NA USE REGULAR-LY IN THE CLOSET!
YOUR SCHOOL STUFF ON TOP OF THE DESK!
GET YOUR TRASH TO-GETH-ER!
WRONG! ALL THAT LITTLE CRAP GOES IN PLASTIC WASTE!
PHEW...
OKAY, YOU'RE DONE!
NOW GO AND BUY ANY-THING YOU STILL NEED!
YOU CAN GET ANYTHING ELSE YOU NEED AT THE STATION!
ROGER THAT!!
TERRIFYINGLY QUICK

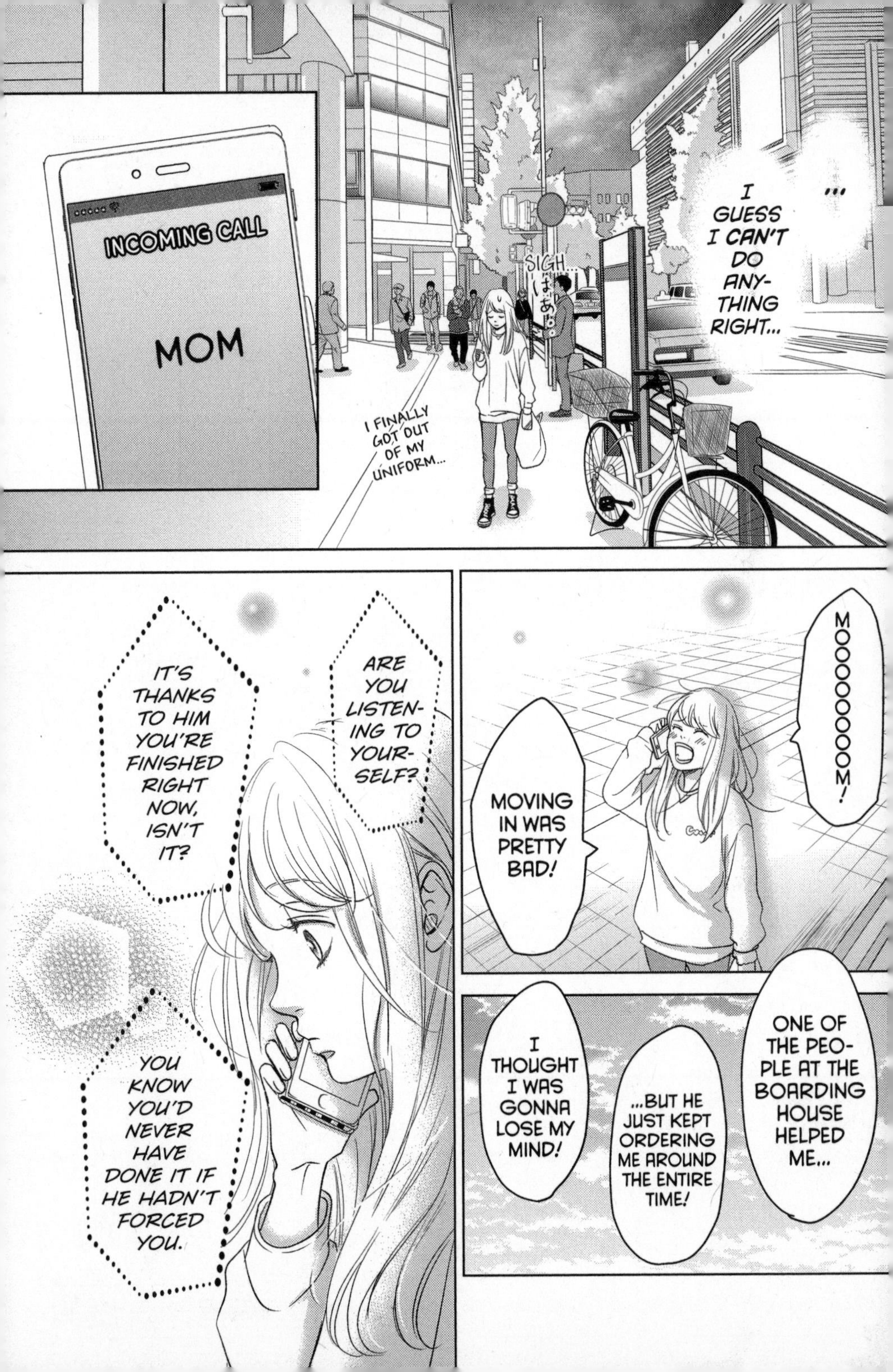

...
I GUESS I CAN'T DO ANYTHING RIGHT...
SIGH... はぁ
I FINALLY GOT OUT OF MY UNIFORM...
INCOMING CALL
MOM
MOOOOOOOOM!
MOVING IN WAS PRETTY BAD!
ONE OF THE PEOPLE AT THE BOARDING HOUSE HELPED ME...
...BUT HE JUST KEPT ORDERING ME AROUND THE ENTIRE TIME!
I THOUGHT I WAS GONNA LOSE MY MIND!
ARE YOU LISTENING TO YOURSELF?
IT'S THANKS TO HIM YOU'RE FINISHED RIGHT NOW, ISN'T IT?
YOU KNOW YOU'D NEVER HAVE DONE IT IF HE HADN'T FORCED YOU.

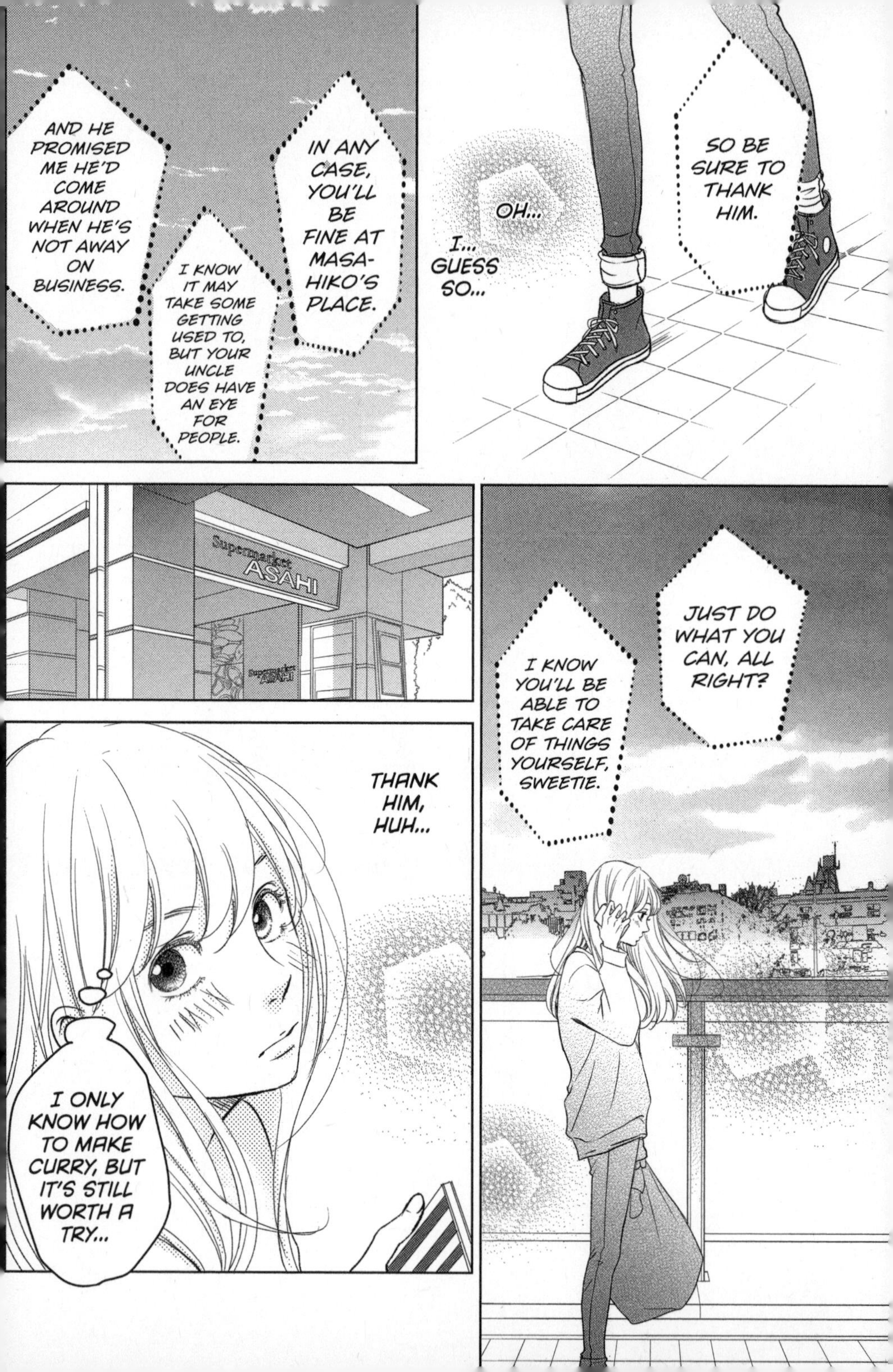
IN ANY CASE, YOU'LL BE FINE AT MASA-HIKO'S PLACE.
I KNOW IT MAY TAKE SOME GETTING USED TO, BUT YOUR UNCLE DOES HAVE AN EYE FOR PEOPLE.
AND HE PROMISED ME HE'D COME AROUND WHEN HE'S NOT AWAY ON BUSINESS.
SO BE SURE TO THANK HIM.
OH...
I... GUESS SO...
JUST DO WHAT YOU CAN, ALL RIGHT?
I KNOW YOU'LL BE ABLE TO TAKE CARE OF THINGS YOURSELF, SWEETIE.
Supermarket ASAHI
THANK HIM, HUH...
I ONLY KNOW HOW TO MAKE CURRY, BUT IT'S STILL WORTH A TRY...

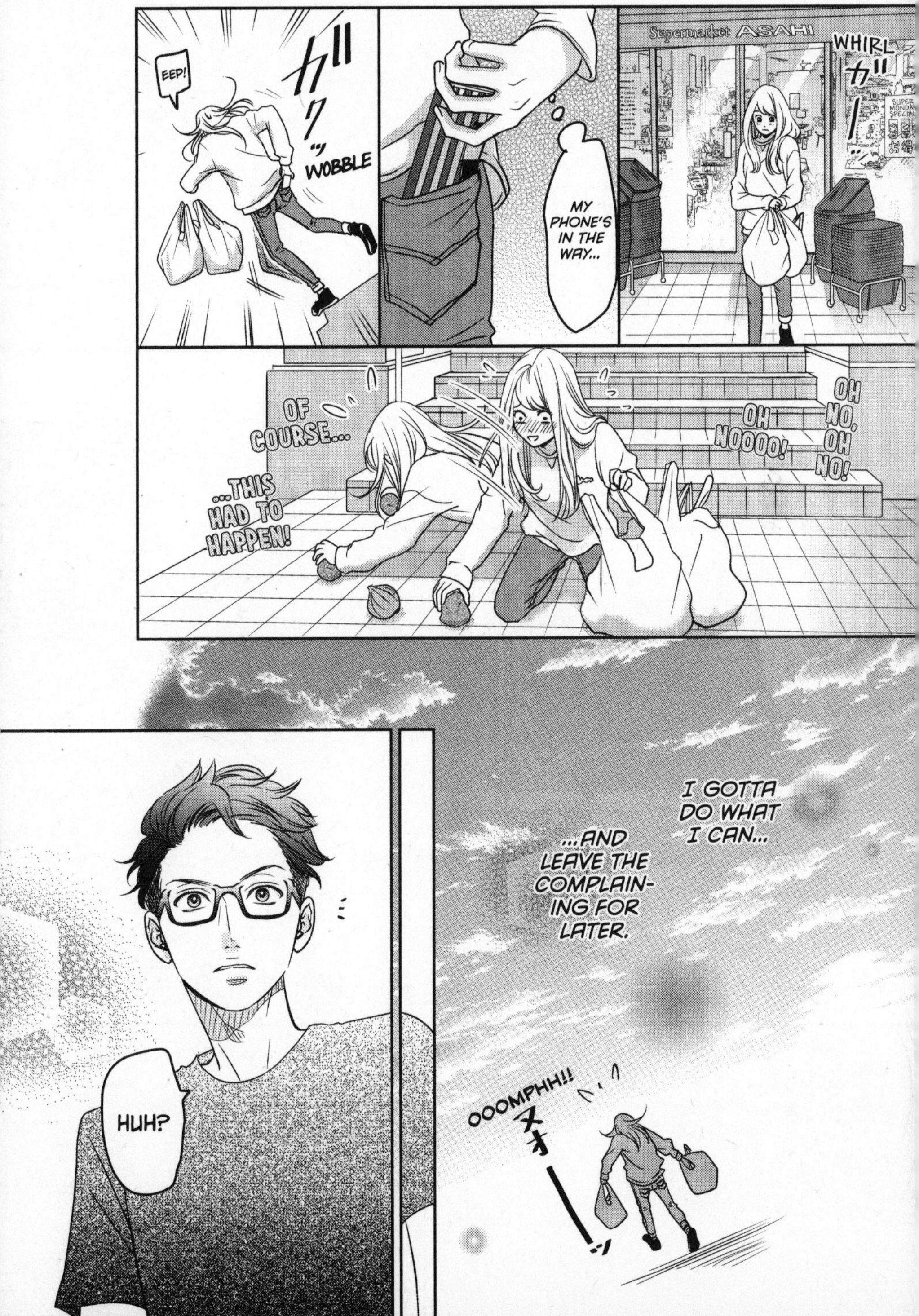
Supermarket ASAHI
WHIRL
カー
MY PHONE'S IN THE WAY...
EEP!
カクッ
WOBBLE
OH NO, OH NO!
OH NOOOO!
OF COURSE...
...THIS HAD TO HAPPEN!
I GOTTA DO WHAT I CAN...
...AND LEAVE THE COMPLAIN-ING FOR LATER.
OOOMPHH!!
ヌオー
HUH?

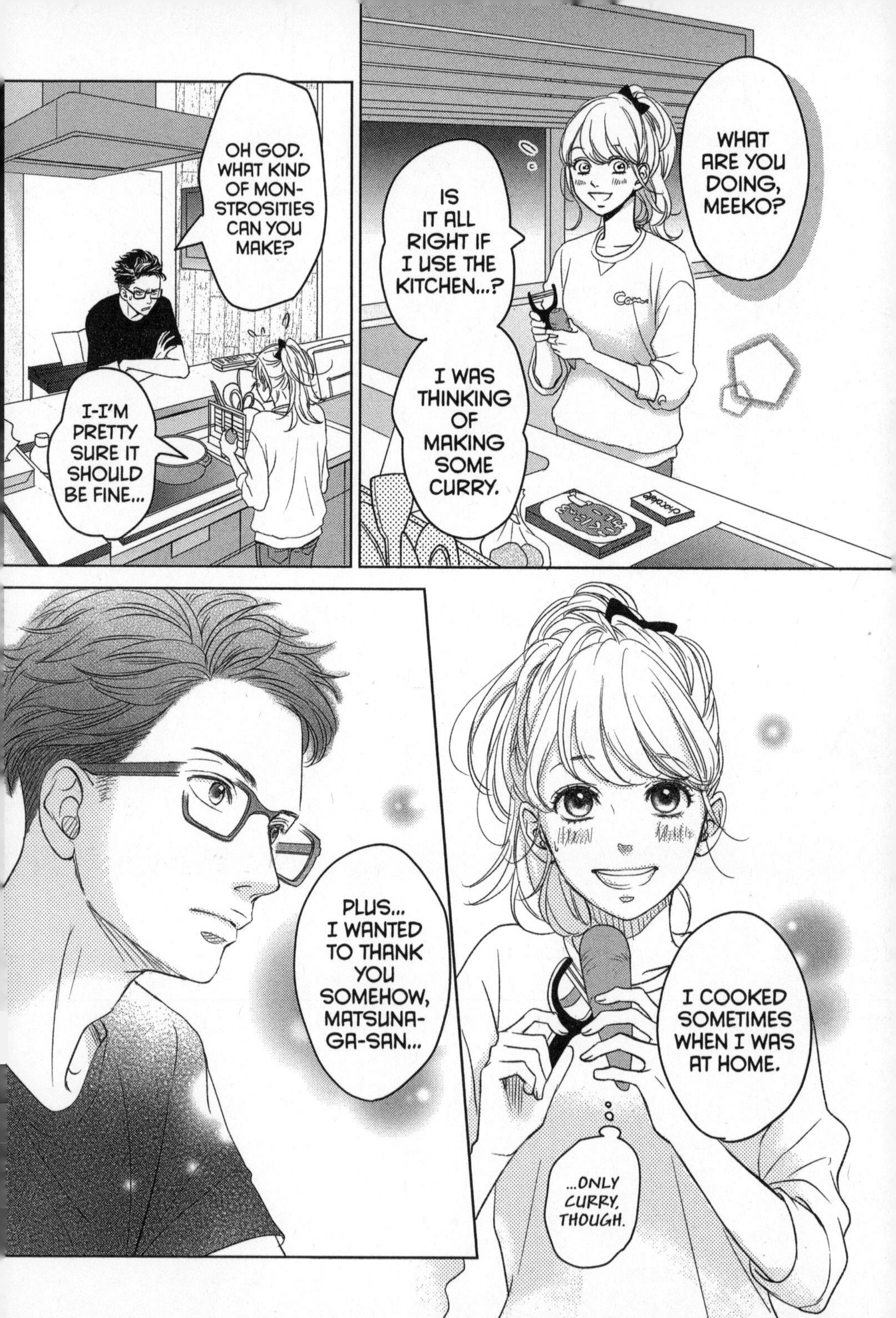

WHAT ARE YOU DOING, MEEKO?
IS IT ALL RIGHT IF I USE THE KITCHEN...?
I WAS THINKING OF MAKING SOME CURRY.
OH GOD. WHAT KIND OF MON-STROSITIES CAN YOU MAKE?
I-I'M PRETTY SURE IT SHOULD BE FINE...
I COOKED SOMETIMES WHEN I WAS AT HOME.
...ONLY CURRY, THOUGH.
PLUS... I WANTED TO THANK YOU SOMEHOW, MATSUNAGA-SAN...

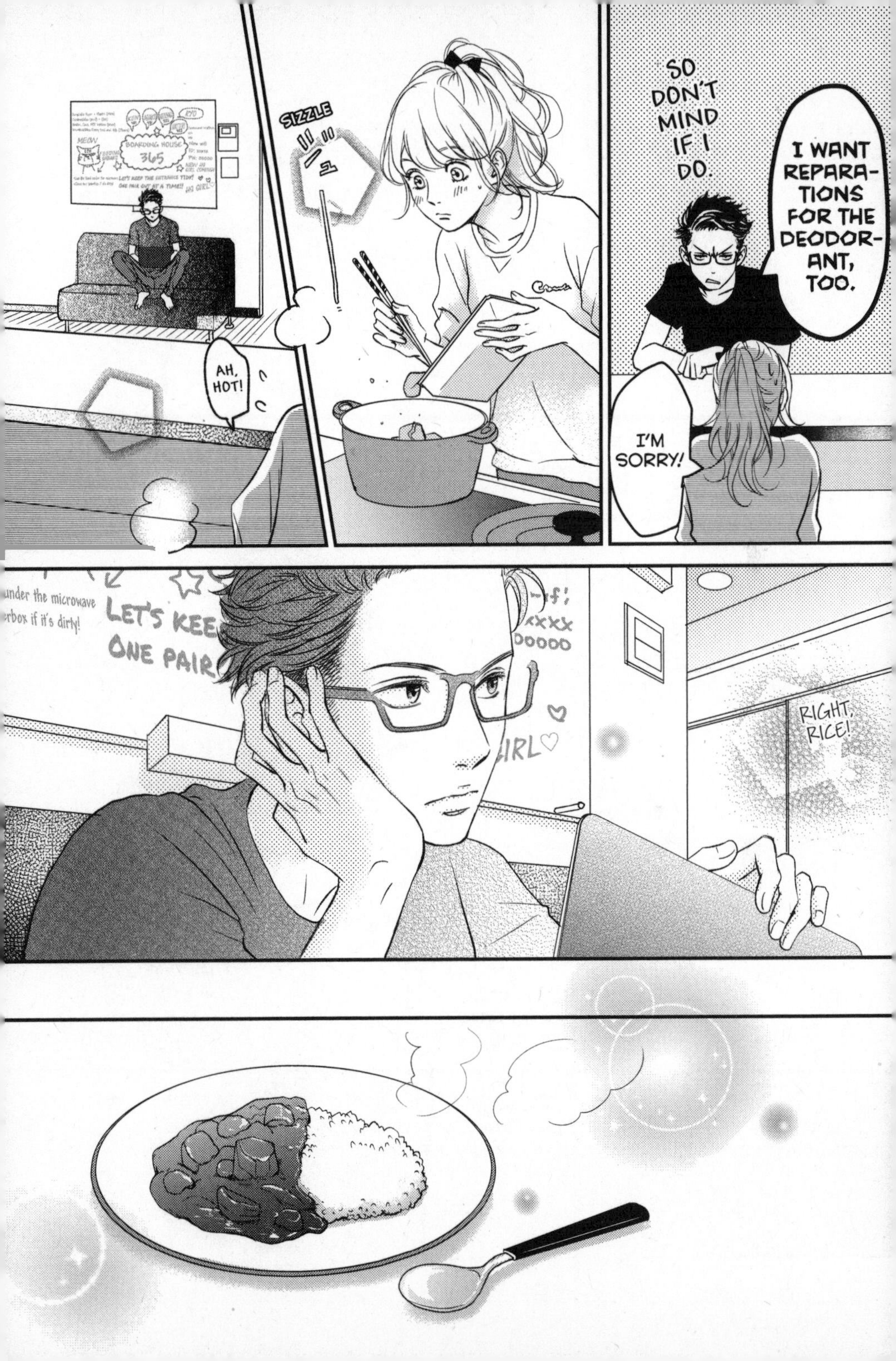
I WANT REPARATIONS FOR THE DEODORANT, TOO.
SO DON'T MIND IF I DO.
I'M SORRY!
SIZZLE
AH, HOT!
BOARDING HOUSE 365
under the microwave
erbox if it's dirty!
LET'S KEE
ONE PAIR
GIRL♡
RIGHT, RICE!

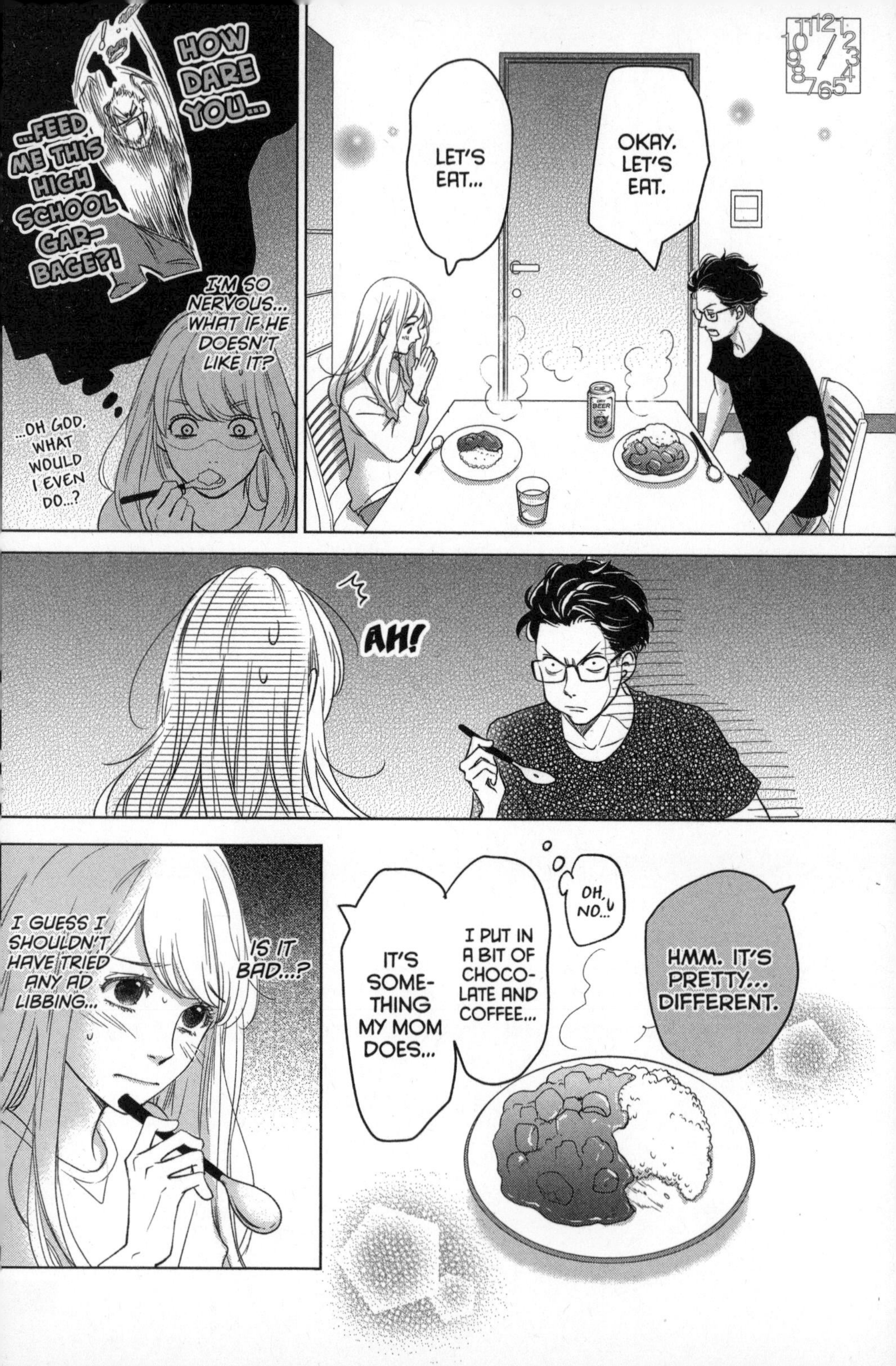

OKAY. LET'S EAT.
LET'S EAT...
HOW DARE YOU...
...FEED ME THIS HIGH SCHOOL GAR-BAGE?!
I'M SO NERVOUS... WHAT IF HE DOESN'T LIKE IT?
...OH GOD, WHAT WOULD I EVEN DO...?
AH!
HMM. IT'S PRETTY... DIFFERENT.
OH, NO...
I PUT IN A BIT OF CHOCO-LATE AND COFFEE...
IT'S SOME-THING MY MOM DOES...
IS IT BAD...?
I GUESS I SHOULDN'T HAVE TRIED ANY AD LIBBING...

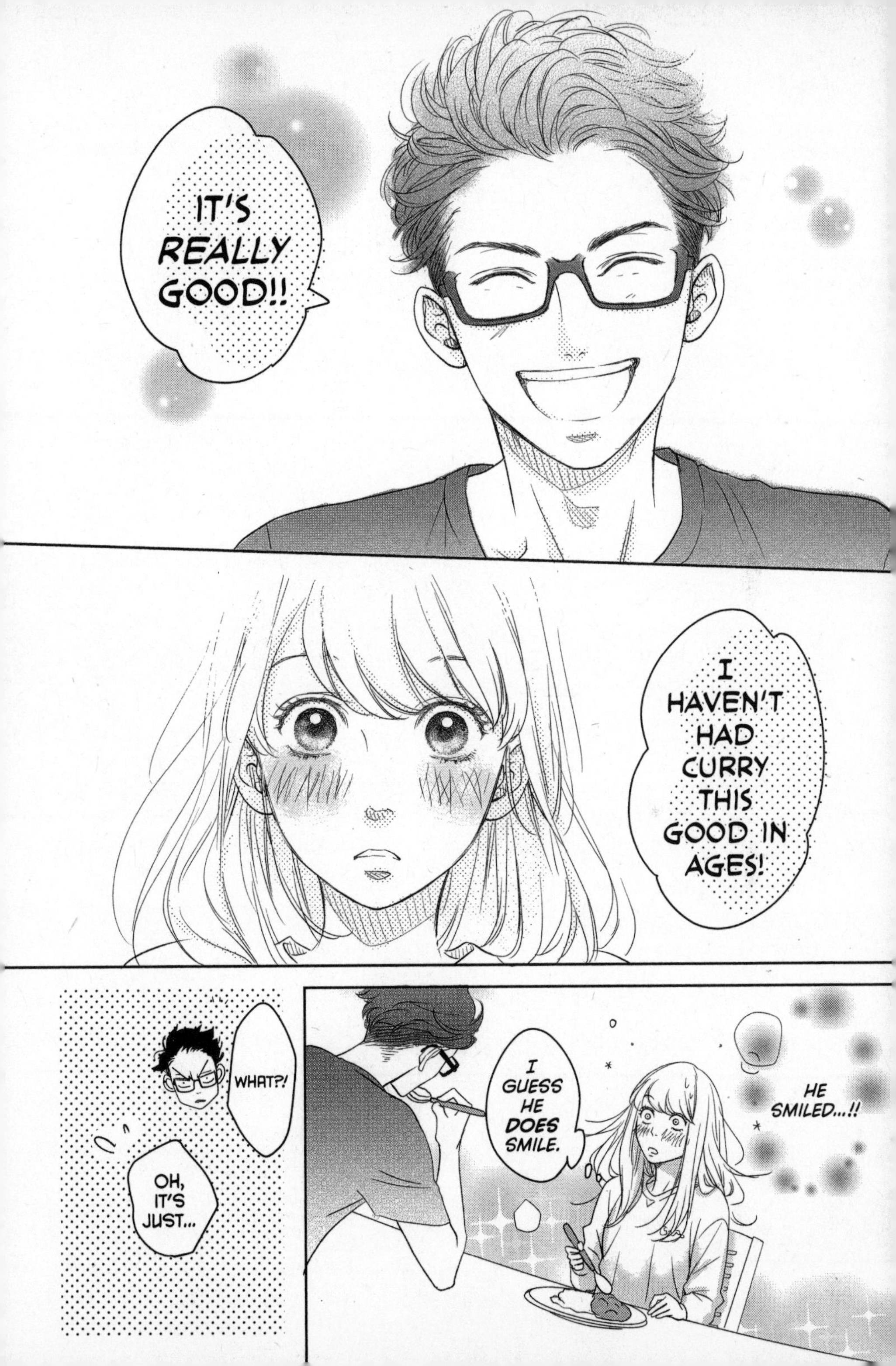
IT'S REALLY GOOD!!
I HAVEN'T HAD CURRY THIS GOOD IN AGES!
HE SMILED...!!
I GUESS HE DOES SMILE.
WHAT?!
OH, IT'S JUST...

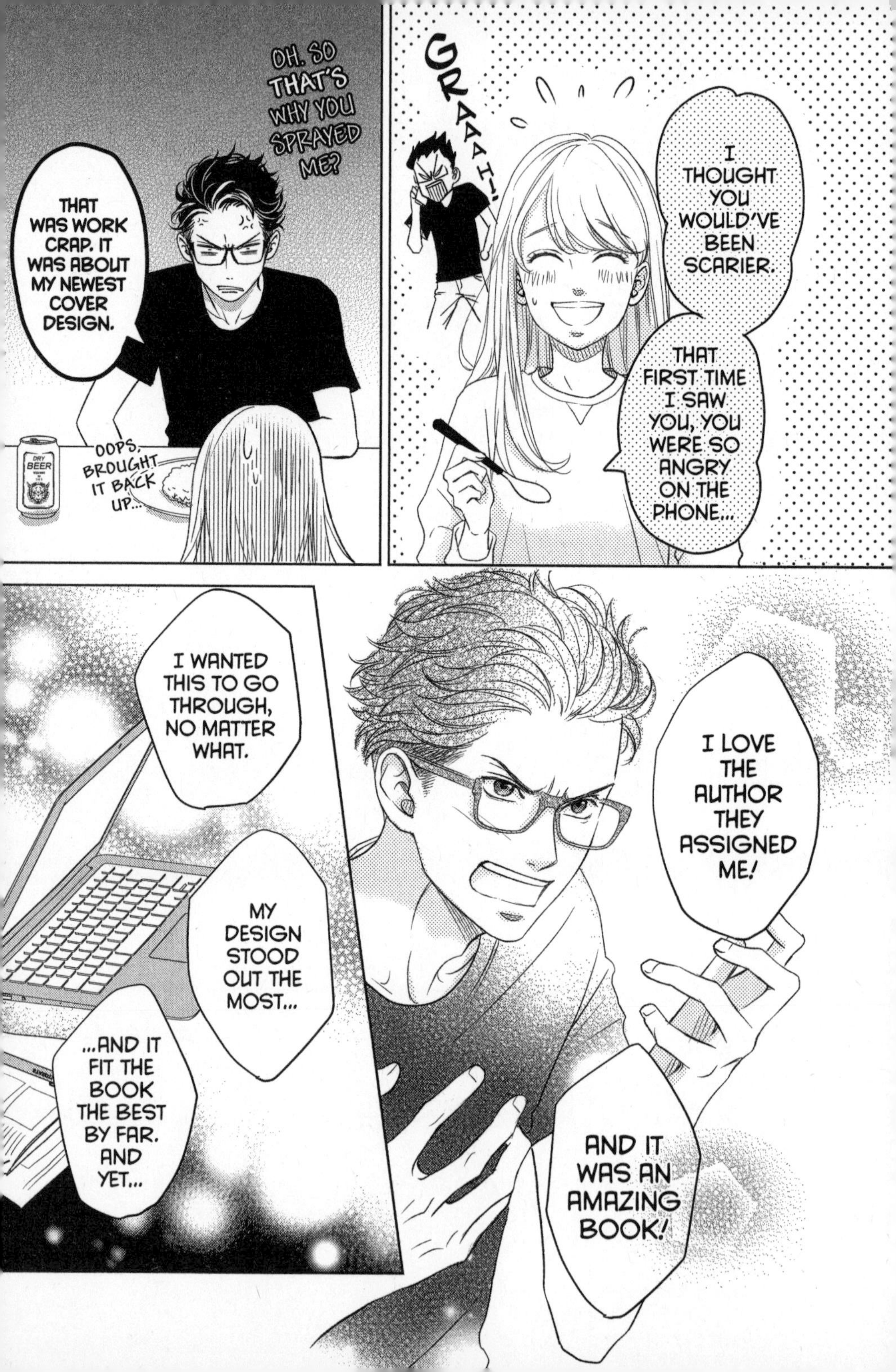
I THOUGHT YOU WOULD'VE BEEN SCARIER.
GRAAAH!
THAT FIRST TIME I SAW YOU, YOU WERE SO ANGRY ON THE PHONE...
OH. SO THAT'S WHY YOU SPRAYED ME?
THAT WAS WORK CRAP. IT WAS ABOUT MY NEWEST COVER DESIGN.
DRY BEER
OOPS, BROUGHT IT BACK UP...
I LOVE THE AUTHOR THEY ASSIGNED ME!
AND IT WAS AN AMAZING BOOK!
I WANTED THIS TO GO THROUGH, NO MATTER WHAT.
MY DESIGN STOOD OUT THE MOST...
...AND IT FIT THE BOOK THE BEST BY FAR. AND YET...

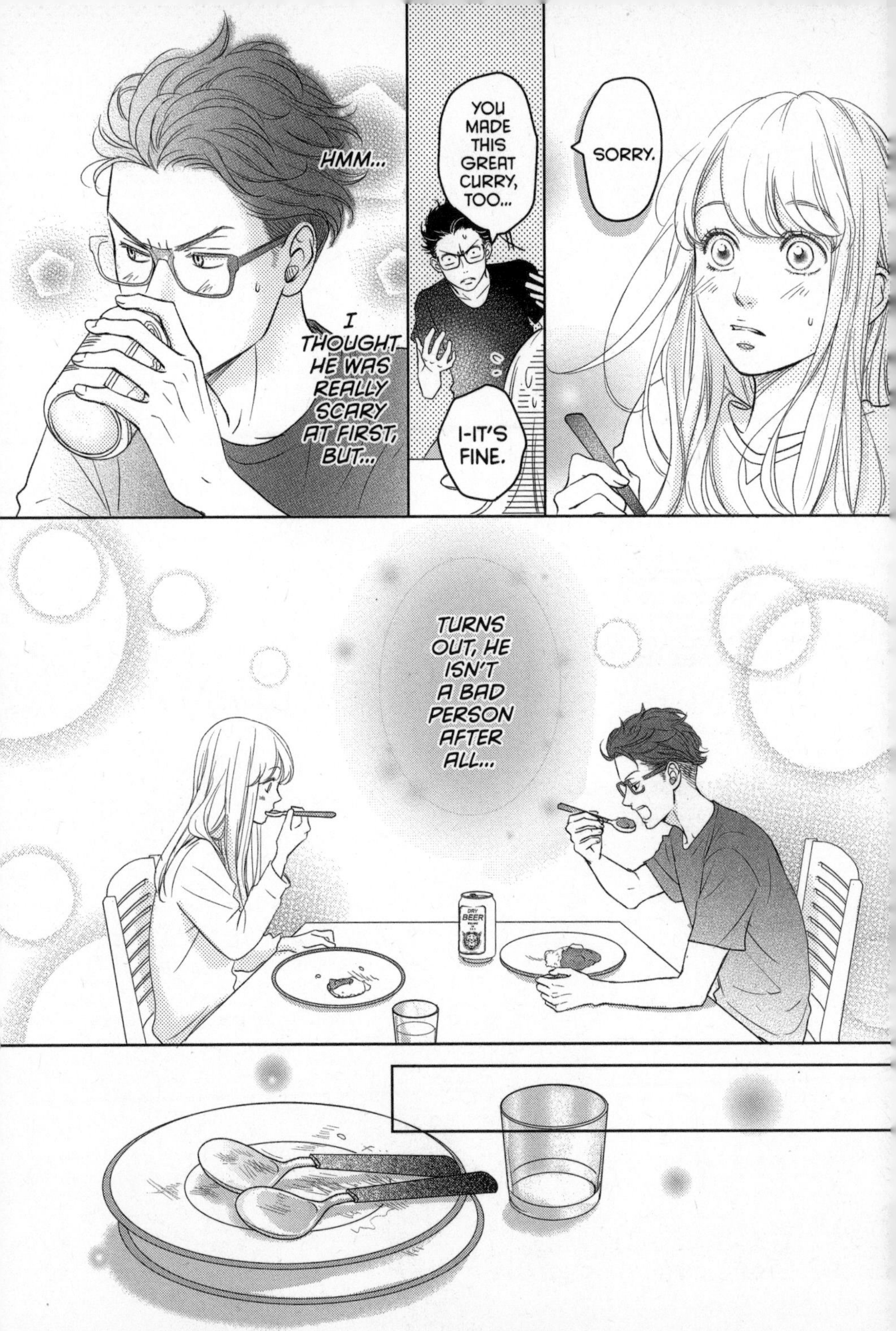
SORRY.
YOU MADE THIS GREAT CURRY, TOO...
I-IT'S FINE.
HMM...
I THOUGHT HE WAS REALLY SCARY AT FIRST, BUT...
TURNS OUT, HE ISN'T A BAD PERSON AFTER ALL...

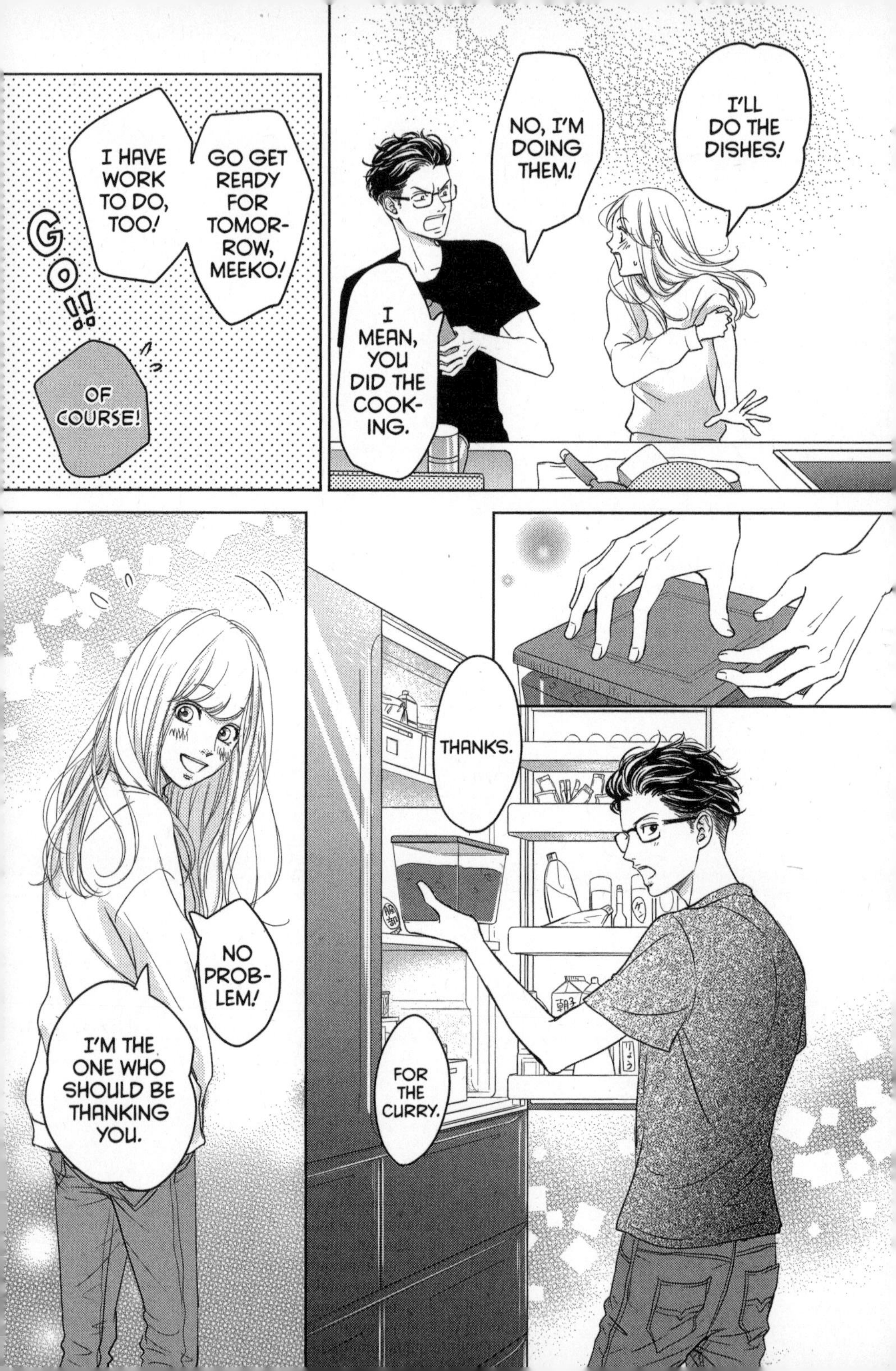
I'LL DO THE DISHES!
NO, I'M DOING THEM!
I MEAN, YOU DID THE COOK-ING.
GO GET READY FOR TOMOR-ROW, MEEKO!
I HAVE WORK TO DO, TOO!
GO!!
OF COURSE!
THANKS.
FOR THE CURRY.
NO PROB-LEM!
I'M THE ONE WHO SHOULD BE THANKING YOU.

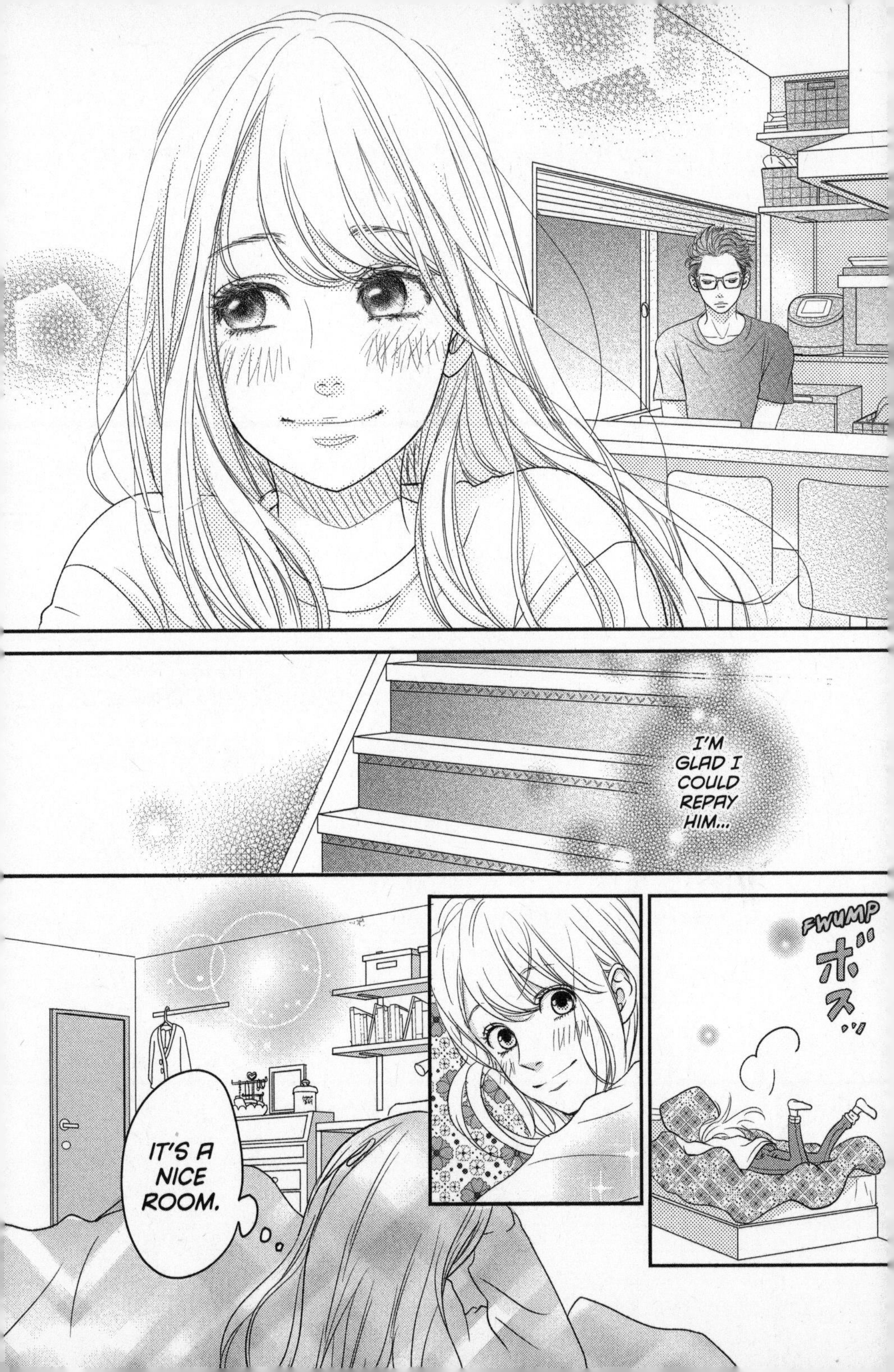
I'M GLAD I COULD REPAY HIM...
FWUMP
ボスッ
IT'S A NICE ROOM.

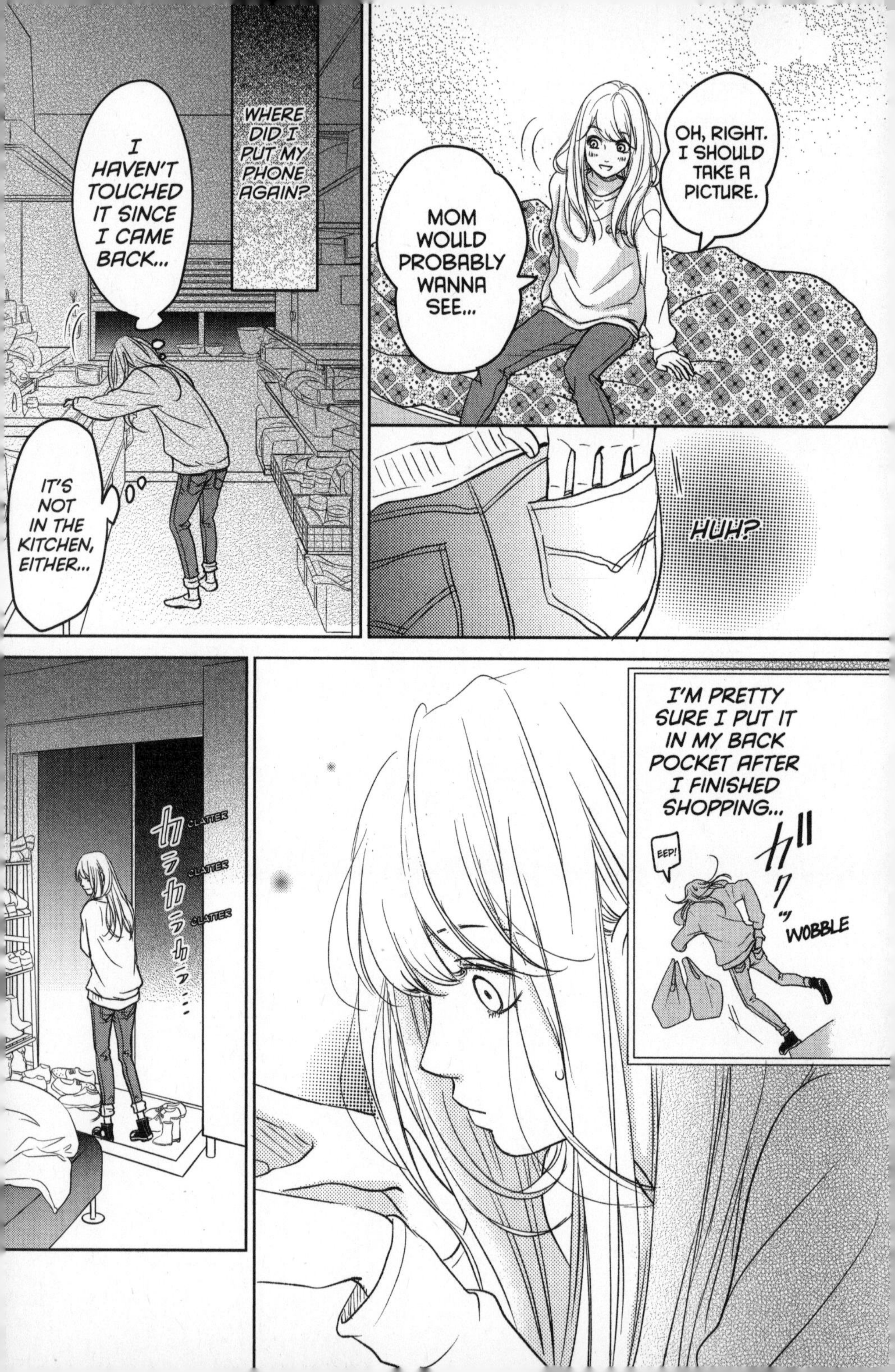
OH, RIGHT. I SHOULD TAKE A PICTURE.
MOM WOULD PROBABLY WANNA SEE...
HUH?
WHERE DID I PUT MY PHONE AGAIN?
I HAVEN'T TOUCHED IT SINCE I CAME BACK...
IT'S NOT IN THE KITCHEN, EITHER...
I'M PRETTY SURE I PUT IT IN MY BACK POCKET AFTER I FINISHED SHOPPING...
EEP!
ガク
WOBBLE
カラカラカラ…
CLATTER
CLATTER
CLATTER

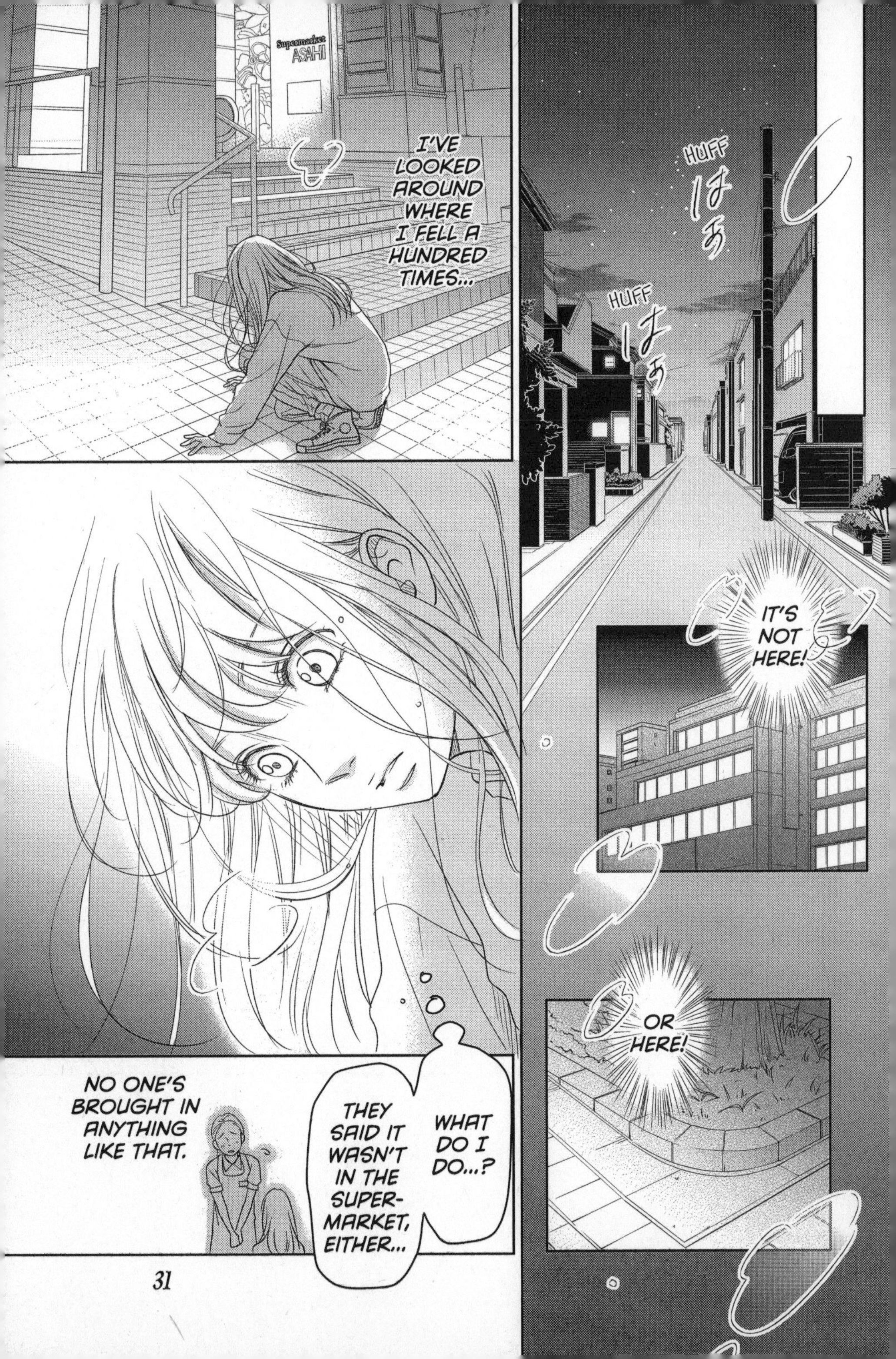
HUFF
はあ
HUFF
はあ
IT'S NOT HERE!
OR HERE!
Supermarket ASAHI
I'VE LOOKED AROUND WHERE I FELL A HUNDRED TIMES...
WHAT DO I DO...?
THEY SAID IT WASN'T IN THE SUPER-MARKET, EITHER...
NO ONE'S BROUGHT IN ANYTHING LIKE THAT.

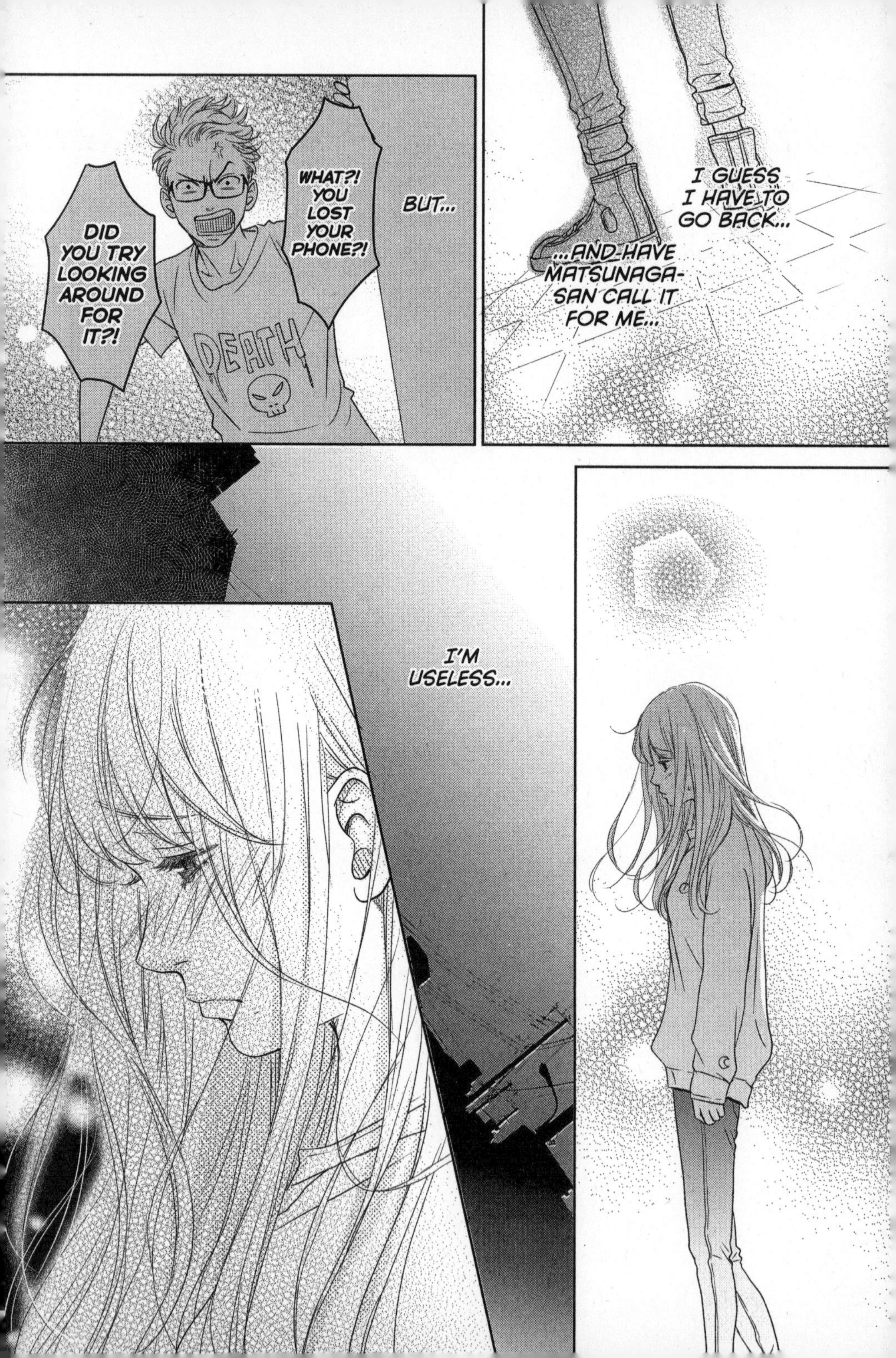
I GUESS I HAVE TO GO BACK...
...AND HAVE MATSUNAGA-SAN CALL IT FOR ME...
BUT...
WHAT?! YOU LOST YOUR PHONE?!
DID YOU TRY LOOKING AROUND FOR IT?!
I'M USELESS...

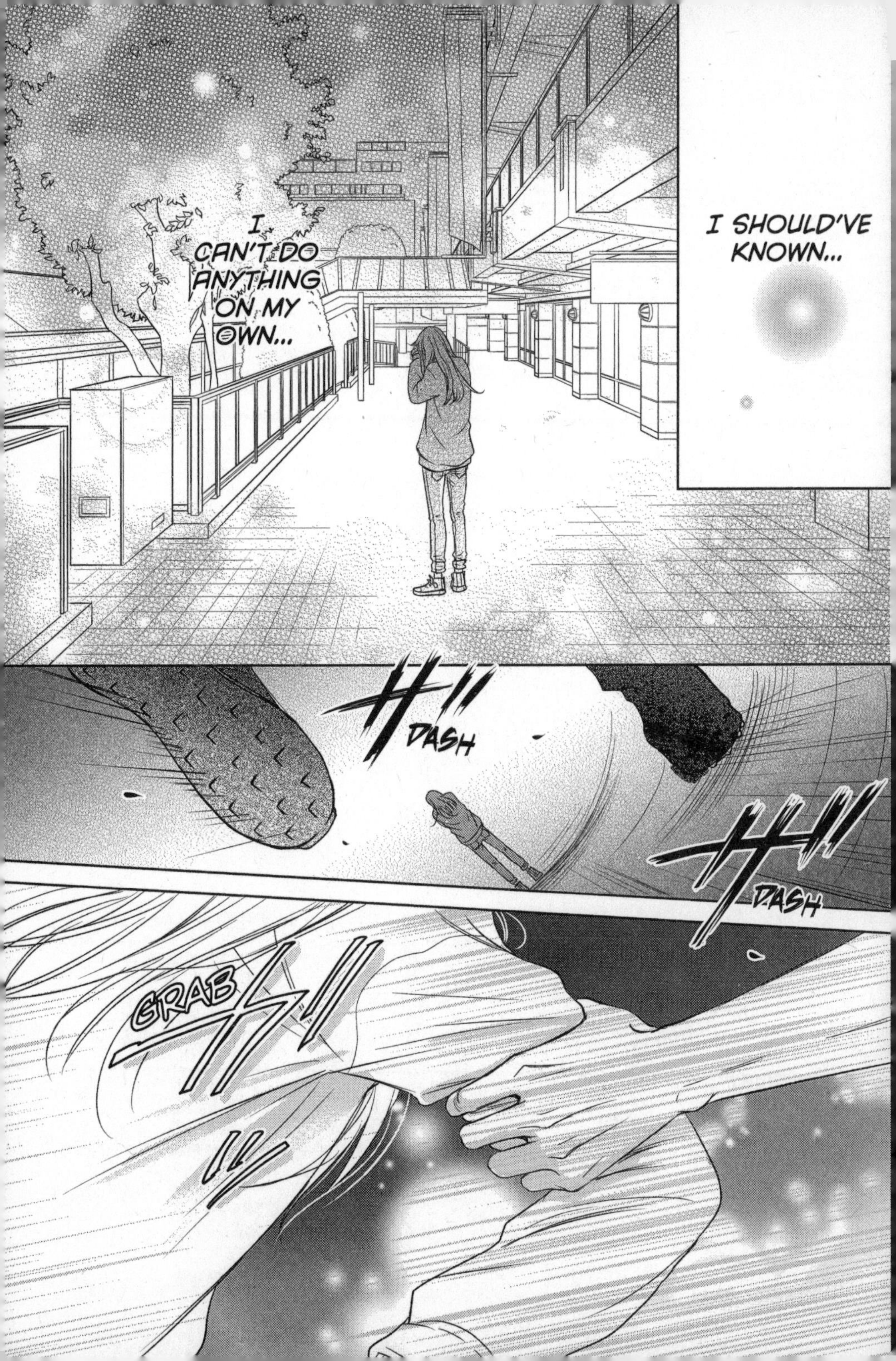
I SHOULD'VE KNOWN...
I CAN'T DO ANYTHING ON MY OWN...
DASH
DASH
GRAB

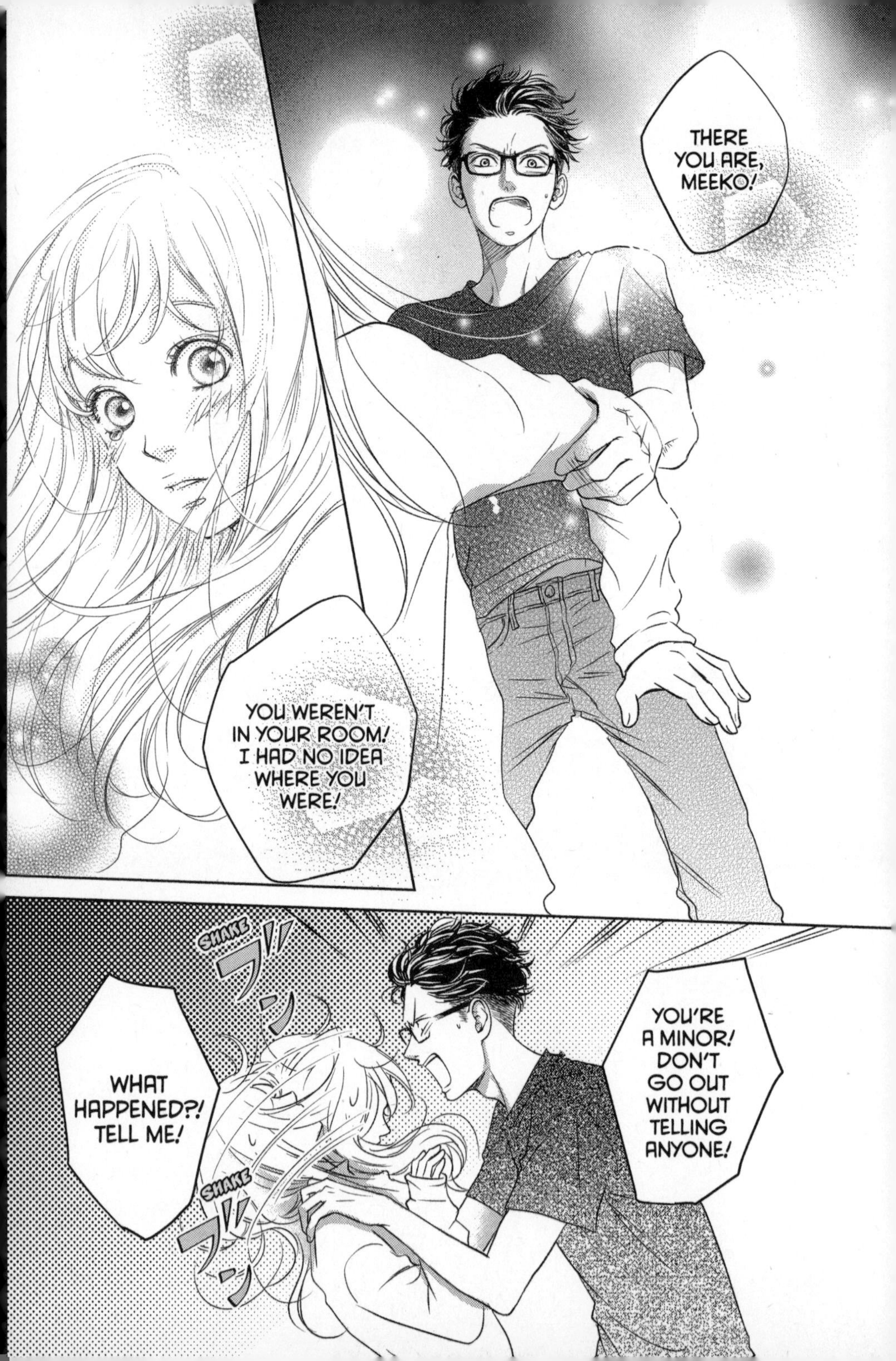
THERE YOU ARE, MEEKO!
YOU WEREN'T IN YOUR ROOM! I HAD NO IDEA WHERE YOU WERE!
SHAKE
YOU'RE A MINOR! DON'T GO OUT WITHOUT TELLING ANYONE!
WHAT HAPPENED?! TELL ME!
SHAKE

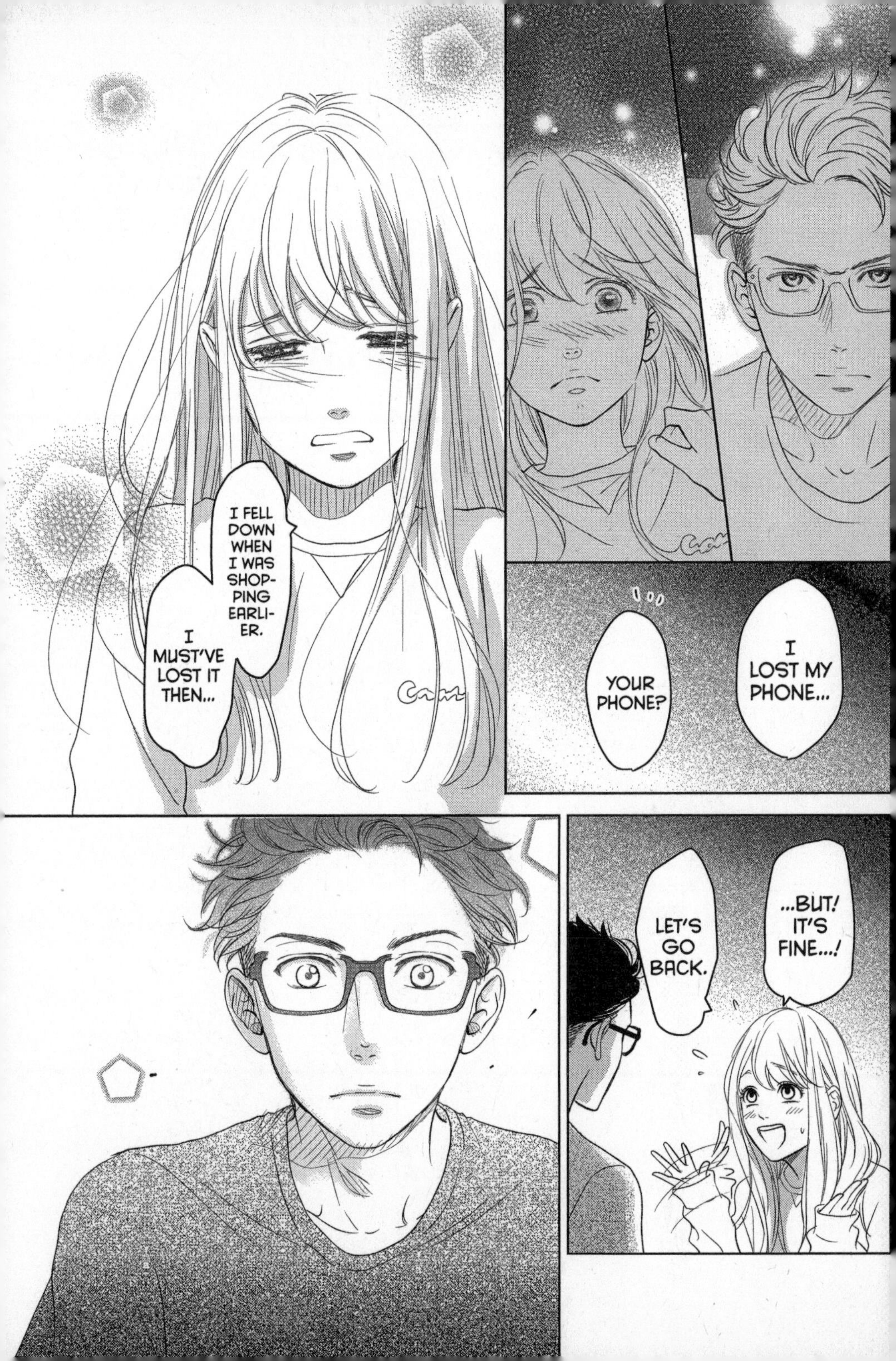
I LOST MY PHONE...
YOUR PHONE?
I FELL DOWN WHEN I WAS SHOPPING EARLIER.
I MUST'VE LOST IT THEN...
...BUT! IT'S FINE...!
LET'S GO BACK.

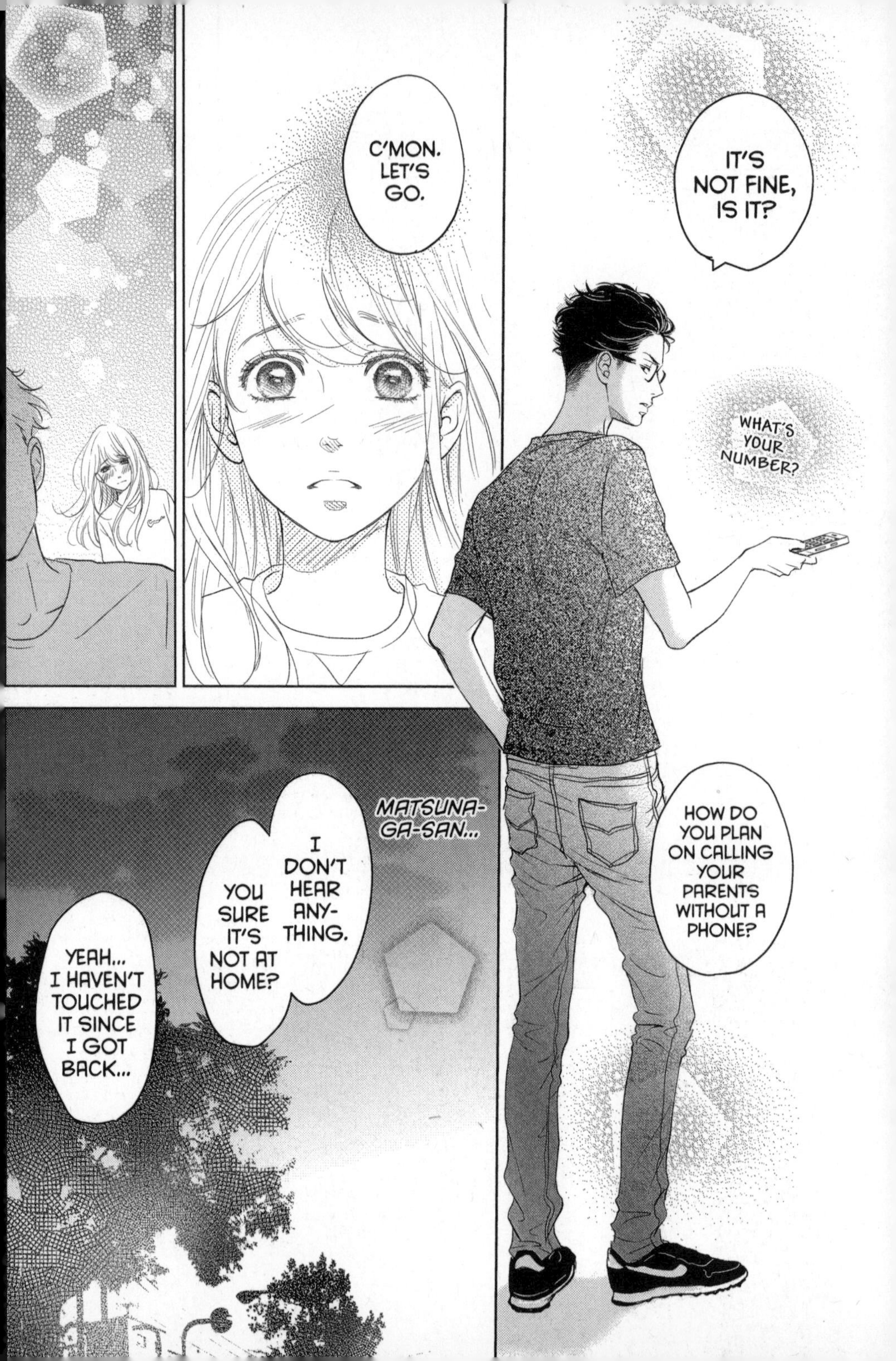
IT'S NOT FINE, IS IT?
WHAT'S YOUR NUMBER?
HOW DO YOU PLAN ON CALLING YOUR PARENTS WITHOUT A PHONE?
C'MON. LET'S GO.
MATSUNA-GA-SAN...
I DON'T HEAR ANY-THING.
YOU SURE IT'S NOT AT HOME?
YEAH... I HAVEN'T TOUCHED IT SINCE I GOT BACK...

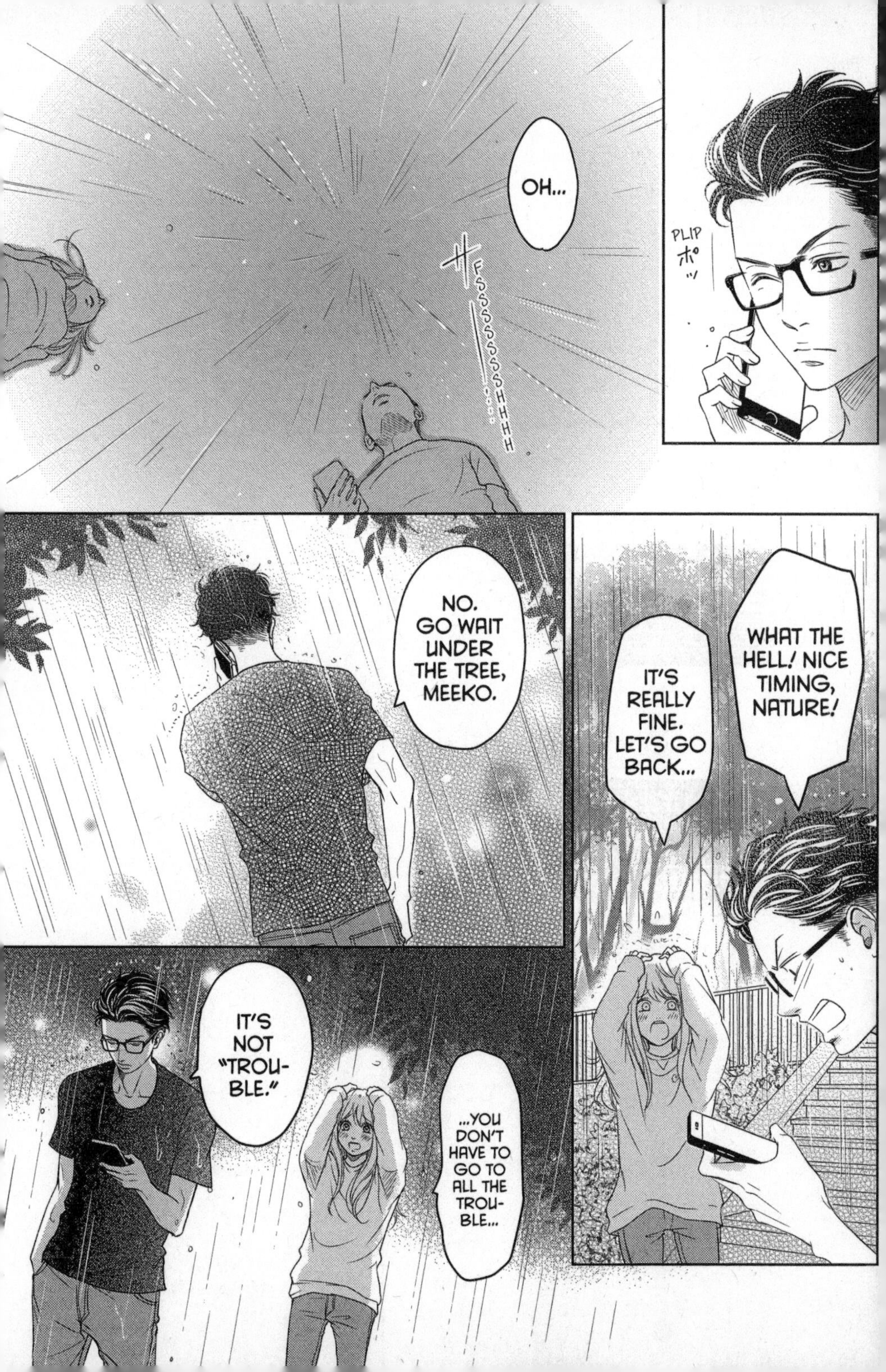
PLIP
ポッ
OH...
FSSSSSSSSHHHH
WHAT THE HELL! NICE TIMING, NATURE!
IT'S REALLY FINE. LET'S GO BACK...
NO. GO WAIT UNDER THE TREE, MEEKO.
...YOU DON'T HAVE TO GO TO ALL THE TROU-BLE...
IT'S NOT "TROU-BLE."

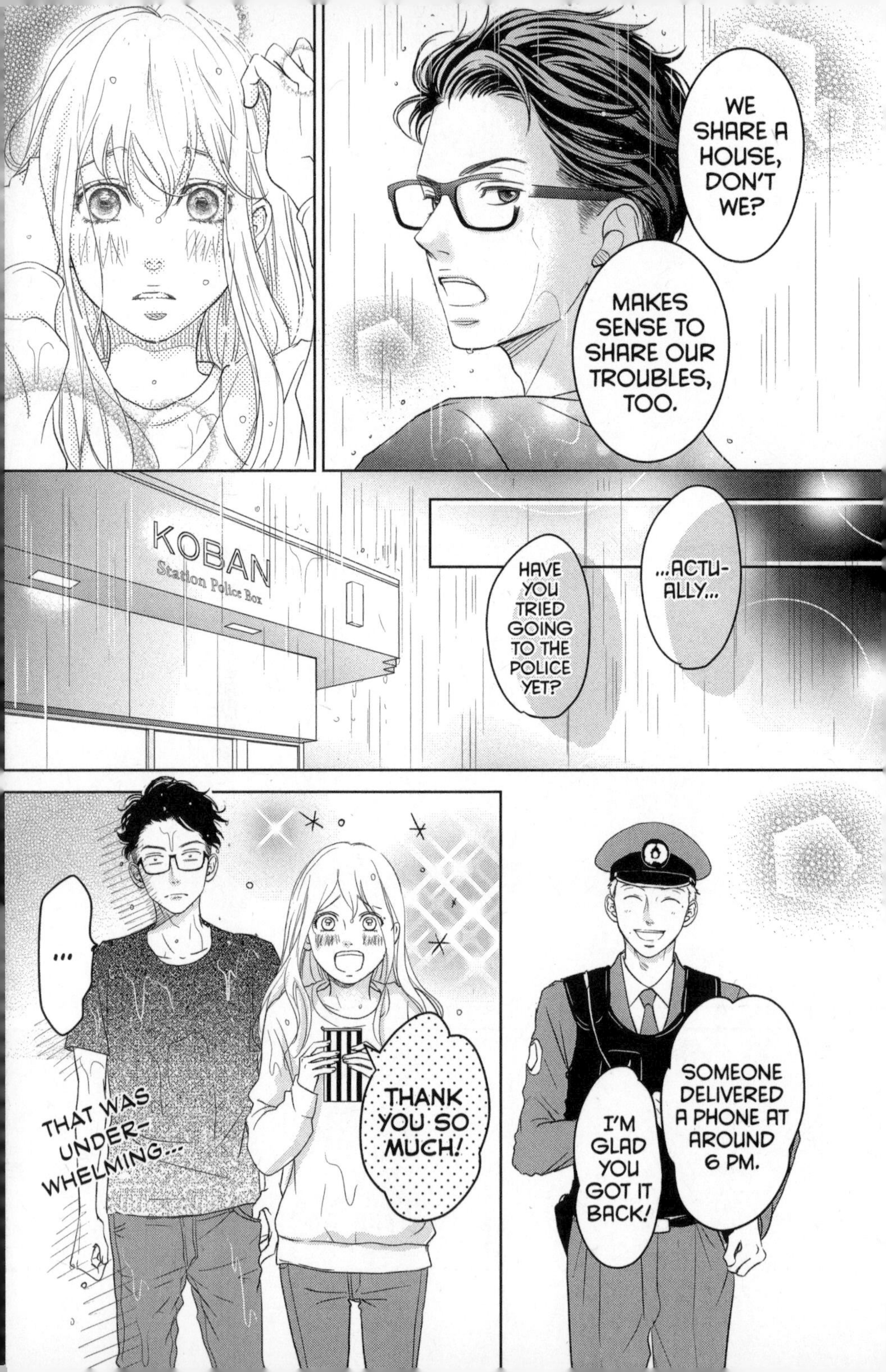
WE SHARE A HOUSE, DON'T WE?
MAKES SENSE TO SHARE OUR TROUBLES, TOO.
...ACTU-ALLY...
HAVE YOU TRIED GOING TO THE POLICE YET?
KOBAN
Station Police Box
SOMEONE DELIVERED A PHONE AT AROUND 6 PM.
I'M GLAD YOU GOT IT BACK!
THANK YOU SO MUCH!
...
THAT WAS UNDER-WHELMING...

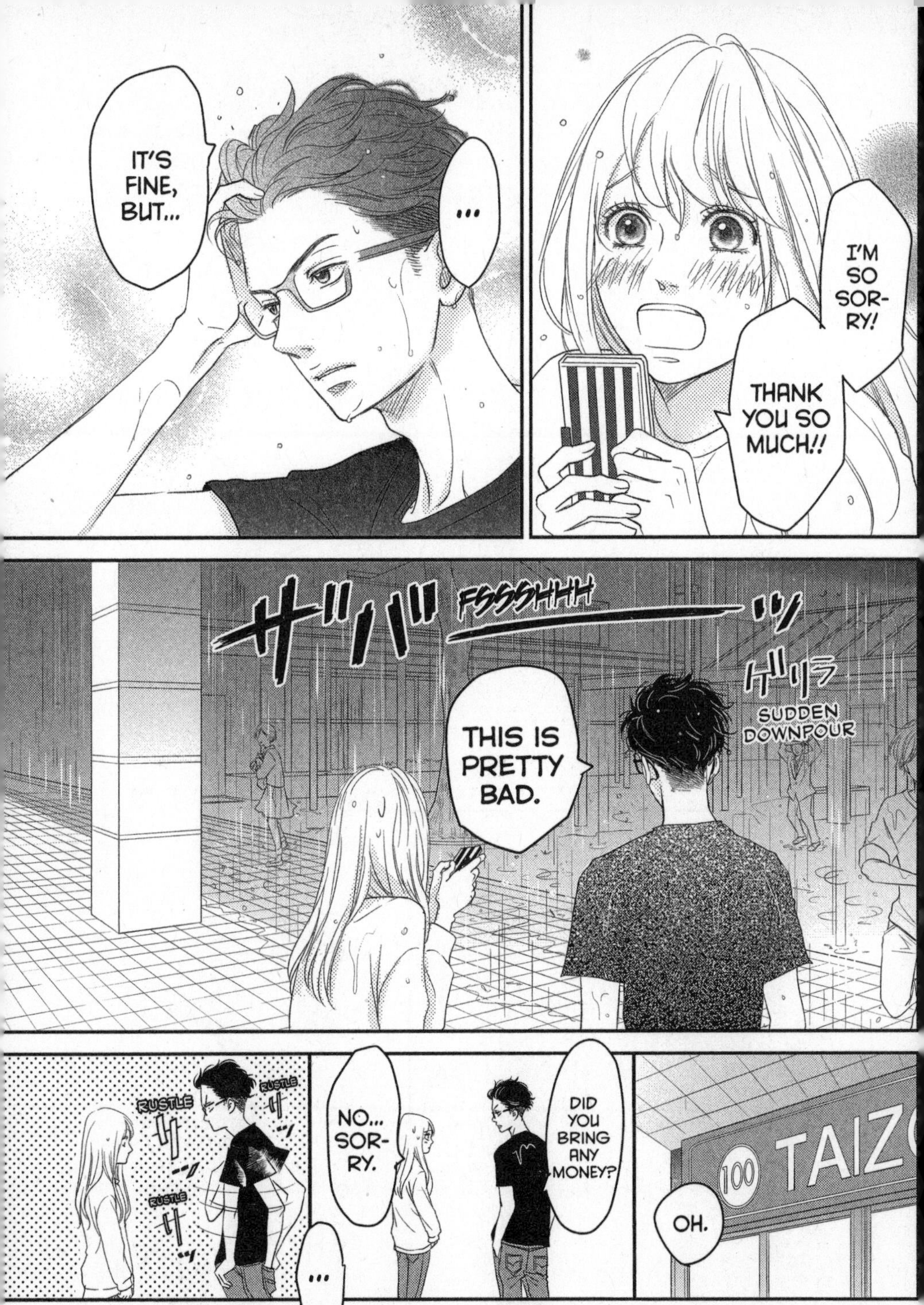
I'M SO SORRY!
THANK YOU SO MUCH!!
IT'S FINE, BUT...
...
ザバ
FSSSHHH
ッ
ゲリラ
SUDDEN DOWNPOUR
THIS IS PRETTY BAD.
100 TAIZ
OH.
DID YOU BRING ANY MONEY?
NO... SORRY.
...
RUSTLE
RUSTLE
RUSTLE

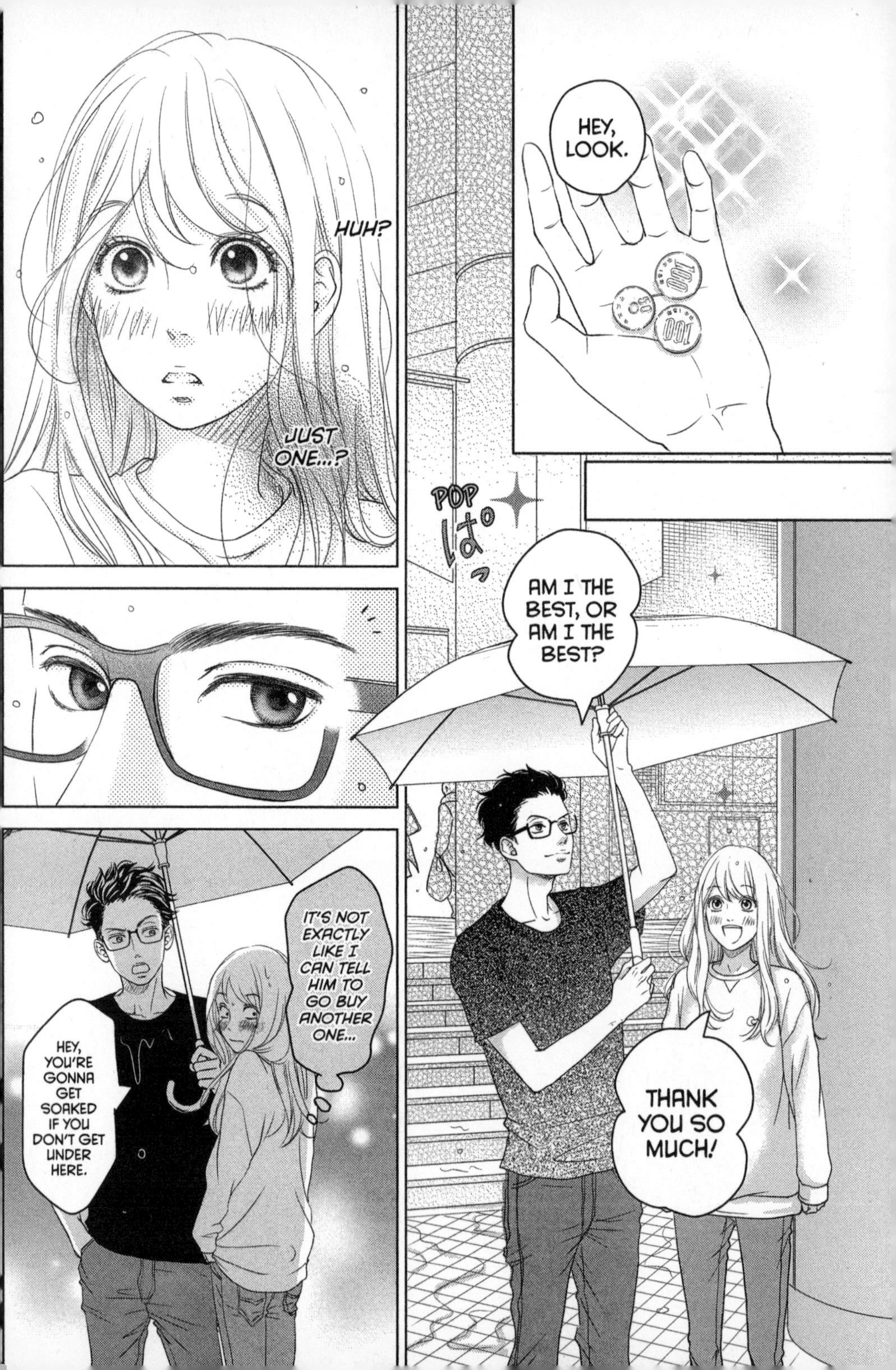
HEY, LOOK.
POP
AM I THE BEST, OR AM I THE BEST?
THANK YOU SO MUCH!
HUH?
JUST ONE...?
IT'S NOT EXACTLY LIKE I CAN TELL HIM TO GO BUY ANOTHER ONE...
HEY, YOU'RE GONNA GET SOAKED IF YOU DON'T GET UNDER HERE.

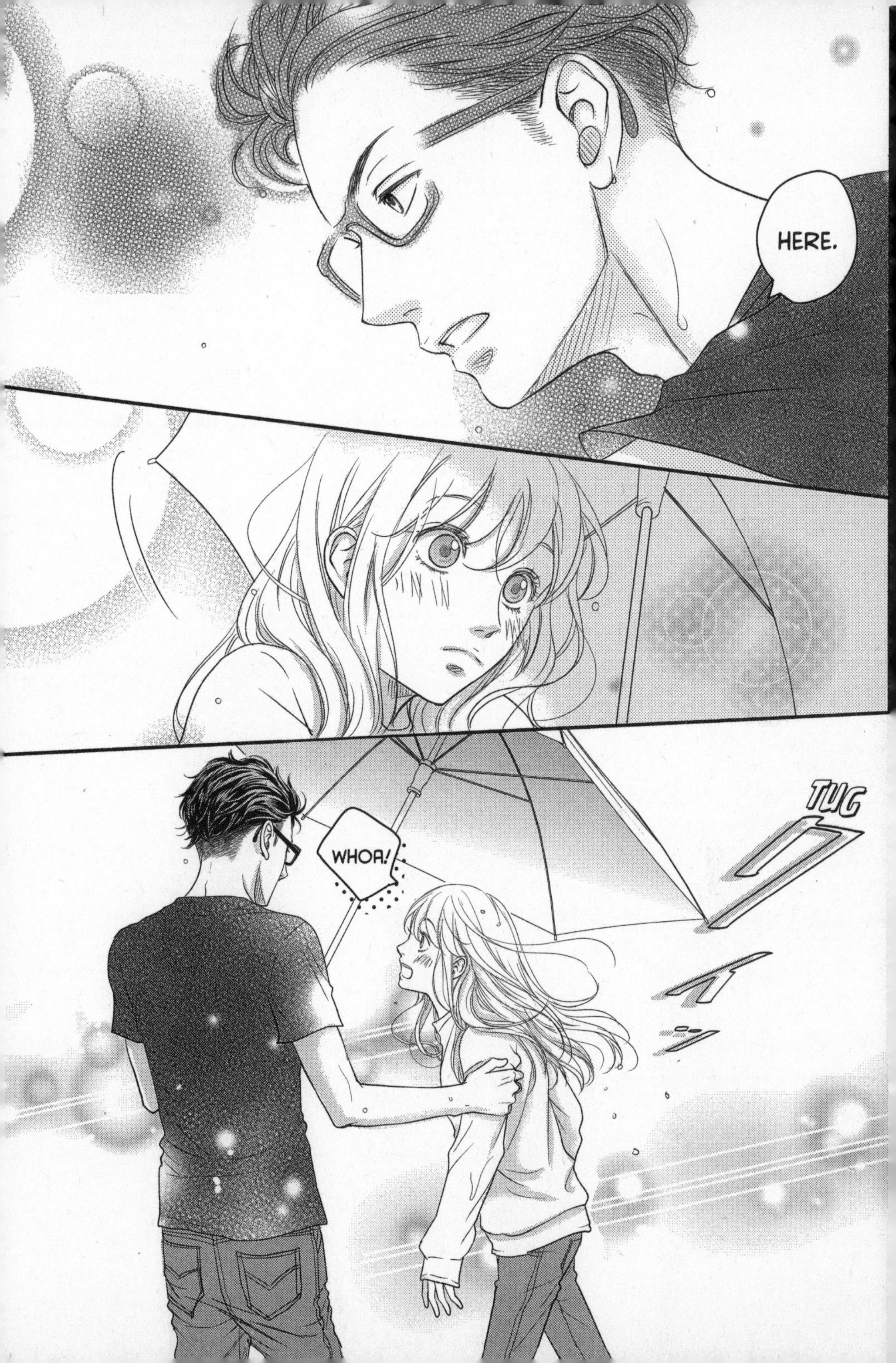
HERE.
TUG
WHOA!

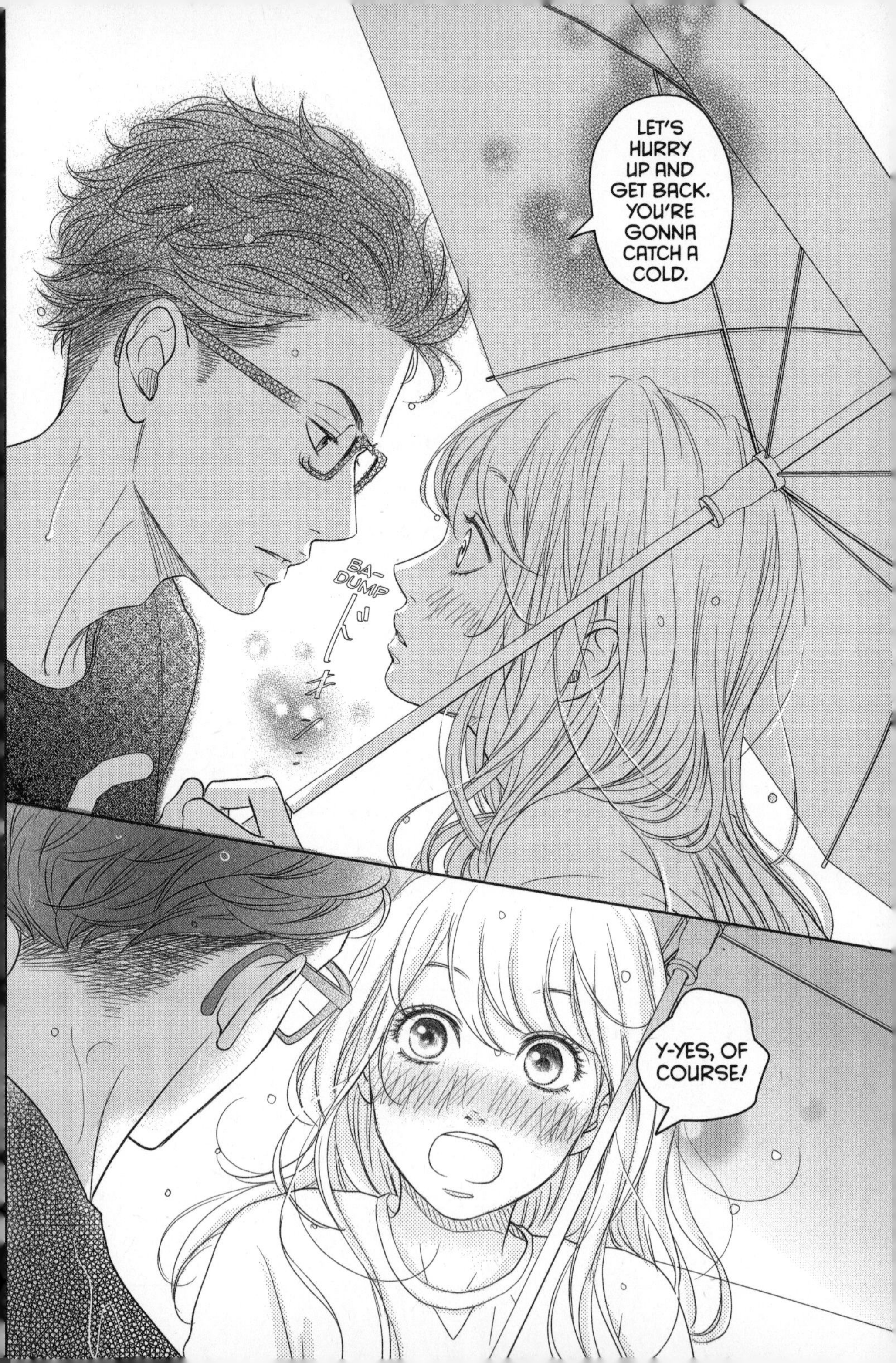
LET'S HURRY UP AND GET BACK. YOU'RE GONNA CATCH A COLD.
BA-DUMP
ドキ
Y-YES, OF COURSE!

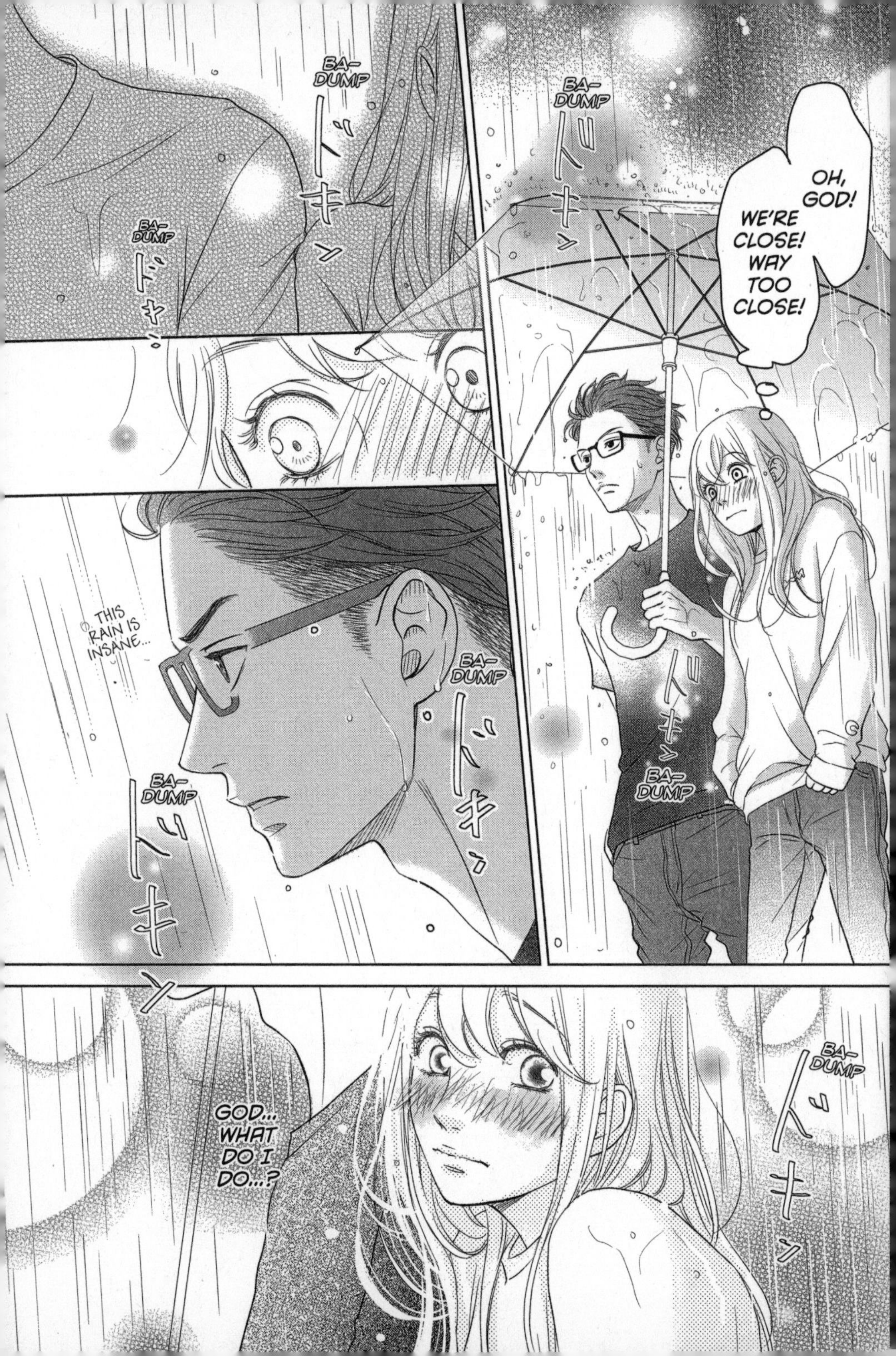
BA-DUMP
OH, GOD! WE'RE CLOSE! WAY TOO CLOSE!
BA-DUMP
BA-DUMP
BA-DUMP
THIS RAIN IS INSANE...
BA-DUMP
BA-DUMP
BA-DUMP
GOD... WHAT DO I DO...?

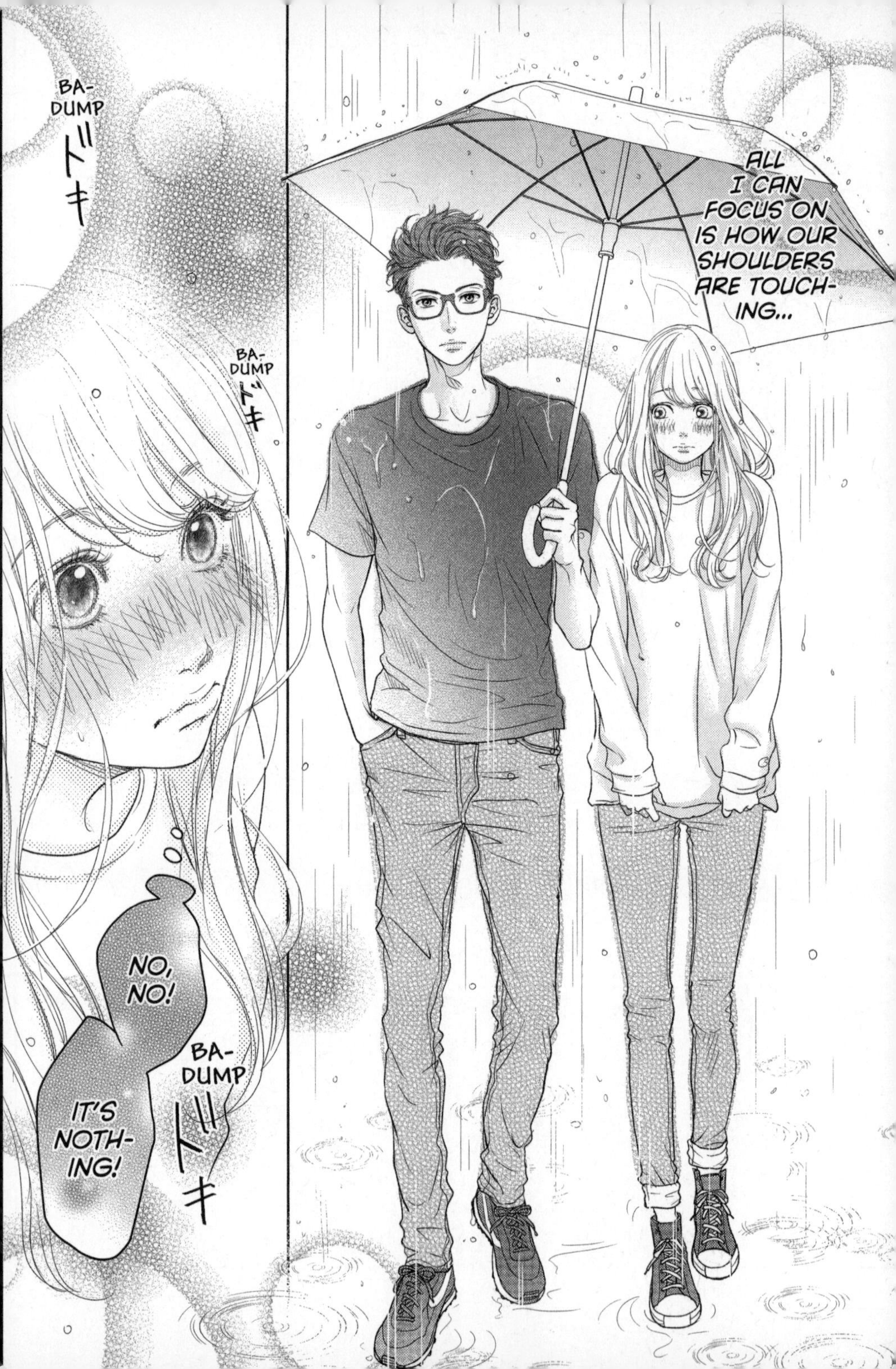
ALL I CAN FOCUS ON IS HOW OUR SHOULDERS ARE TOUCHING...
BA-DUMP
ドキ
BA-DUMP
ドキ
NO, NO!
IT'S NOTHING!
BA-DUMP
ドキ

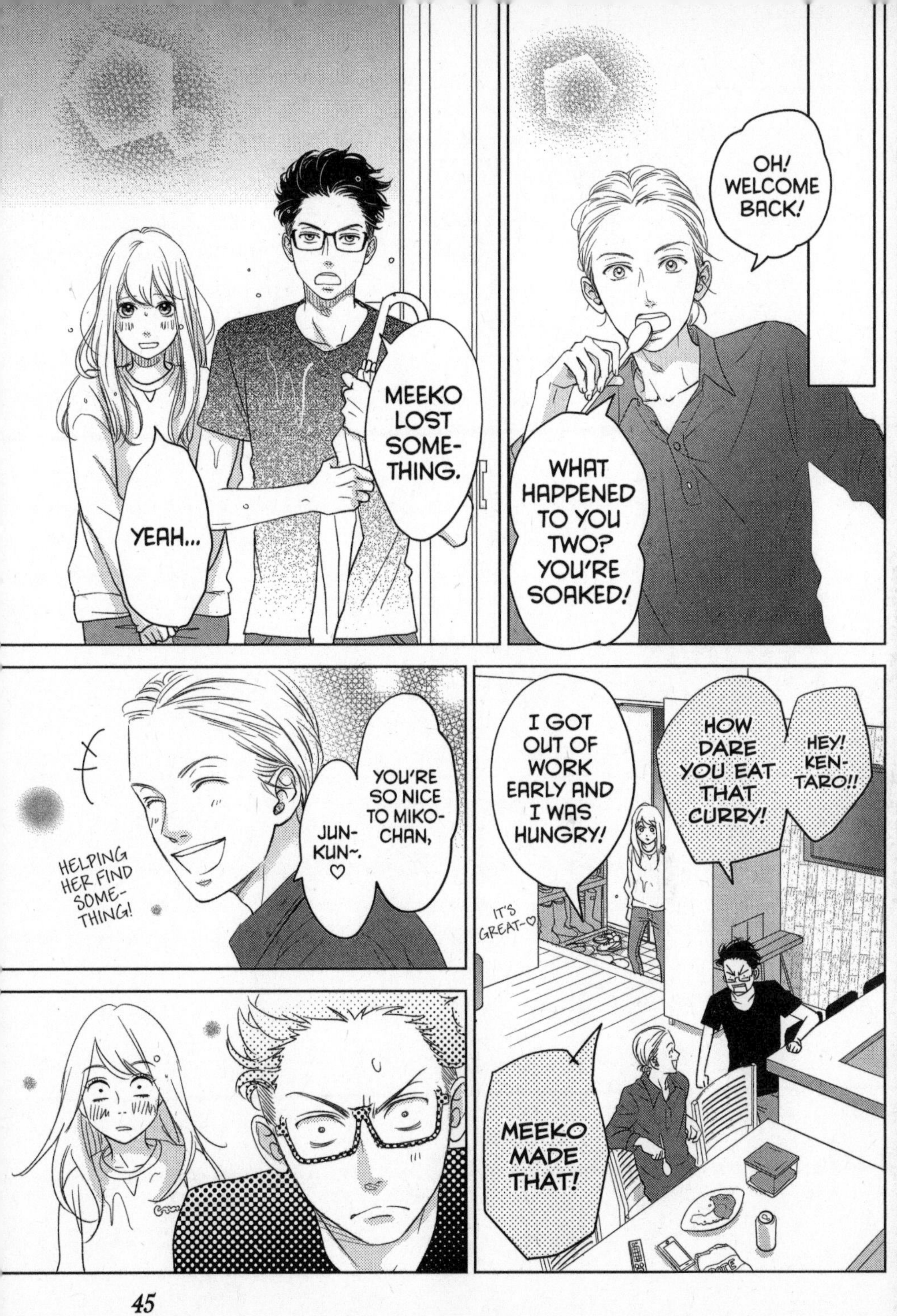
OH! WELCOME BACK!
WHAT HAPPENED TO YOU TWO? YOU'RE SOAKED!
MEEKO LOST SOME-THING.
YEAH...
HEY! KEN-TARO!!
HOW DARE YOU EAT THAT CURRY!
I GOT OUT OF WORK EARLY AND I WAS HUNGRY!
IT'S GREAT-♡
MEEKO MADE THAT!
YOU'RE SO NICE TO MIKO-CHAN,
JUN-KUN~.♡
HELPING HER FIND SOME-THING!

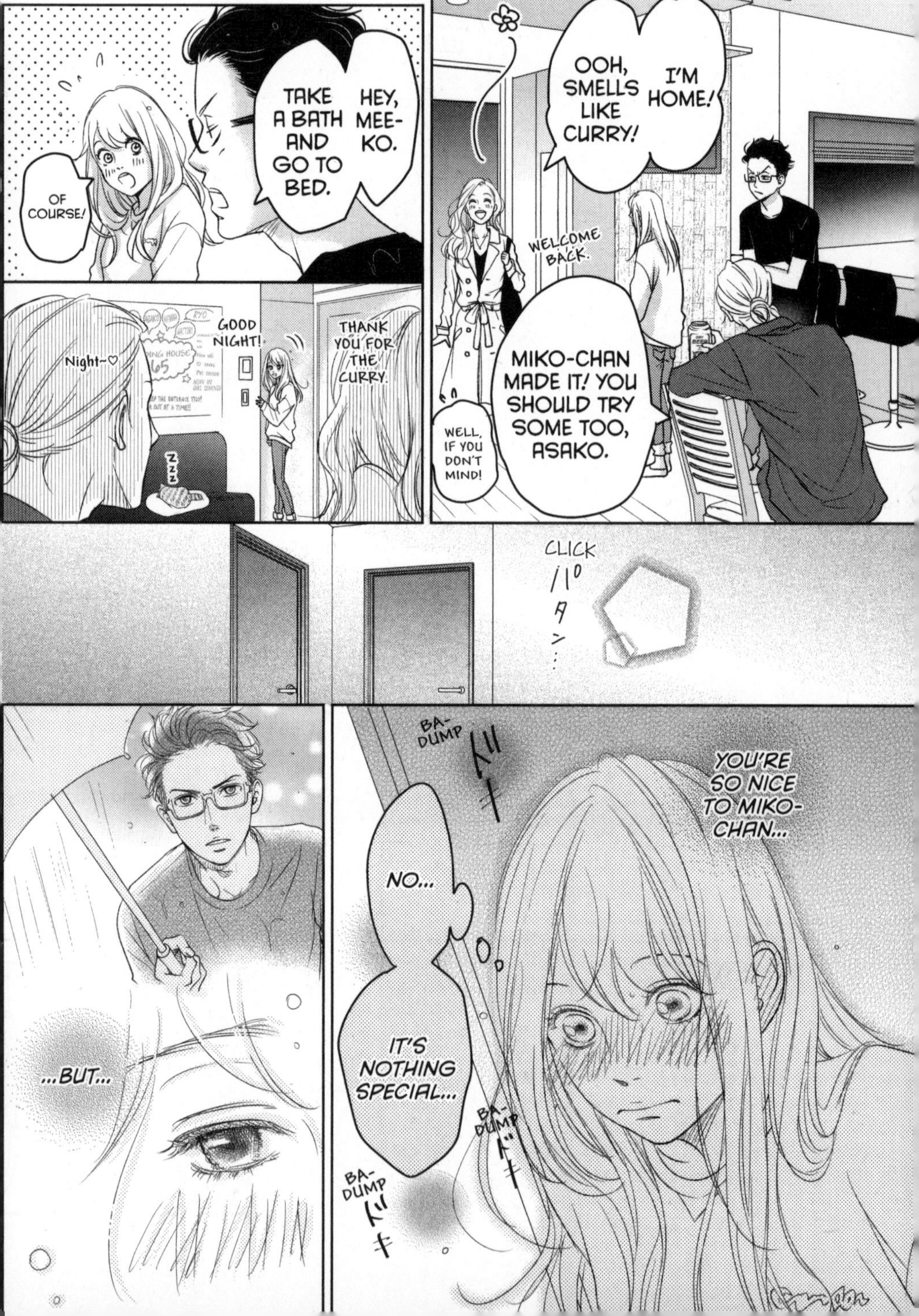
I'M HOME!
OOH, SMELLS LIKE CURRY!
WELCOME BACK.
MIKO-CHAN MADE IT! YOU SHOULD TRY SOME TOO, ASAKO.
WELL, IF YOU DON'T MIND!
HEY, MEE-KO. TAKE A BATH AND GO TO BED.
OF COURSE!
THANK YOU FOR THE CURRY.
GOOD NIGHT!
Night~♡
CLICK
パタン…
BA-DUMP ドキ
YOU'RE SO NICE TO MIKO-CHAN...
NO...
IT'S NOTHING SPECIAL...
BA-DUMP ドキ
BA-DUMP ドキ
...BUT...

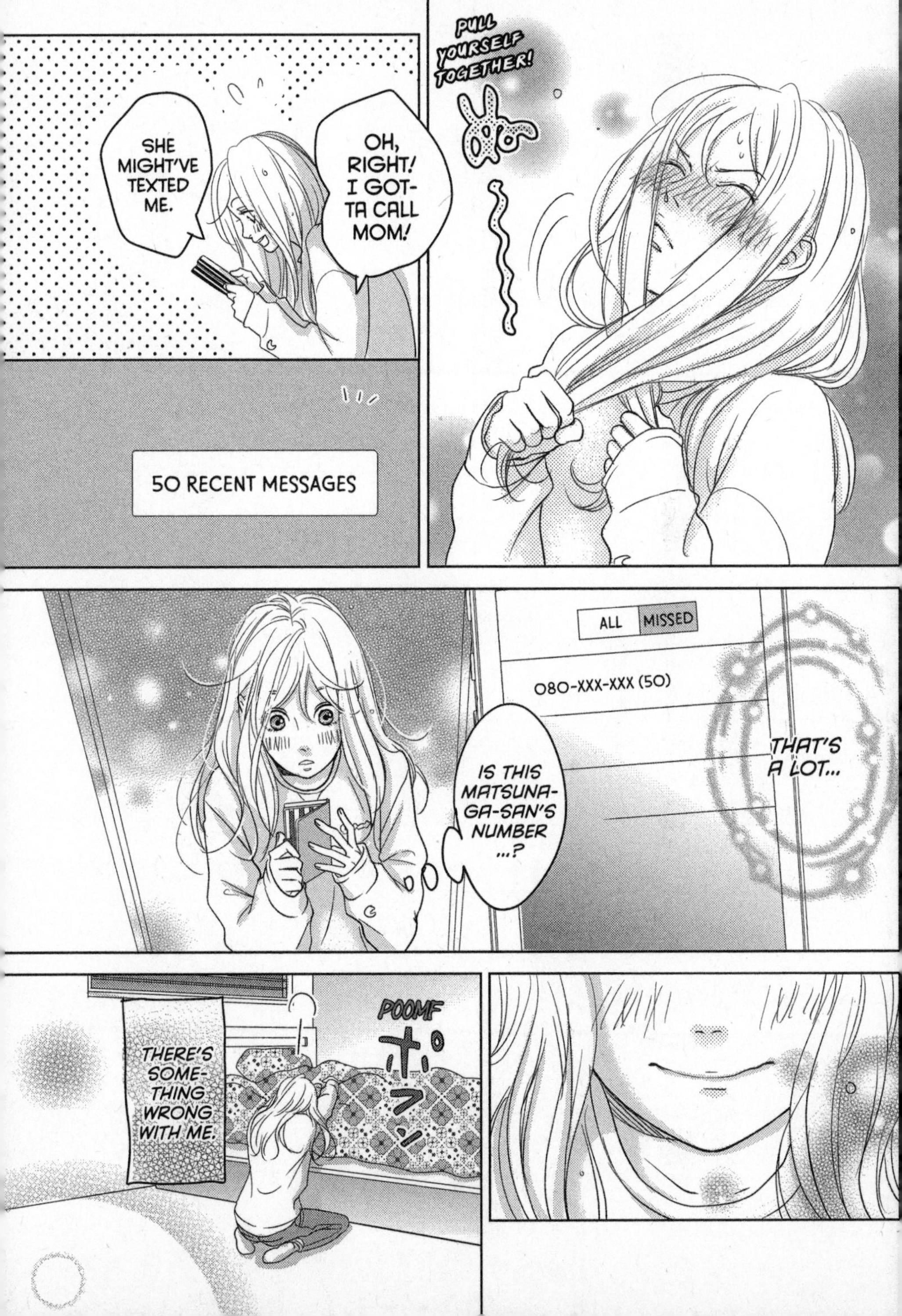
PULL YOURSELF TOGETHER!
OH, RIGHT! I GOTTA CALL MOM!
SHE MIGHT'VE TEXTED ME.
50 RECENT MESSAGES
ALL
MISSED
080-XXX-XXX (50)
THAT'S A LOT...
IS THIS MATSUNAGA-SAN'S NUMBER ...?
POOMF
THERE'S SOMETHING WRONG WITH ME.

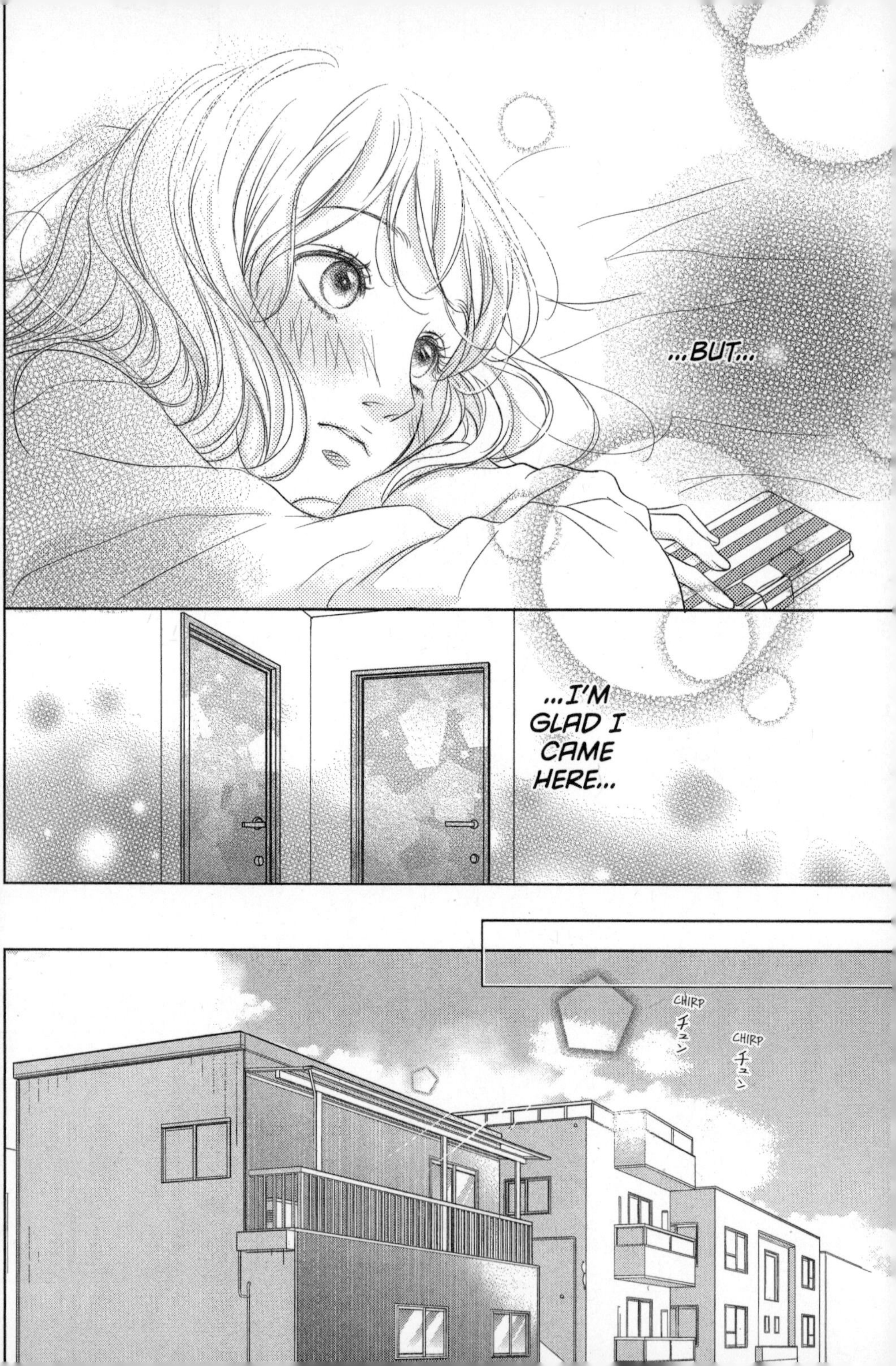
...BUT...
...I'M GLAD I CAME HERE...
CHIRP
チュン
CHIRP
チュン

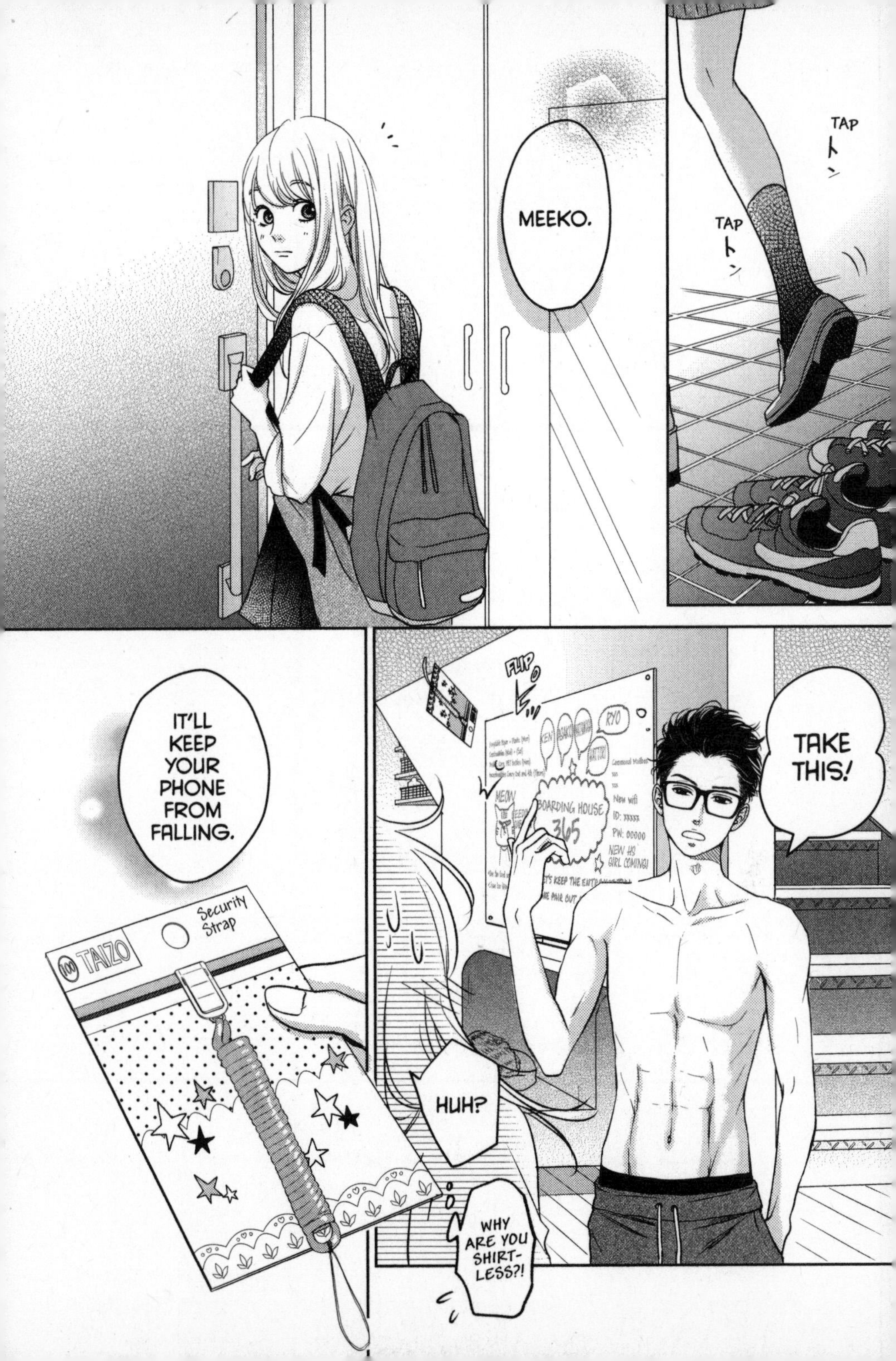

TAP
TAP
MEEKO.
TAKE THIS!
FLIP
RYO
BOARDING HOUSE 365
New wifi
ID: xxxxx
PW: 00000
NEW HS GIRL COMING!
HUH?
WHY ARE YOU SHIRT-LESS?!
IT'LL KEEP YOUR PHONE FROM FALLING.
TAIZO
Security Strap

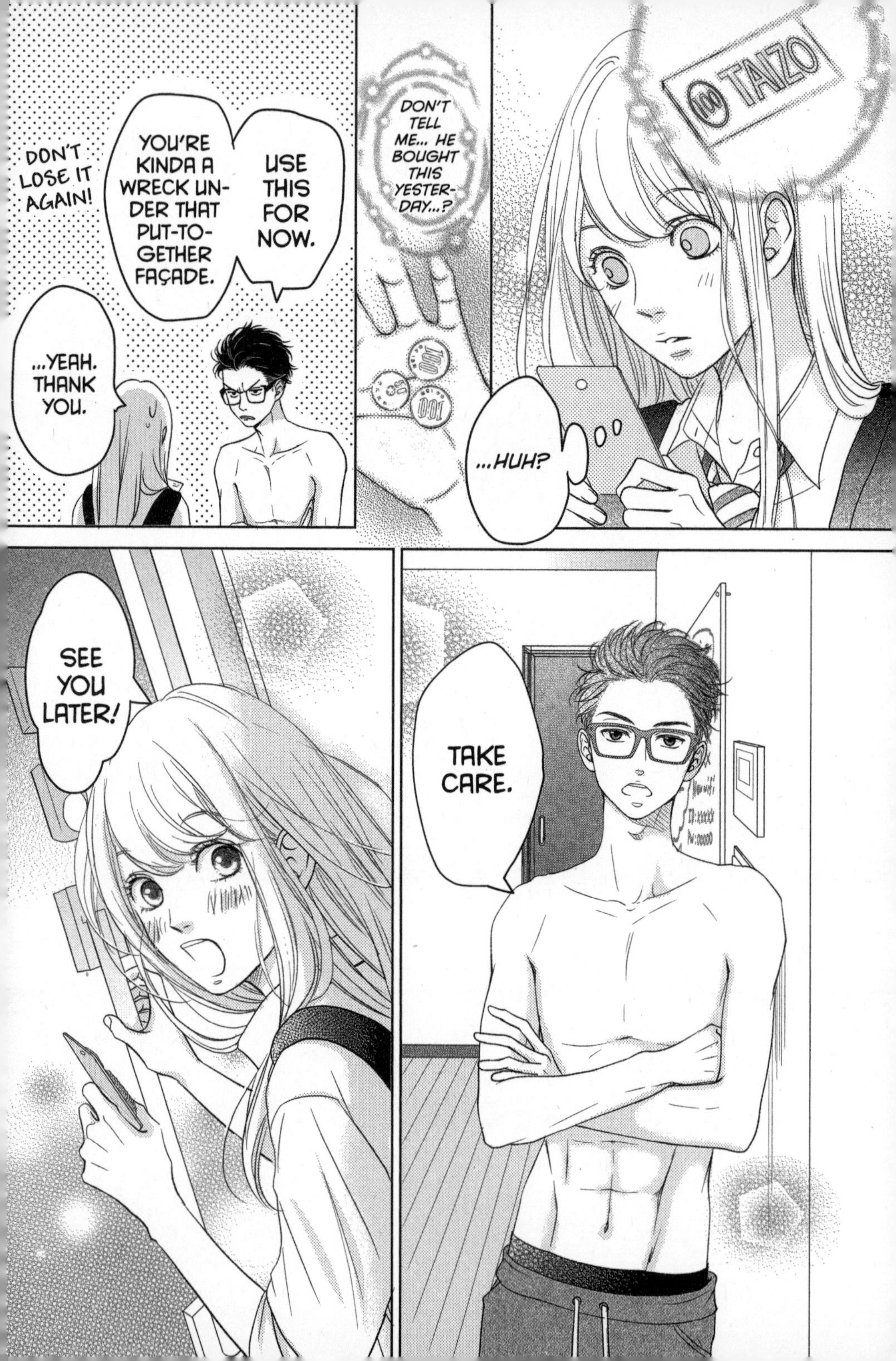
TAIZO
...HUH?
DON'T TELL ME... HE BOUGHT THIS YESTER-DAY...?
USE THIS FOR NOW.
YOU'RE KINDA A WRECK UN-DER THAT PUT-TO-GETHER FAÇADE.
DON'T LOSE IT AGAIN!
...YEAH. THANK YOU.
TAKE CARE.
SEE YOU LATER!

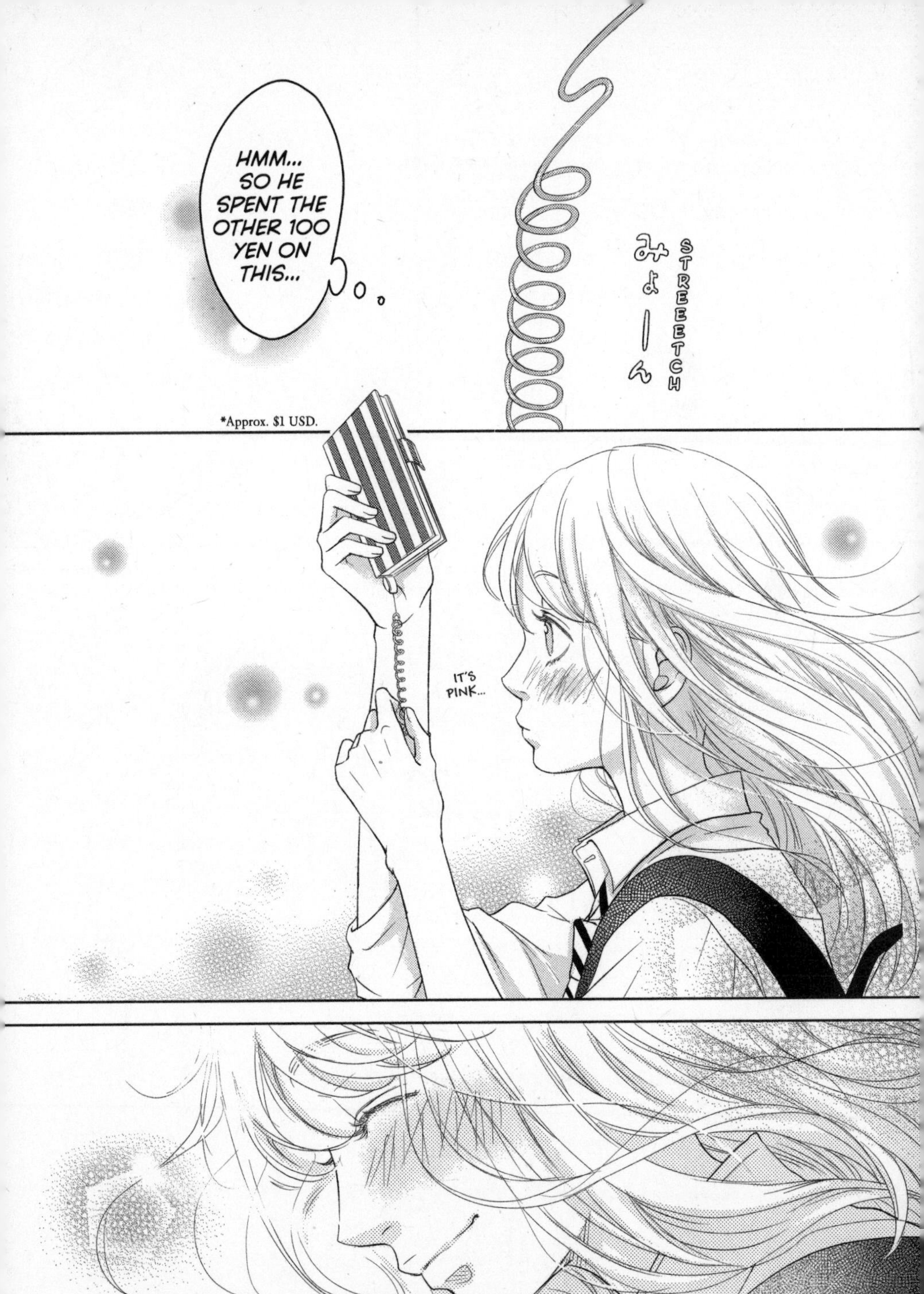

STREETCH
みよーん
HMM... SO HE SPENT THE OTHER 100 YEN ON THIS...
IT'S PINK...

*Approx. $1 USD.

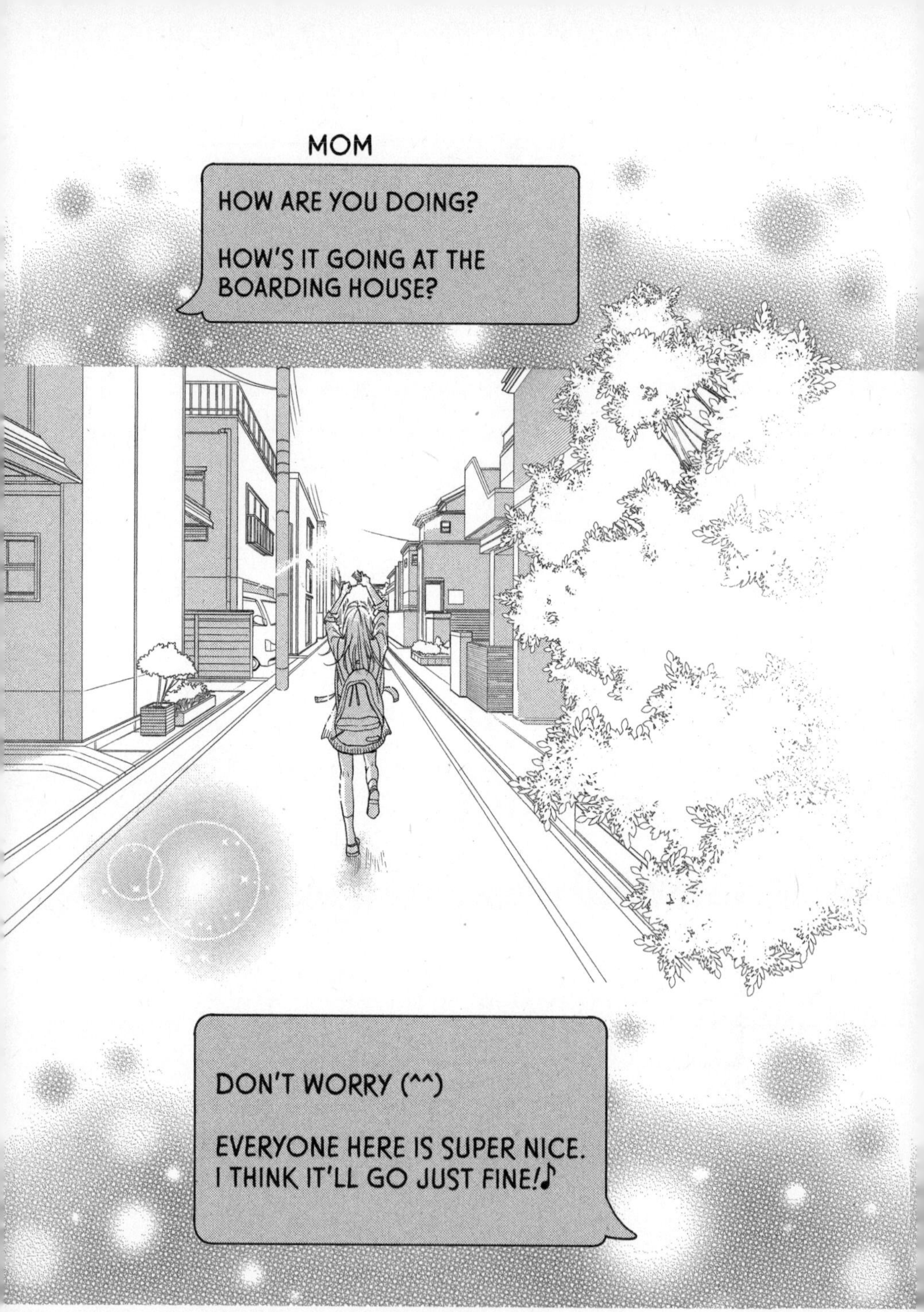
MOM
HOW ARE YOU DOING?
HOW'S IT GOING AT THE BOARDING HOUSE?
DON'T WORRY (^^)
EVERYONE HERE IS SUPER NICE. I THINK IT'LL GO JUST FINE!♪

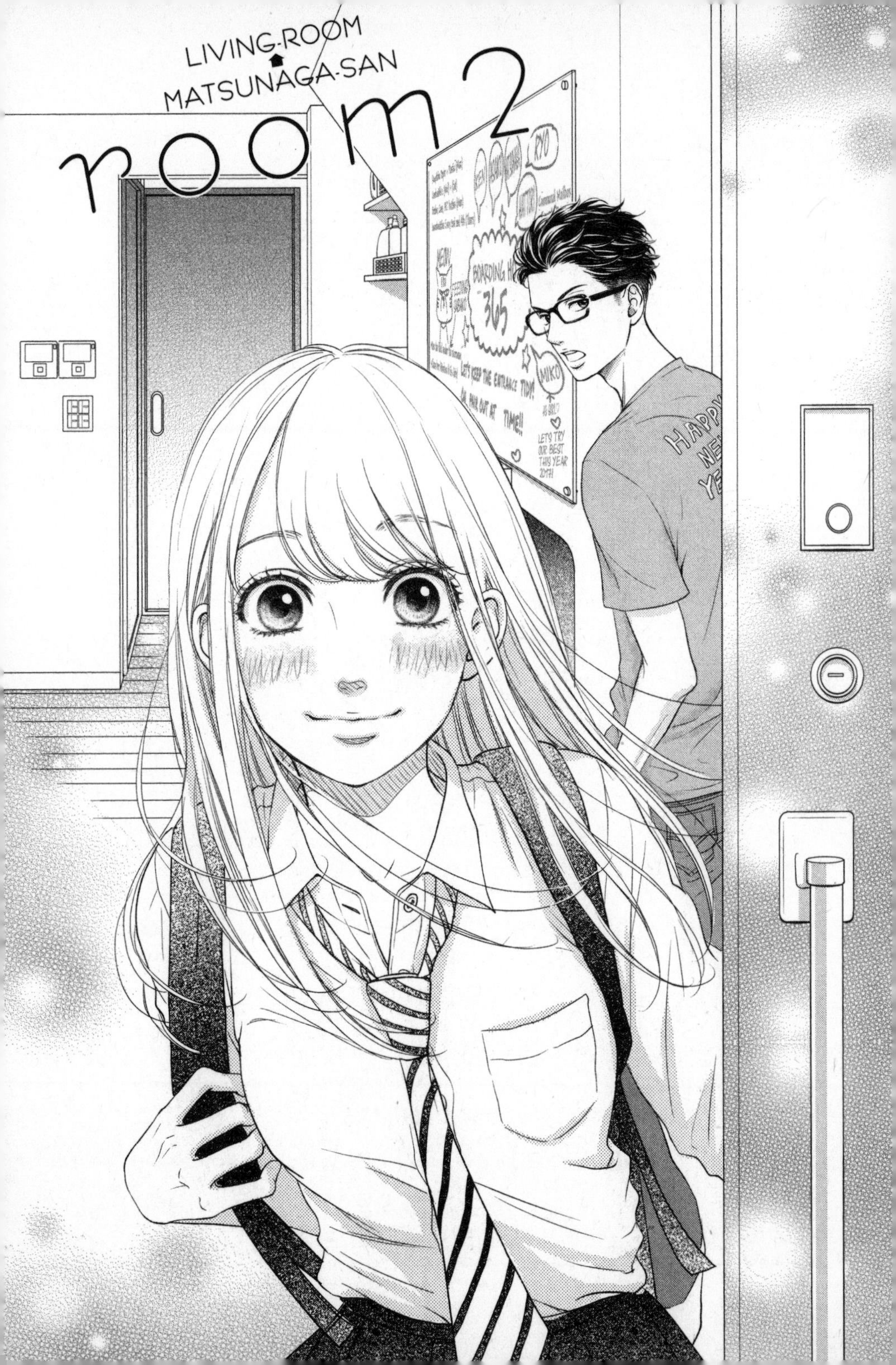
LIVING-ROOM MATSUNAGA-SAN
room 2
RYO
BOARDING H
365
MIKO
LET'S KEEP THE ENTRANCE TIDY!
LET'S TRY OUR BEST THIS YEAR 20TH!
HAPPY NE YE

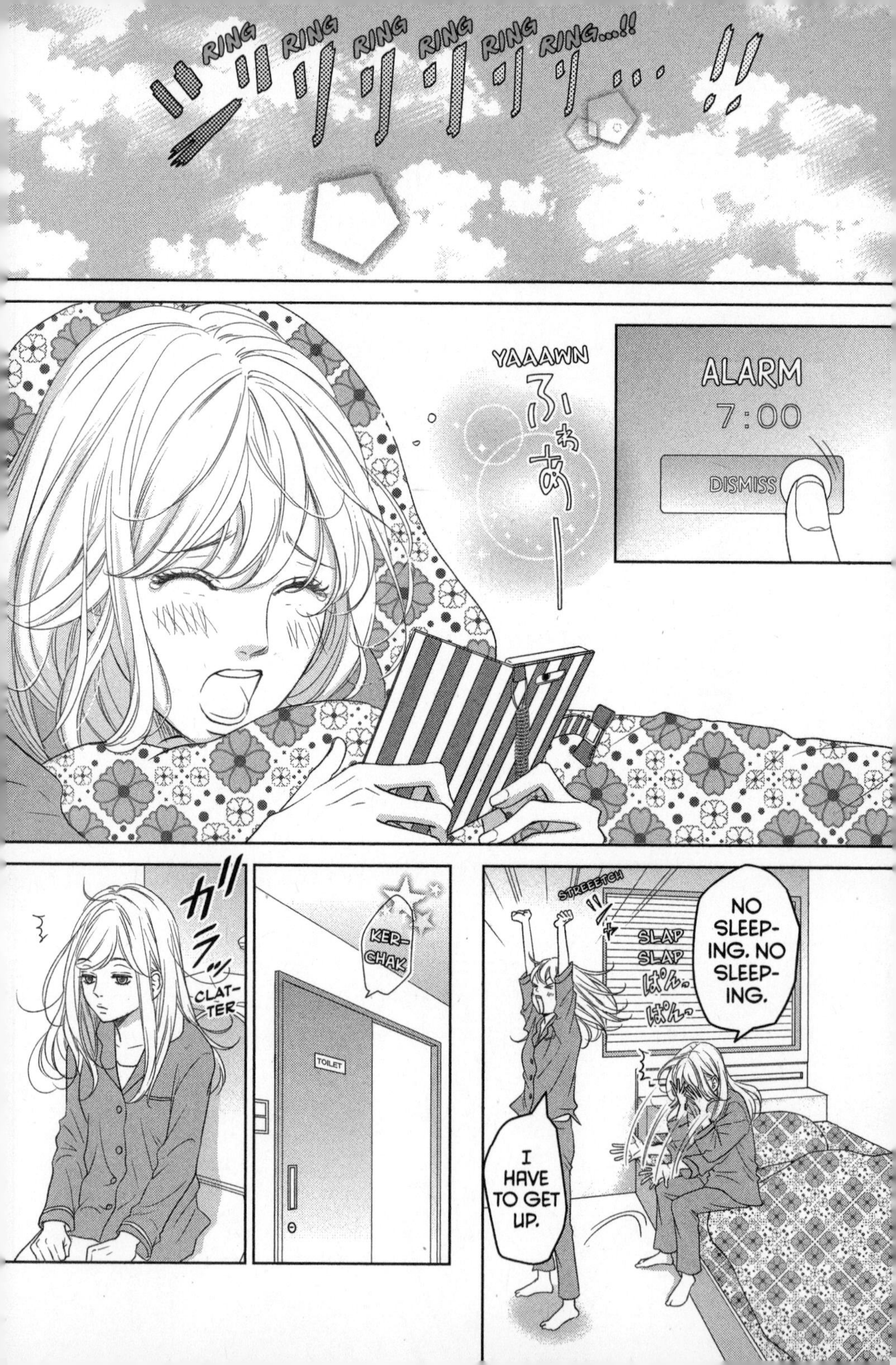
RING RING RING RING RING RING...!!
ALARM
7:00
DISMISS
YAAAWN
STREEETCH
NO SLEEP-ING. NO SLEEP-ING.
SLAP SLAP
I HAVE TO GET UP.
KER-CHAK
TOILET
CLAT-TER

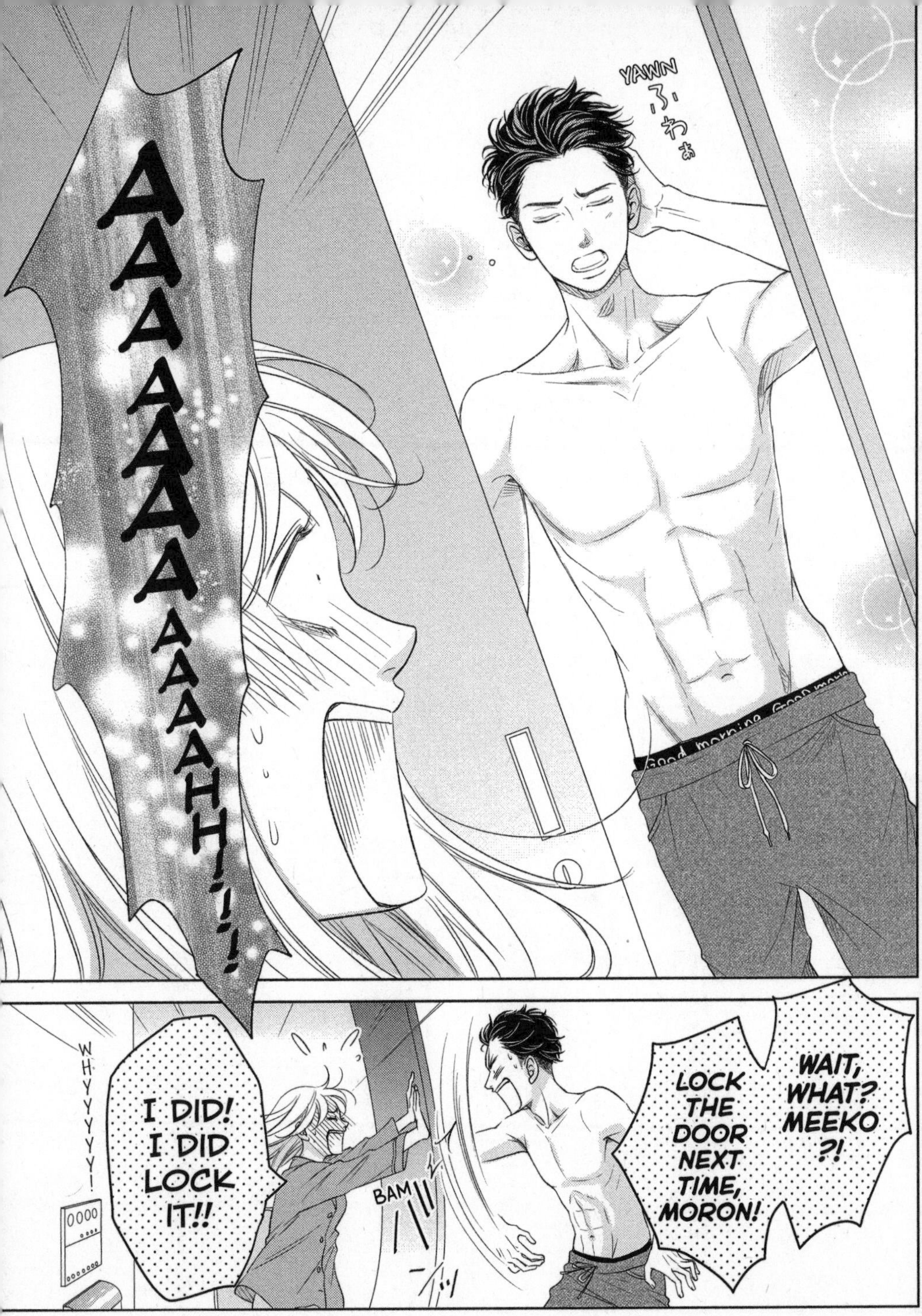
YAWN
ふわぁ
AAAAAAAAAAAAAAAH!!!!
WAIT, WHAT? MEEKO?!
LOCK THE DOOR NEXT TIME, MORON!
BAM
I DID! I DID LOCK IT!!
WHYYYYY!

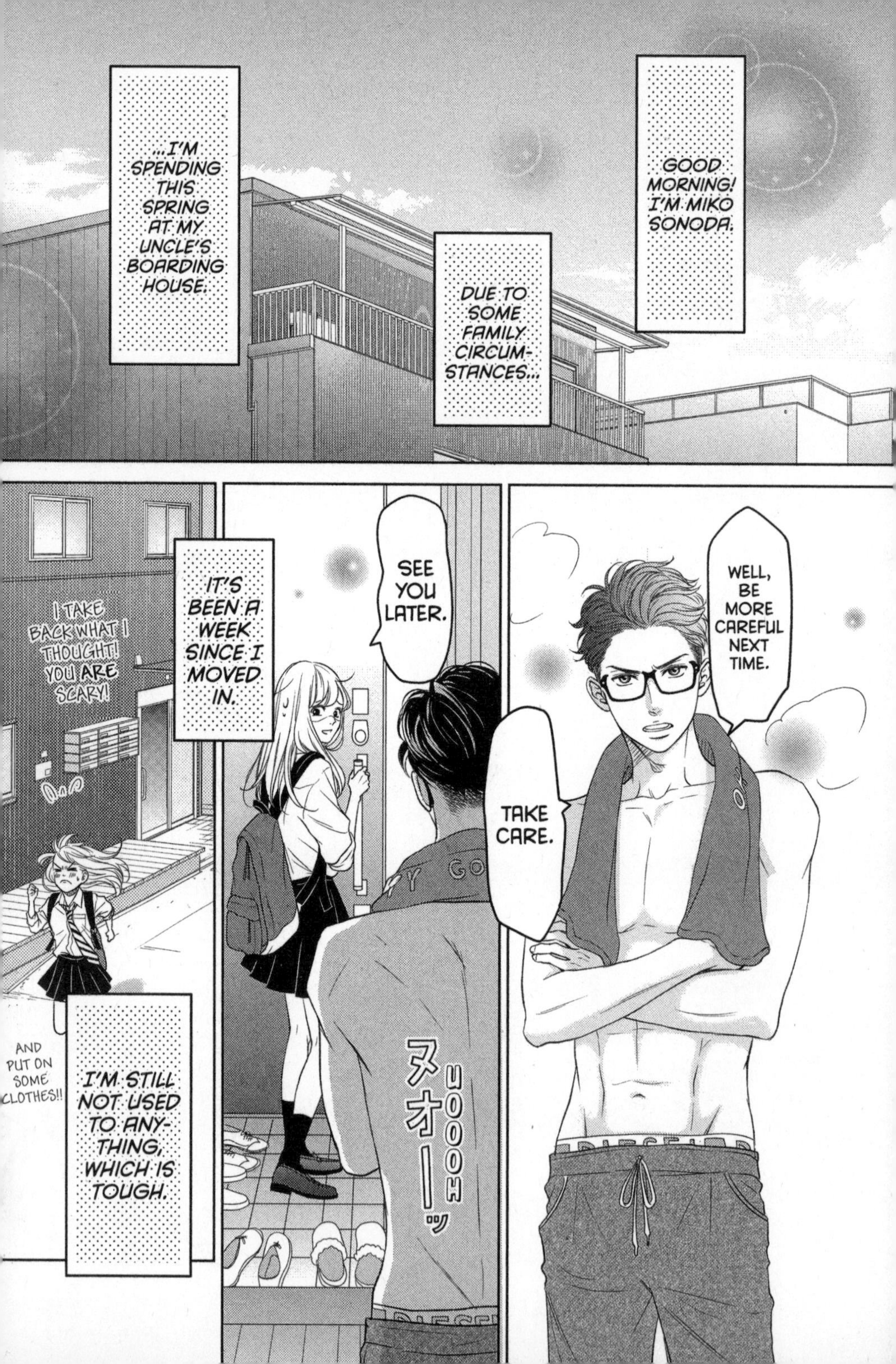
GOOD MORNING! I'M MIKO SONODA.
DUE TO SOME FAMILY CIRCUMSTANCES...
...I'M SPENDING THIS SPRING AT MY UNCLE'S BOARDING HOUSE.
WELL, BE MORE CAREFUL NEXT TIME.
TAKE CARE.
SEE YOU LATER.
IT'S BEEN A WEEK SINCE I MOVED IN.
ヌオーッ
UOOOOH
I TAKE BACK WHAT I THOUGHT! YOU ARE SCARY!
I'M STILL NOT USED TO ANYTHING, WHICH IS TOUGH.
AND PUT ON SOME CLOTHES!!

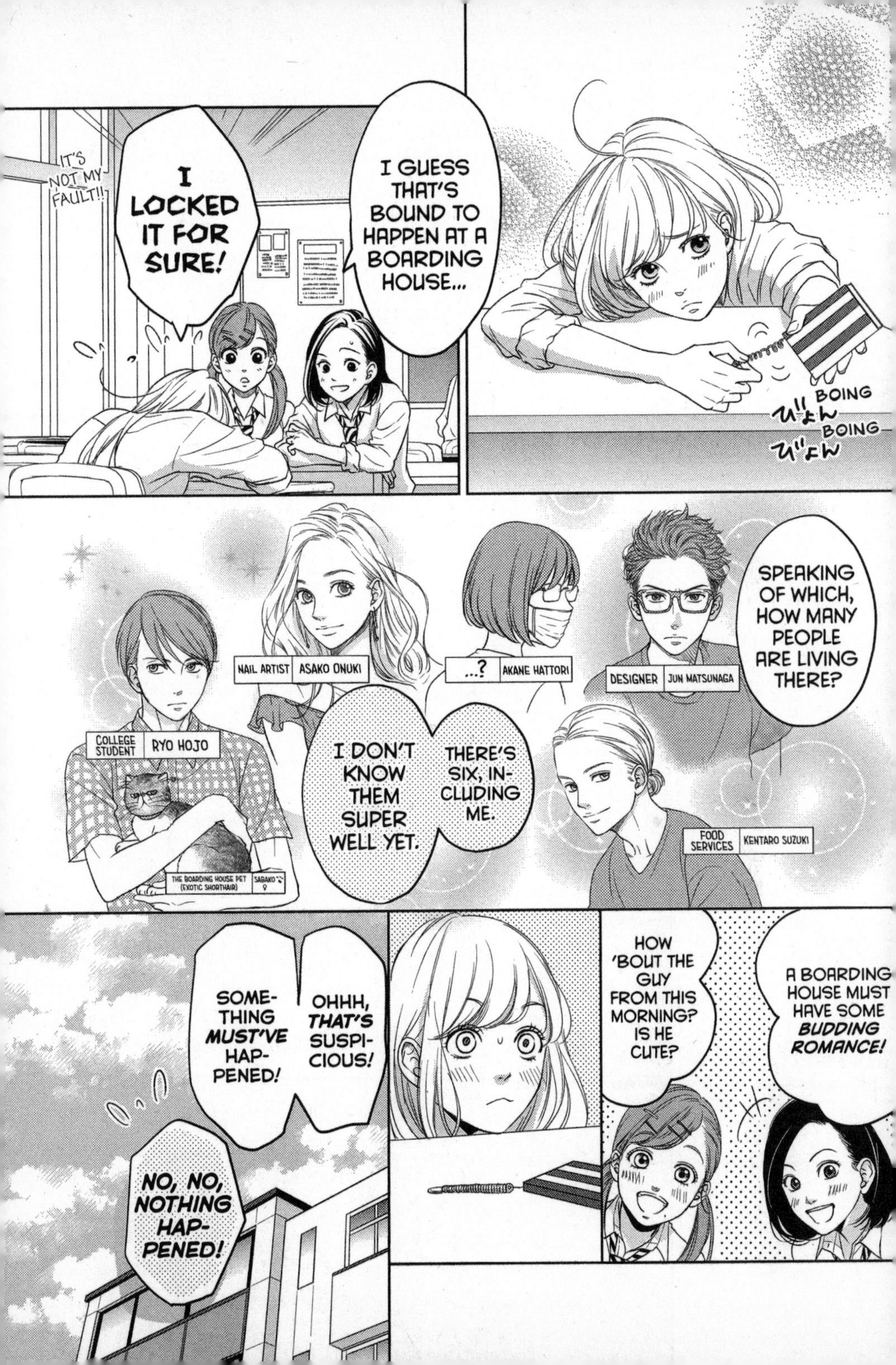

BOING
びょん
BOING
びょん
I GUESS THAT'S BOUND TO HAPPEN AT A BOARDING HOUSE...
I LOCKED IT FOR SURE!
IT'S NOT MY FAULT!!
SPEAKING OF WHICH, HOW MANY PEOPLE ARE LIVING THERE?
DESIGNER JUN MATSUNAGA
...? AKANE HATTORI
NAIL ARTIST ASAKO ONUKI
FOOD SERVICES KENTARO SUZUKI
THERE'S SIX, INCLUDING ME.
I DON'T KNOW THEM SUPER WELL YET.
COLLEGE STUDENT RYO HOJO
THE BOARDING HOUSE PET (EXOTIC SHORTHAIR) SABAKO ♀
A BOARDING HOUSE MUST HAVE SOME BUDDING ROMANCE!
HOW 'BOUT THE GUY FROM THIS MORNING? IS HE CUTE?
OHHH, THAT'S SUSPICIOUS!
SOMETHING MUST'VE HAPPENED!
NO, NO, NOTHING HAPPENED!

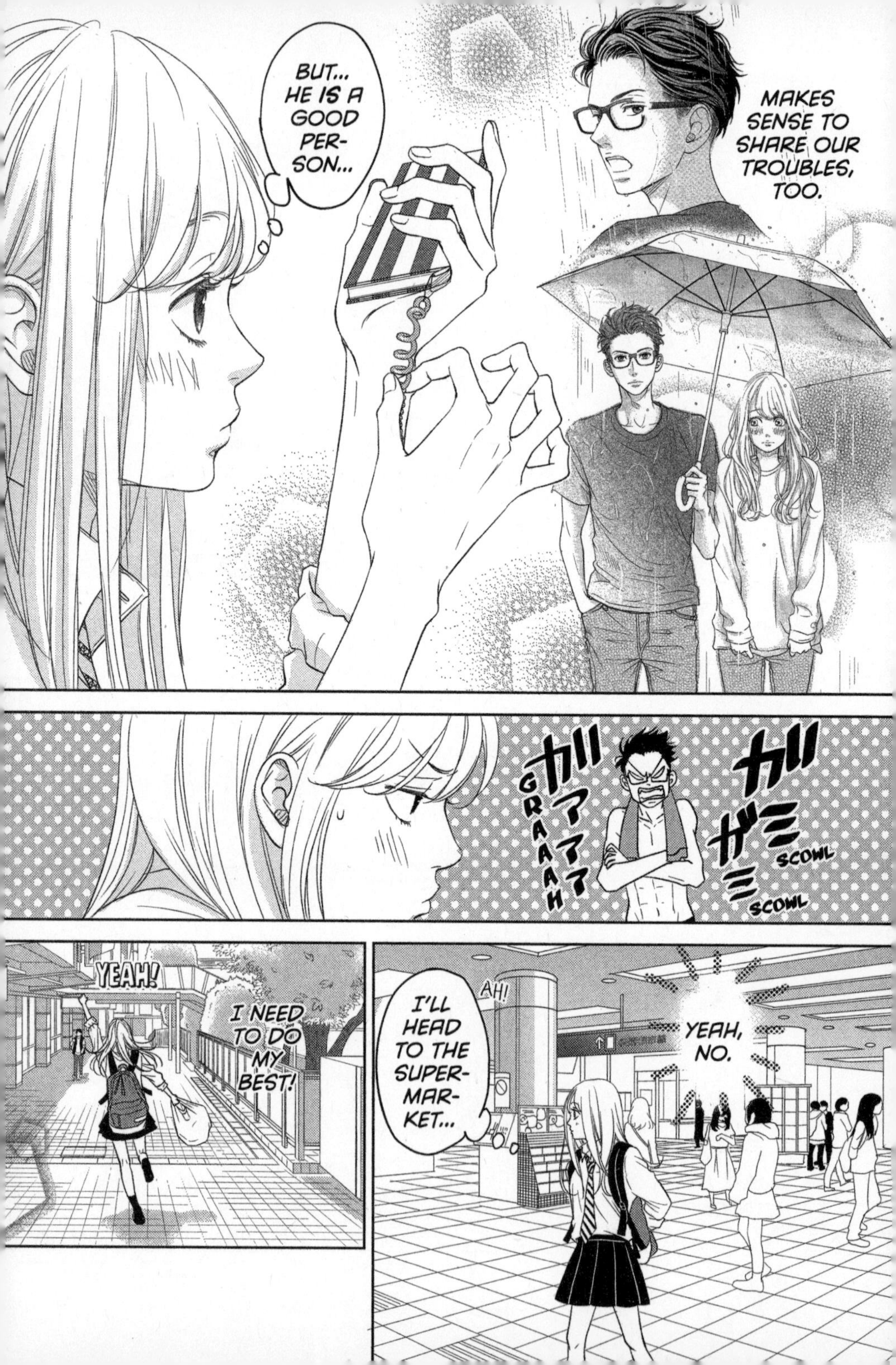
MAKES SENSE TO SHARE OUR TROUBLES, TOO.
BUT... HE IS A GOOD PER-SON...
SCOWL
SCOWL
GRAAAAH
YEAH, NO.
AH!
I'LL HEAD TO THE SUPER-MAR-KET...
YEAH!
I NEED TO DO MY BEST!

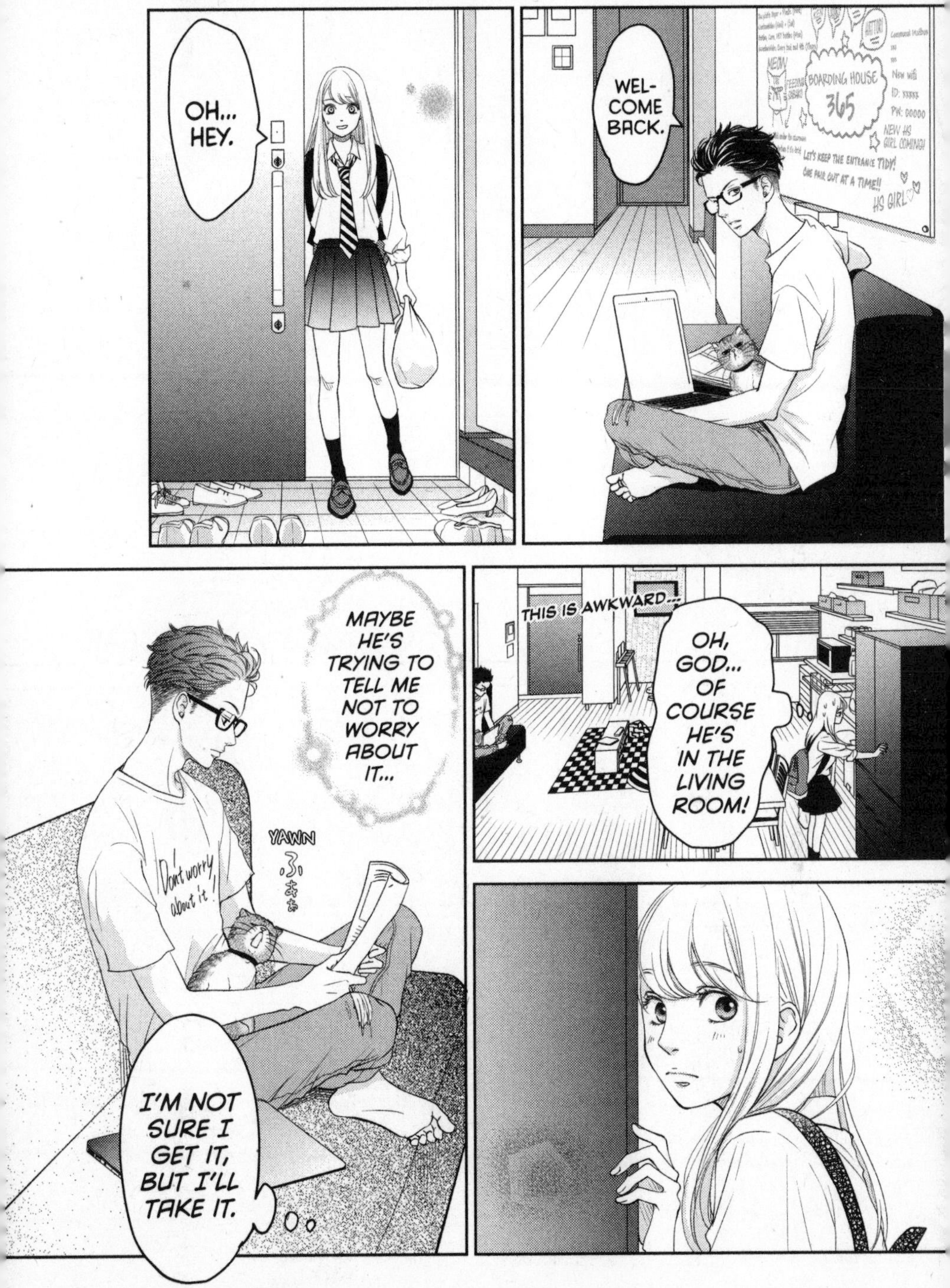
WEL-COME BACK.
BOARDING HOUSE 365
New wifi
ID: xxxxx
PW: 00000
NEW HS GIRL COMING!
LET'S KEEP THE ENTRANCE TIDY! ONE PAIR OUT AT A TIME!!
HS GIRL♡
OH... HEY.
THIS IS AWKWARD...
OH, GOD... OF COURSE HE'S IN THE LIVING ROOM!
MAYBE HE'S TRYING TO TELL ME NOT TO WORRY ABOUT IT...
YAWN
ふあぁ
Don't worry about it
I'M NOT SURE I GET IT, BUT I'LL TAKE IT.

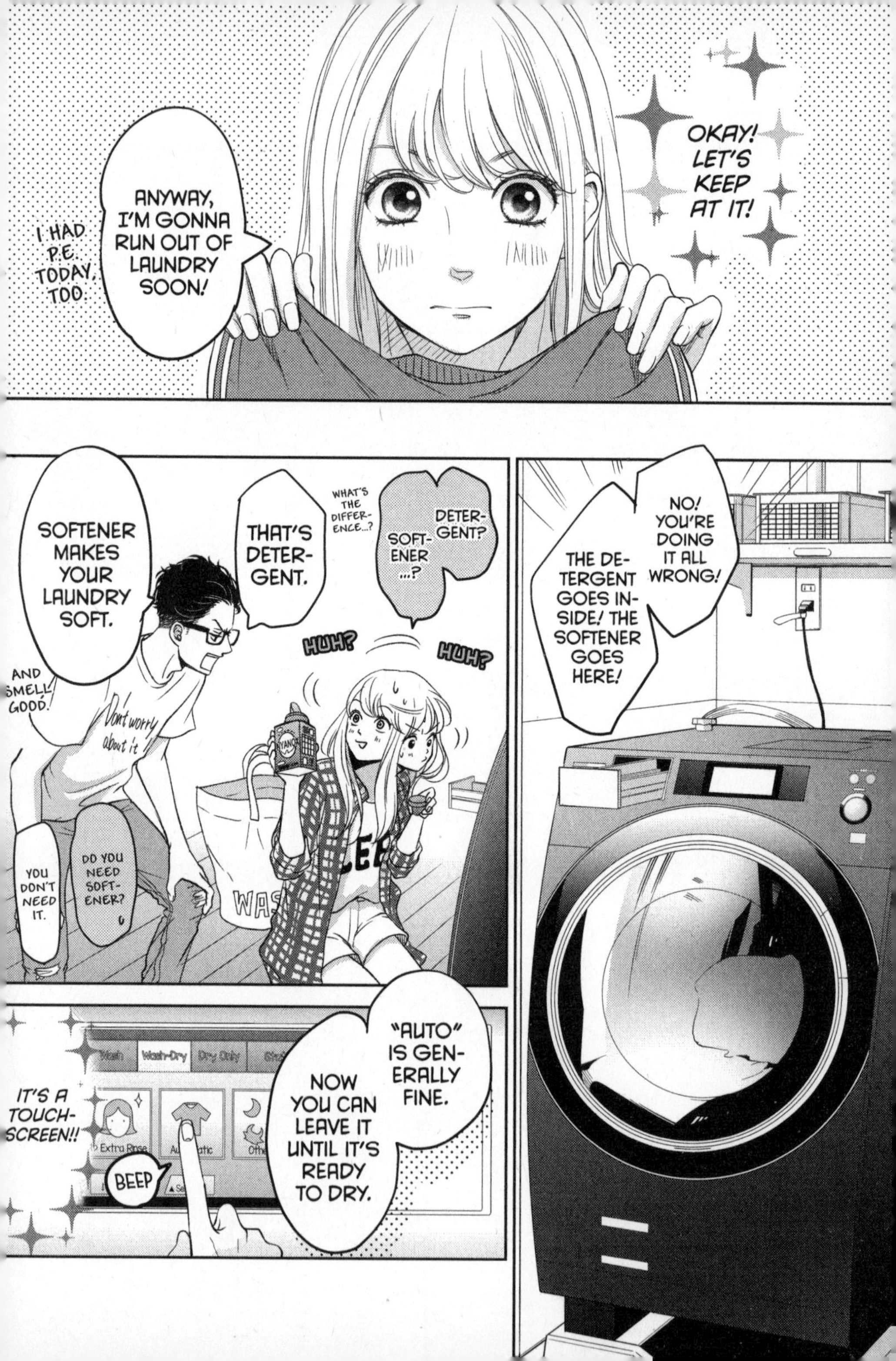
OKAY! LET'S KEEP AT IT!
ANYWAY, I'M GONNA RUN OUT OF LAUNDRY SOON!
I HAD P.E. TODAY, TOO.
NO! YOU'RE DOING IT ALL WRONG!
THE DE-TERGENT GOES IN-SIDE! THE SOFTENER GOES HERE!
DETER-GENT?
SOFT-ENER ...?
WHAT'S THE DIFFER-ENCE...?
THAT'S DETER-GENT.
SOFTENER MAKES YOUR LAUNDRY SOFT.
AND SMELL GOOD.
HUH?
HUH?
DO YOU NEED SOFT-ENER?
YOU DON'T NEED IT.
"AUTO" IS GEN-ERALLY FINE.
NOW YOU CAN LEAVE IT UNTIL IT'S READY TO DRY.
Wash-Dry
Dry Only
BEEP
IT'S A TOUCH-SCREEN!!

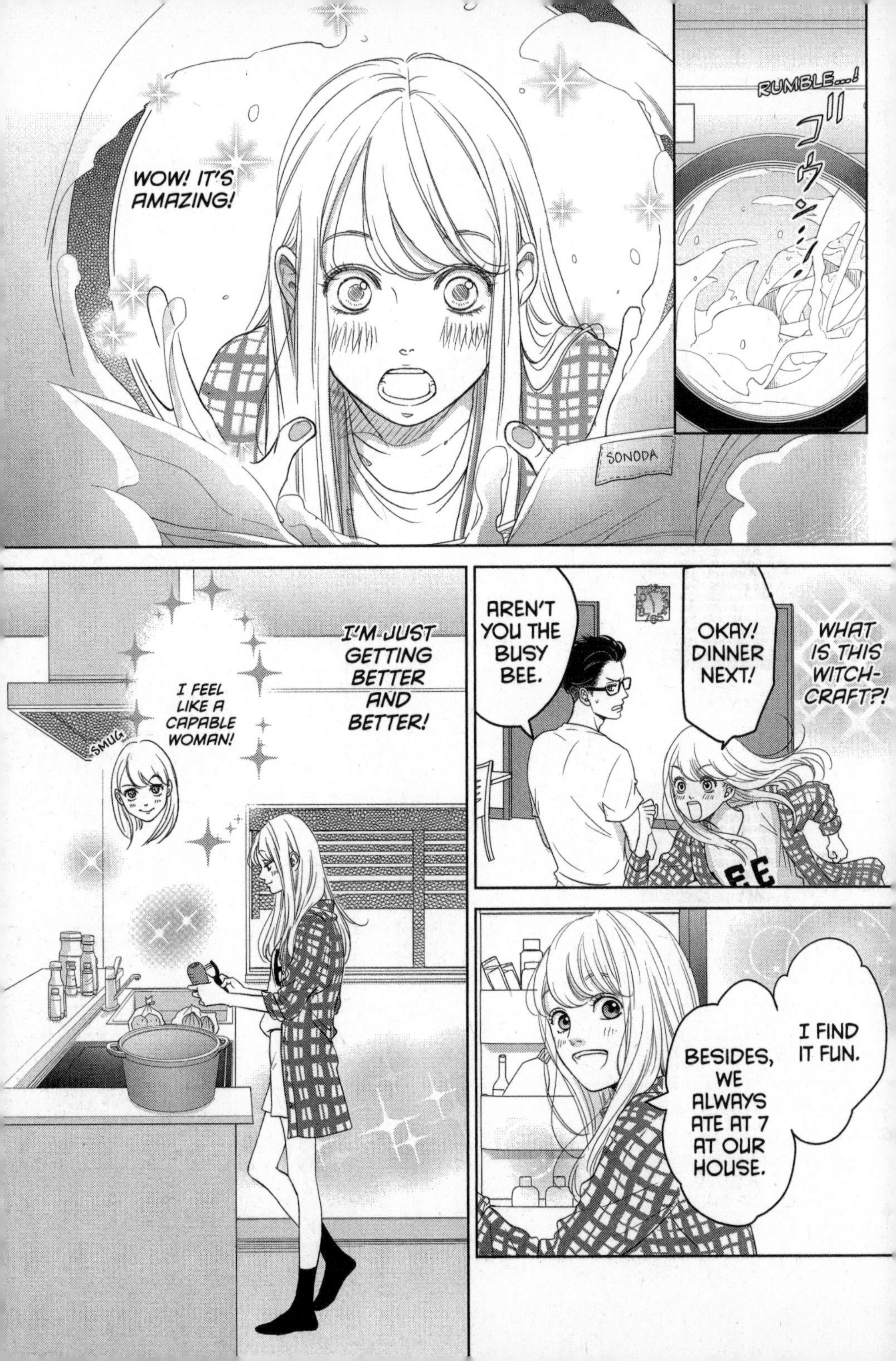
RUMBLE...!
ゴウン…!
WOW! IT'S AMAZING!
SONODA
WHAT IS THIS WITCH-CRAFT?!
OKAY! DINNER NEXT!
AREN'T YOU THE BUSY BEE.
I FIND IT FUN.
BESIDES, WE ALWAYS ATE AT 7 AT OUR HOUSE.
I'M JUST GETTING BETTER AND BETTER!
I FEEL LIKE A CAPABLE WOMAN!
SMUG

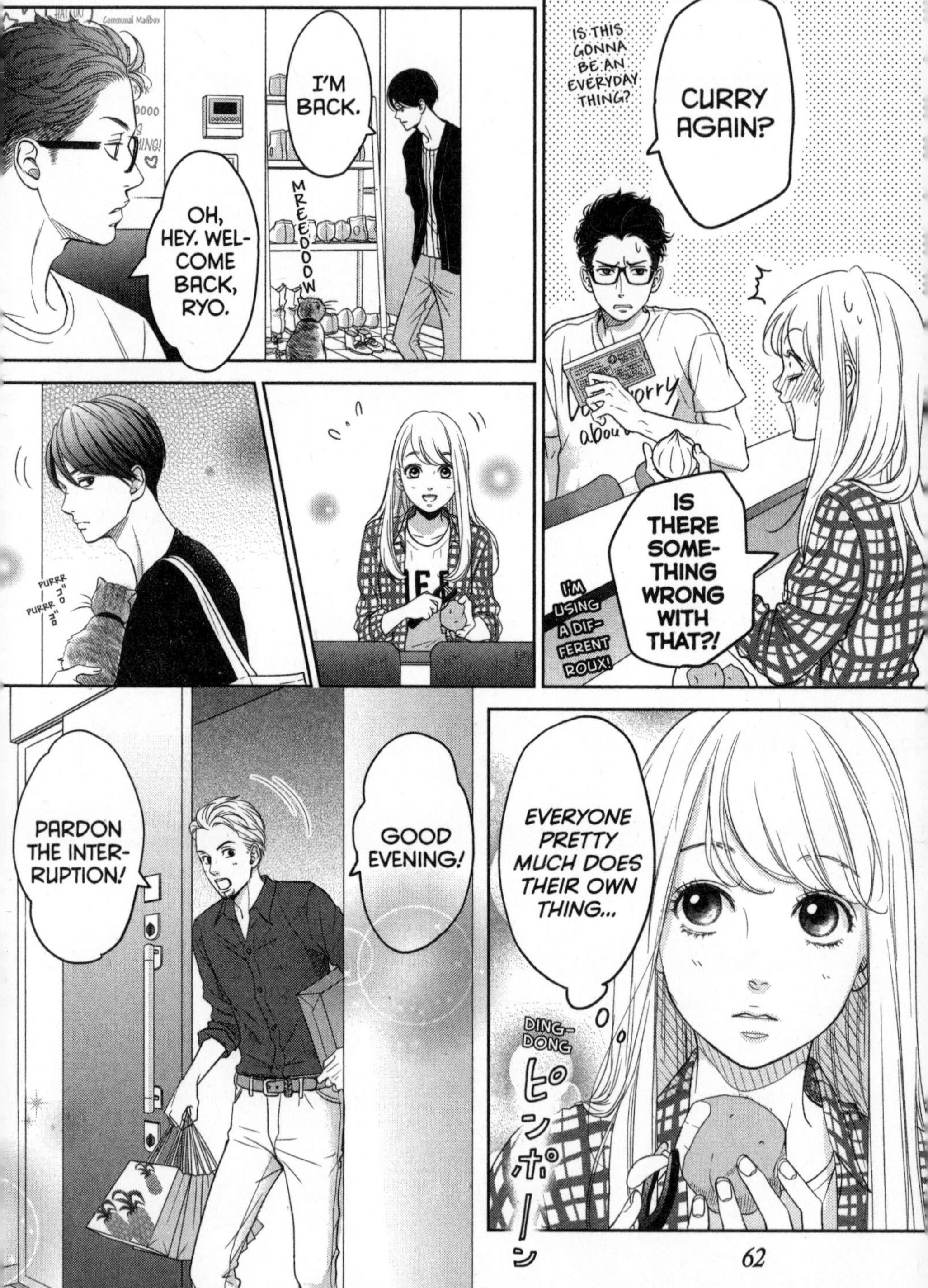
IS THIS GONNA BE AN EVERYDAY THING?
CURRY AGAIN?
IS THERE SOMETHING WRONG WITH THAT?!
I'M USING A DIFFERENT ROUX!
Communal Mailbox
I'M BACK.
OH, HEY. WELCOME BACK, RYO.
MREEOOOW
PURRR PURRR
EVERYONE PRETTY MUCH DOES THEIR OWN THING...
DING-DONG
GOOD EVENING!
PARDON THE INTERRUPTION!

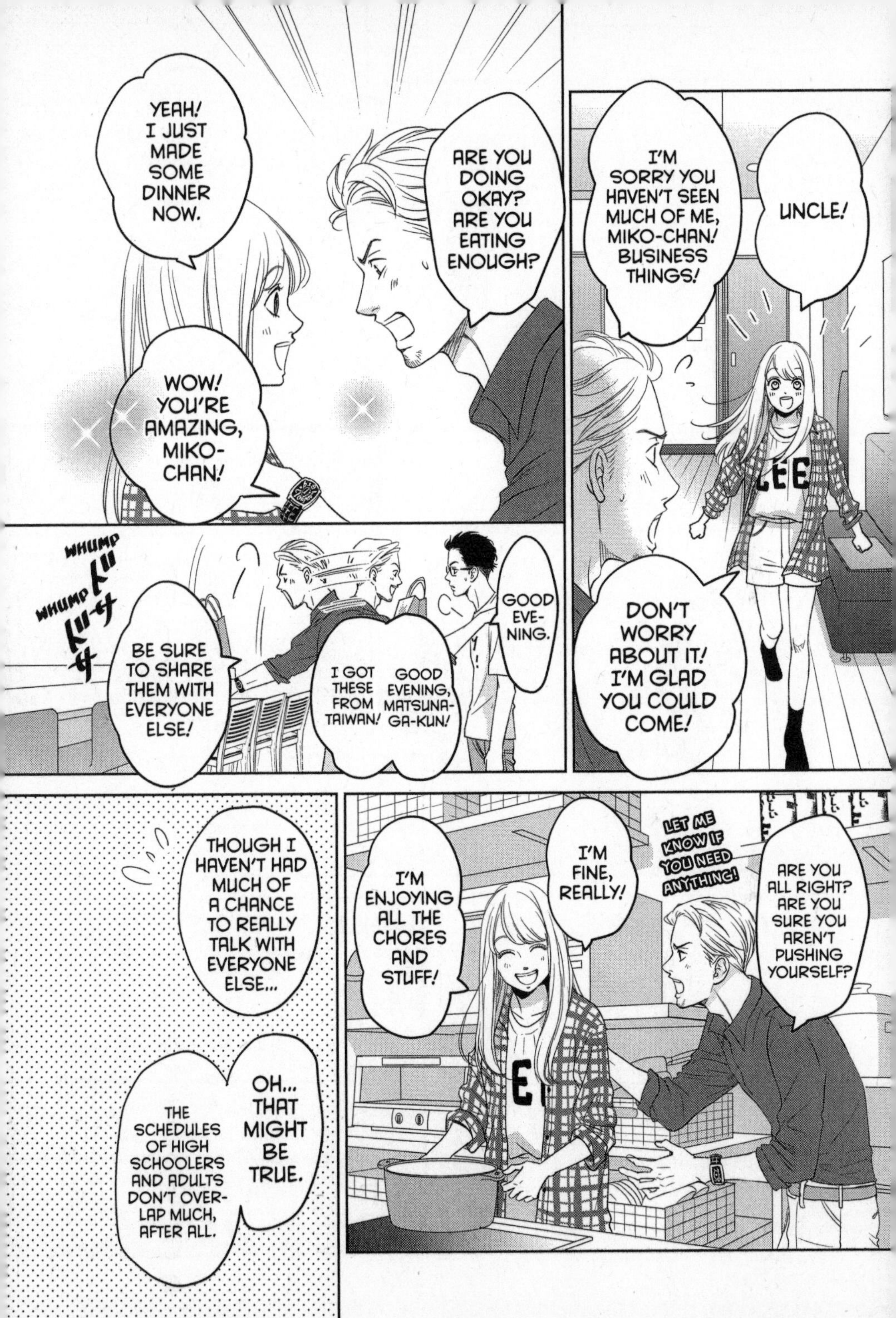
UNCLE!
I'M SORRY YOU HAVEN'T SEEN MUCH OF ME, MIKO-CHAN! BUSINESS THINGS!
DON'T WORRY ABOUT IT! I'M GLAD YOU COULD COME!
ARE YOU DOING OKAY? ARE YOU EATING ENOUGH?
YEAH! I JUST MADE SOME DINNER NOW.
WOW! YOU'RE AMAZING, MIKO-CHAN!
GOOD EVENING.
GOOD EVENING, MATSUNAGA-KUN!
I GOT THESE FROM TAIWAN!
BE SURE TO SHARE THEM WITH EVERYONE ELSE!
WHUMP ドサ
WHUMP ドサ
ARE YOU ALL RIGHT? ARE YOU SURE YOU AREN'T PUSHING YOURSELF?
LET ME KNOW IF YOU NEED ANYTHING!
I'M FINE, REALLY!
I'M ENJOYING ALL THE CHORES AND STUFF!
THOUGH I HAVEN'T HAD MUCH OF A CHANCE TO REALLY TALK WITH EVERYONE ELSE...
OH... THAT MIGHT BE TRUE.
THE SCHEDULES OF HIGH SCHOOLERS AND ADULTS DON'T OVERLAP MUCH, AFTER ALL.

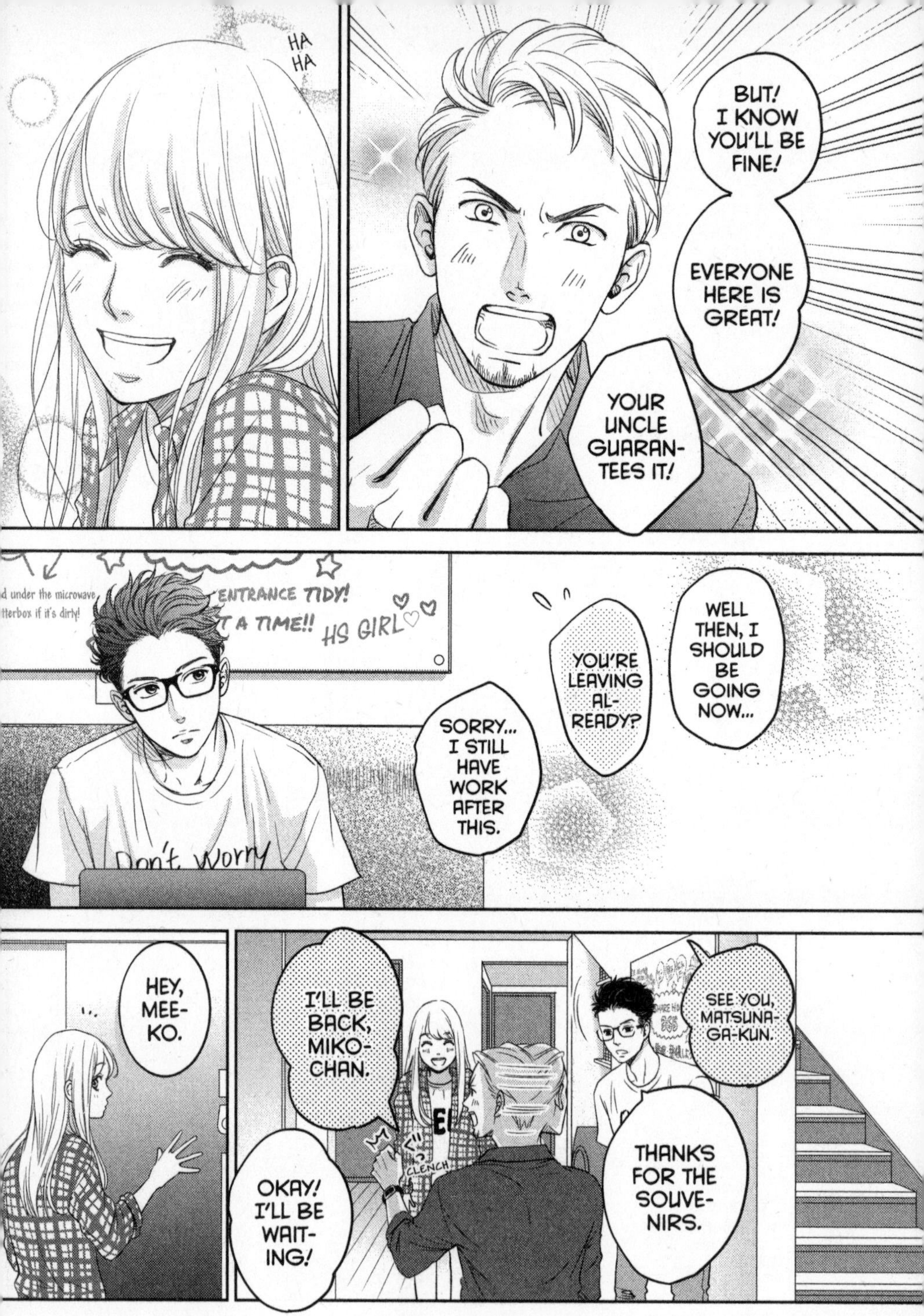
BUT! I KNOW YOU'LL BE FINE!
EVERYONE HERE IS GREAT!
YOUR UNCLE GUARANTEES IT!
HA HA
d under the microwave
tterbox if it's dirty!
ENTRANCE TIDY!
T A TIME!!
HS GIRL
WELL THEN, I SHOULD BE GOING NOW...
YOU'RE LEAVING ALREADY?
SORRY... I STILL HAVE WORK AFTER THIS.
Don't worry
SEE YOU, MATSUNAGA-KUN.
I'LL BE BACK, MIKO-CHAN.
THANKS FOR THE SOUVENIRS.
OKAY! I'LL BE WAITING!
CLENCH
HEY, MEE-KO.

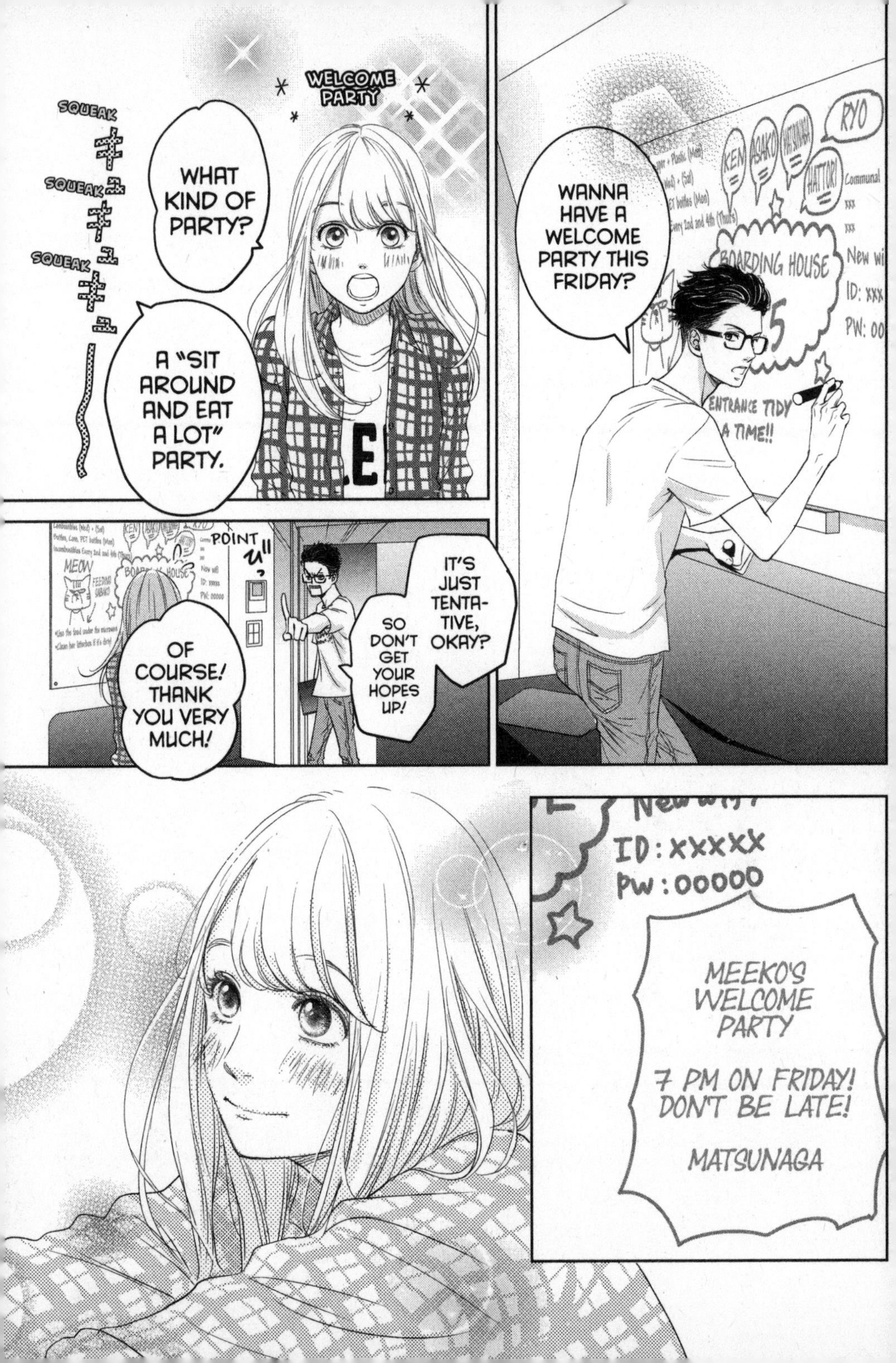
WANNA HAVE A WELCOME PARTY THIS FRIDAY?
KEN
ASAKO
MATSUNAGA
RYO
HATTORI
Communal
BOARDING HOUSE
New wi
ID: xxx
PW: 00
ENTRANCE TIDY
A TIME!!
WELCOME PARTY
WHAT KIND OF PARTY?
A "SIT AROUND AND EAT A LOT" PARTY.
SQUEAK
SQUEAK
SQUEAK
IT'S JUST TENTATIVE, OKAY?
SO DON'T GET YOUR HOPES UP!
POINT
OF COURSE! THANK YOU VERY MUCH!
ID : XXXXX
PW : 00000
MEEKO'S WELCOME PARTY
7 PM ON FRIDAY! DON'T BE LATE!
MATSUNAGA

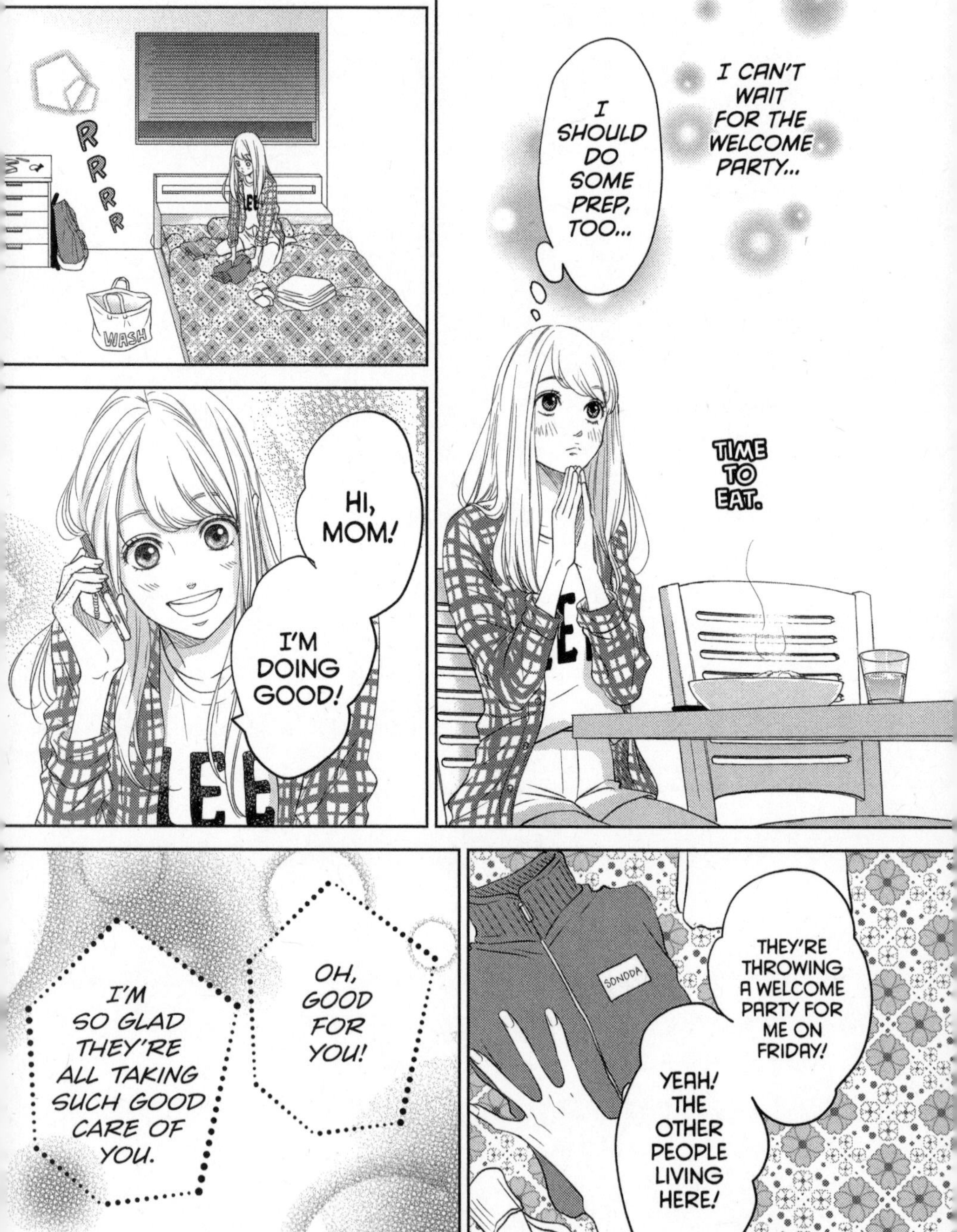
I CAN'T WAIT FOR THE WELCOME PARTY...
I SHOULD DO SOME PREP, TOO...
TIME TO EAT.
RRRR
WASH
HI, MOM!
I'M DOING GOOD!
THEY'RE THROWING A WELCOME PARTY FOR ME ON FRIDAY!
SONODA
YEAH! THE OTHER PEOPLE LIVING HERE!
OH, GOOD FOR YOU!
I'M SO GLAD THEY'RE ALL TAKING SUCH GOOD CARE OF YOU.

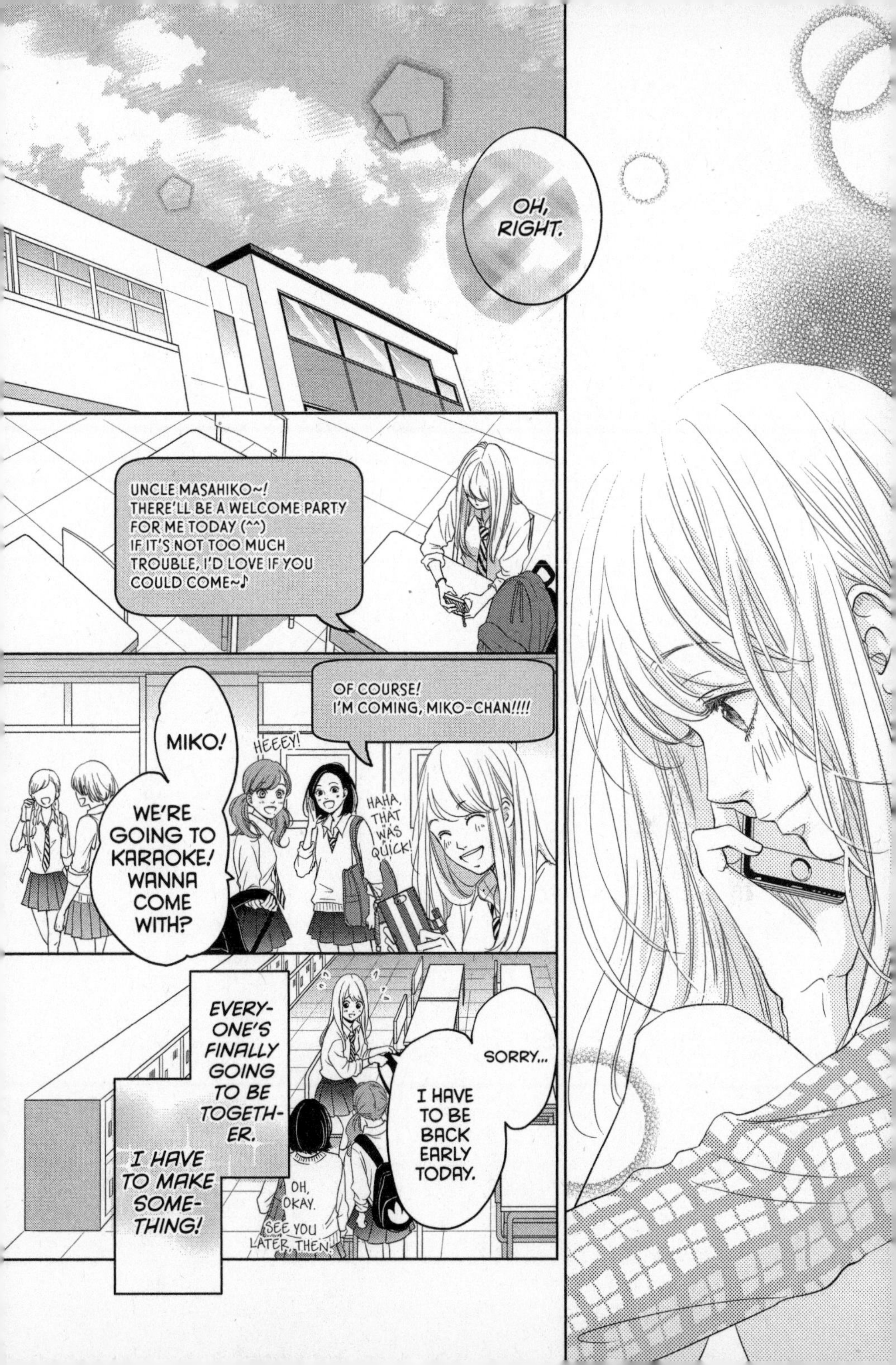
OH, RIGHT.
UNCLE MASAHIKO~! THERE'LL BE A WELCOME PARTY FOR ME TODAY (^^) IF IT'S NOT TOO MUCH TROUBLE, I'D LOVE IF YOU COULD COME~♪
OF COURSE! I'M COMING, MIKO-CHAN!!!!
HAHA, THAT WAS QUICK!
HEEEY!
MIKO! WE'RE GOING TO KARAOKE! WANNA COME WITH?
SORRY... I HAVE TO BE BACK EARLY TODAY.
OH, OKAY. SEE YOU LATER, THEN.
EVERYONE'S FINALLY GOING TO BE TOGETHER.
I HAVE TO MAKE SOMETHING!

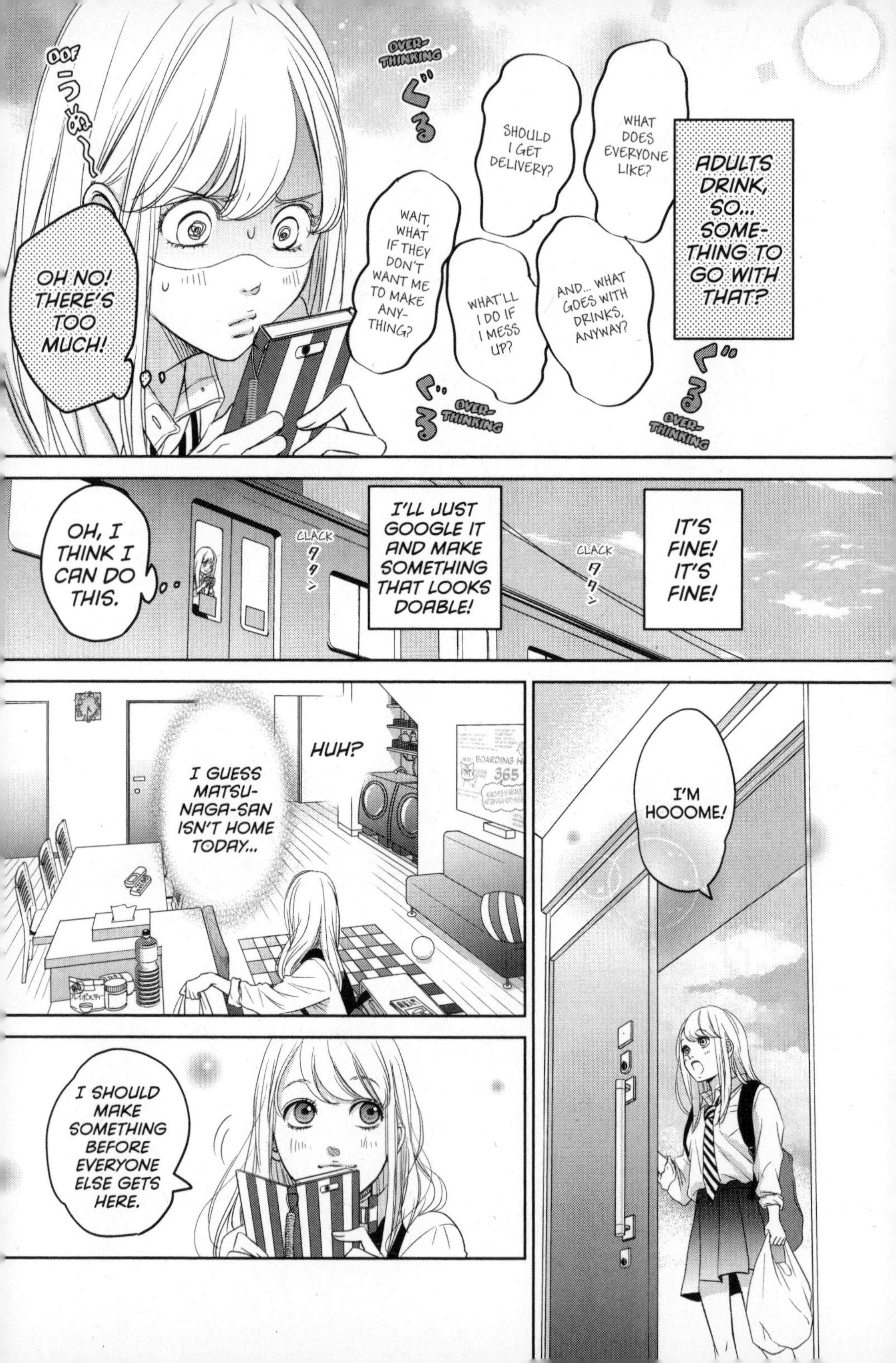
ADULTS DRINK, SO... SOMETHING TO GO WITH THAT?
WHAT DOES EVERYONE LIKE?
SHOULD I GET DELIVERY?
OVER-THINKING
AND... WHAT GOES WITH DRINKS, ANYWAY?
WHAT'LL I DO IF I MESS UP?
WAIT, WHAT IF THEY DON'T WANT ME TO MAKE ANYTHING?
OVER-THINKING
OVER-THINKING
OOF
OH NO! THERE'S TOO MUCH!
IT'S FINE! IT'S FINE!
CLACK
I'LL JUST GOOGLE IT AND MAKE SOMETHING THAT LOOKS DOABLE!
CLACK
OH, I THINK I CAN DO THIS.
I'M HOOOME!
HUH?
I GUESS MATSUNAGA-SAN ISN'T HOME TODAY...
I SHOULD MAKE SOMETHING BEFORE EVERYONE ELSE GETS HERE.

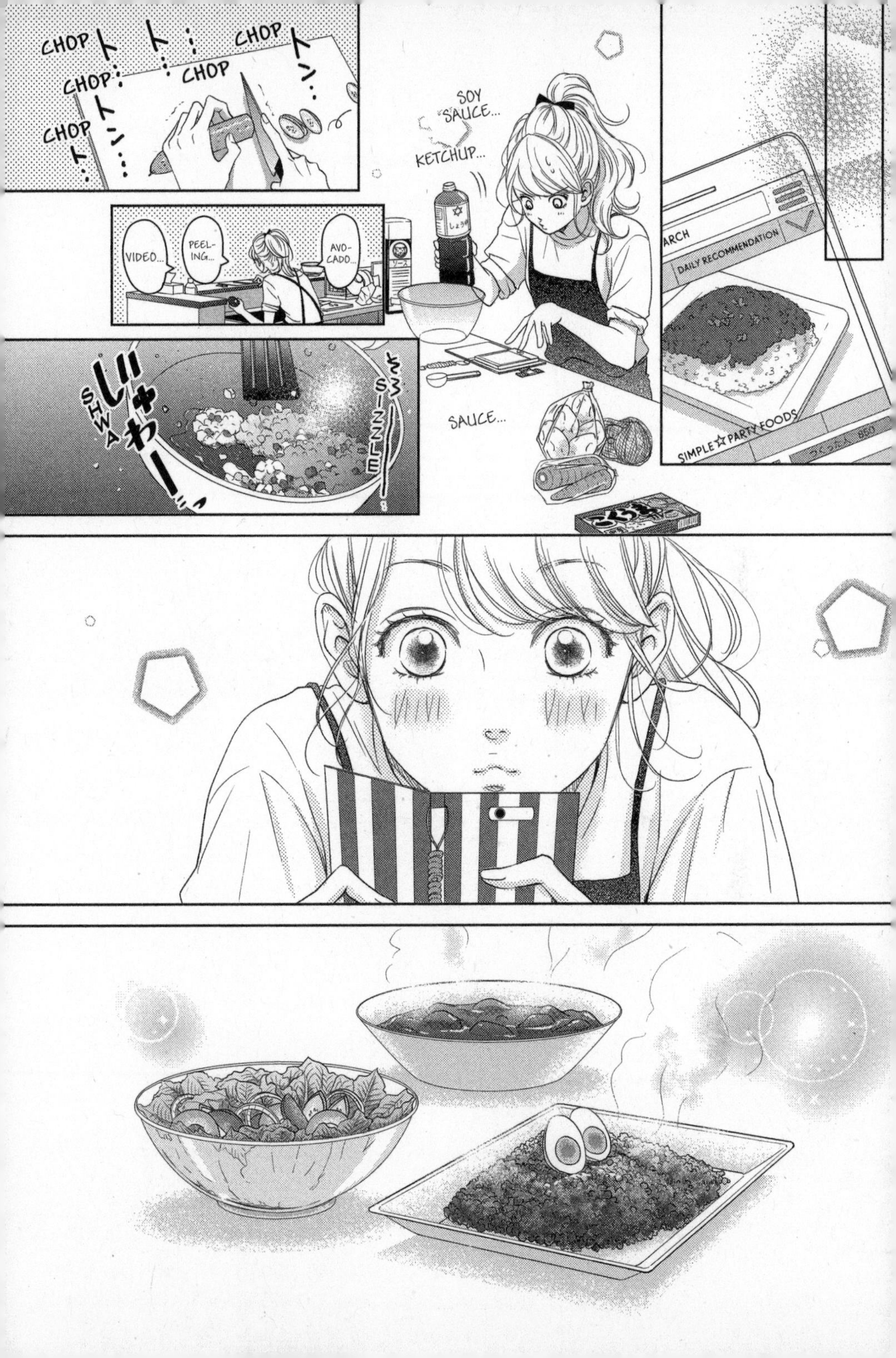

...ARCH
DAILY RECOMMENDATION
SIMPLE☆PARTY FOODS
SOY SAUCE...
KETCHUP...
SAUCE...
CHOP トン…
CHOP
CHOP ト
CHOP ト
CHOP トン…
CHOP ト…
AVO-CADO...
PEEL-ING...
VIDEO...
SIZZLE
じゅわー
SHWA

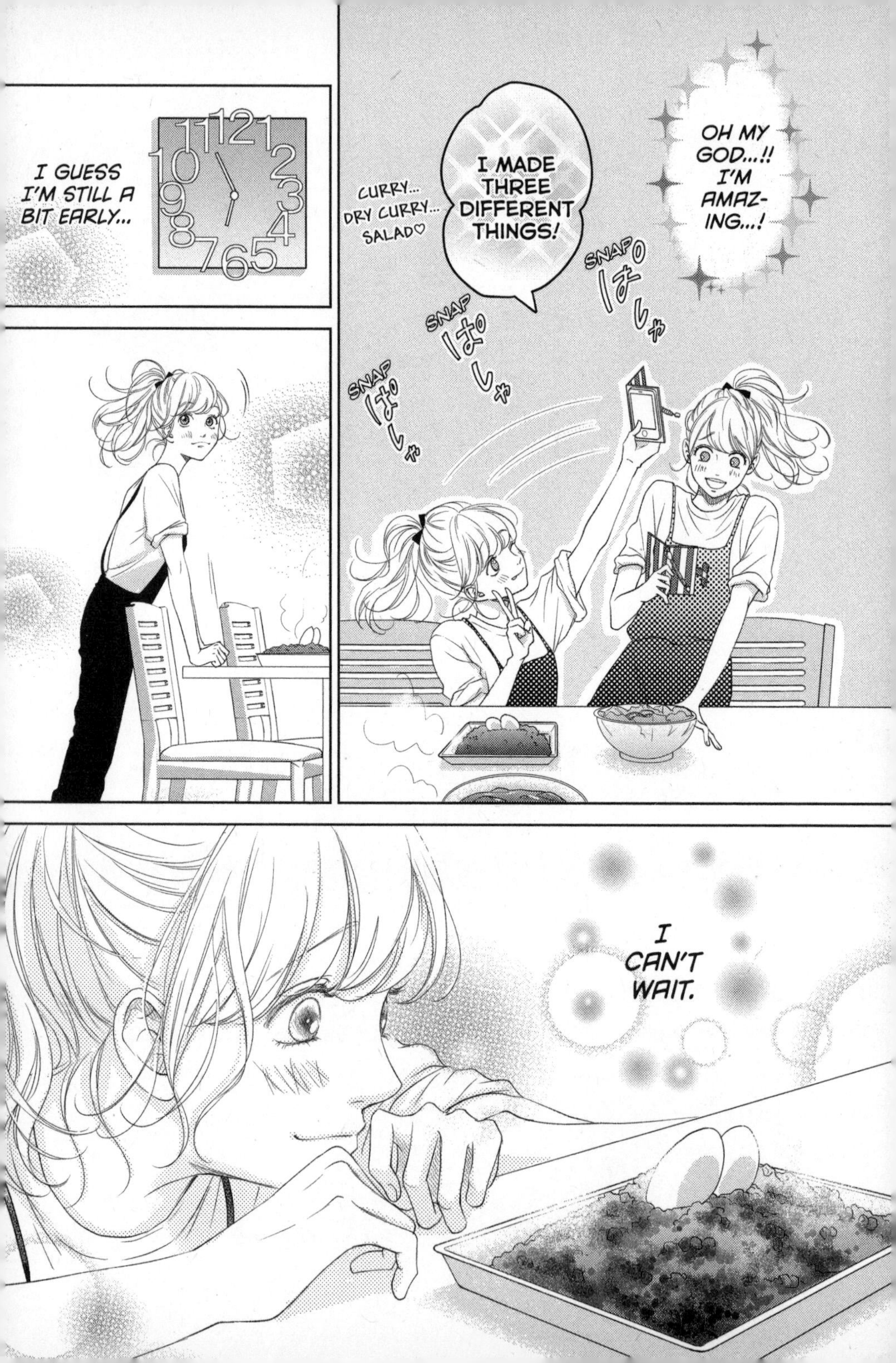

OH MY GOD...!! I'M AMAZ-ING...!
I MADE THREE DIFFERENT THINGS!
CURRY... DRY CURRY... SALAD♡
SNAP ぱしゃ
SNAP ぱしゃ
SNAP ぱしゃ
I GUESS I'M STILL A BIT EARLY...
I CAN'T WAIT.

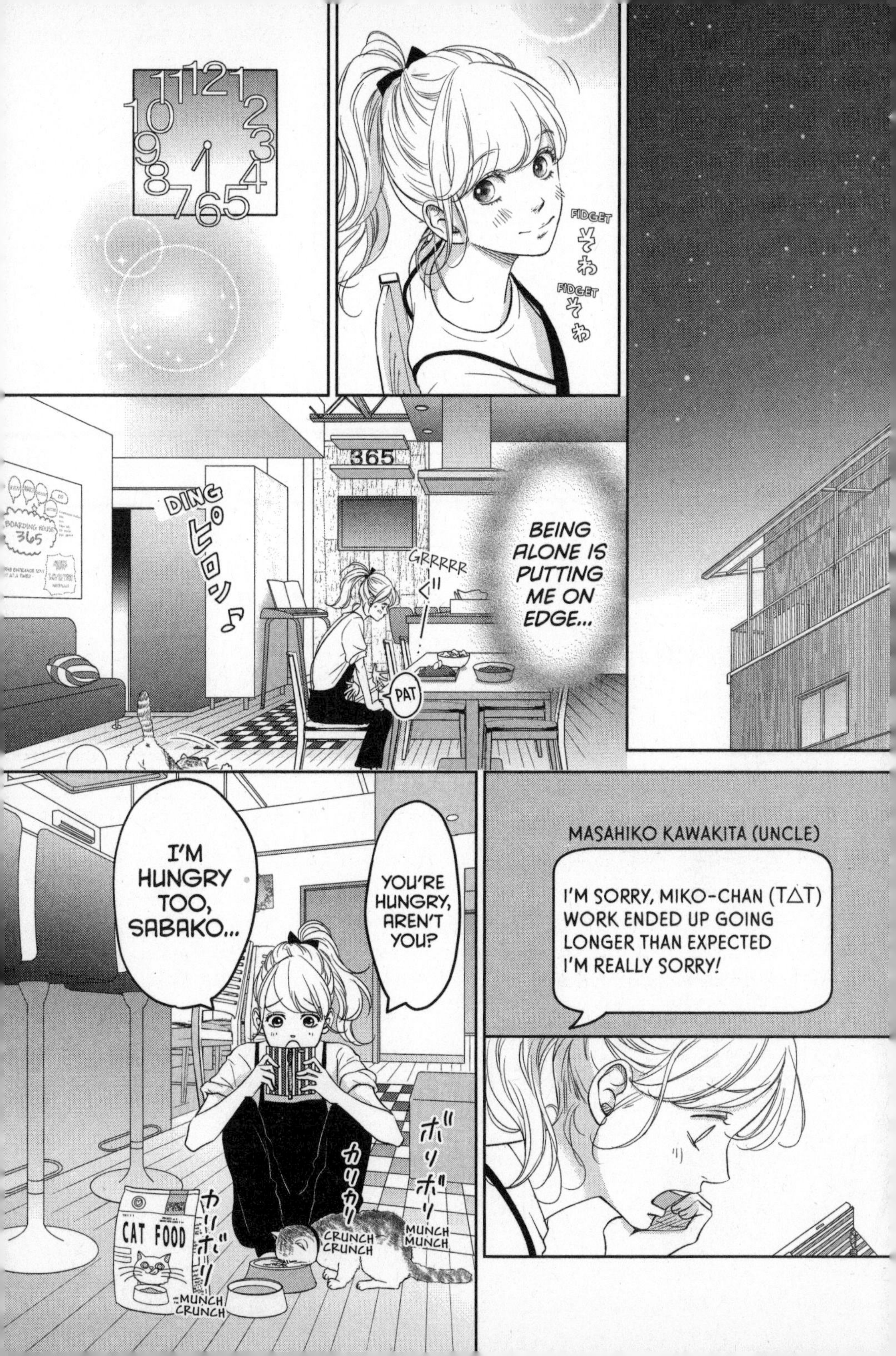

FIDGET
そわ
FIDGET
そわ
BEING ALONE IS PUTTING ME ON EDGE...
365
GRRRRR
DING
ピロッ♪
BOARDING HOUSE 365
PAT
MASAHIKO KAWAKITA (UNCLE)
I'M SORRY, MIKO-CHAN (T△T)
WORK ENDED UP GOING LONGER THAN EXPECTED
I'M REALLY SORRY!
YOU'RE HUNGRY, AREN'T YOU?
I'M HUNGRY TOO, SABAKO...
ボリボリ
MUNCH MUNCH
カリカリ
CRUNCH CRUNCH
カリボリ
MUNCH CRUNCH
CAT FOOD

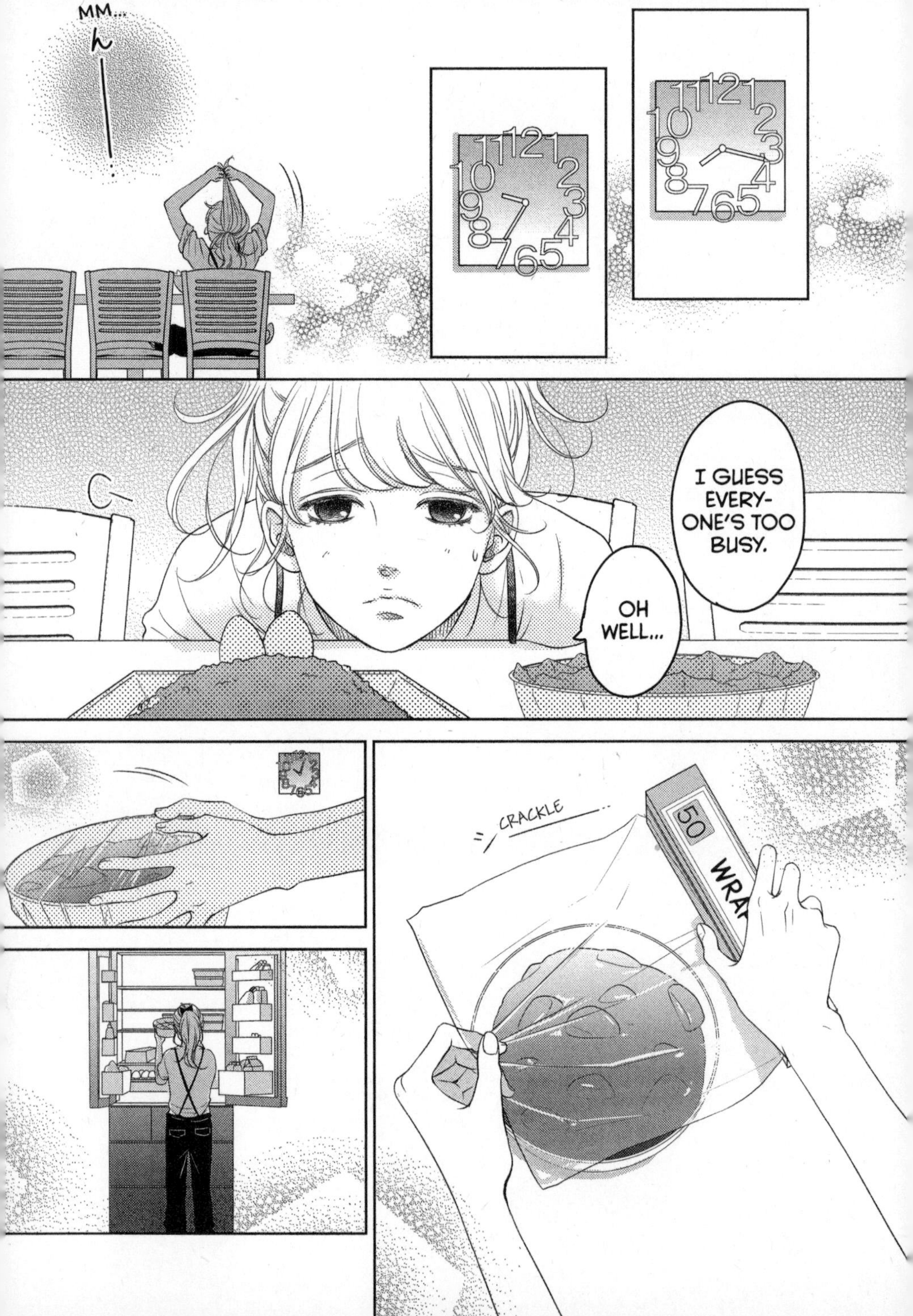
MM...
ん—
I GUESS EVERY-ONE'S TOO BUSY.
OH WELL...
CRACKLE
50
WRA

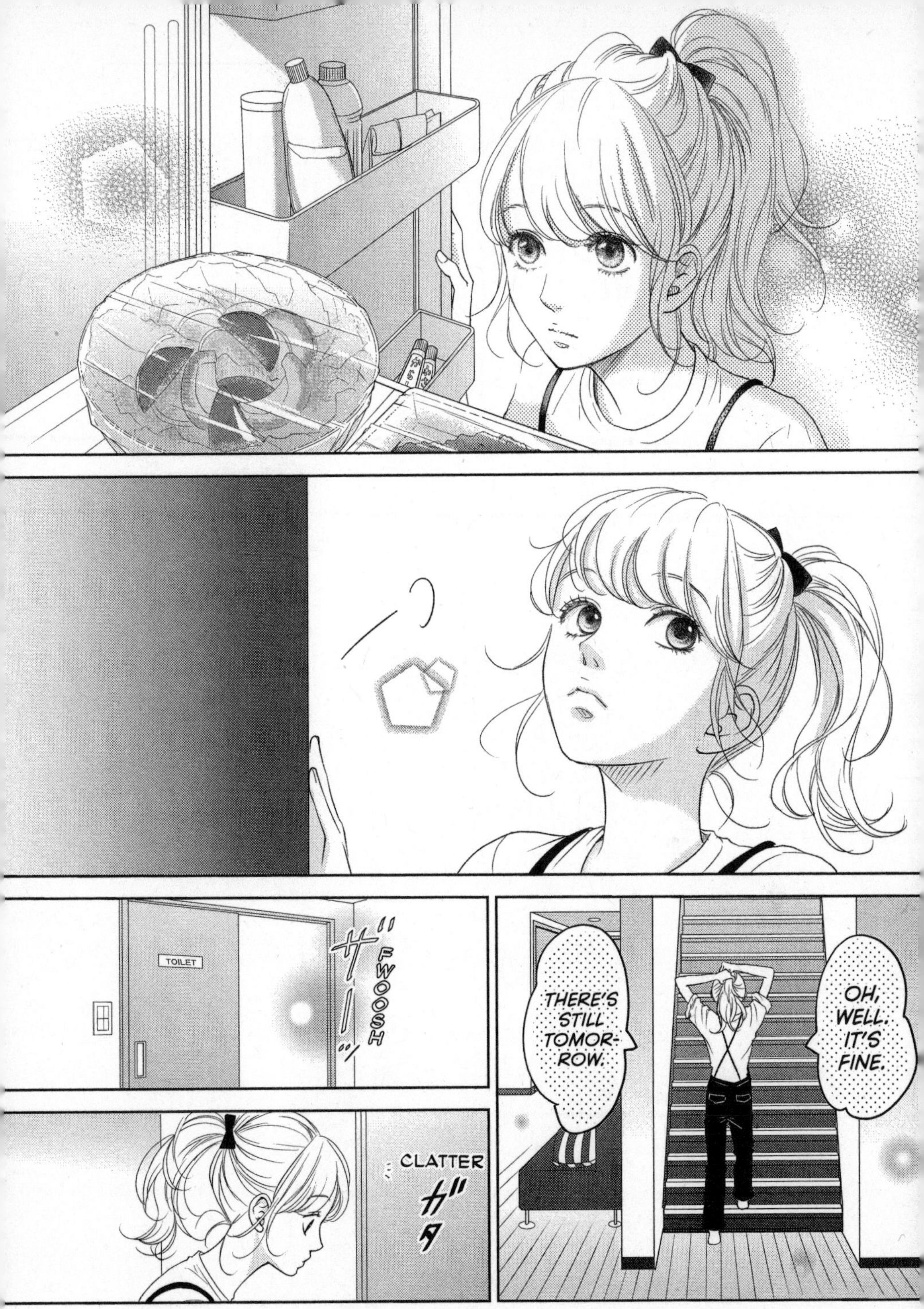
OH, WELL. IT'S FINE.
THERE'S STILL TOMOR-ROW.
TOILET
FWOOSH
CLATTER

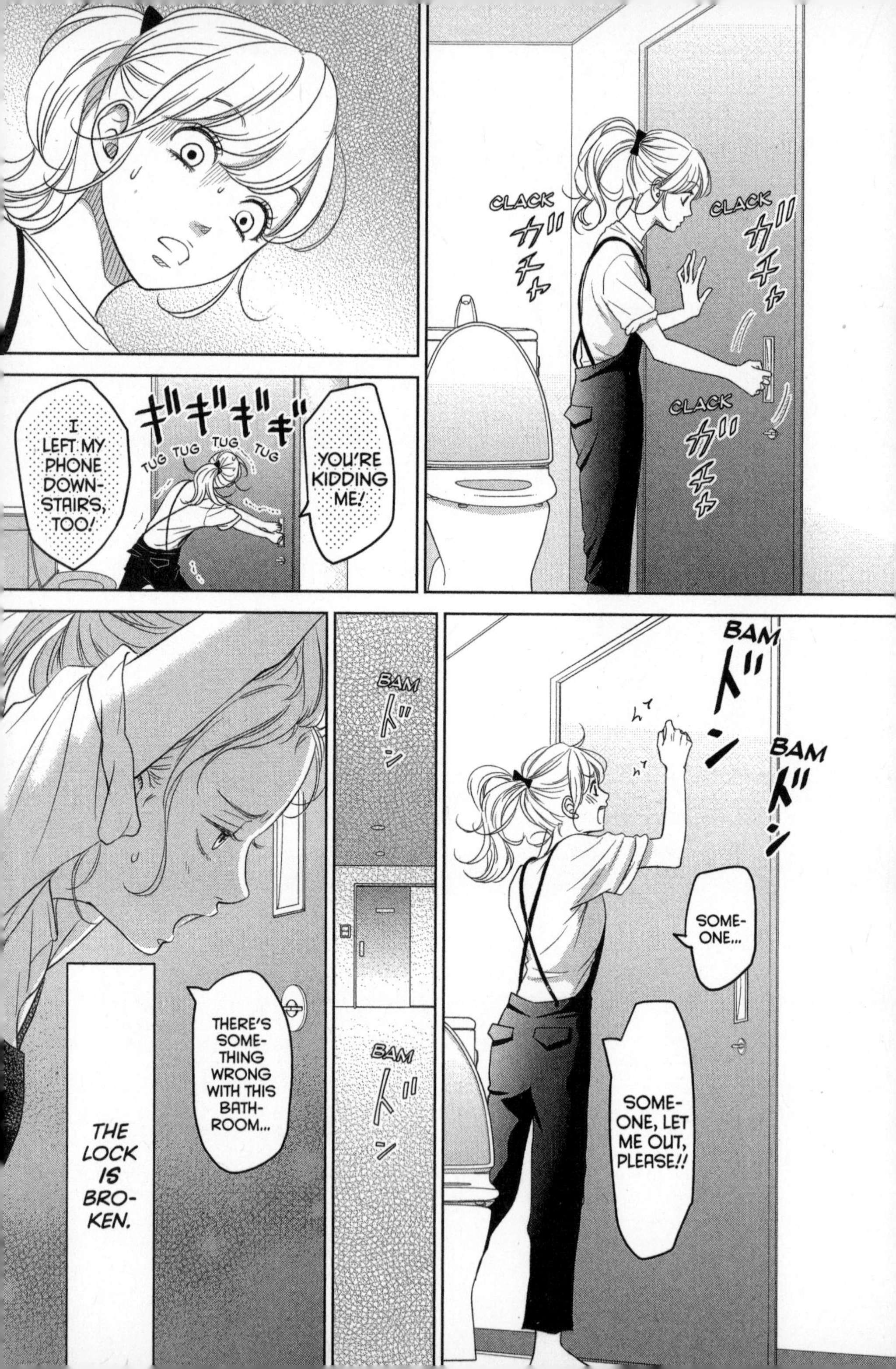
CLACK
カチャ
CLACK
カチャ
CLACK
カチャ
YOU'RE KIDDING ME!
ギギギギ
TUG TUG TUG TUG
I LEFT MY PHONE DOWN-STAIRS, TOO!
BAM
ドン
BAM
ドン
SOME-ONE...
SOME-ONE, LET ME OUT, PLEASE!!
BAM
ドン
BAM
ドン
THERE'S SOME-THING WRONG WITH THIS BATH-ROOM...
THE LOCK IS BRO-KEN.

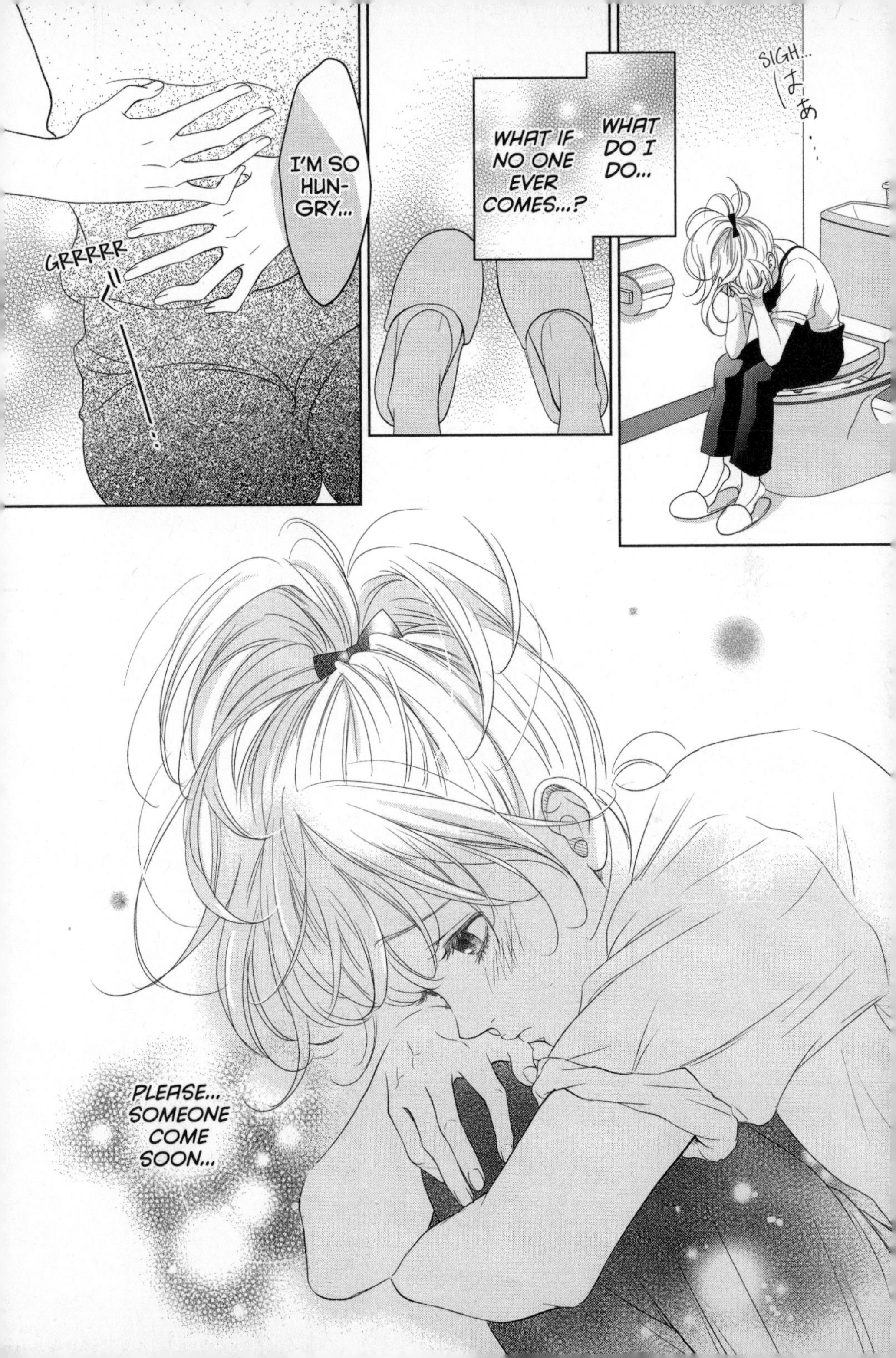
SIGH...
はあ…
WHAT DO I DO...
WHAT IF NO ONE EVER COMES...?
I'M SO HUN-GRY...
GRRRRR
PLEASE... SOMEONE COME SOON...

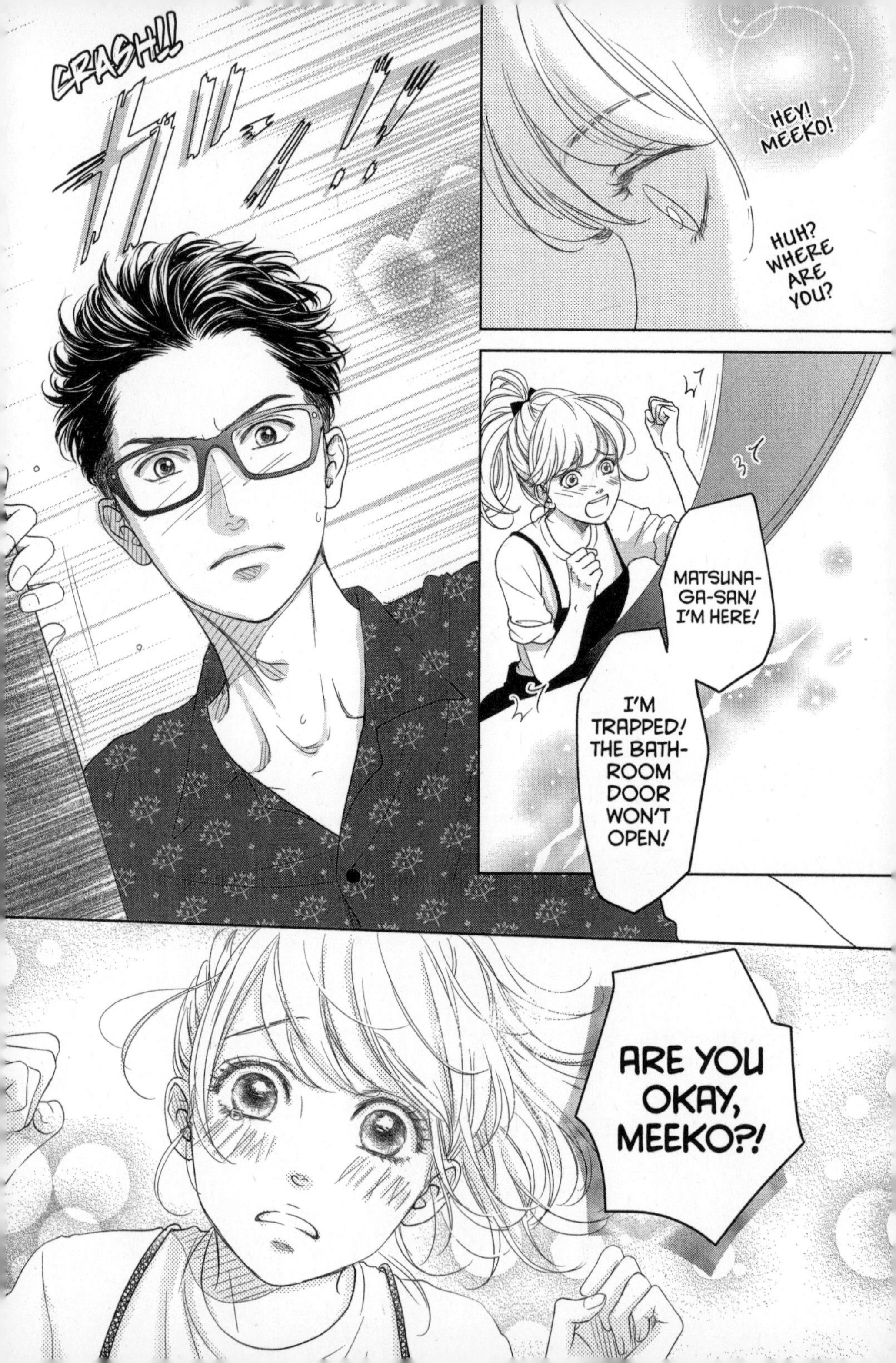
HEY! MEEKO!
HUH? WHERE ARE YOU?
MATSUNAGA-SAN! I'M HERE!
I'M TRAPPED! THE BATHROOM DOOR WON'T OPEN!
CRASH!!
ARE YOU OKAY, MEEKO?!

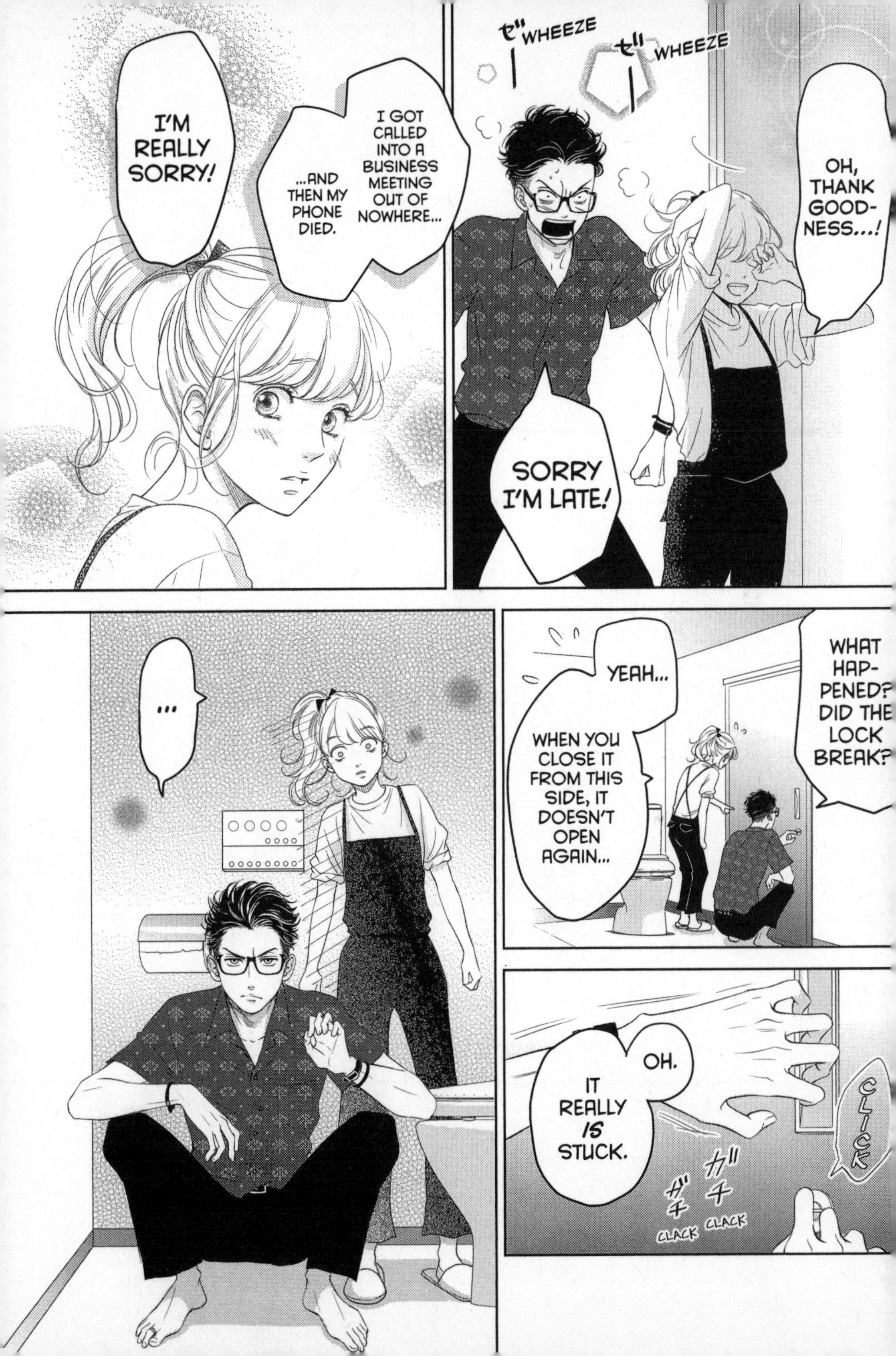
ゼー WHEEZE
ゼー WHEEZE
OH, THANK GOODNESS...!
SORRY I'M LATE!
I GOT CALLED INTO A BUSINESS MEETING OUT OF NOWHERE...
...AND THEN MY PHONE DIED.
I'M REALLY SORRY!
WHAT HAPPENED? DID THE LOCK BREAK?
YEAH...
WHEN YOU CLOSE IT FROM THIS SIDE, IT DOESN'T OPEN AGAIN...
CLICK
OH.
IT REALLY *IS* STUCK.
ガチ CLACK
ガチ CLACK
...

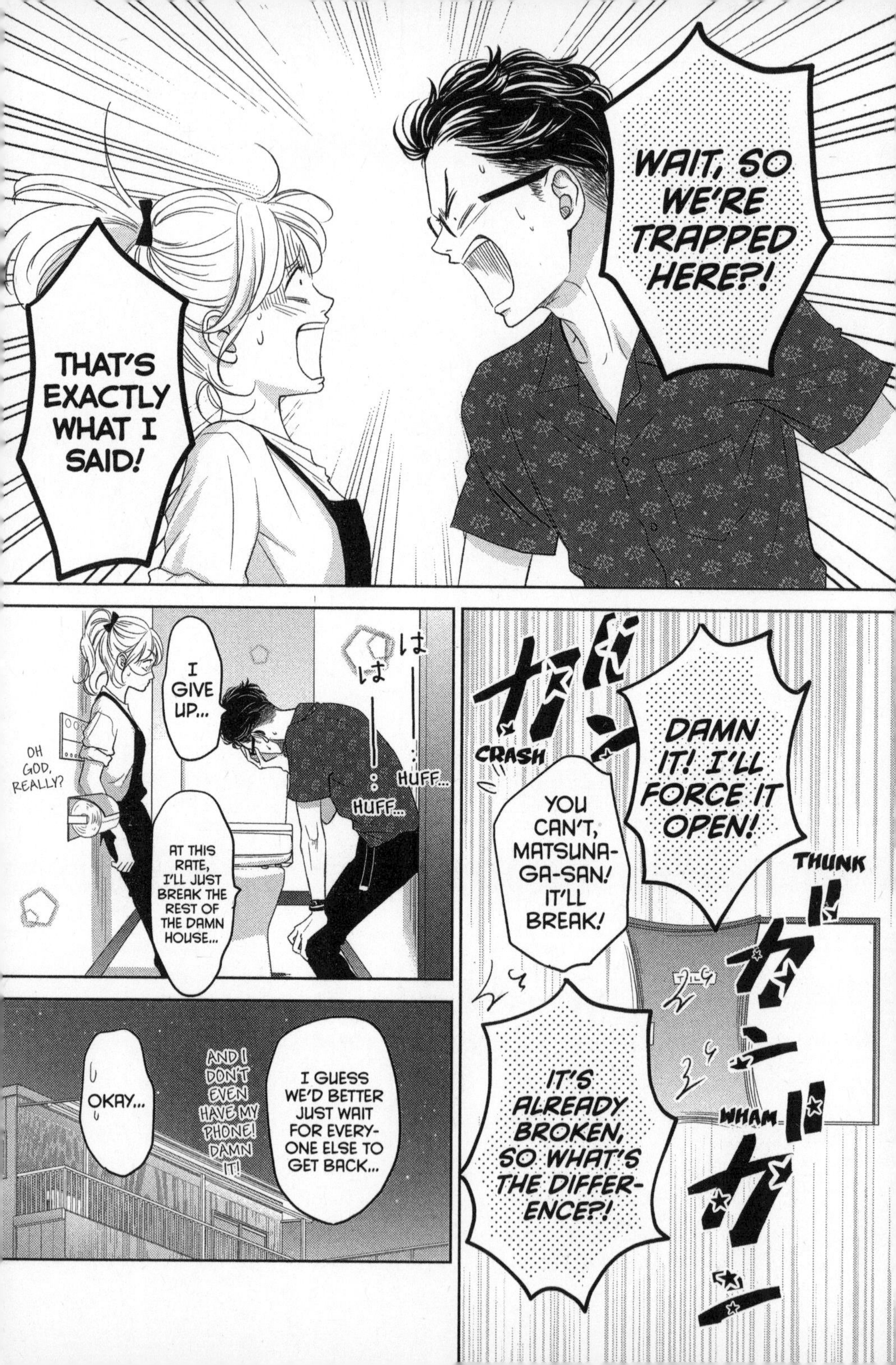
WAIT, SO WE'RE TRAPPED HERE?!
THAT'S EXACTLY WHAT I SAID!
CRASH
DAMN IT! I'LL FORCE IT OPEN!
YOU CAN'T, MATSUNAGA-SAN! IT'LL BREAK!
THUNK
IT'S ALREADY BROKEN, SO WHAT'S THE DIFFERENCE?!
WHAM
はーー
はーー
HUFF...
HUFF...
I GIVE UP...
OH GOD, REALLY?
AT THIS RATE, I'LL JUST BREAK THE REST OF THE DAMN HOUSE...
I GUESS WE'D BETTER JUST WAIT FOR EVERYONE ELSE TO GET BACK...
AND I DON'T EVEN HAVE MY PHONE! DAMN IT!
OKAY...

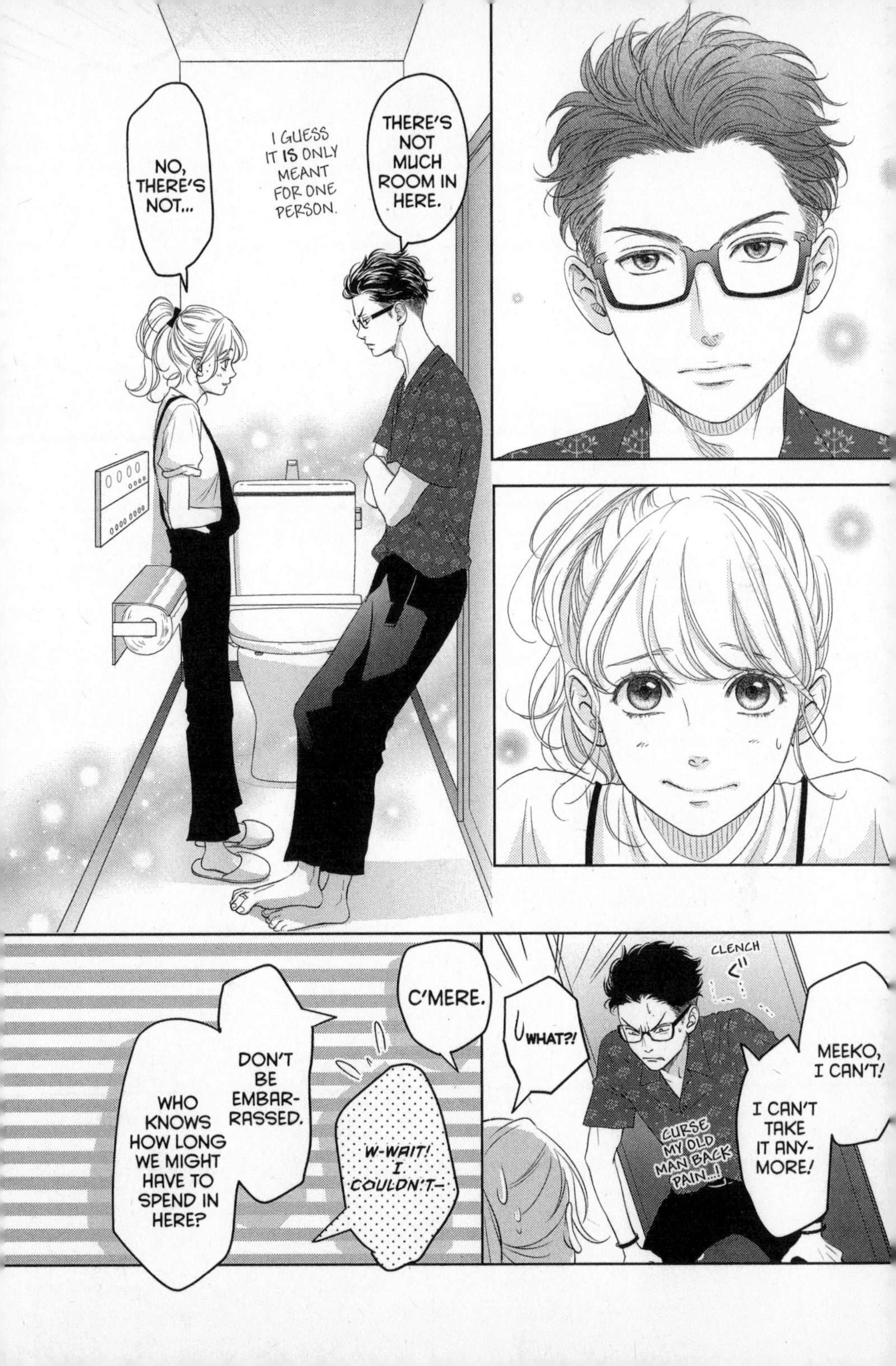
THERE'S NOT MUCH ROOM IN HERE.
I GUESS IT IS ONLY MEANT FOR ONE PERSON.
NO, THERE'S NOT...
CLENCH
MEEKO, I CAN'T!
I CAN'T TAKE IT ANYMORE!
CURSE MY OLD MAN BACK PAIN...!
WHAT?!
C'MERE.
W-WAIT! I COULDN'T—
DON'T BE EMBARRASSED.
WHO KNOWS HOW LONG WE MIGHT HAVE TO SPEND IN HERE?

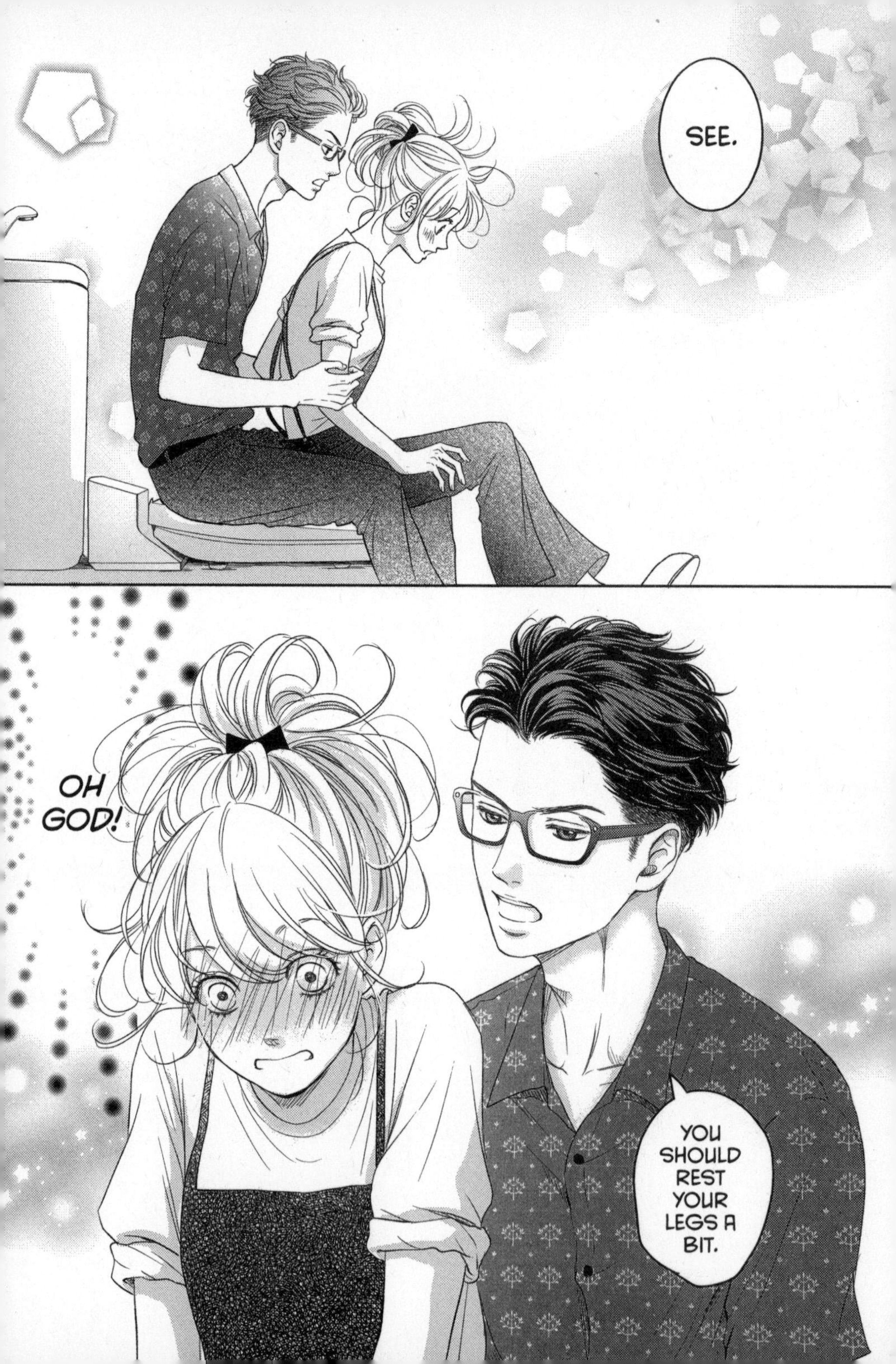
SEE.
YOU SHOULD REST YOUR LEGS A BIT.
OH GOD!

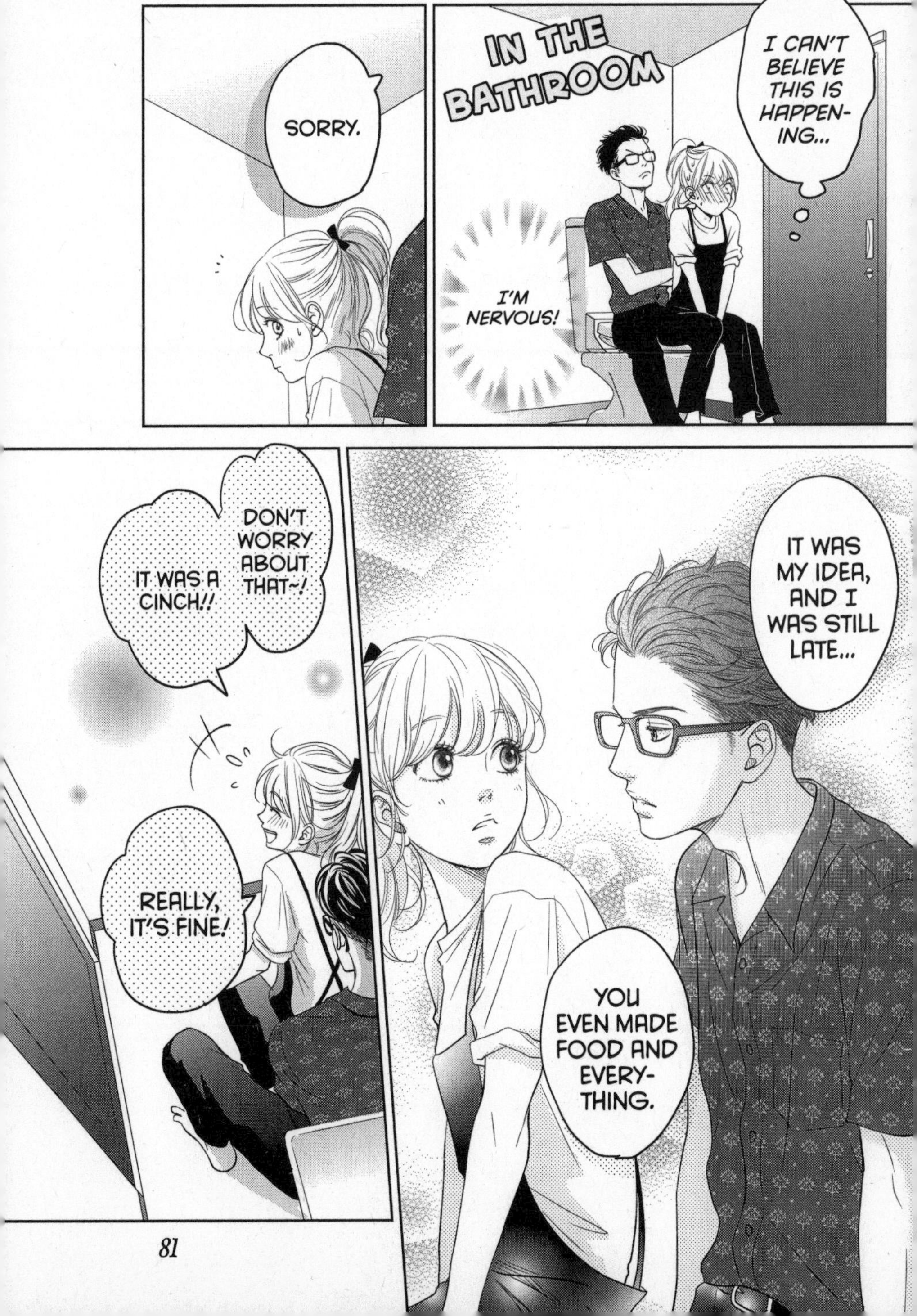
IN THE BATHROOM
I CAN'T BELIEVE THIS IS HAPPEN-ING...
I'M NERVOUS!
SORRY.
IT WAS MY IDEA, AND I WAS STILL LATE...
YOU EVEN MADE FOOD AND EVERY-THING.
DON'T WORRY ABOUT THAT~!
IT WAS A CINCH!!
REALLY, IT'S FINE!

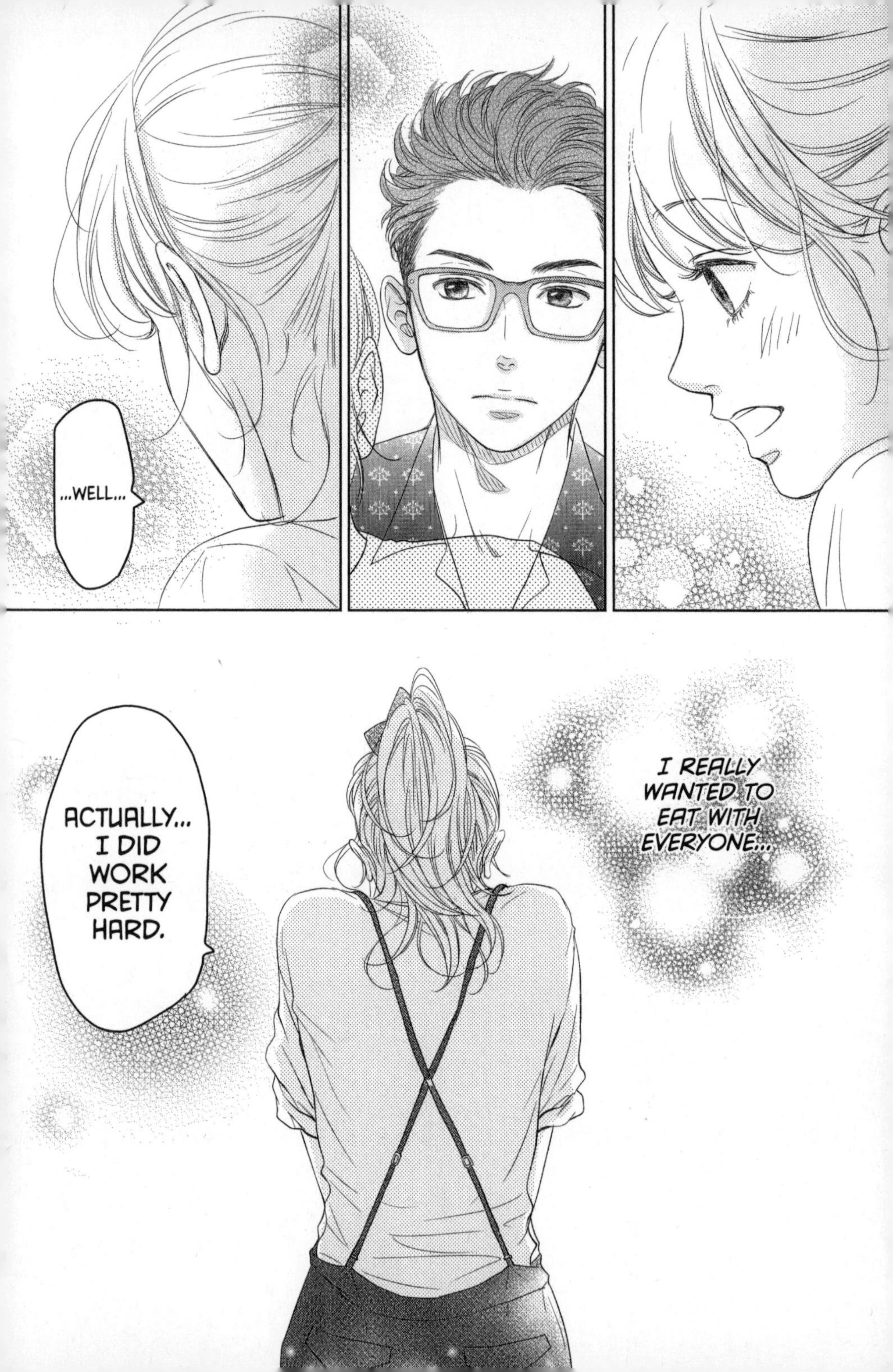

...WELL...
I REALLY WANTED TO EAT WITH EVERYONE...
ACTUALLY... I DID WORK PRETTY HARD.

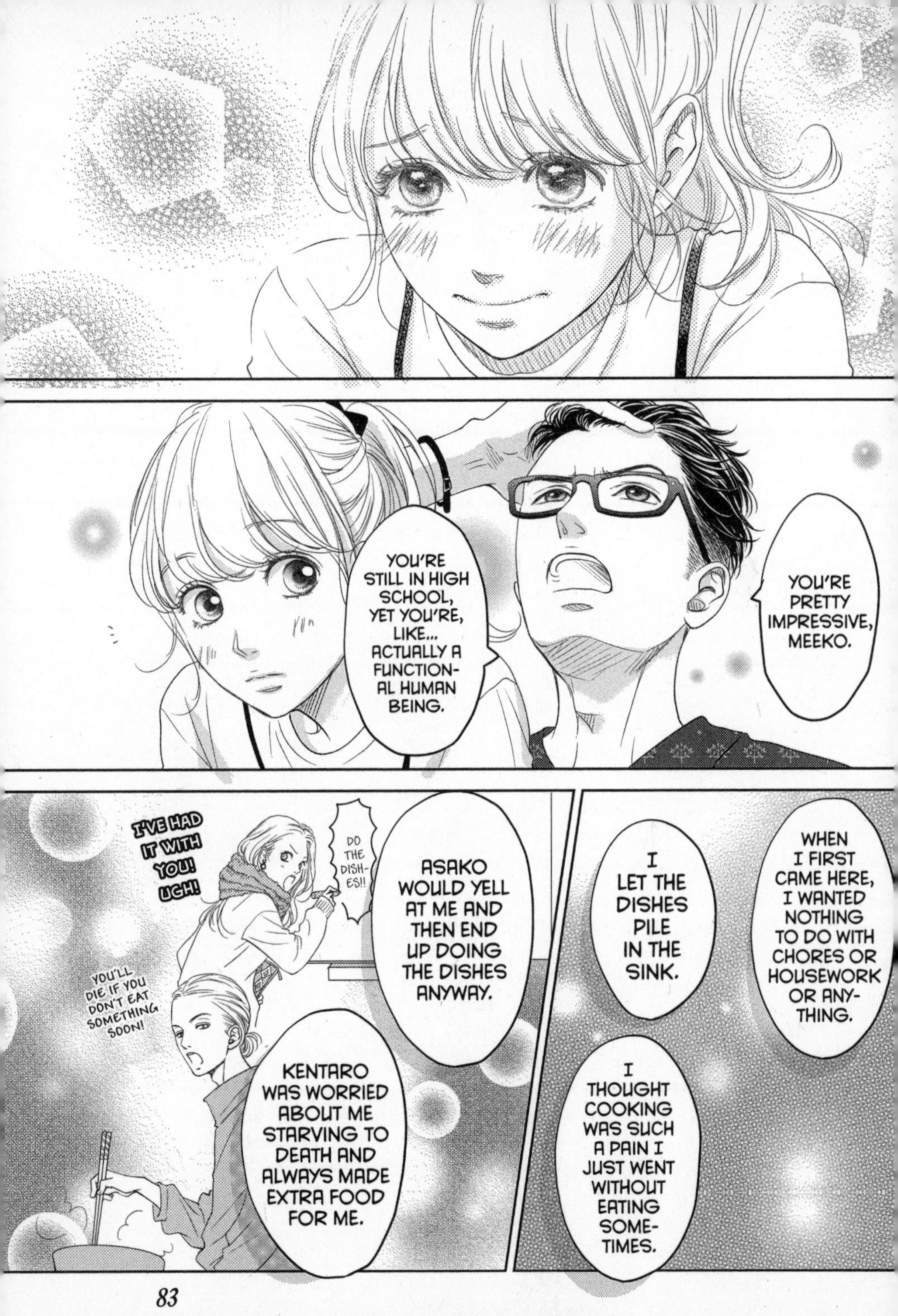
YOU'RE PRETTY IMPRESSIVE, MEEKO.
YOU'RE STILL IN HIGH SCHOOL, YET YOU'RE, LIKE... ACTUALLY A FUNCTIONAL HUMAN BEING.
WHEN I FIRST CAME HERE, I WANTED NOTHING TO DO WITH CHORES OR HOUSEWORK OR ANYTHING.
I LET THE DISHES PILE IN THE SINK.
I THOUGHT COOKING WAS SUCH A PAIN I JUST WENT WITHOUT EATING SOMETIMES.
ASAKO WOULD YELL AT ME AND THEN END UP DOING THE DISHES ANYWAY.
DO THE DISHES!!
I'VE HAD IT WITH YOU! UGH!
KENTARO WAS WORRIED ABOUT ME STARVING TO DEATH AND ALWAYS MADE EXTRA FOOD FOR ME.
YOU'LL DIE IF YOU DON'T EAT SOMETHING SOON!

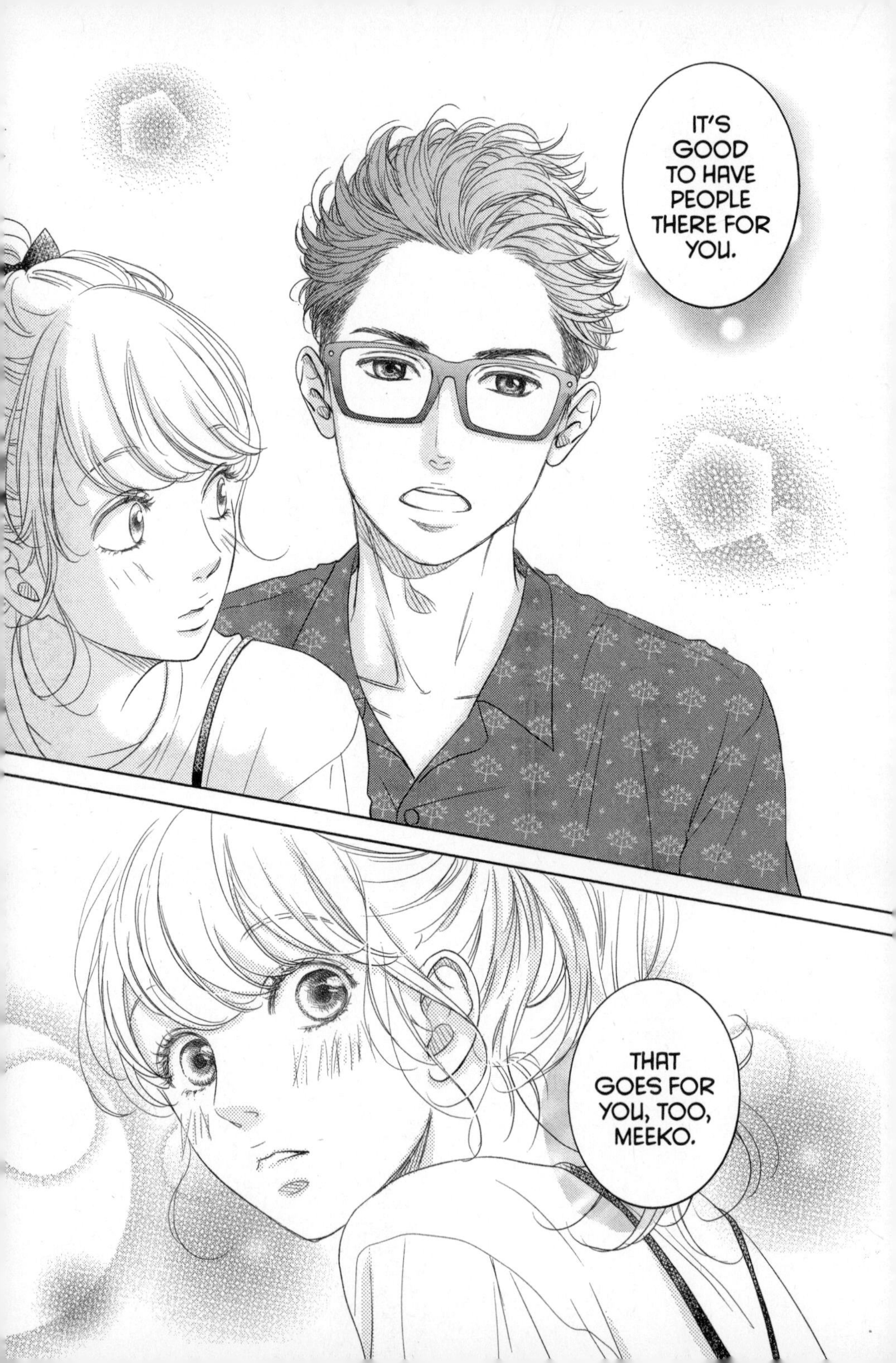
IT'S GOOD TO HAVE PEOPLE THERE FOR YOU.
THAT GOES FOR YOU, TOO, MEEKO.

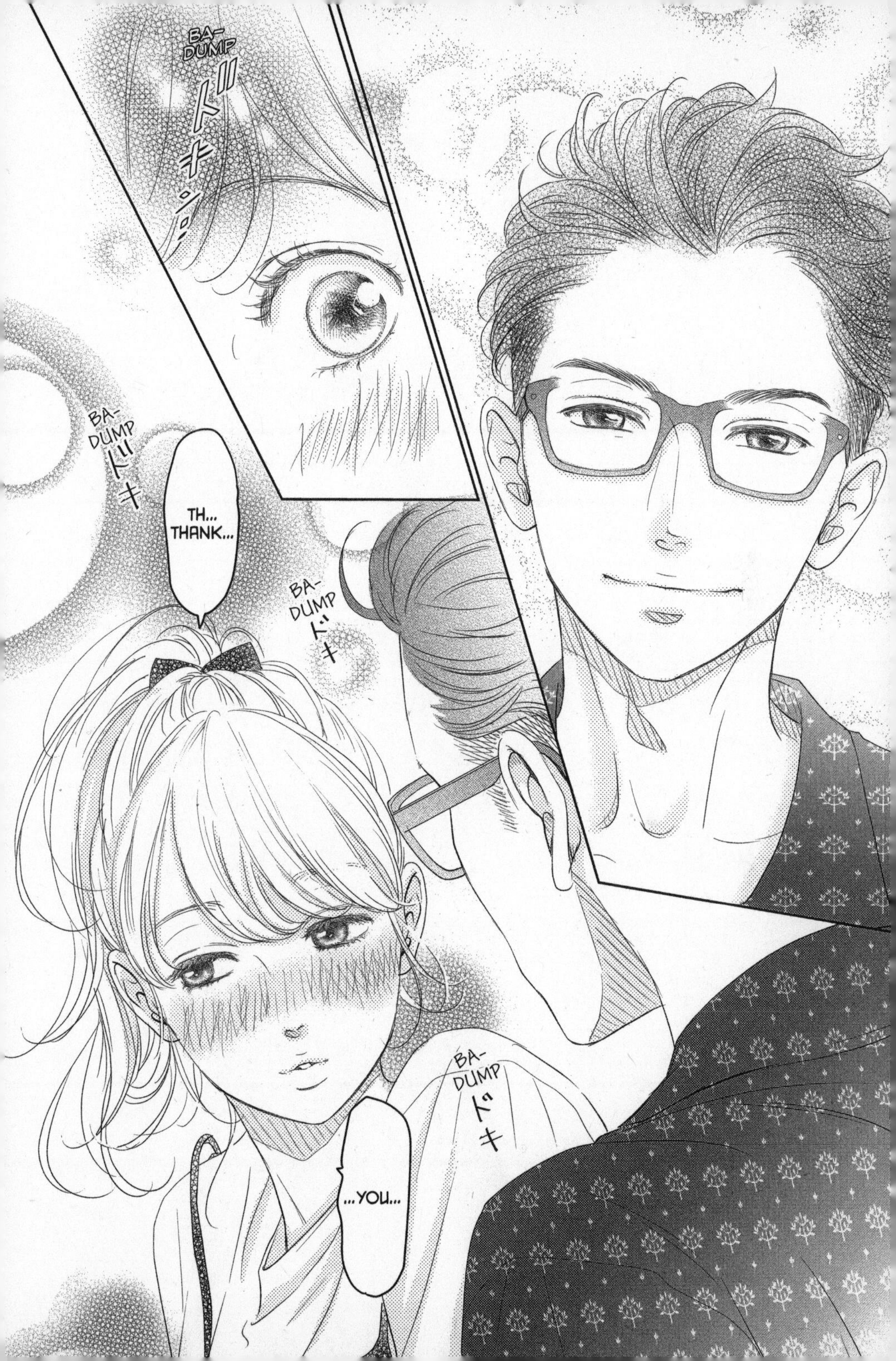
BA-DUMP
ドッキン…
BA-DUMP
ドキ
TH... THANK...
BA-DUMP
ドキ
BA-DUMP
ドキ
...YOU...

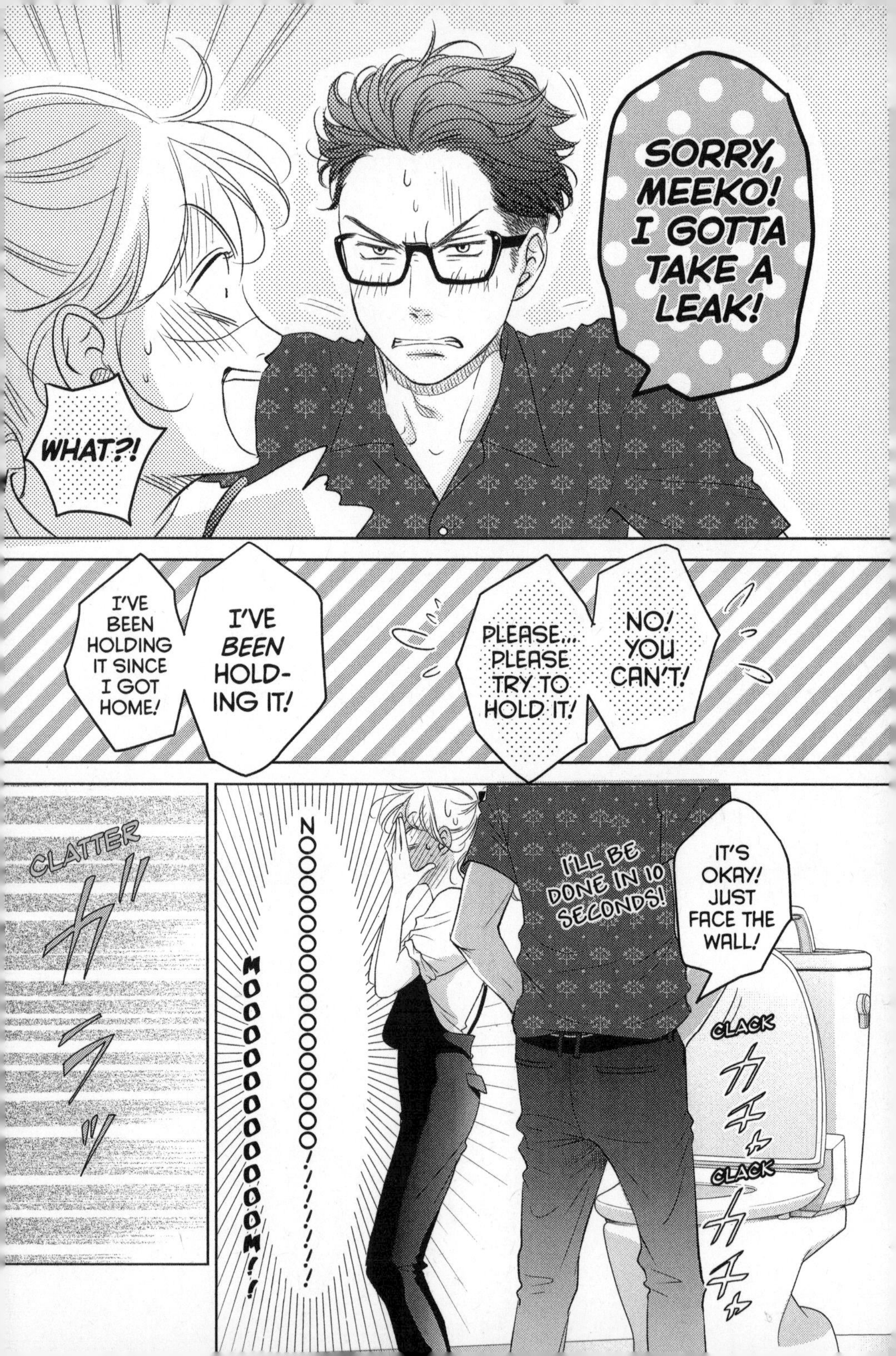
SORRY, MEEKO! I GOTTA TAKE A LEAK!
WHAT?!
NO! YOU CAN'T!
PLEASE... PLEASE TRY TO HOLD IT!
I'VE BEEN HOLDING IT!
I'VE BEEN HOLDING IT SINCE I GOT HOME!
IT'S OKAY! JUST FACE THE WALL!
I'LL BE DONE IN 10 SECONDS!
CLACK
CLACK
NOOOOOOOOOOOOOO!!!!!!
MOOOOOOOOOOOOOOOM!!
CLATTER

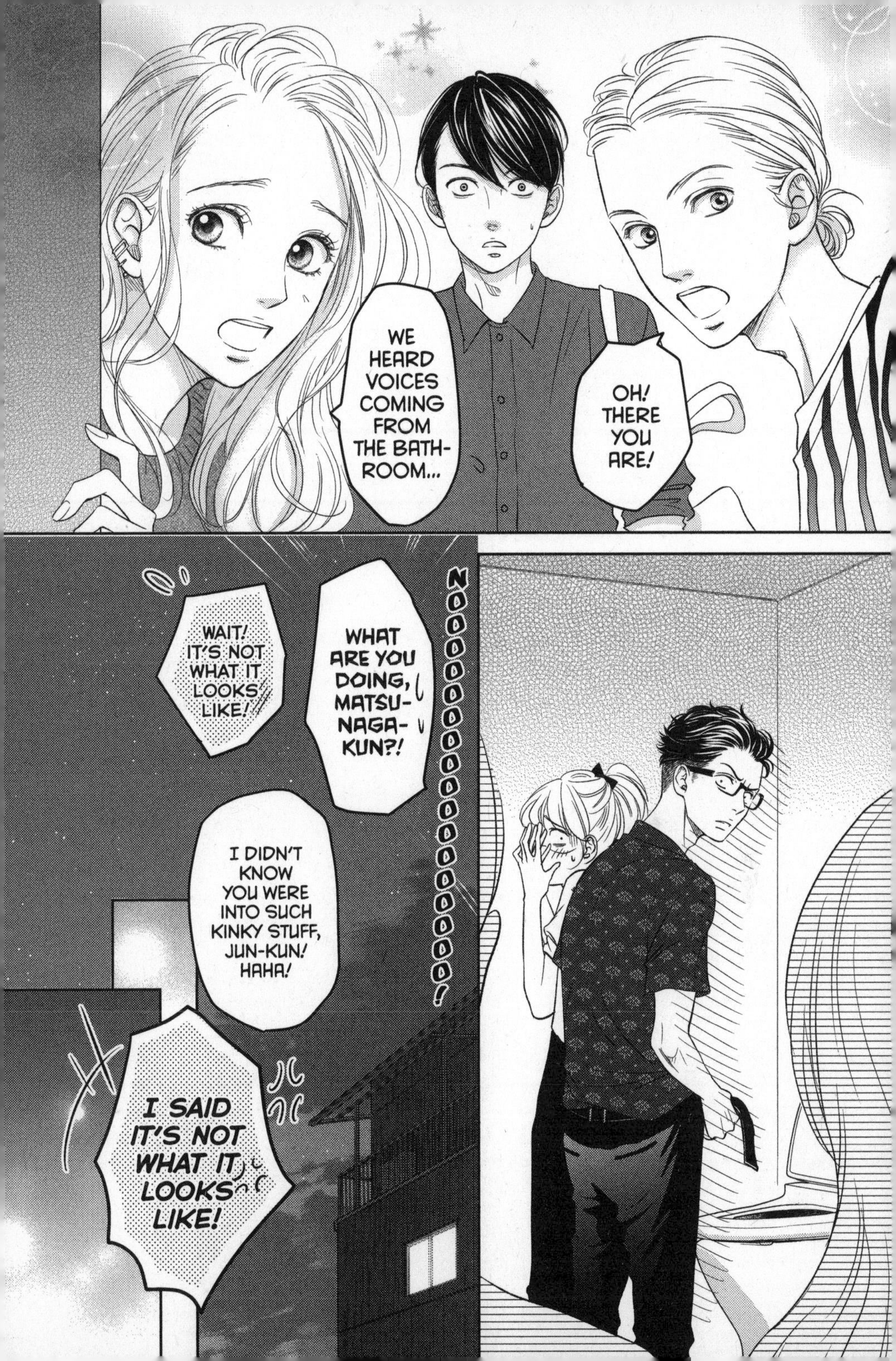
OH! THERE YOU ARE!
WE HEARD VOICES COMING FROM THE BATH-ROOM...
NOOOOOOOOOOOOOOOOOOOOOOOOOO!
WHAT ARE YOU DOING, MATSU-NAGA-KUN?!
WAIT! IT'S NOT WHAT IT LOOKS LIKE!
I DIDN'T KNOW YOU WERE INTO SUCH KINKY STUFF, JUN-KUN! HAHA!
I SAID IT'S NOT WHAT IT LOOKS LIKE!

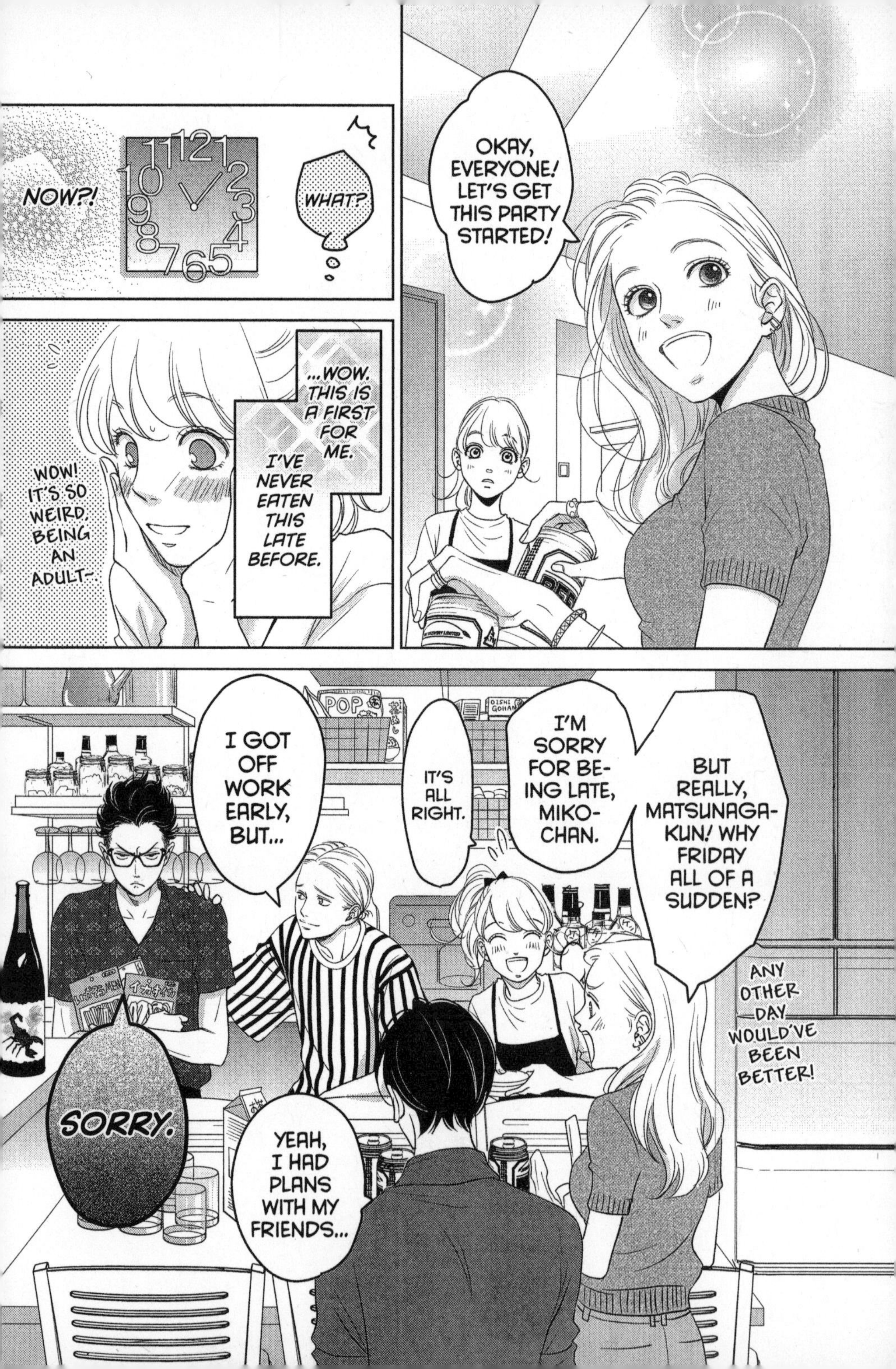
OKAY, EVERYONE! LET'S GET THIS PARTY STARTED!
WHAT?
NOW?!
...WOW. THIS IS A FIRST FOR ME.
I'VE NEVER EATEN THIS LATE BEFORE.
WOW! IT'S SO WEIRD, BEING AN ADULT~
ANY OTHER DAY WOULD'VE BEEN BETTER!
BUT REALLY, MATSUNAGA-KUN! WHY FRIDAY ALL OF A SUDDEN?
I'M SORRY FOR BE-ING LATE, MIKO-CHAN.
IT'S ALL RIGHT.
I GOT OFF WORK EARLY, BUT...
YEAH, I HAD PLANS WITH MY FRIENDS...
SORRY.

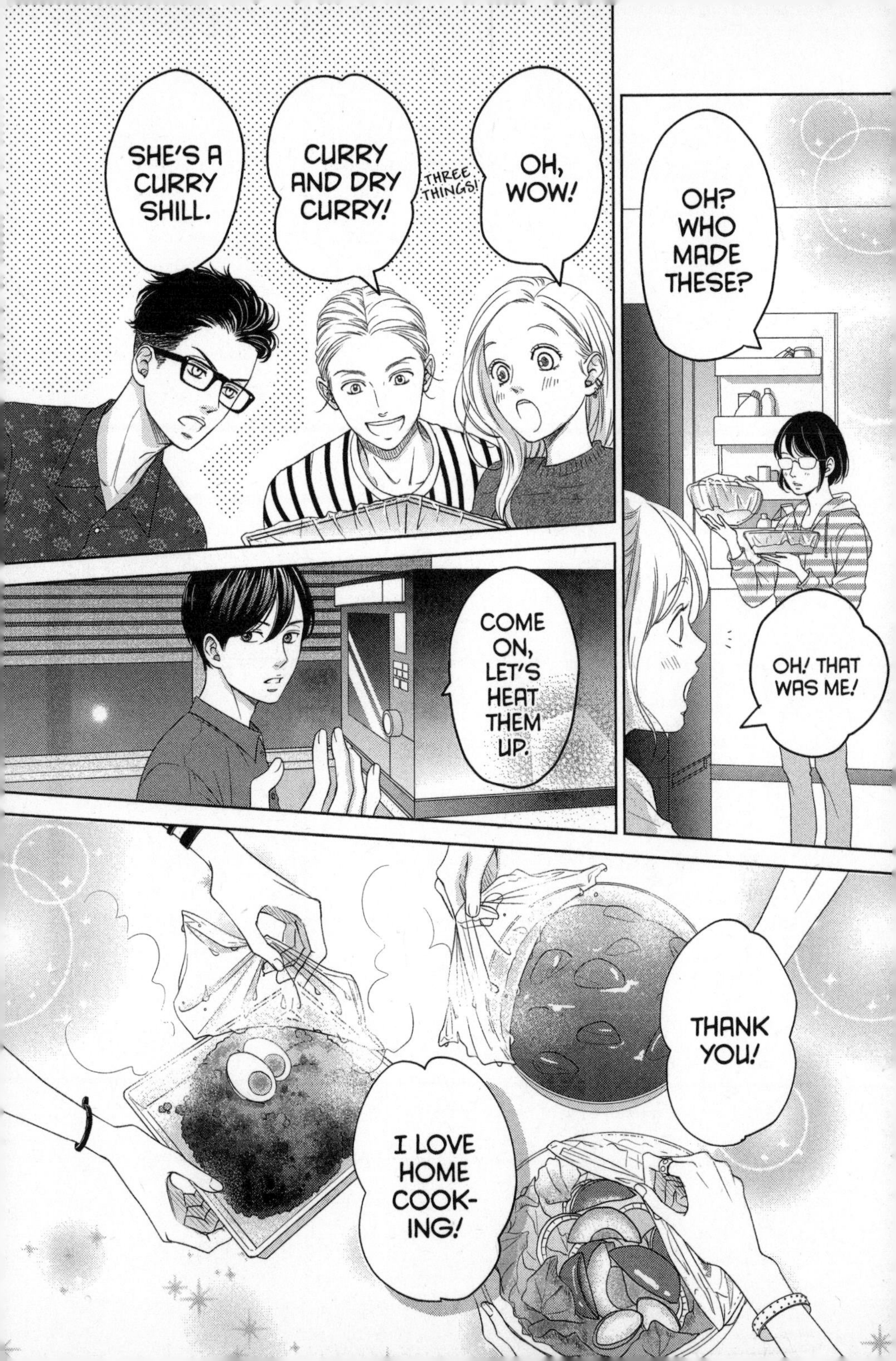
OH? WHO MADE THESE?
OH! THAT WAS ME!
OH, WOW!
THREE THINGS!
CURRY AND DRY CURRY!
SHE'S A CURRY SHILL.
COME ON, LET'S HEAT THEM UP.
THANK YOU!
I LOVE HOME COOK-ING!

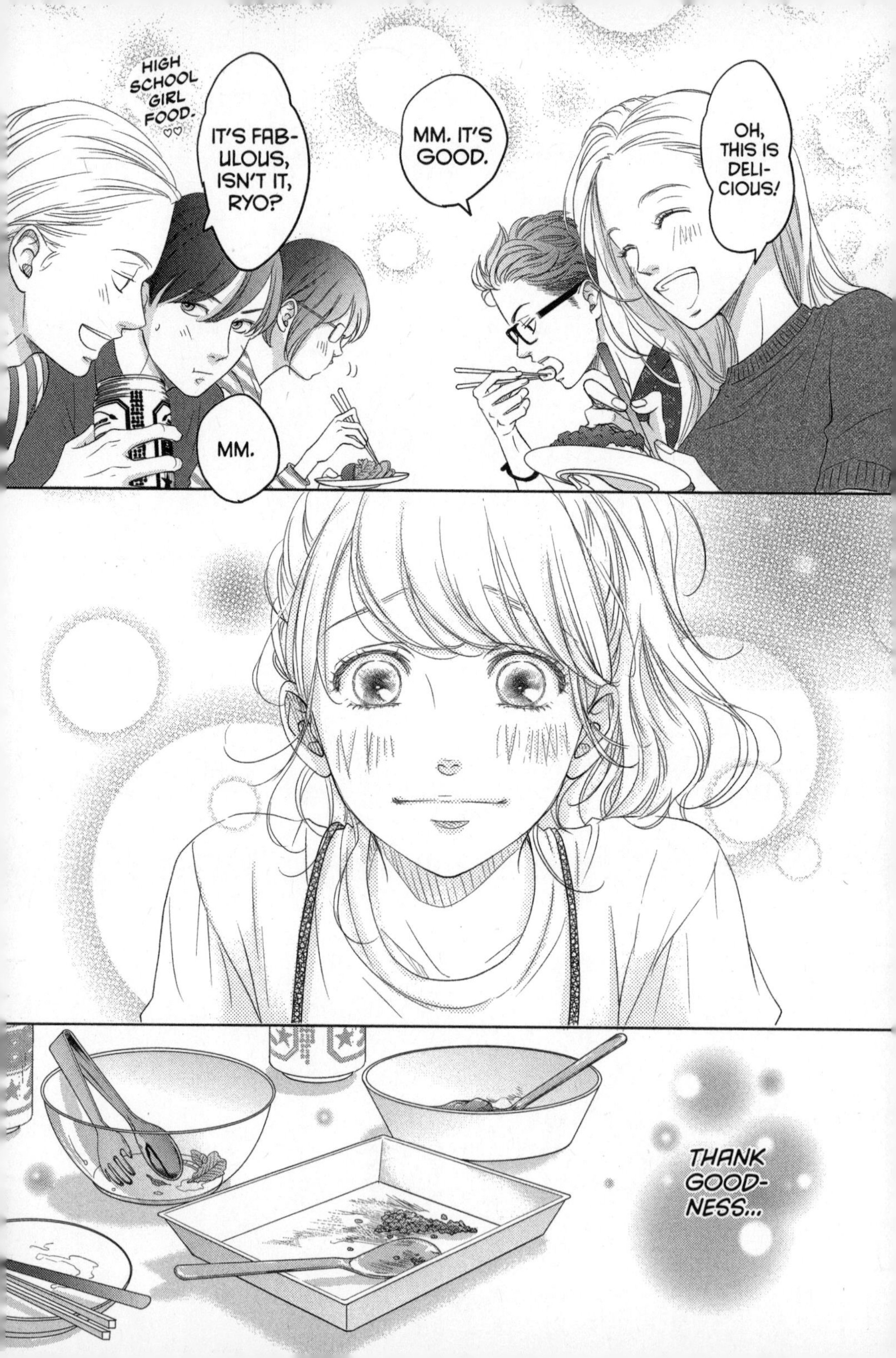
OH, THIS IS DELICIOUS!
MM. IT'S GOOD.
IT'S FABULOUS, ISN'T IT, RYO?
HIGH SCHOOL GIRL FOOD.♡♡
MM.
THANK GOODNESS...

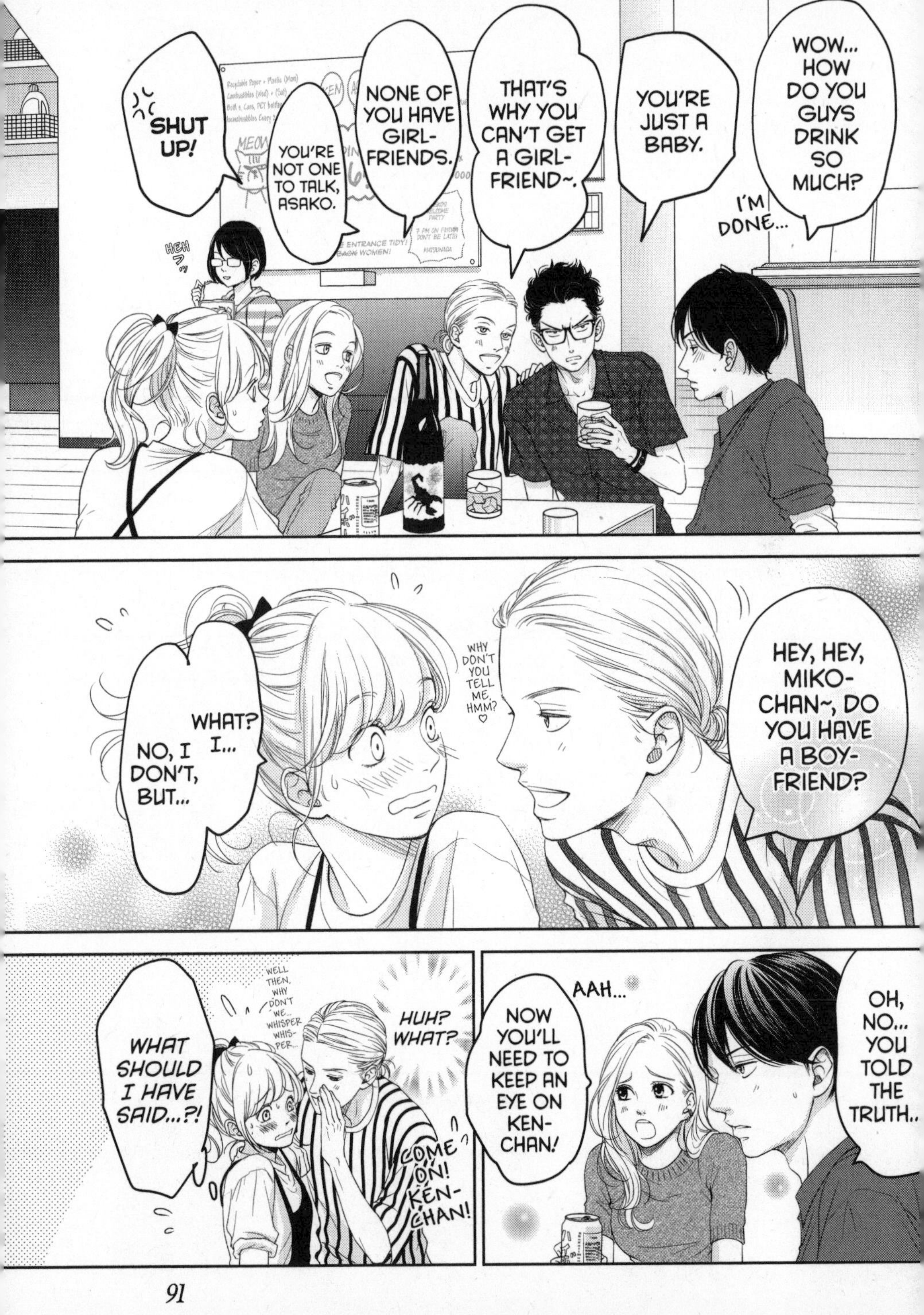
WOW... HOW DO YOU GUYS DRINK SO MUCH?
I'M DONE...
YOU'RE JUST A BABY.
THAT'S WHY YOU CAN'T GET A GIRL-FRIEND~.
NONE OF YOU HAVE GIRL-FRIENDS.
YOU'RE NOT ONE TO TALK, ASAKO.
SHUT UP!
HEH
HEY, HEY, MIKO-CHAN~, DO YOU HAVE A BOY-FRIEND?
WHY DON'T YOU TELL ME, HMM? ♡
WHAT? I...
NO, I DON'T, BUT...
OH, NO... YOU TOLD THE TRUTH..
AAH...
NOW YOU'LL NEED TO KEEP AN EYE ON KEN-CHAN!
HUH? WHAT?
COME ON! KEN-CHAN!
WELL THEN, WHY DON'T WE... WHISPER WHISPER...
WHAT SHOULD I HAVE SAID...?!

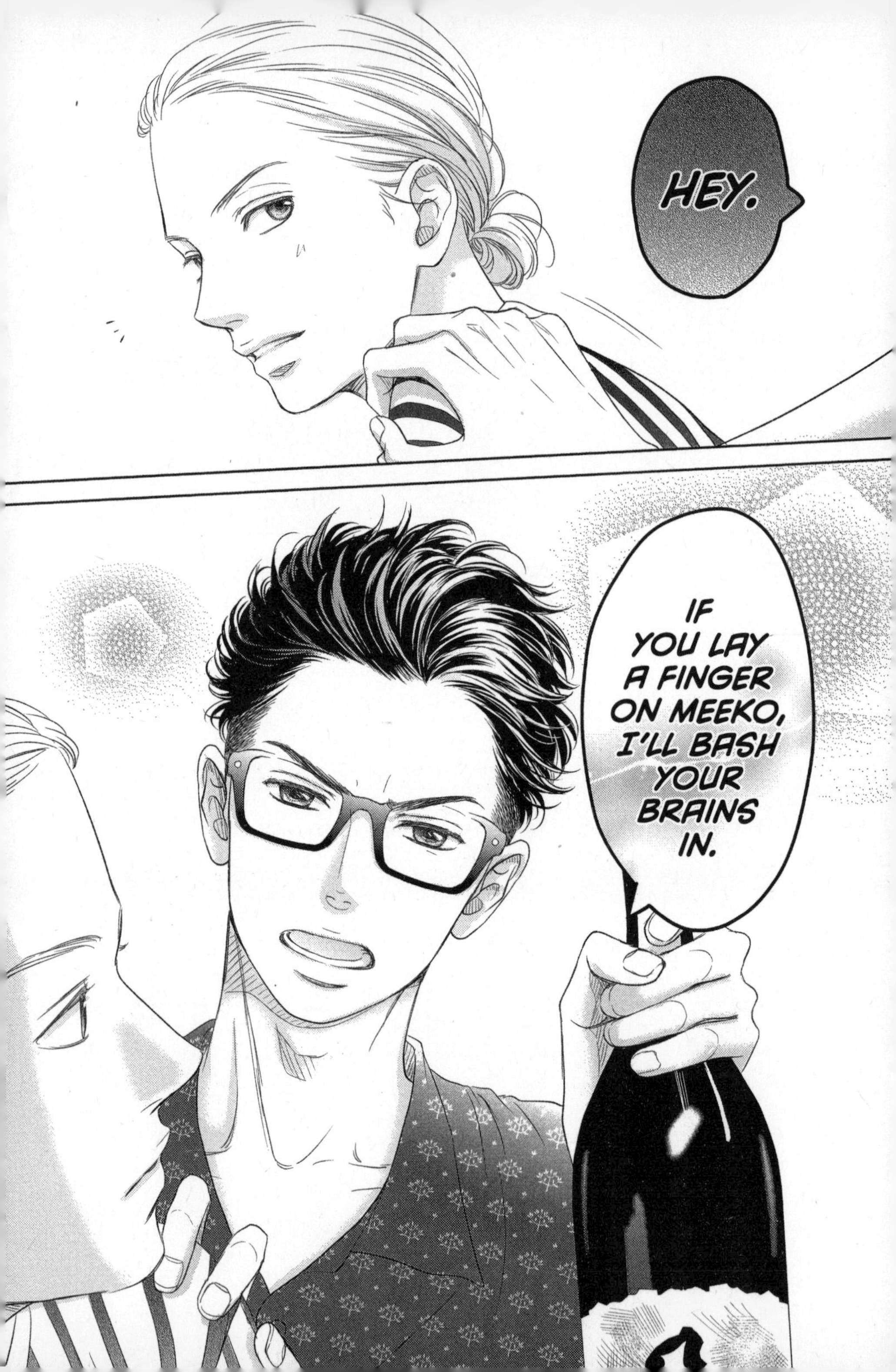
HEY.
IF YOU LAY A FINGER ON MEEKO, I'LL BASH YOUR BRAINS IN.

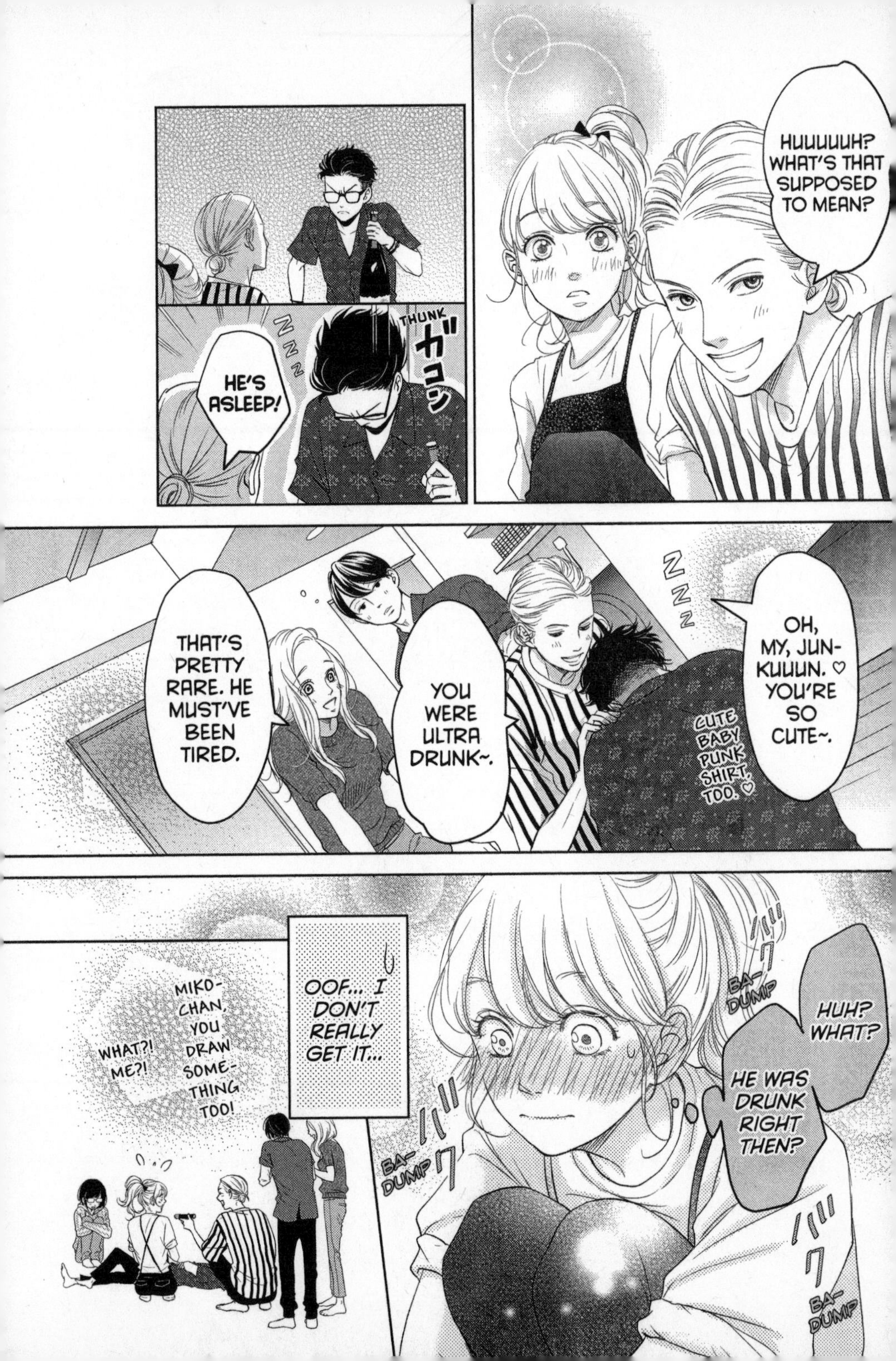
HUUUUUH? WHAT'S THAT SUPPOSED TO MEAN?
THUNK
ガコン
Z Z Z
HE'S ASLEEP!
Z Z Z
OH, MY, JUN-KUUUN. ♡ YOU'RE SO CUTE~.
CUTE BABY PUNK SHIRT, TOO. ♡
YOU WERE ULTRA DRUNK~.
THAT'S PRETTY RARE. HE MUST'VE BEEN TIRED.
BA-DUMP
HUH? WHAT?
HE WAS DRUNK RIGHT THEN?
BA-DUMP
BA-DUMP
OOF... I DON'T REALLY GET IT...
MIKO-CHAN, YOU DRAW SOME-THING TOO!
WHAT?! ME?!

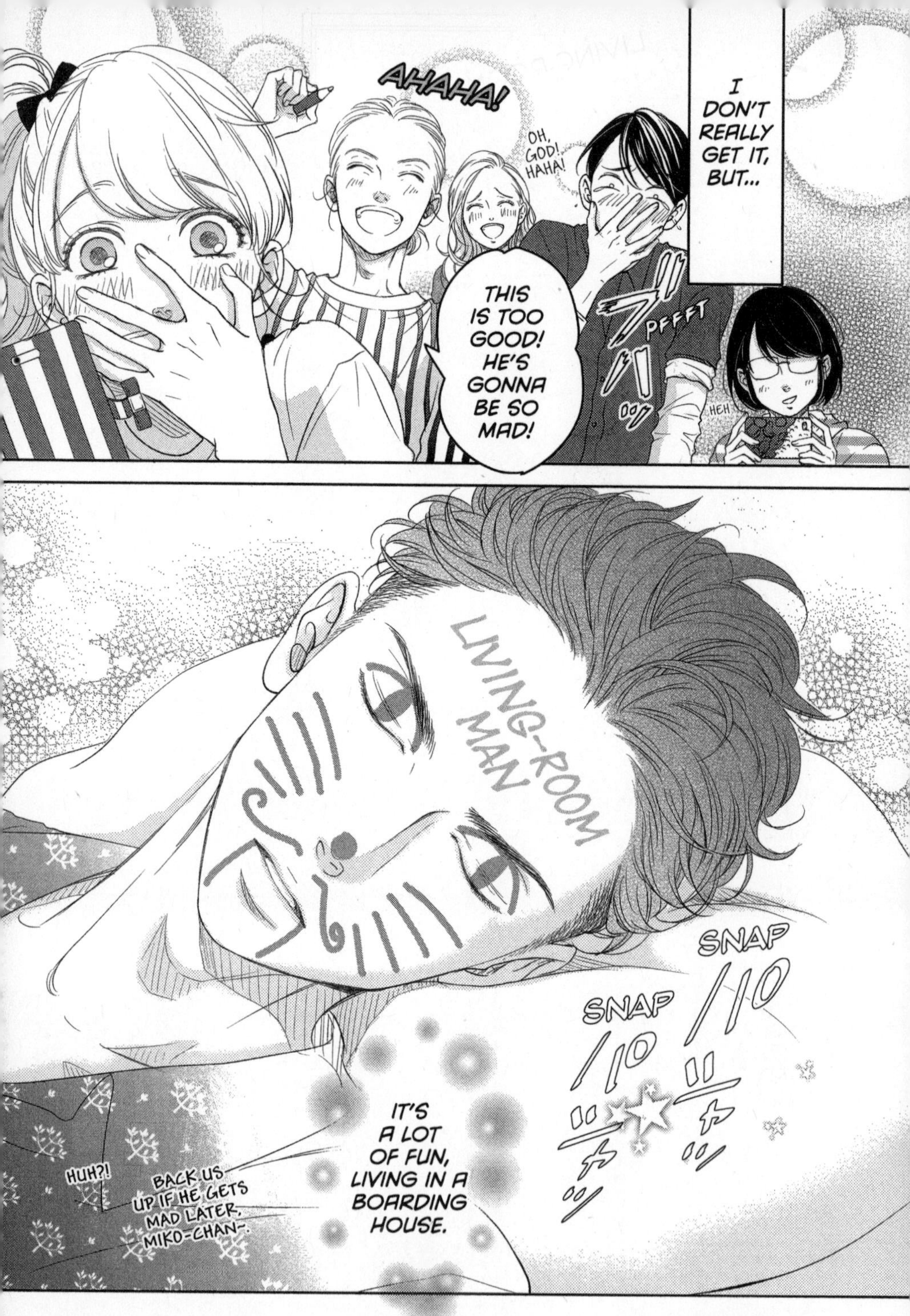
I DON'T REALLY GET IT, BUT...
OH, GOD! HAHA!
AHAHA!
THIS IS TOO GOOD! HE'S GONNA BE SO MAD!
PFFFT
HEH
SNAP
SNAP
LIVING-ROOM MAN
IT'S A LOT OF FUN, LIVING IN A BOARDING HOUSE.
BACK US UP IF HE GETS MAD LATER, MIKO-CHAN~.
HUH?!

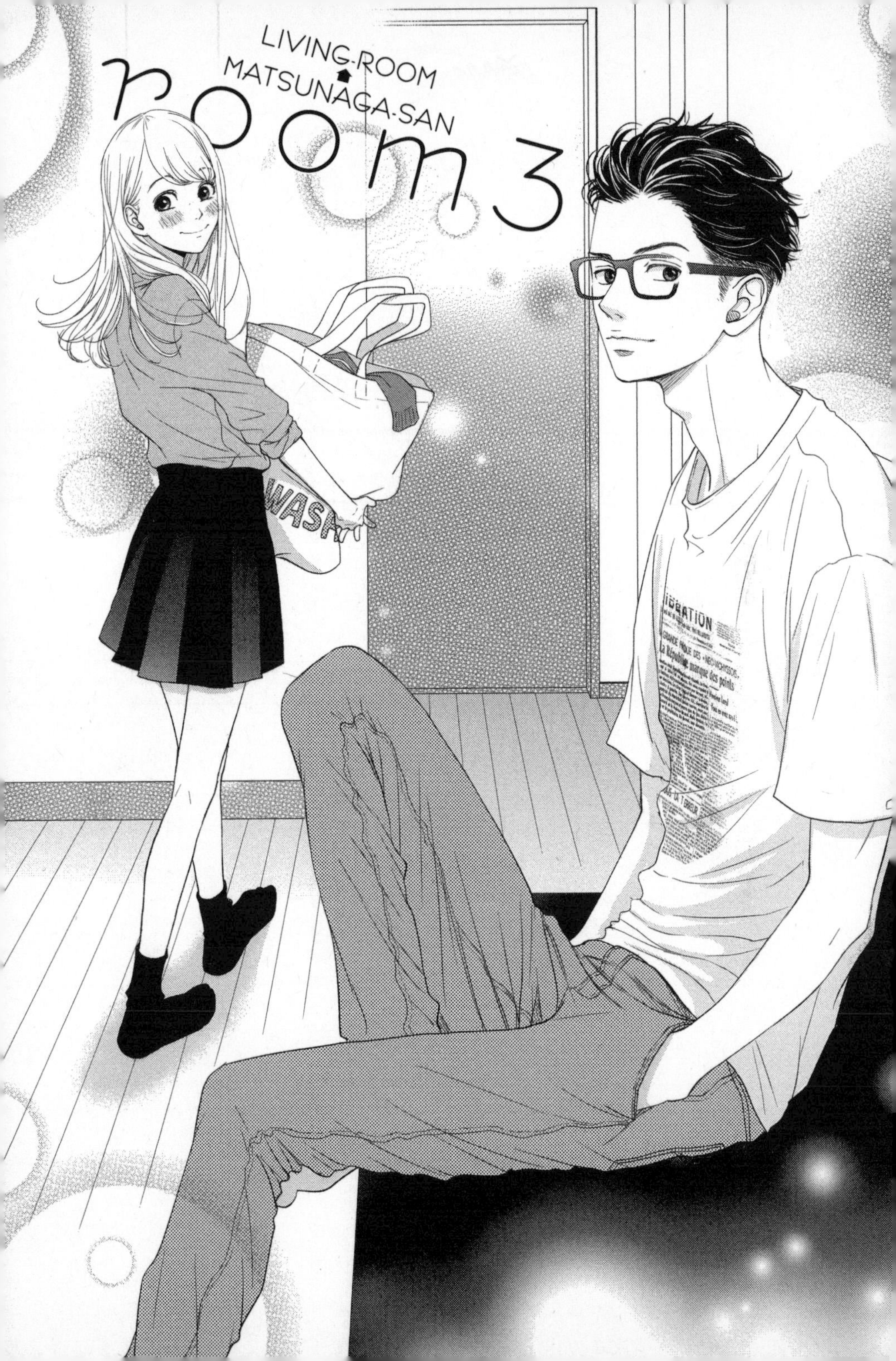
LIVING-ROOM
MATSUNAGA-SAN
room 3
WASH

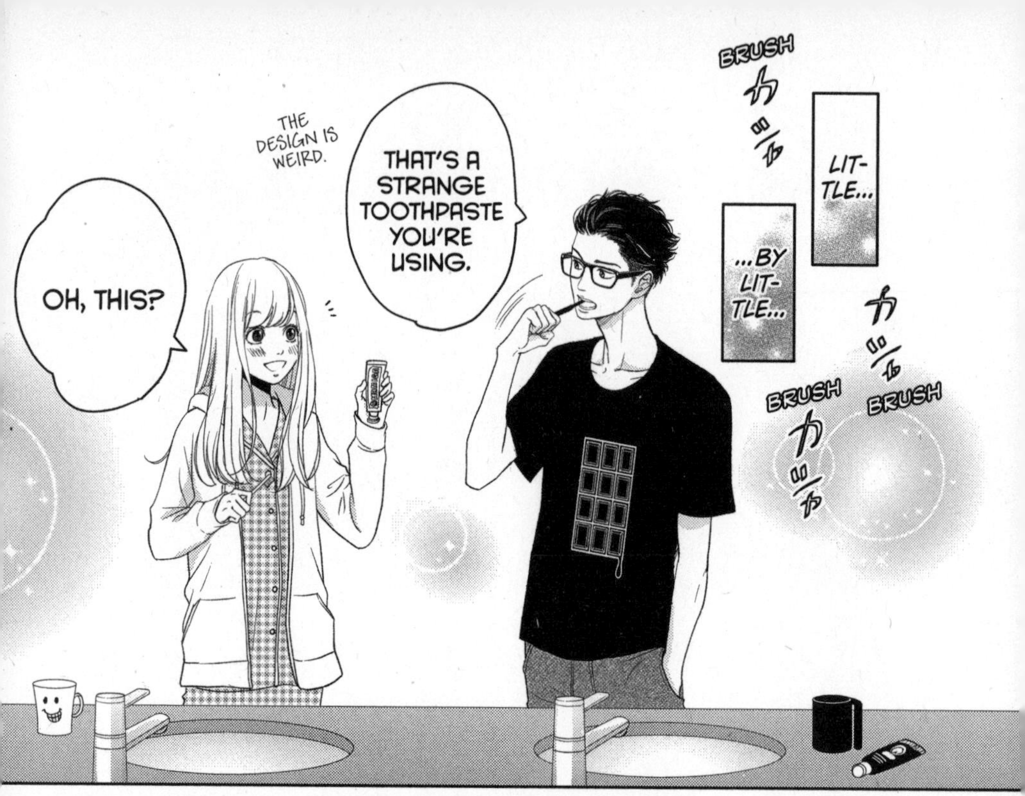
BRUSH
LIT-TLE...
...BY LIT-TLE...
BRUSH BRUSH
THAT'S A STRANGE TOOTHPASTE YOU'RE USING.
THE DESIGN IS WEIRD.
OH, THIS?

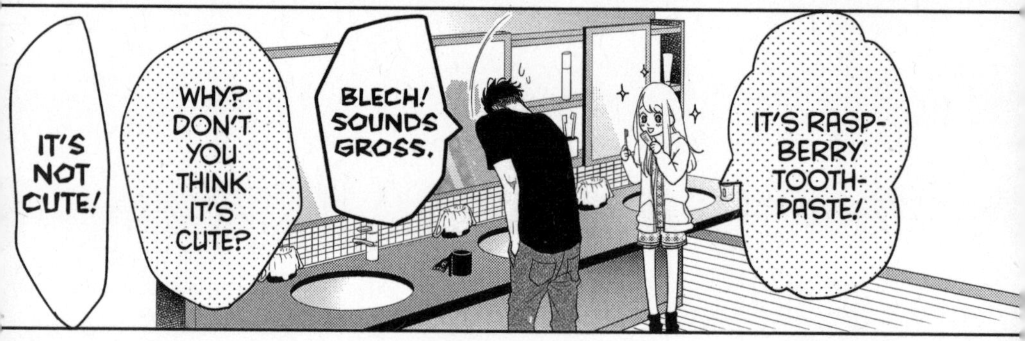
IT'S RASP-BERRY TOOTH-PASTE!
BLECH! SOUNDS GROSS.
WHY? DON'T YOU THINK IT'S CUTE?
IT'S NOT CUTE!

Boarding House Trivia

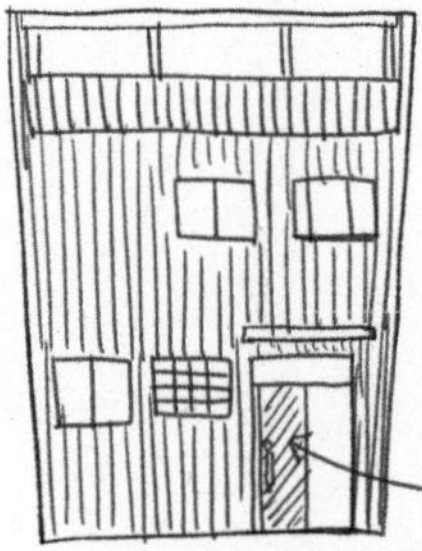

I modeled their boarding house on a real boarding house in the city! I'm indebted to the owner's kindness!!

The red entrance looks really incredible!

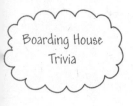

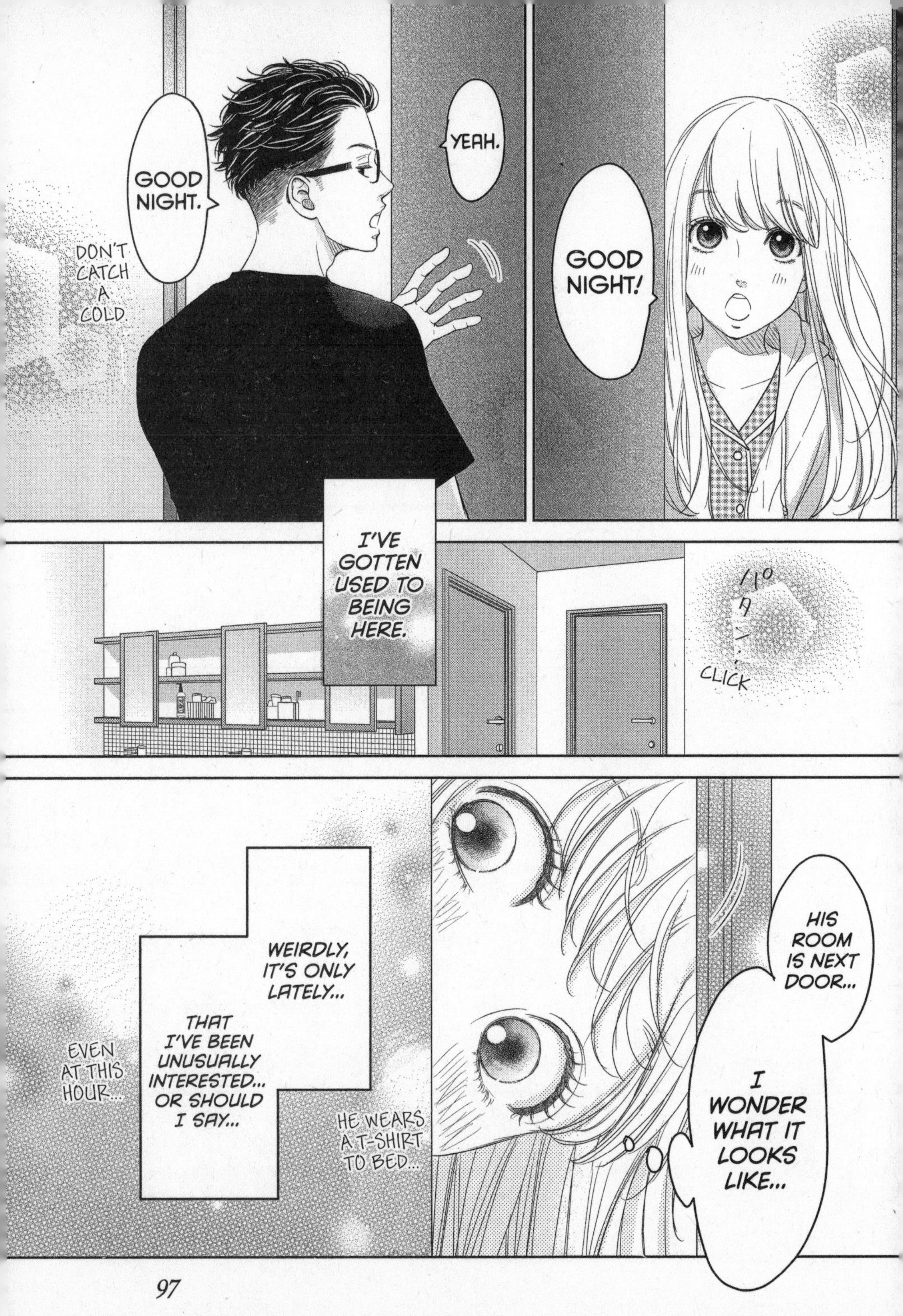
GOOD NIGHT!
YEAH.
GOOD NIGHT.
DON'T CATCH A COLD.
I'VE GOTTEN USED TO BEING HERE.
CLICK
HIS ROOM IS NEXT DOOR...
I WONDER WHAT IT LOOKS LIKE...
WEIRDLY, IT'S ONLY LATELY...
THAT I'VE BEEN UNUSUALLY INTERESTED... OR SHOULD I SAY...
EVEN AT THIS HOUR...
HE WEARS A T-SHIRT TO BED...

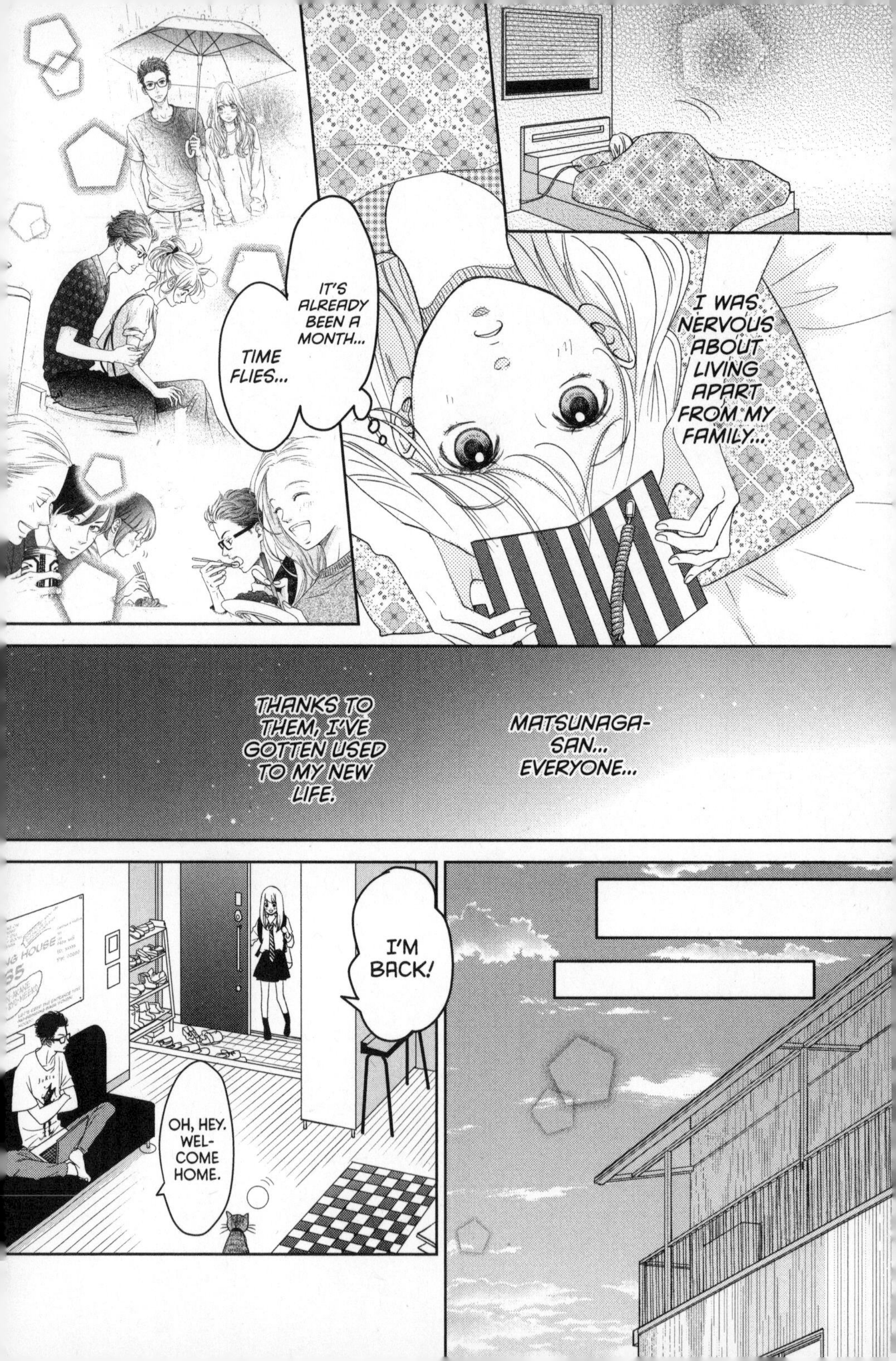
I WAS NERVOUS ABOUT LIVING APART FROM MY FAMILY...
IT'S ALREADY BEEN A MONTH... TIME FLIES...
MATSUNAGA-SAN... EVERYONE...
THANKS TO THEM, I'VE GOTTEN USED TO MY NEW LIFE.
I'M BACK!
OH, HEY. WEL-COME HOME.

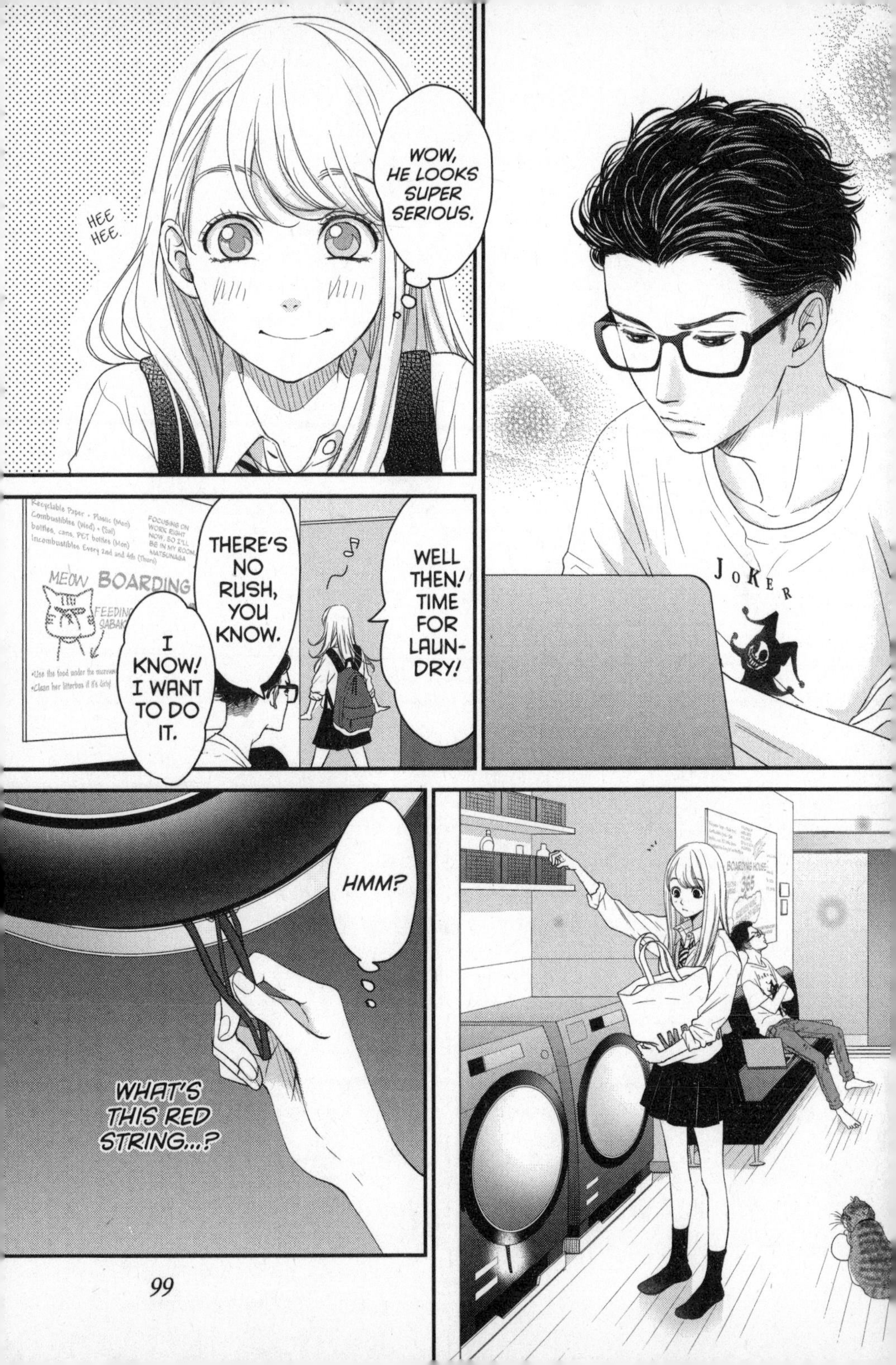
JoKER
WOW, HE LOOKS SUPER SERIOUS.
HEE HEE.
WELL THEN! TIME FOR LAUNDRY!
THERE'S NO RUSH, YOU KNOW.
I KNOW! I WANT TO DO IT.
FOCUSING ON WORK RIGHT NOW, SO I'LL BE IN MY ROOM. MATSUNAGA
Recyclable Paper + Plastic (Mon)
Combustibles (Wed) + (Sat)
bottles, cans, PET bottles (Mon)
Incombustibles Every 2nd and 4th (Thurs)
MEOW BOARDING
HMM?
WHAT'S THIS RED STRING...?

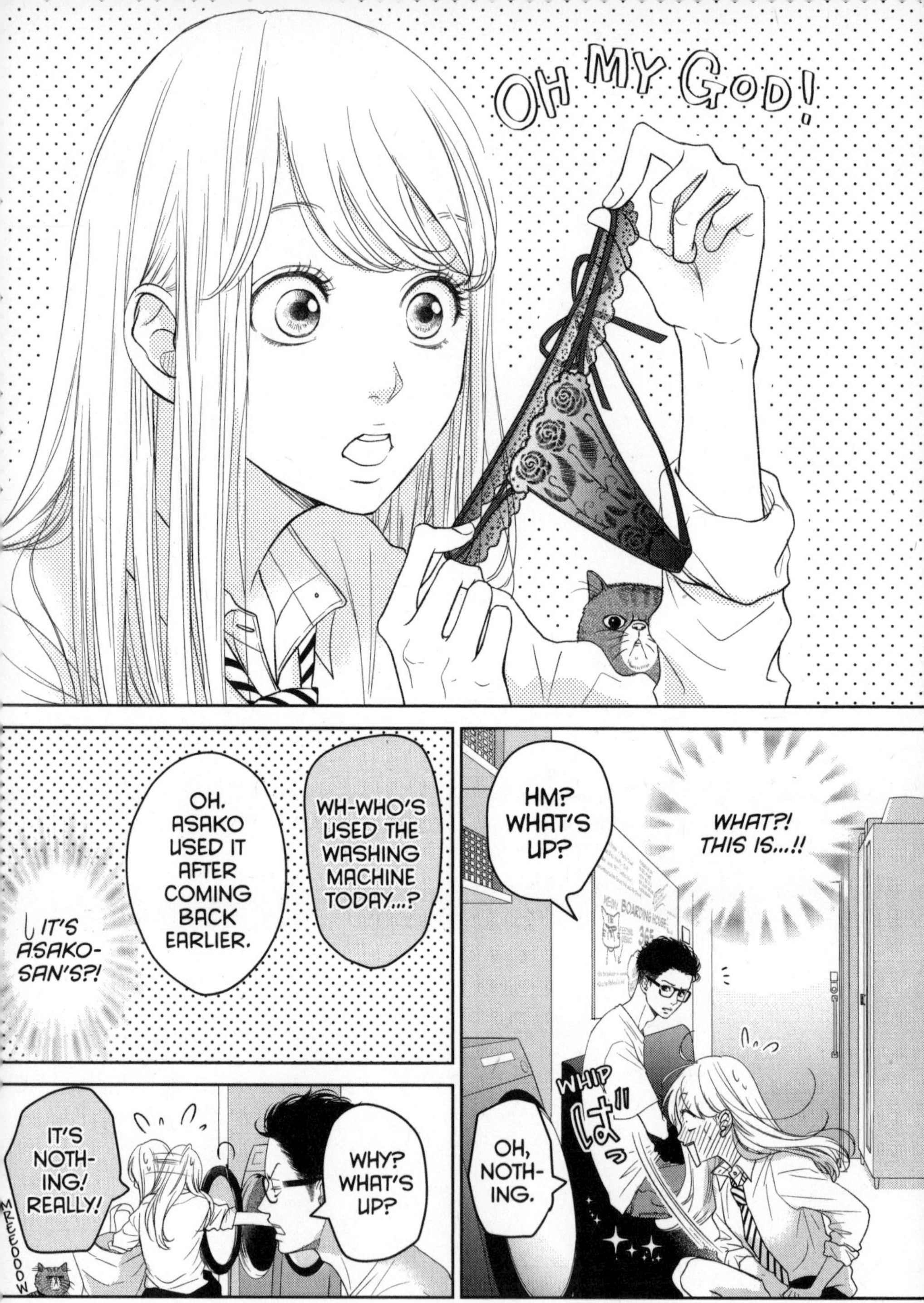

OH MY GOD!
WHAT?! THIS IS...!!
HM? WHAT'S UP?
WHIP
OH, NOTHING.
WH-WHO'S USED THE WASHING MACHINE TODAY...?
OH. ASAKO USED IT AFTER COMING BACK EARLIER.
IT'S ASAKO-SAN'S?!
WHY? WHAT'S UP?
IT'S NOTHING! REALLY!
MREEOOOW

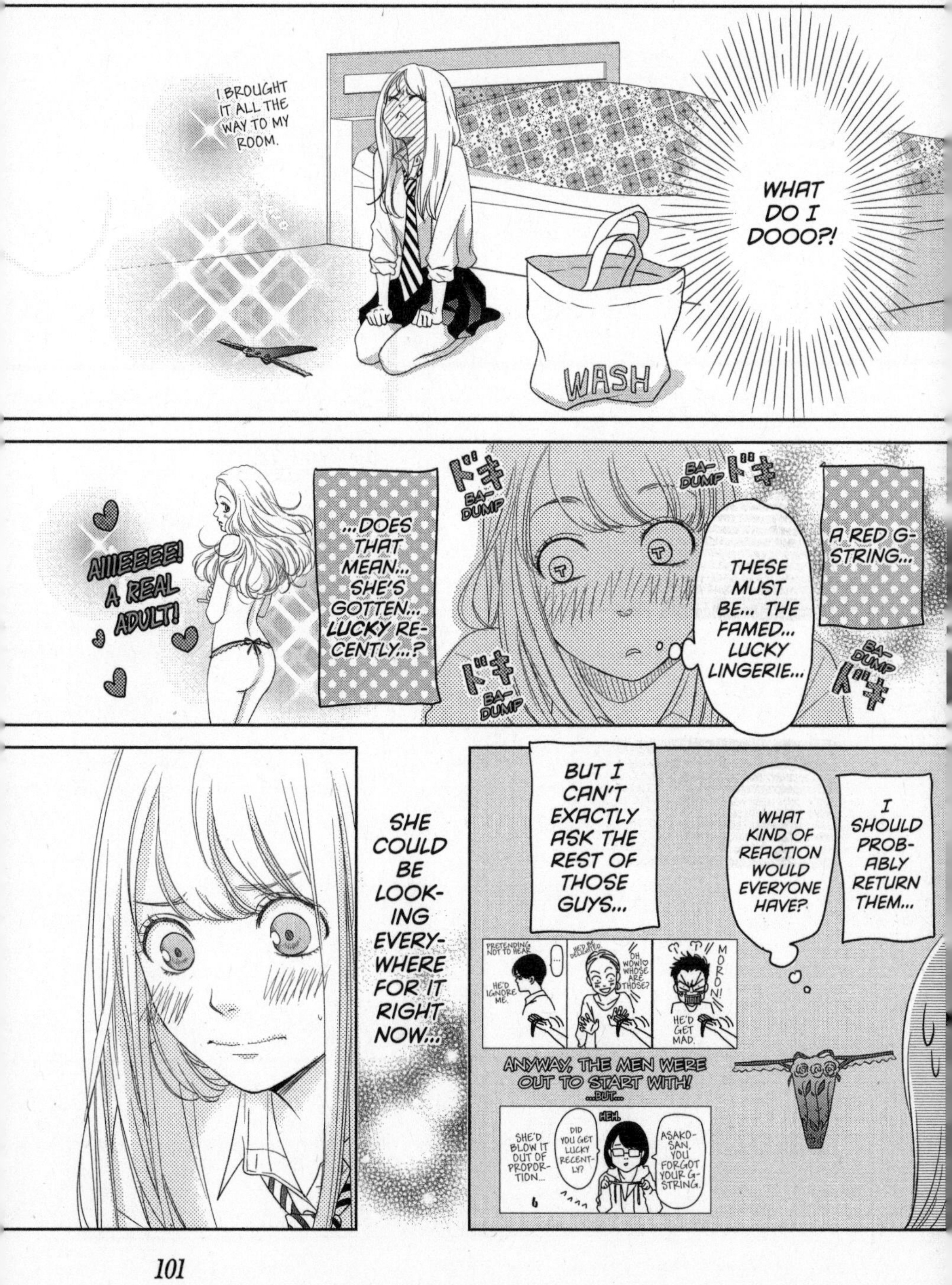
I BROUGHT IT ALL THE WAY TO MY ROOM.
WHAT DO I DOOO?!
WASH
A RED G-STRING...
BA-DUMP
ドキ
THESE MUST BE... THE FAMED... LUCKY LINGERIE...
BA-DUMP
ドキ
...DOES THAT MEAN... SHE'S GOTTEN... LUCKY RECENTLY...?
AIIIEEEE! A REAL ADULT!
I SHOULD PROBABLY RETURN THEM...
WHAT KIND OF REACTION WOULD EVERYONE HAVE?
BUT I CAN'T EXACTLY ASK THE REST OF THOSE GUYS...
MORON!
HE'D GET MAD.
HE'D BE DELIGHTED
OH WOW! WHOSE ARE THOSE?
PRETENDING NOT TO HEAR
...
HE'D IGNORE ME.
ANYWAY, THE MEN WERE OUT TO START WITH!
...BUT...
ASAKO-SAN, YOU FORGOT YOUR G-STRING.
HEH.
DID YOU GET LUCKY RECENTLY?
SHE'D BLOW IT OUT OF PROPORTION...
SHE COULD BE LOOKING EVERYWHERE FOR IT RIGHT NOW...

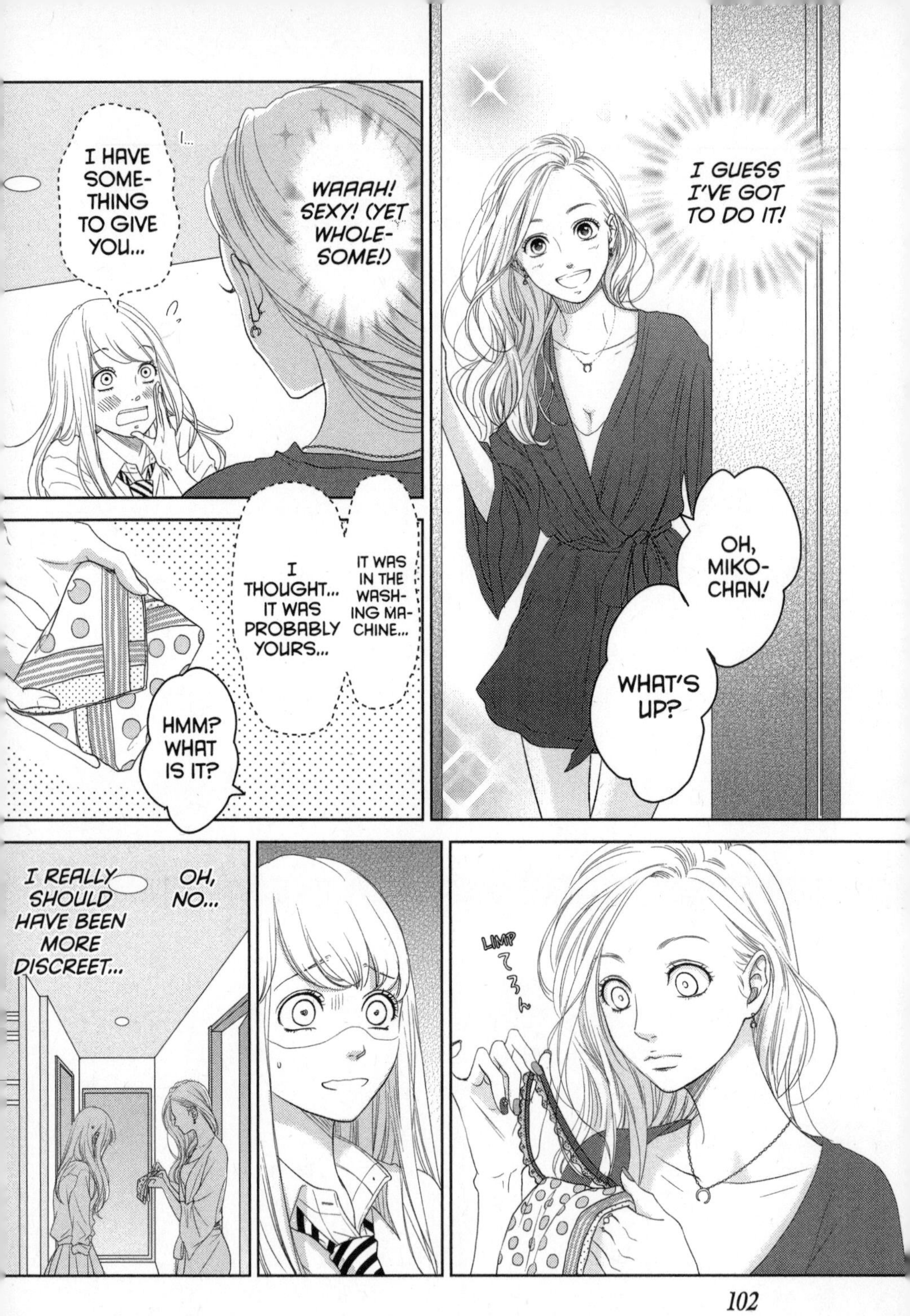
I GUESS I'VE GOT TO DO IT!
OH, MIKO-CHAN!
WHAT'S UP?
WAAAH! SEXY! (YET WHOLE-SOME!)
I...
I HAVE SOME-THING TO GIVE YOU...
IT WAS IN THE WASH-ING MA-CHINE...
I THOUGHT... IT WAS PROBABLY YOURS...
HMM? WHAT IS IT?
LIMP
てろん
OH, NO...
I REALLY SHOULD HAVE BEEN MORE DISCREET...

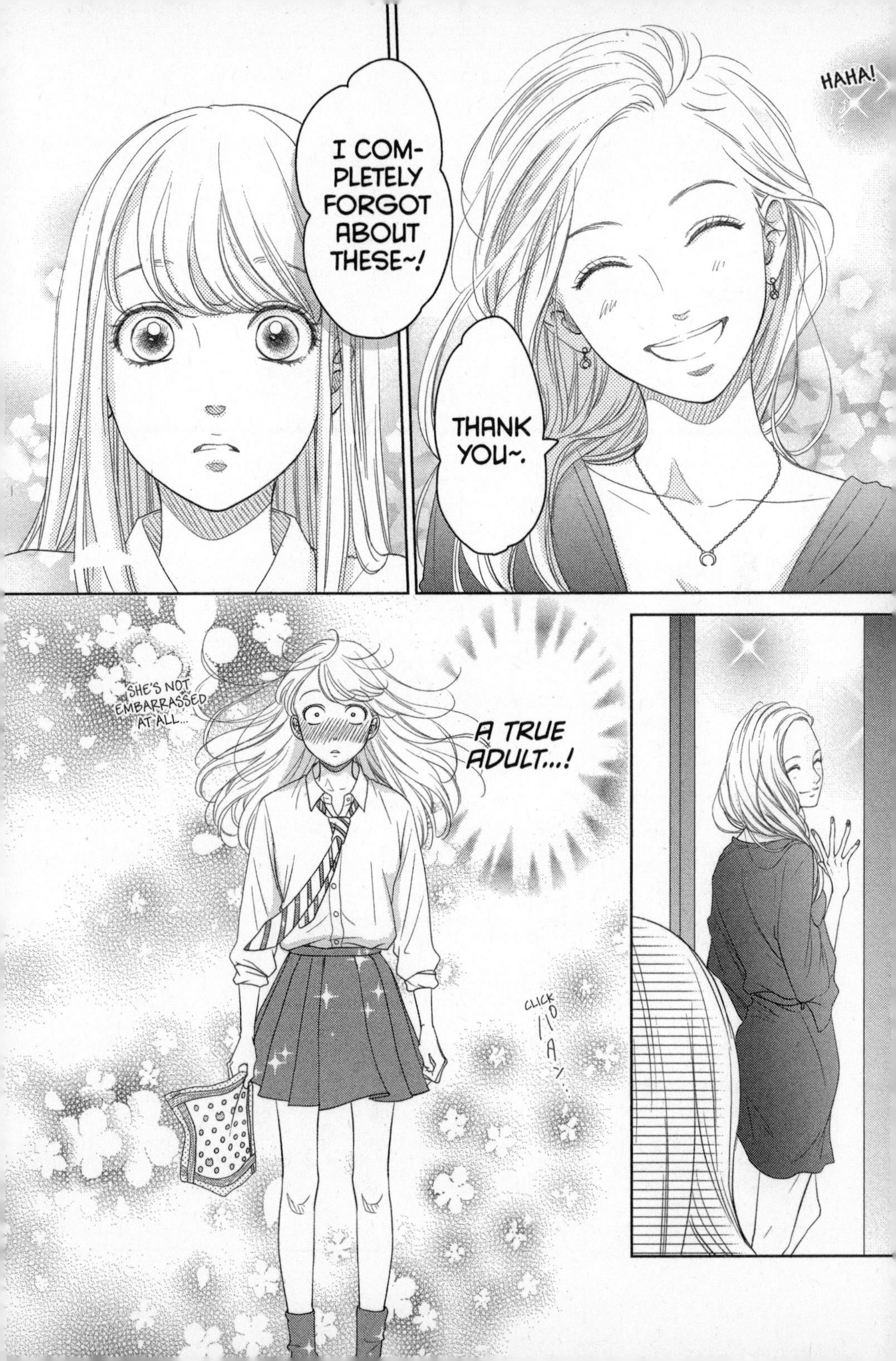
HAHA!
I COM-PLETELY FORGOT ABOUT THESE~!
THANK YOU~.
SHE'S NOT EMBARRASSED AT ALL...
A TRUE ADULT...!
CLICK

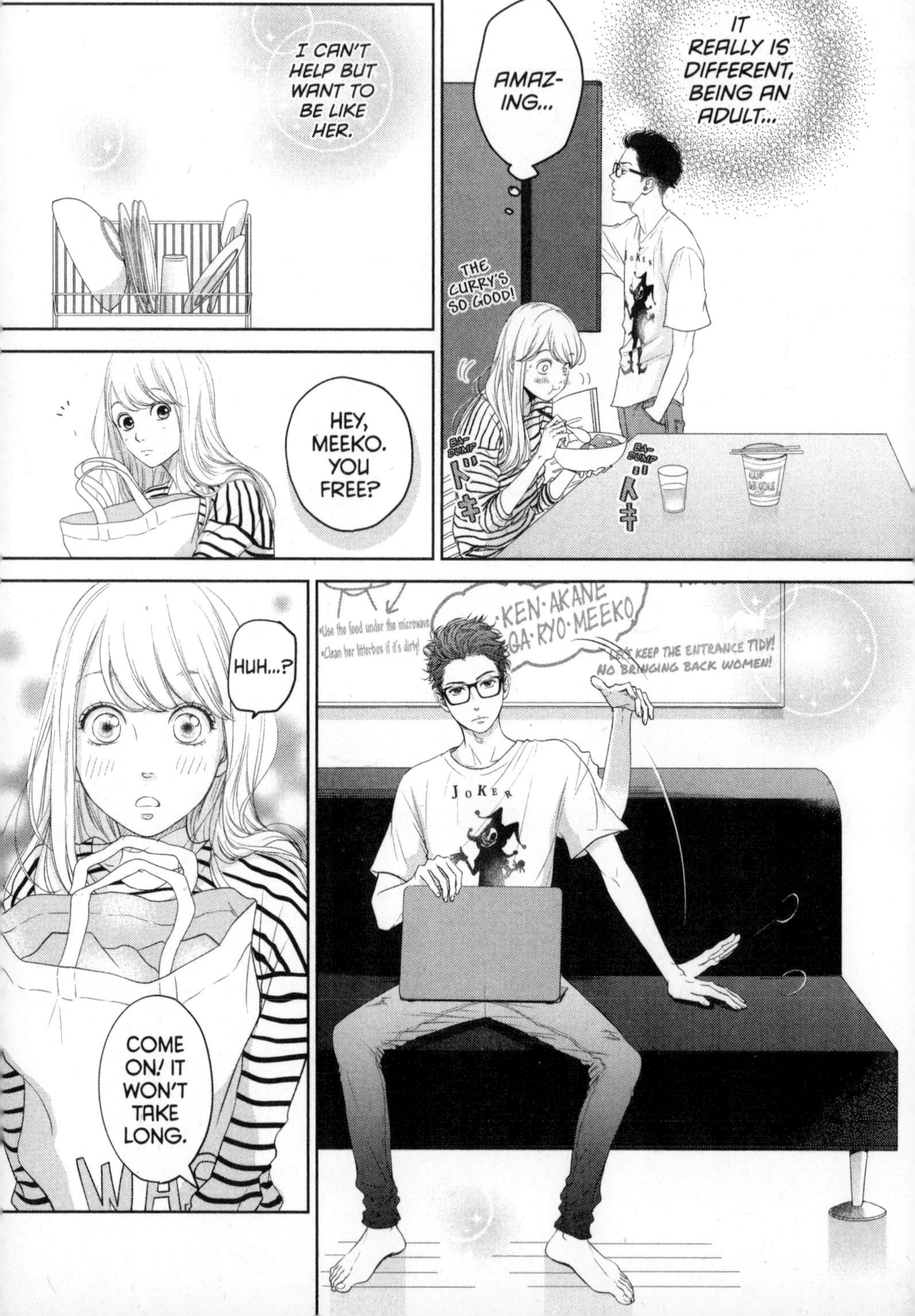

IT REALLY IS DIFFERENT, BEING AN ADULT...
AMAZ-ING...
THE CURRY'S SO GOOD!
BA-DUMP
ドキ
BA-DUMP
ドキ
JOKER
I CAN'T HELP BUT WANT TO BE LIKE HER.
HEY, MEEKO. YOU FREE?
KEN·AKANE
GA·RYO·MEEKO
•Use the food under the microwave
•Clean her litterbox if it's dirty!
LET'S KEEP THE ENTRANCE TIDY!
NO BRINGING BACK WOMEN!
JOKER
HUH...?
COME ON! IT WON'T TAKE LONG.

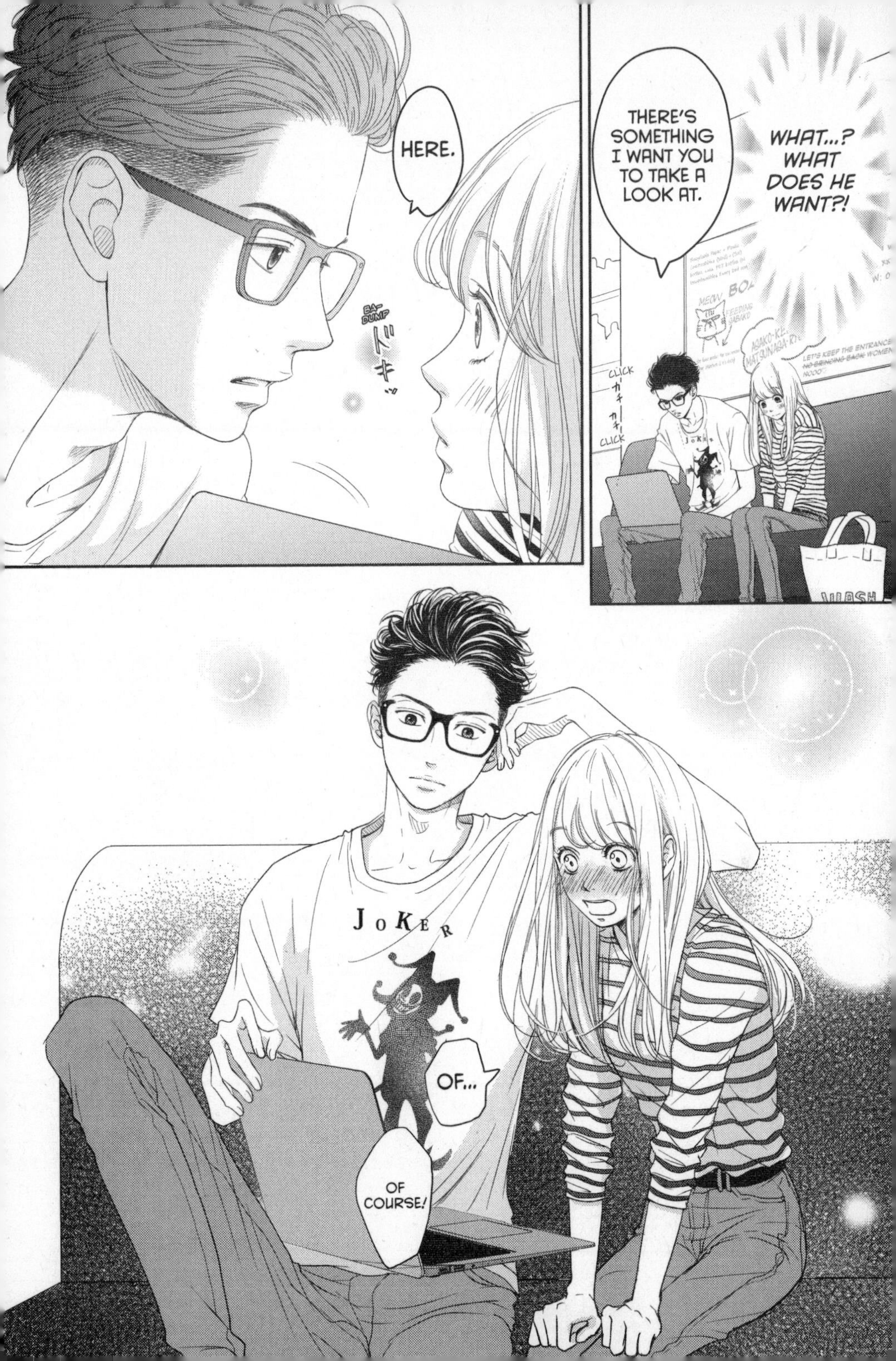
THERE'S SOMETHING I WANT YOU TO TAKE A LOOK AT.
WHAT...? WHAT DOES HE WANT?!
CLICK
CLICK
HERE.
BA-DUMP
OF...
OF COURSE!

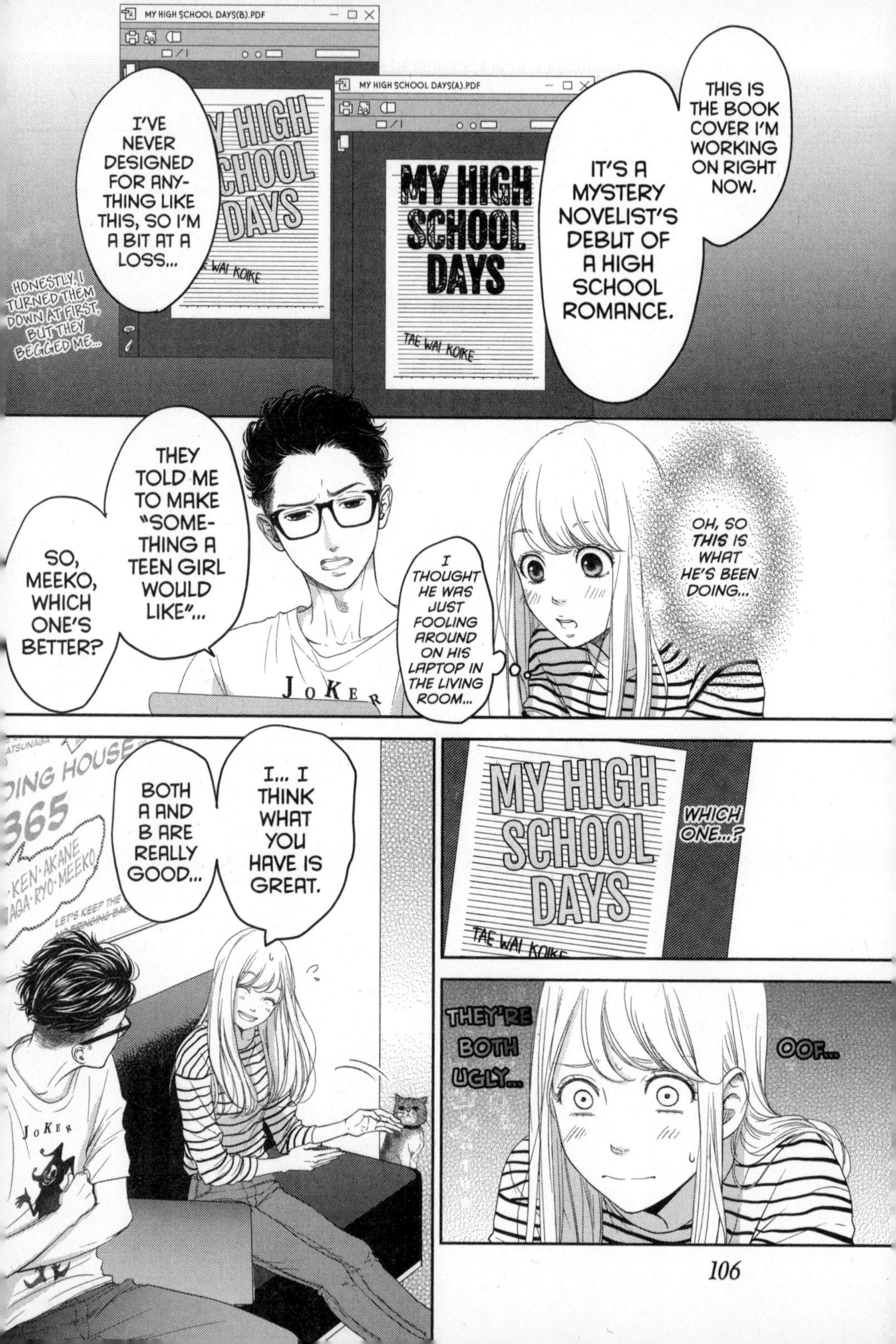
MY HIGH SCHOOL DAYS(A).PDF
MY HIGH SCHOOL DAYS
TAE WAI KOIKE
THIS IS THE BOOK COVER I'M WORKING ON RIGHT NOW.
IT'S A MYSTERY NOVELIST'S DEBUT OF A HIGH SCHOOL ROMANCE.
MY HIGH SCHOOL DAYS(B).PDF
I'VE NEVER DESIGNED FOR ANY-THING LIKE THIS, SO I'M A BIT AT A LOSS...
HONESTLY, I TURNED THEM DOWN AT FIRST, BUT THEY BEGGED ME...
OH, SO *THIS* IS WHAT HE'S BEEN DOING...
I THOUGHT HE WAS JUST FOOLING AROUND ON HIS LAPTOP IN THE LIVING ROOM...
THEY TOLD ME TO MAKE "SOME-THING A TEEN GIRL WOULD LIKE"...
SO, MEEKO, WHICH ONE'S BETTER?
JOKER
MY HIGH SCHOOL DAYS
WHICH ONE...?
OOF...
THEY'RE BOTH UGLY...
I... I THINK WHAT YOU HAVE IS GREAT.
BOTH A AND B ARE REALLY GOOD...
365
KEN·AKANE
RYO·MEEKO

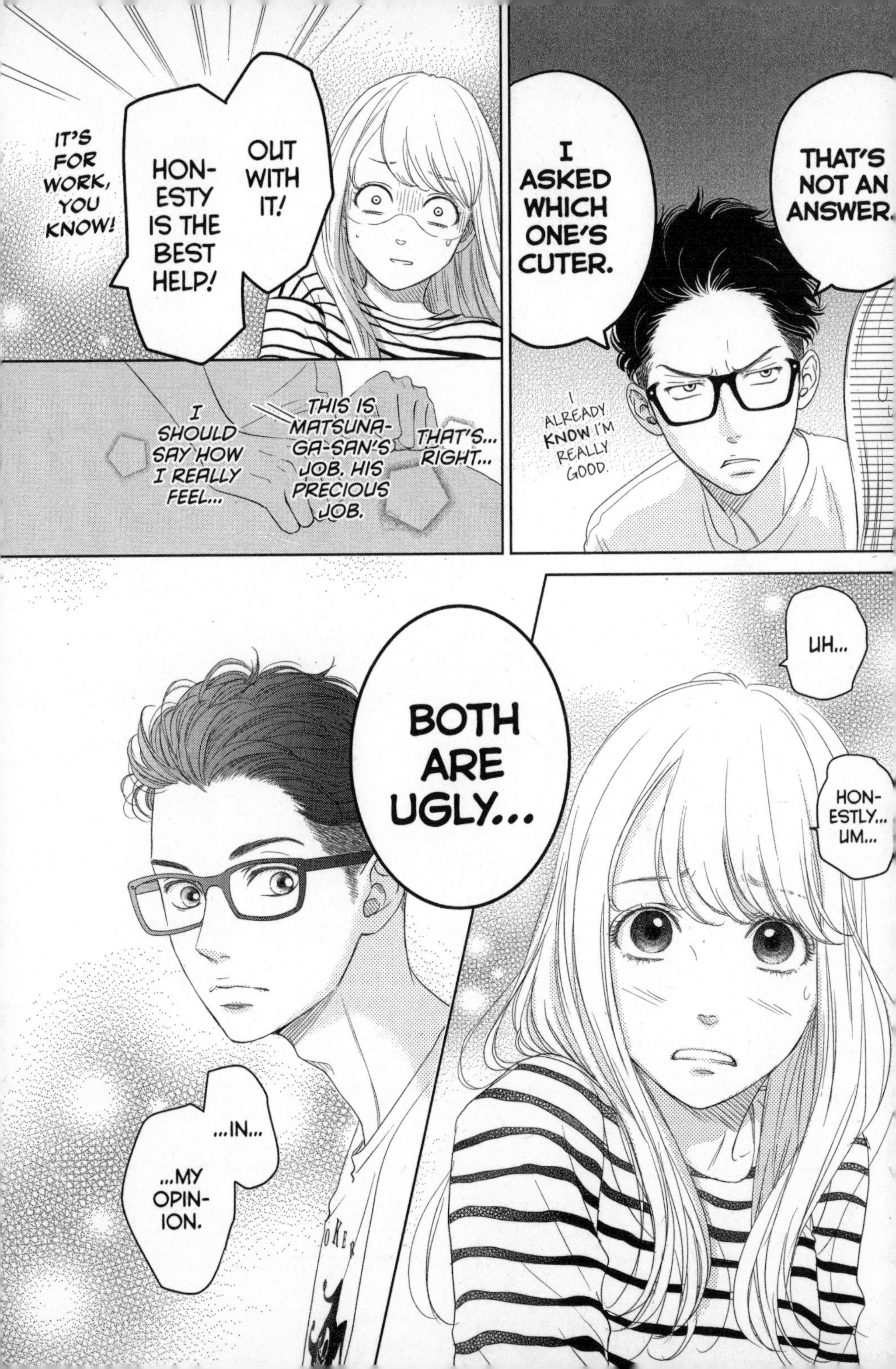
THAT'S NOT AN ANSWER.
I ASKED WHICH ONE'S CUTER.
I ALREADY KNOW I'M REALLY GOOD.
OUT WITH IT!
HONESTY IS THE BEST HELP!
IT'S FOR WORK, YOU KNOW!
THAT'S... RIGHT...
THIS IS MATSUNAGA-SAN'S JOB. HIS PRECIOUS JOB.
I SHOULD SAY HOW I REALLY FEEL...
UH...
HONESTLY... UM...
BOTH ARE UGLY...
...IN...
...MY OPINION.

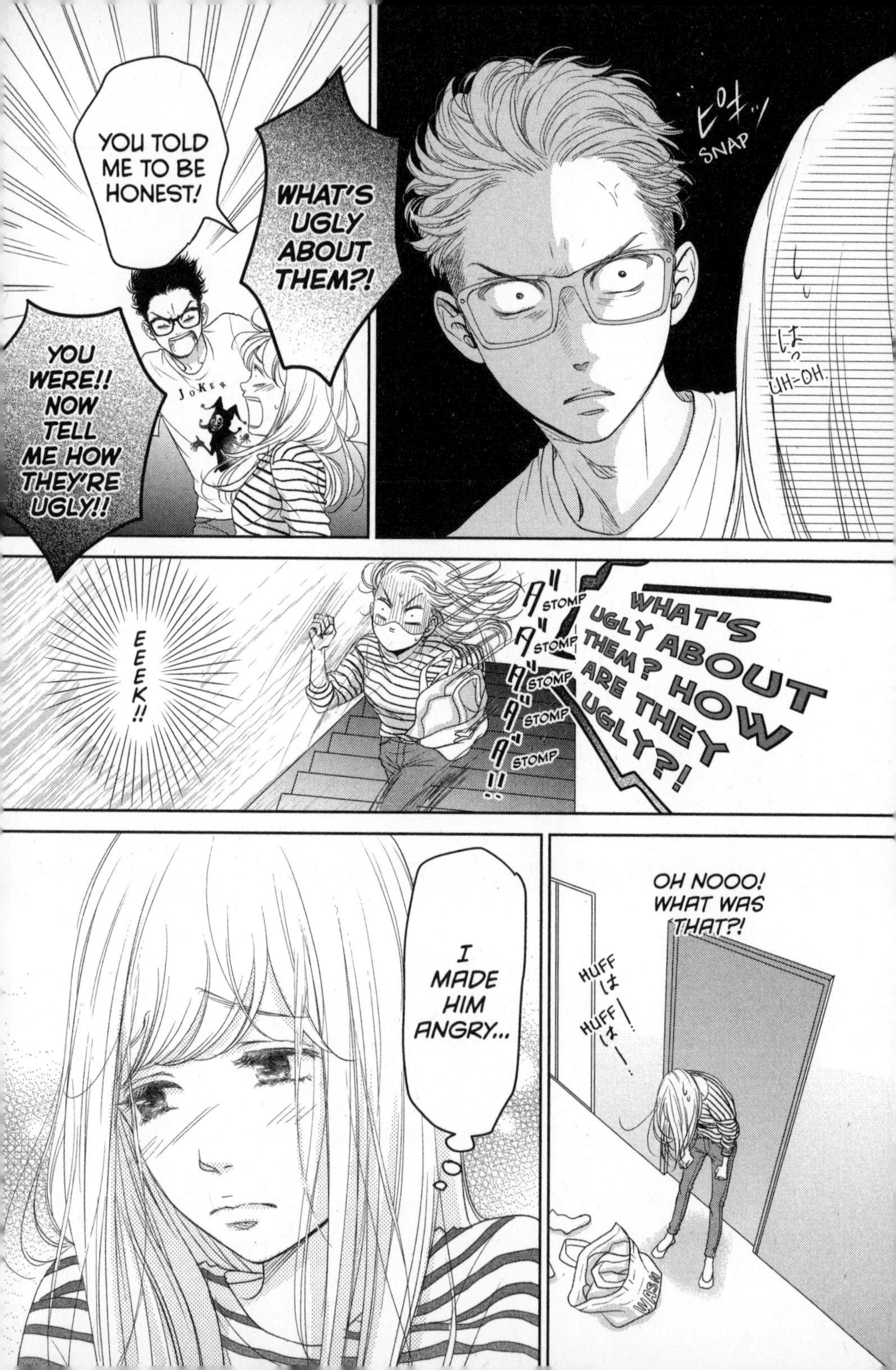

SNAP
UH-OH.
WHAT'S UGLY ABOUT THEM?!
YOU TOLD ME TO BE HONEST!
JOKER
YOU WERE!! NOW TELL ME HOW THEY'RE UGLY!!
WHAT'S UGLY ABOUT THEM? HOW ARE THEY UGLY?!
STOMP
STOMP
STOMP
STOMP
STOMP
EEEK!!
OH NOOO! WHAT WAS THAT?!
HUFF
HUFF
WASH
I MADE HIM ANGRY...

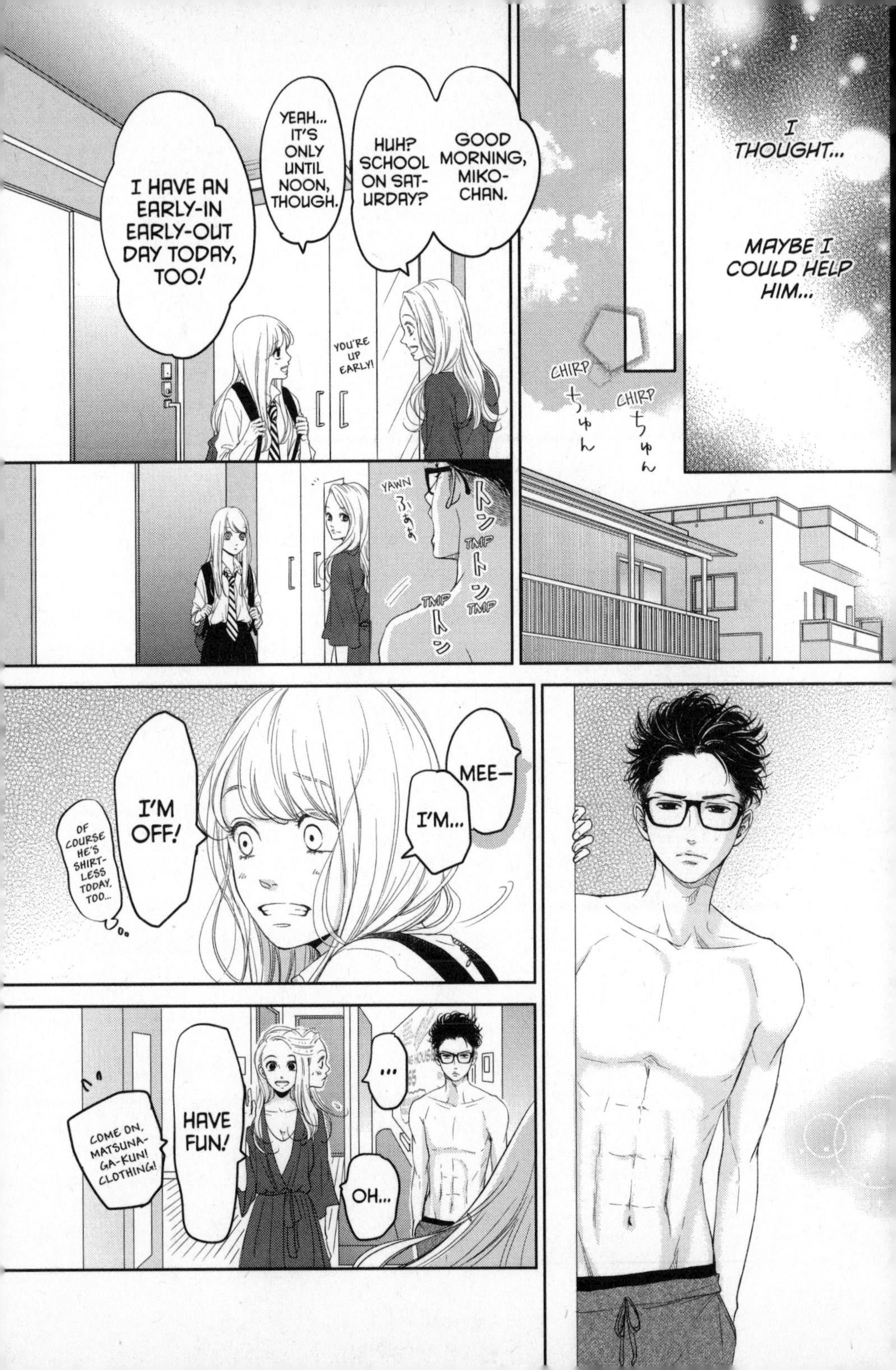
I THOUGHT...
MAYBE I COULD HELP HIM...
CHIRP ちゅん
CHIRP ちゅん
GOOD MORNING, MIKO-CHAN.
HUH? SCHOOL ON SAT-URDAY?
YEAH... IT'S ONLY UNTIL NOON, THOUGH.
YOU'RE UP EARLY!
I HAVE AN EARLY-IN EARLY-OUT DAY TODAY, TOO!
TMP トン
TMP トン
TMP トン
YAWN ふあぁ
MEE—
I'M...
I'M OFF!
OF COURSE HE'S SHIRT-LESS TODAY, TOO...
...
OH...
HAVE FUN!
COME ON, MATSUNA-GA-KUN! CLOTHING!

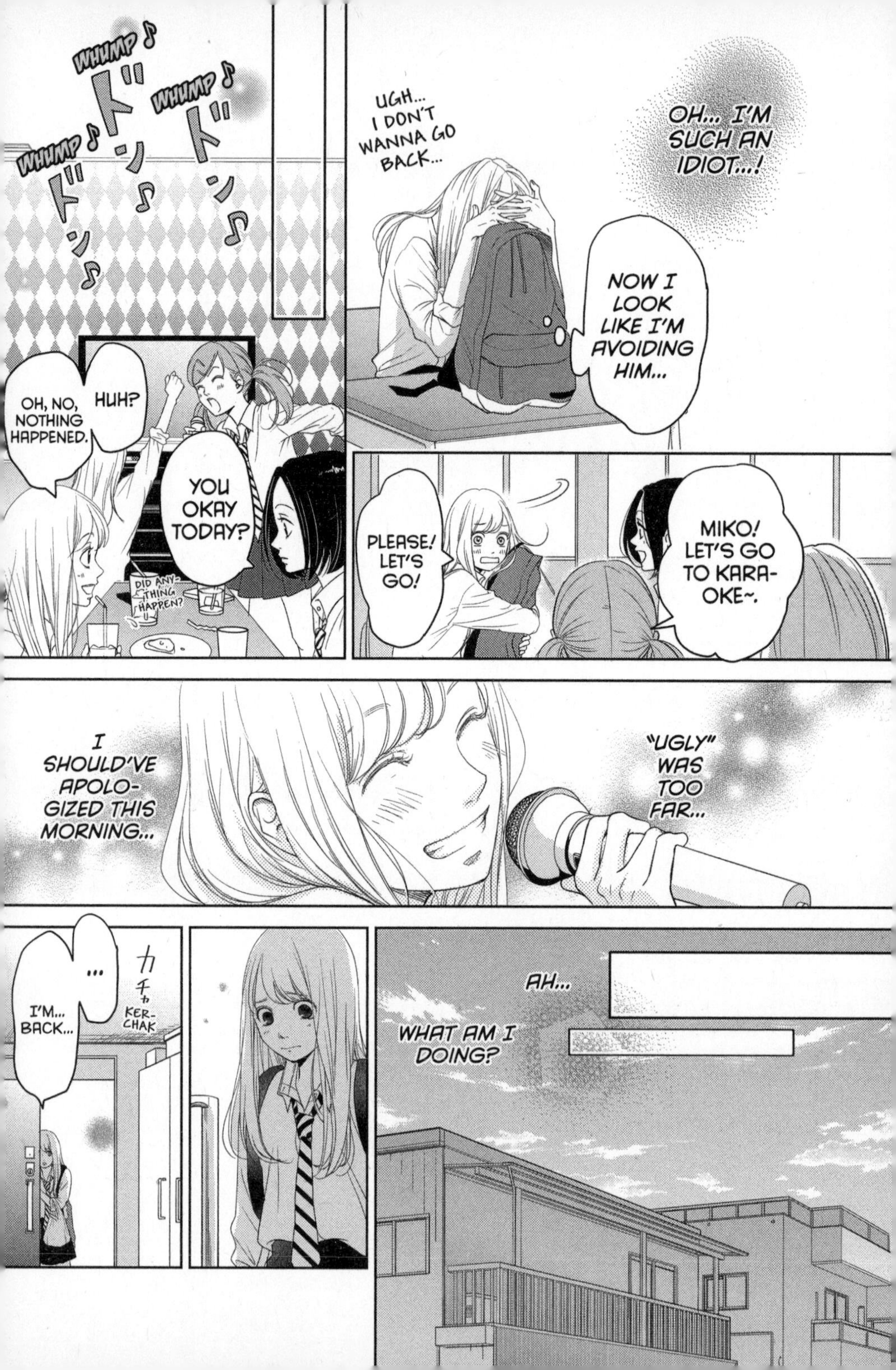
OH... I'M SUCH AN IDIOT...!
UGH... I DON'T WANNA GO BACK...
NOW I LOOK LIKE I'M AVOIDING HIM...
MIKO! LET'S GO TO KARA-OKE~.
PLEASE! LET'S GO!
WHUMP♪ WHUMP♪ WHUMP♪
ドドン♪ ドドン♪ ドドン♪
YOU OKAY TODAY?
DID ANY-THING HAPPEN?
HUH?
OH, NO, NOTHING HAPPENED.
"UGLY" WAS TOO FAR...
I SHOULD'VE APOLO-GIZED THIS MORNING...
AH...
WHAT AM I DOING?
カチャ KER-CHAK
...
I'M... BACK...

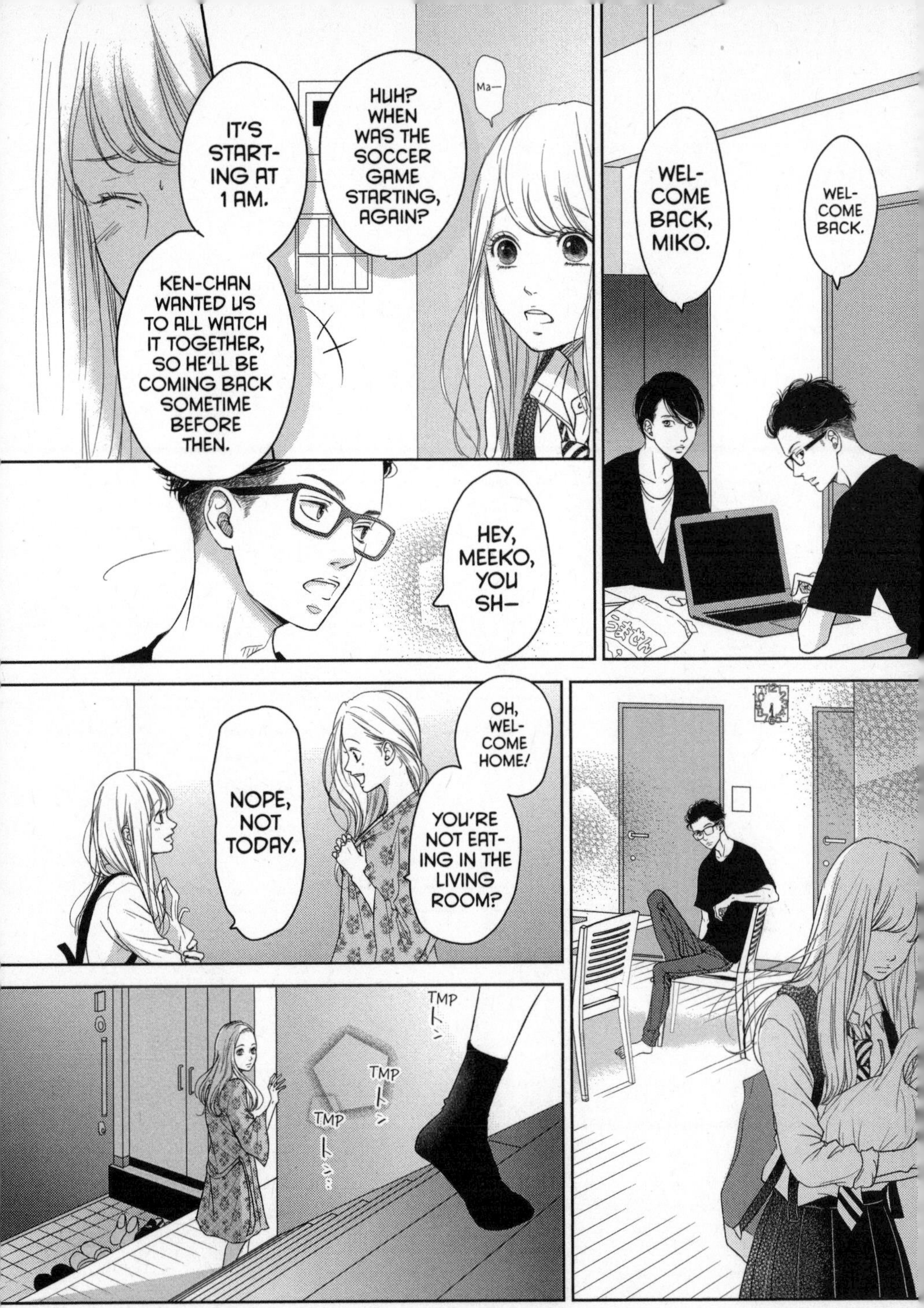
WEL-COME BACK.
WEL-COME BACK, MIKO.
Ma—
HUH? WHEN WAS THE SOCCER GAME STARTING, AGAIN?
IT'S START-ING AT 1 AM.
KEN-CHAN WANTED US TO ALL WATCH IT TOGETHER, SO HE'LL BE COMING BACK SOMETIME BEFORE THEN.
HEY, MEEKO, YOU SH—
OH, WEL-COME HOME!
YOU'RE NOT EAT-ING IN THE LIVING ROOM?
NOPE, NOT TODAY.
TMP
TMP
TMP

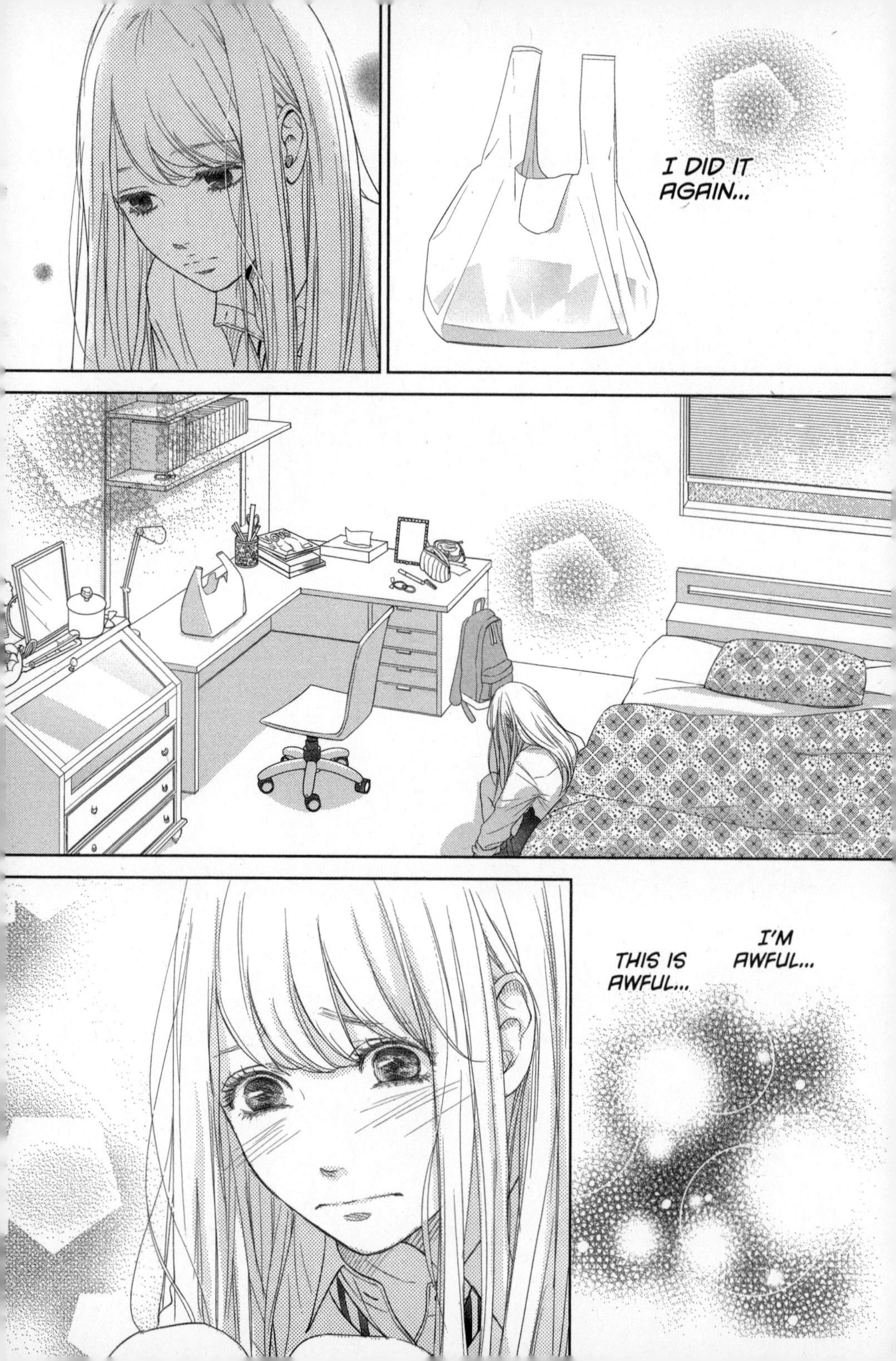
I DID IT AGAIN...
I'M AWFUL...
THIS IS AWFUL...

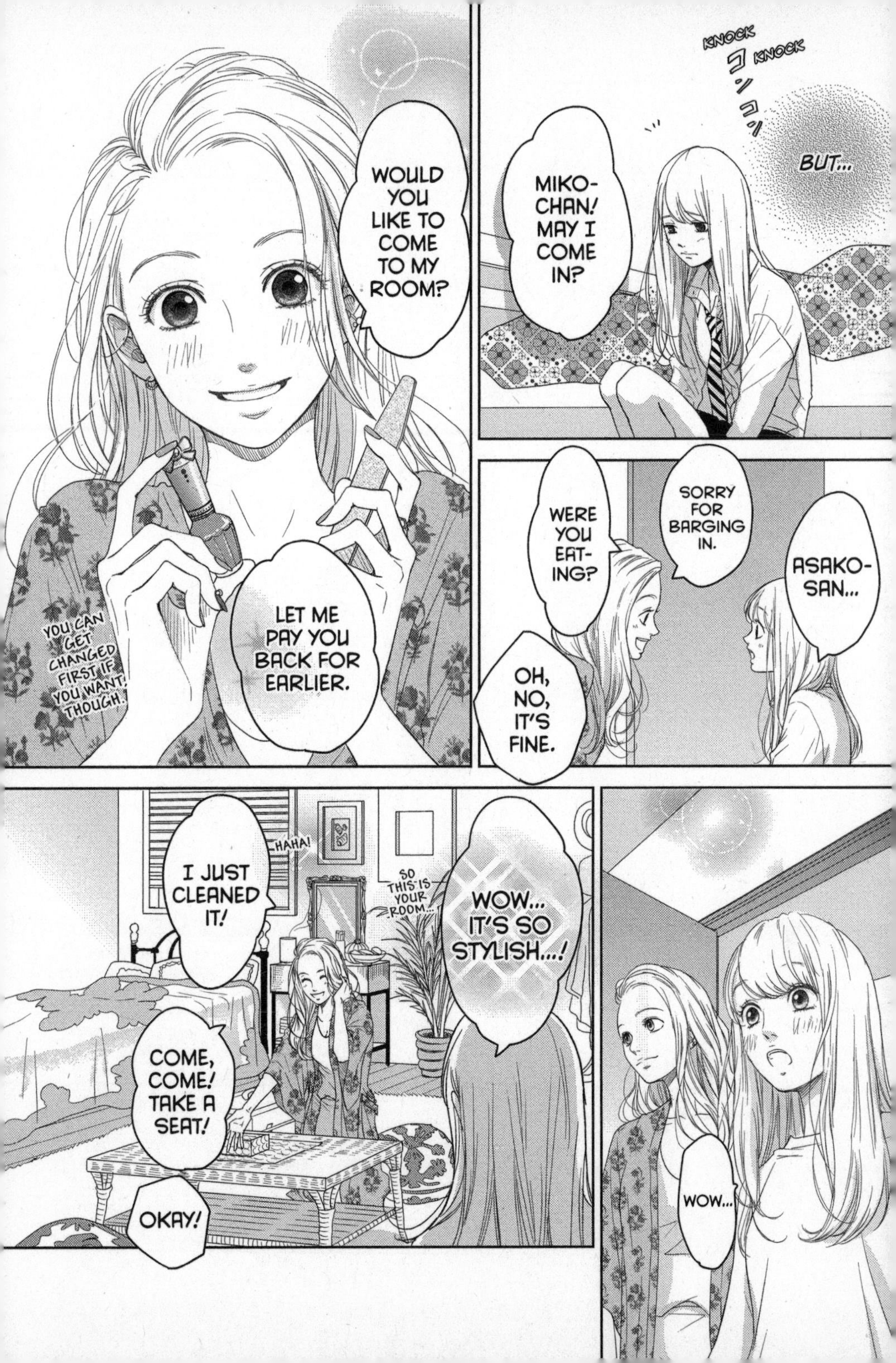
KNOCK KNOCK
コンコン
BUT...
MIKO-CHAN! MAY I COME IN?
ASAKO-SAN...
SORRY FOR BARGING IN.
WERE YOU EAT-ING?
OH, NO, IT'S FINE.
WOULD YOU LIKE TO COME TO MY ROOM?
LET ME PAY YOU BACK FOR EARLIER.
YOU CAN GET CHANGED FIRST IF YOU WANT, THOUGH.
WOW...
WOW... IT'S SO STYLISH...!
SO THIS IS YOUR ROOM...
HAHA!
I JUST CLEANED IT!
COME, COME! TAKE A SEAT!
OKAY!

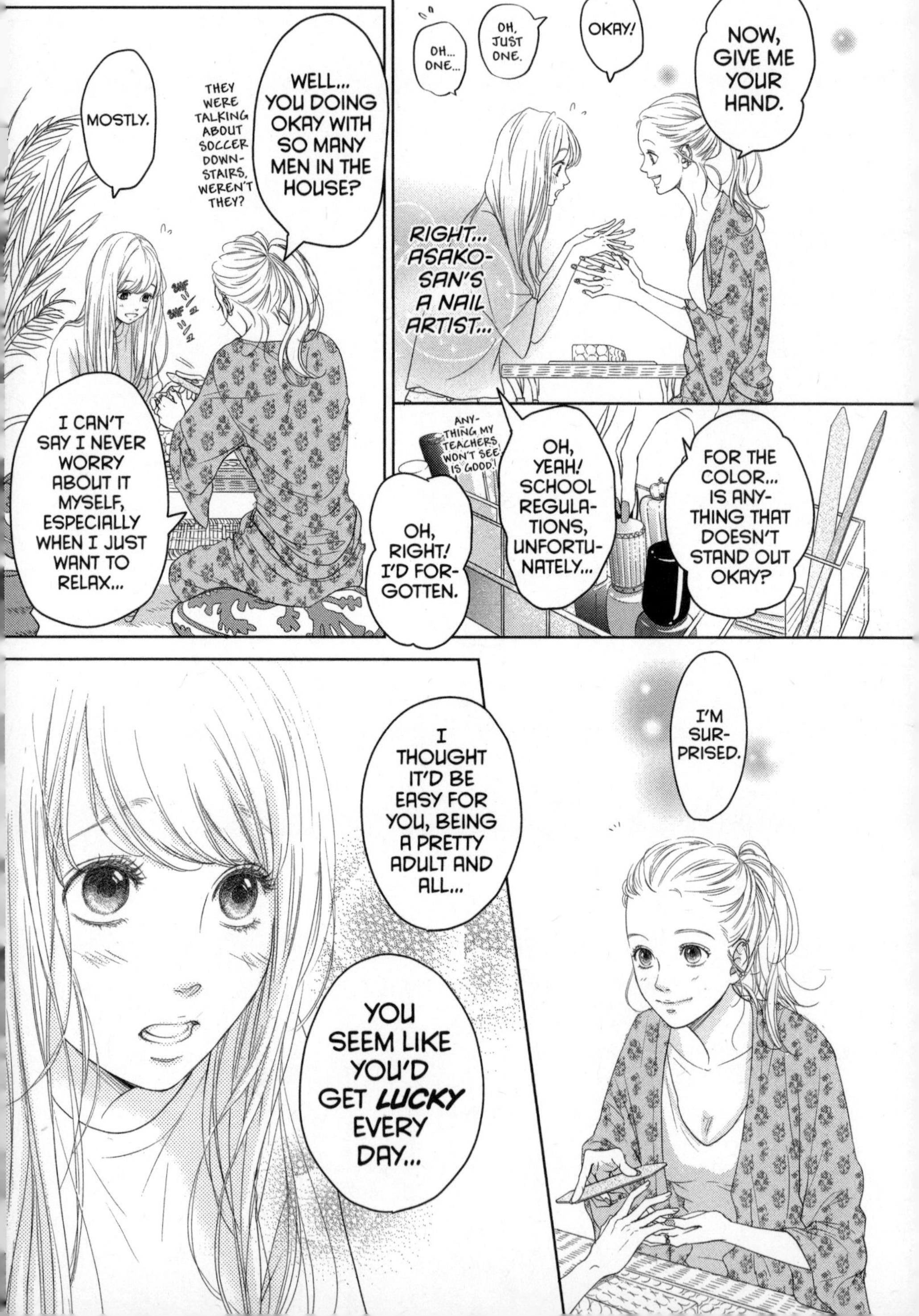
NOW, GIVE ME YOUR HAND.
OKAY!
OH, JUST ONE.
OH... ONE...
RIGHT... ASAKO-SAN'S A NAIL ARTIST...
FOR THE COLOR... IS ANYTHING THAT DOESN'T STAND OUT OKAY?
OH, YEAH! SCHOOL REGULATIONS, UNFORTUNATELY...
ANYTHING MY TEACHERS WON'T SEE IS GOOD!
OH, RIGHT! I'D FORGOTTEN.
WELL... YOU DOING OKAY WITH SO MANY MEN IN THE HOUSE?
THEY WERE TALKING ABOUT SOCCER DOWNSTAIRS, WEREN'T THEY?
MOSTLY.
I CAN'T SAY I NEVER WORRY ABOUT IT MYSELF, ESPECIALLY WHEN I JUST WANT TO RELAX...
I'M SURPRISED.
I THOUGHT IT'D BE EASY FOR YOU, BEING A PRETTY ADULT AND ALL...
YOU SEEM LIKE YOU'D GET *LUCKY* EVERY DAY...

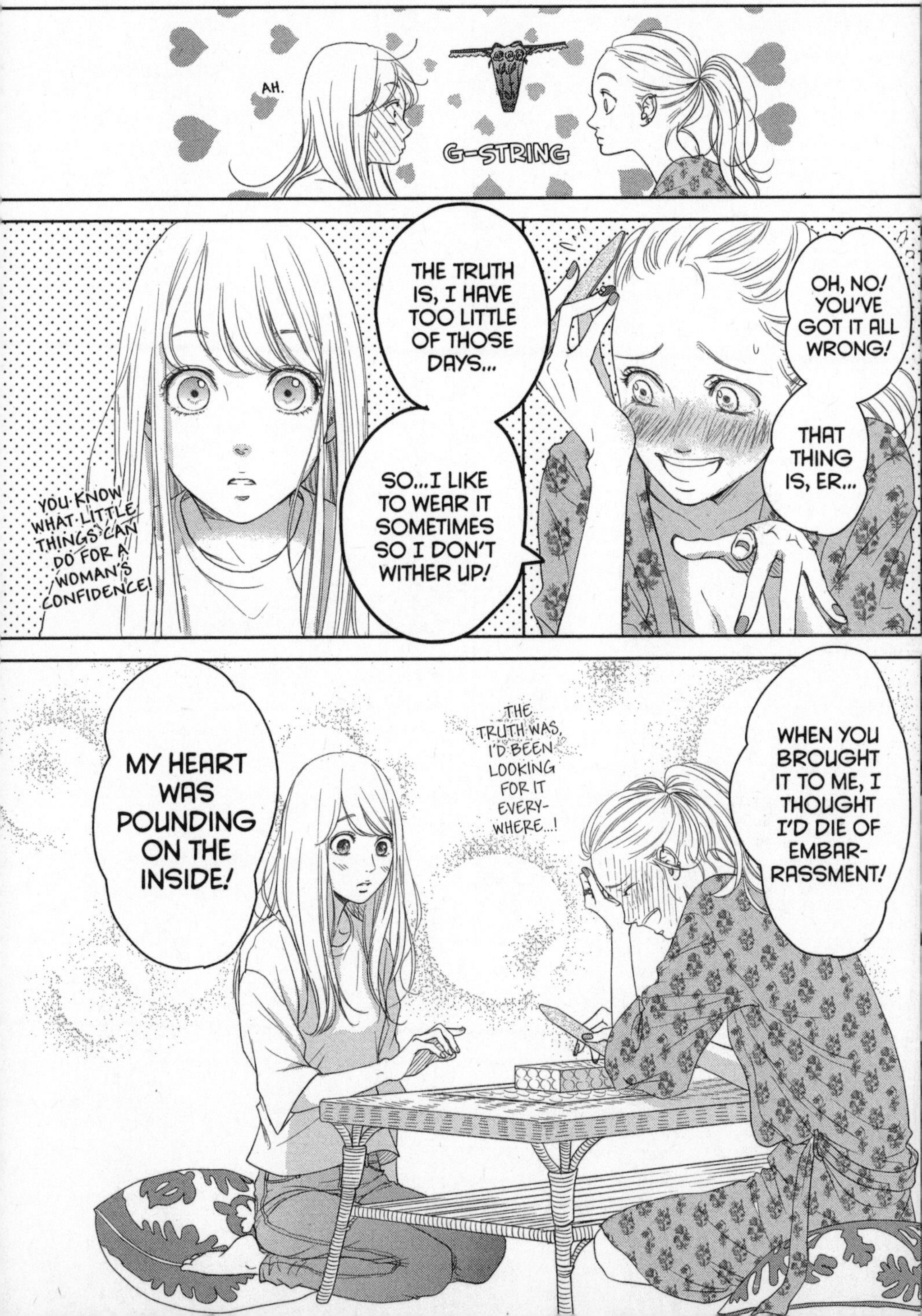

AH.
G-STRING
OH, NO! YOU'VE GOT IT ALL WRONG!
THAT THING IS, ER...
THE TRUTH IS, I HAVE TOO LITTLE OF THOSE DAYS...
SO...I LIKE TO WEAR IT SOMETIMES SO I DON'T WITHER UP!
YOU KNOW WHAT LITTLE THINGS CAN DO FOR A WOMAN'S CONFIDENCE!
WHEN YOU BROUGHT IT TO ME, I THOUGHT I'D DIE OF EMBAR-RASSMENT!
THE TRUTH WAS, I'D BEEN LOOKING FOR IT EVERY-WHERE...!
MY HEART WAS POUNDING ON THE INSIDE!

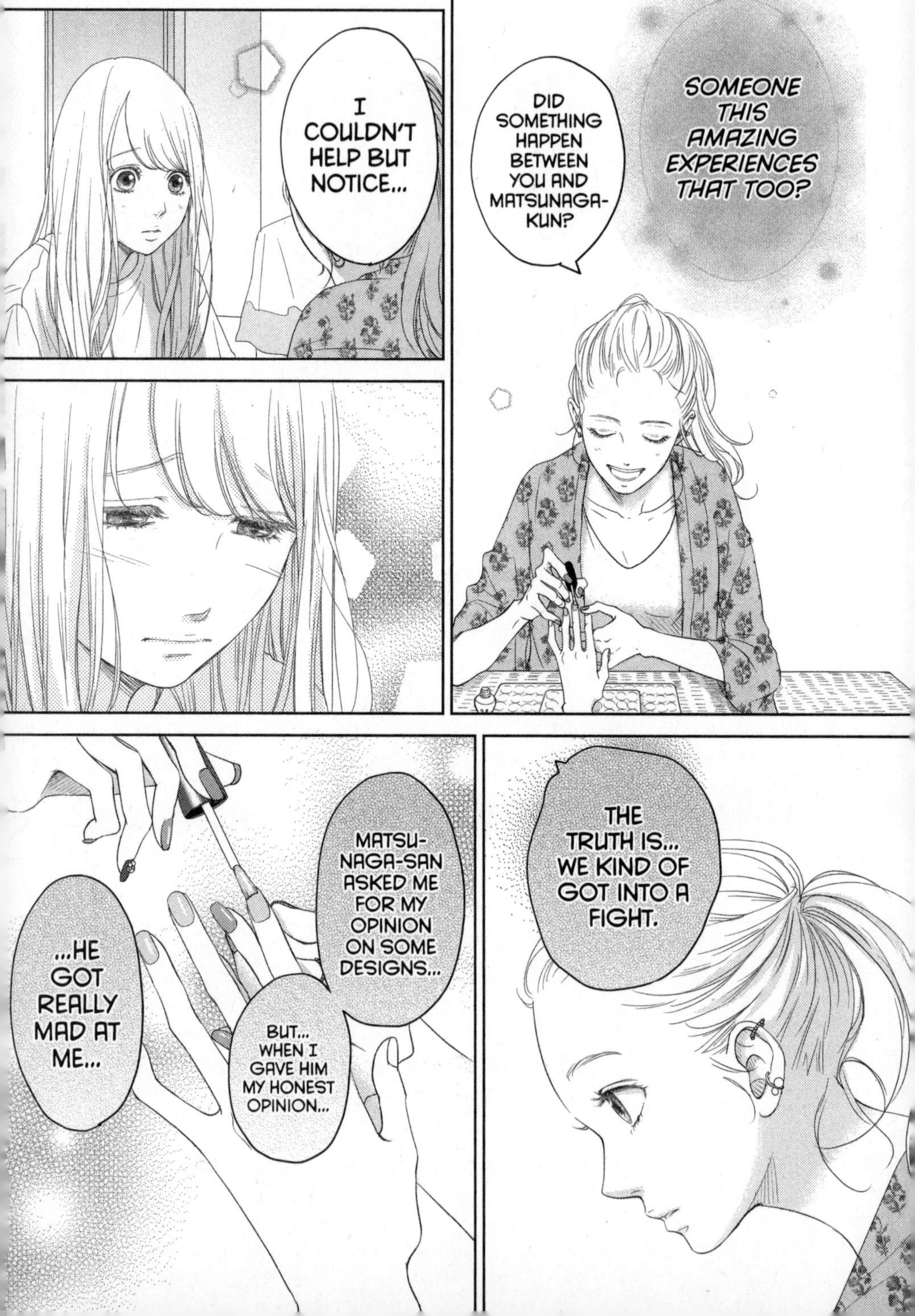
SOMEONE THIS AMAZING EXPERIENCES THAT TOO?
DID SOMETHING HAPPEN BETWEEN YOU AND MATSUNAGA-KUN?
I COULDN'T HELP BUT NOTICE...
THE TRUTH IS... WE KIND OF GOT INTO A FIGHT.
MATSU-NAGA-SAN ASKED ME FOR MY OPINION ON SOME DESIGNS...
BUT... WHEN I GAVE HIM MY HONEST OPINION...
...HE GOT REALLY MAD AT ME...

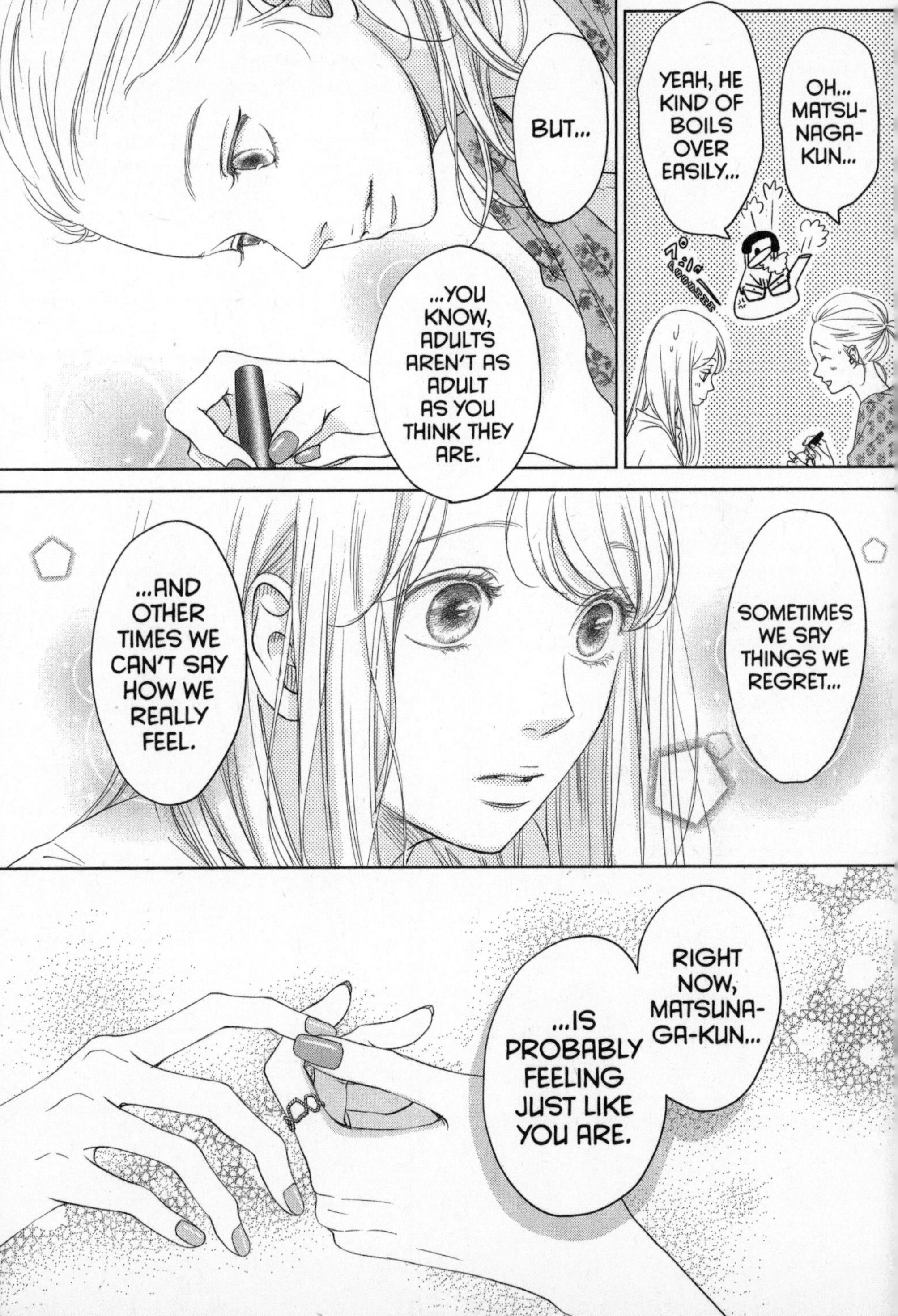
OH... MATSU-NAGA-KUN...
YEAH, HE KIND OF BOILS OVER EASILY...
BUT...
...YOU KNOW, ADULTS AREN'T AS ADULT AS YOU THINK THEY ARE.
SOMETIMES WE SAY THINGS WE REGRET...
...AND OTHER TIMES WE CAN'T SAY HOW WE REALLY FEEL.
RIGHT NOW, MATSUNA-GA-KUN...
...IS PROBABLY FEELING JUST LIKE YOU ARE.

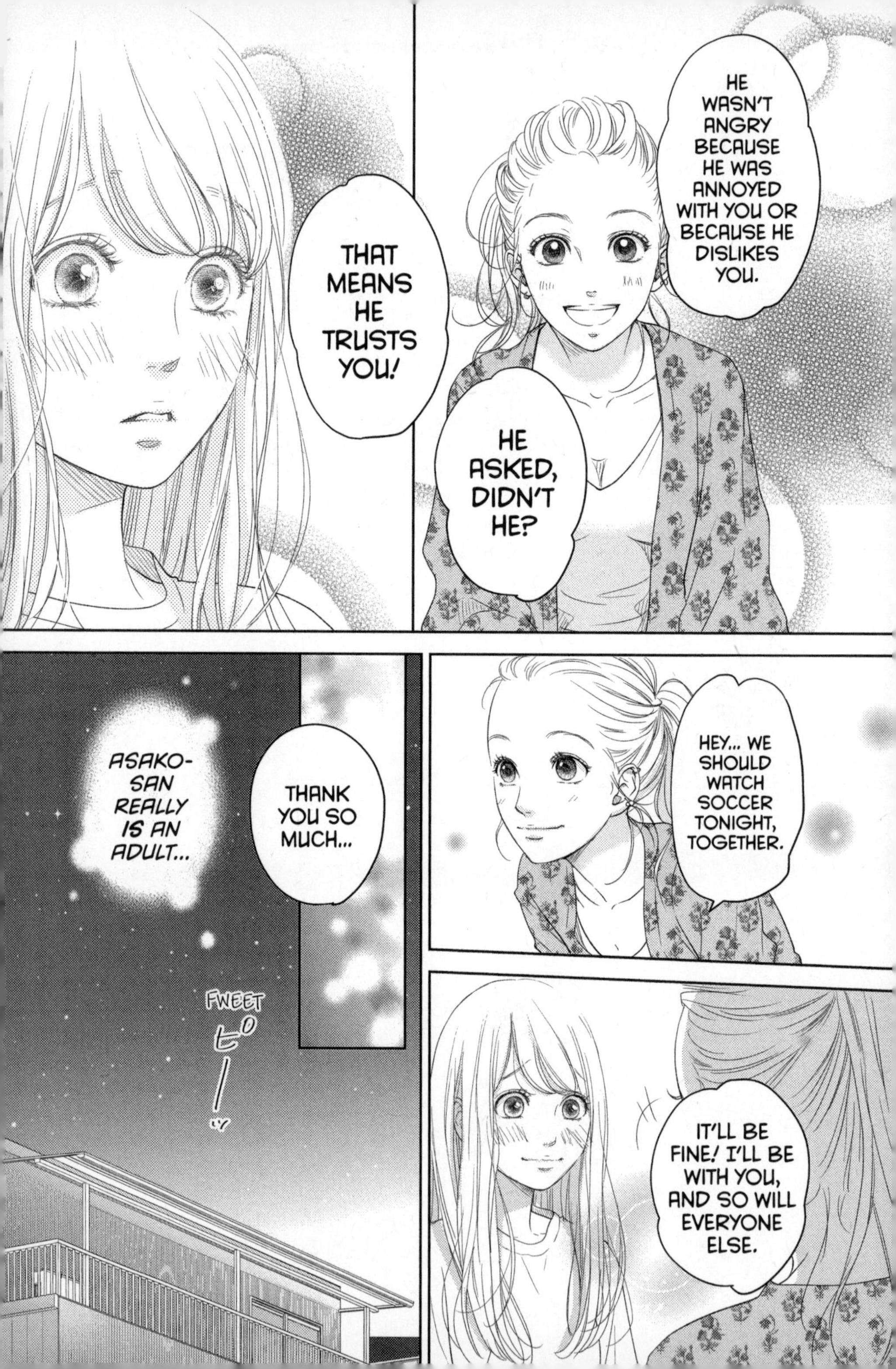
HE WASN'T ANGRY BECAUSE HE WAS ANNOYED WITH YOU OR BECAUSE HE DISLIKES YOU.
HE ASKED, DIDN'T HE?
THAT MEANS HE TRUSTS YOU!
HEY... WE SHOULD WATCH SOCCER TONIGHT, TOGETHER.
IT'LL BE FINE! I'LL BE WITH YOU, AND SO WILL EVERYONE ELSE.
THANK YOU SO MUCH...
ASAKO-SAN REALLY *IS* AN ADULT...
FWEET
ピー

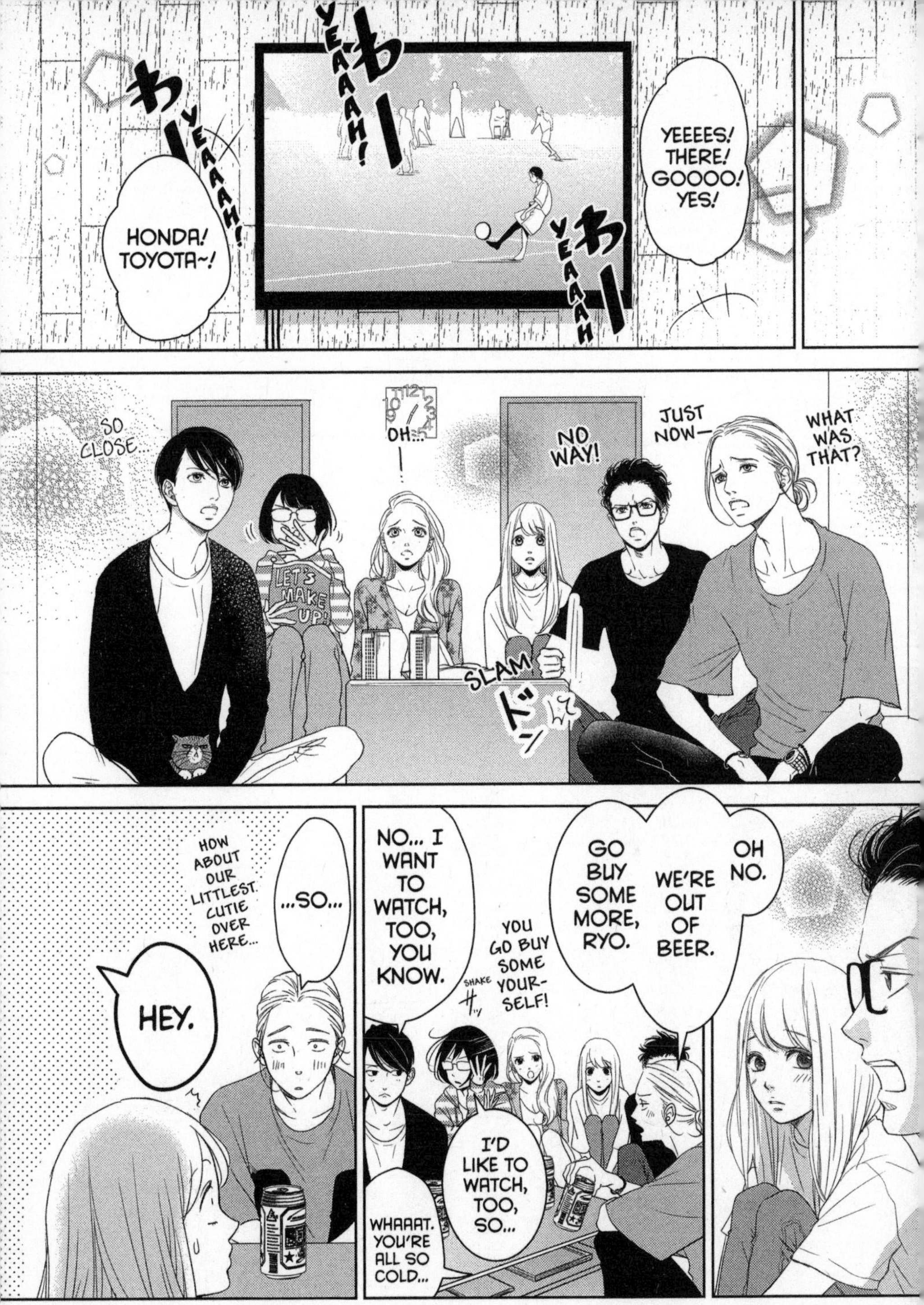
YEEEES! THERE! GOOOO! YES!
わー YEAAAAH
わー YEAAAAH!
わー YEAAAAH!
HONDA! TOYOTA~!
WHAT WAS THAT?
JUST NOW—
NO WAY!
SLAM ドン
OH...!
LET'S MAKE UP!
SO CLOSE...
OH NO.
WE'RE OUT OF BEER.
GO BUY SOME MORE, RYO.
YOU GO BUY SOME YOURSELF!
SHAKE
NO... I WANT TO WATCH, TOO, YOU KNOW.
I'D LIKE TO WATCH, TOO, SO...
WHAAAT. YOU'RE ALL SO COLD...
...SO...
HOW ABOUT OUR LITTLEST CUTIE OVER HERE...
HEY.

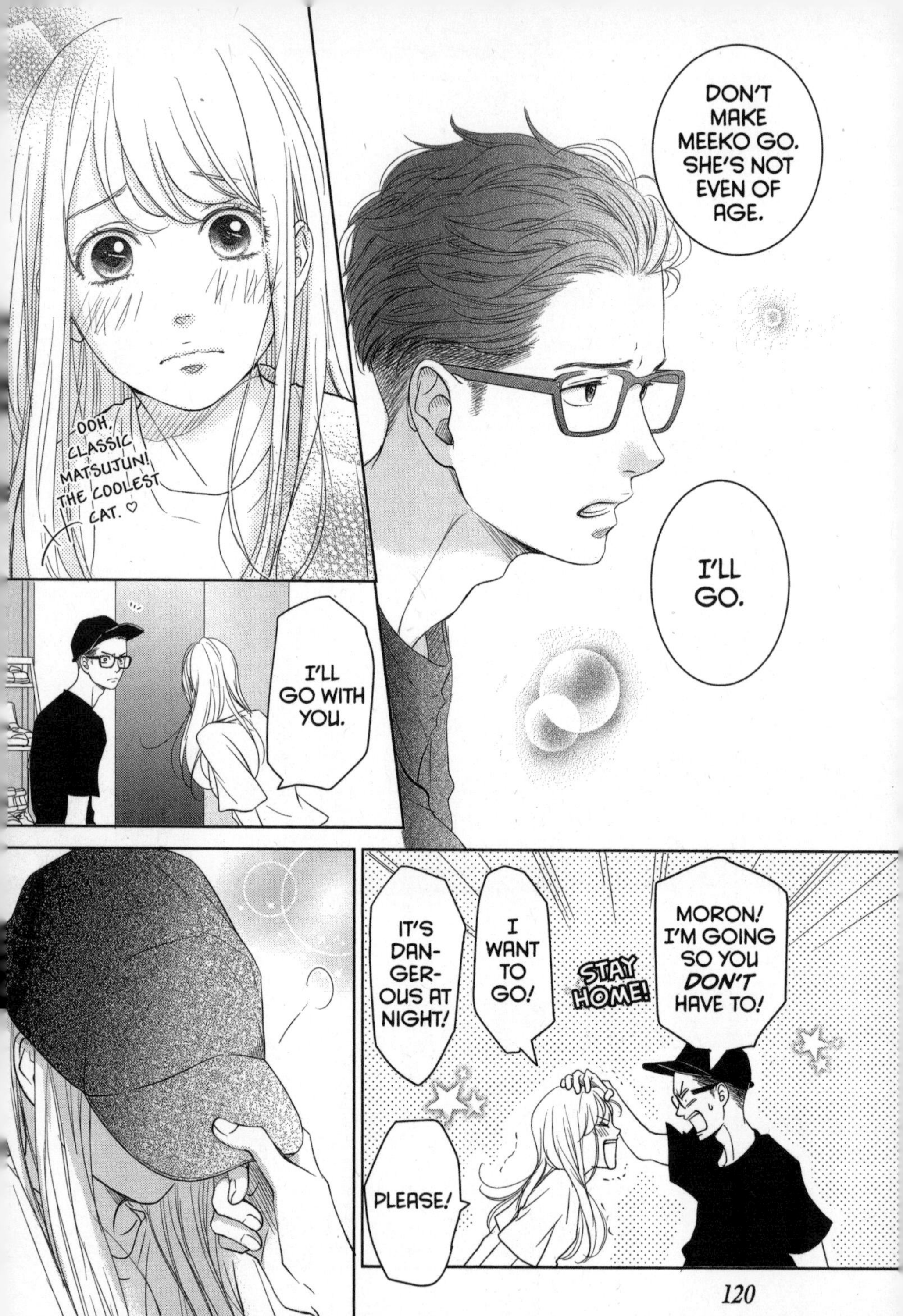
DON'T MAKE MEEKO GO. SHE'S NOT EVEN OF AGE.
I'LL GO.
OOH, CLASSIC MATSUJUN! THE COOLEST CAT. ♡
I'LL GO WITH YOU.
MORON! I'M GOING SO YOU *DON'T* HAVE TO!
STAY HOME!
I WANT TO GO!
IT'S DAN-GER-OUS AT NIGHT!
PLEASE!

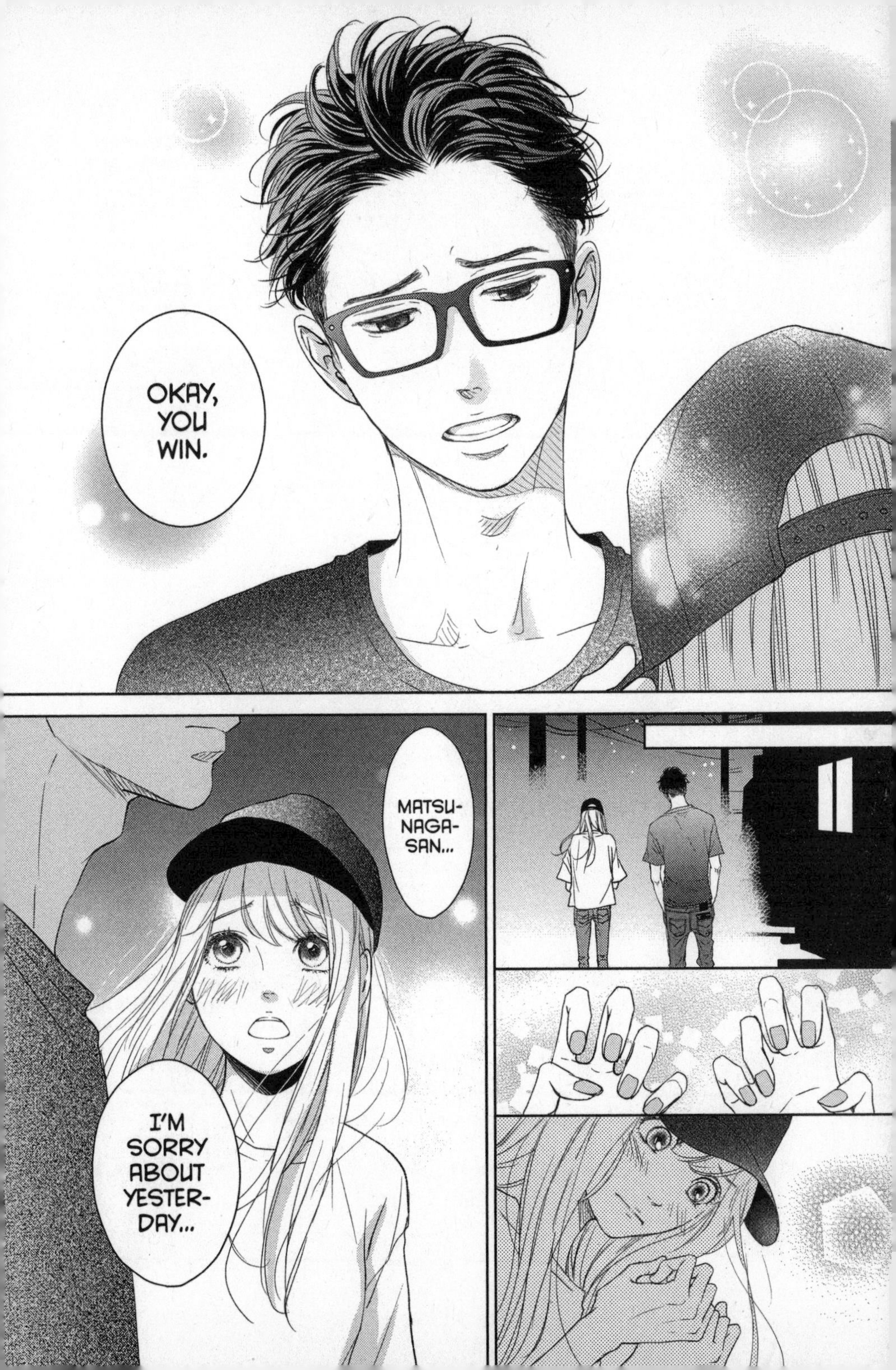
OKAY, YOU WIN.
MATSU-NAGA-SAN...
I'M SORRY ABOUT YESTER-DAY...

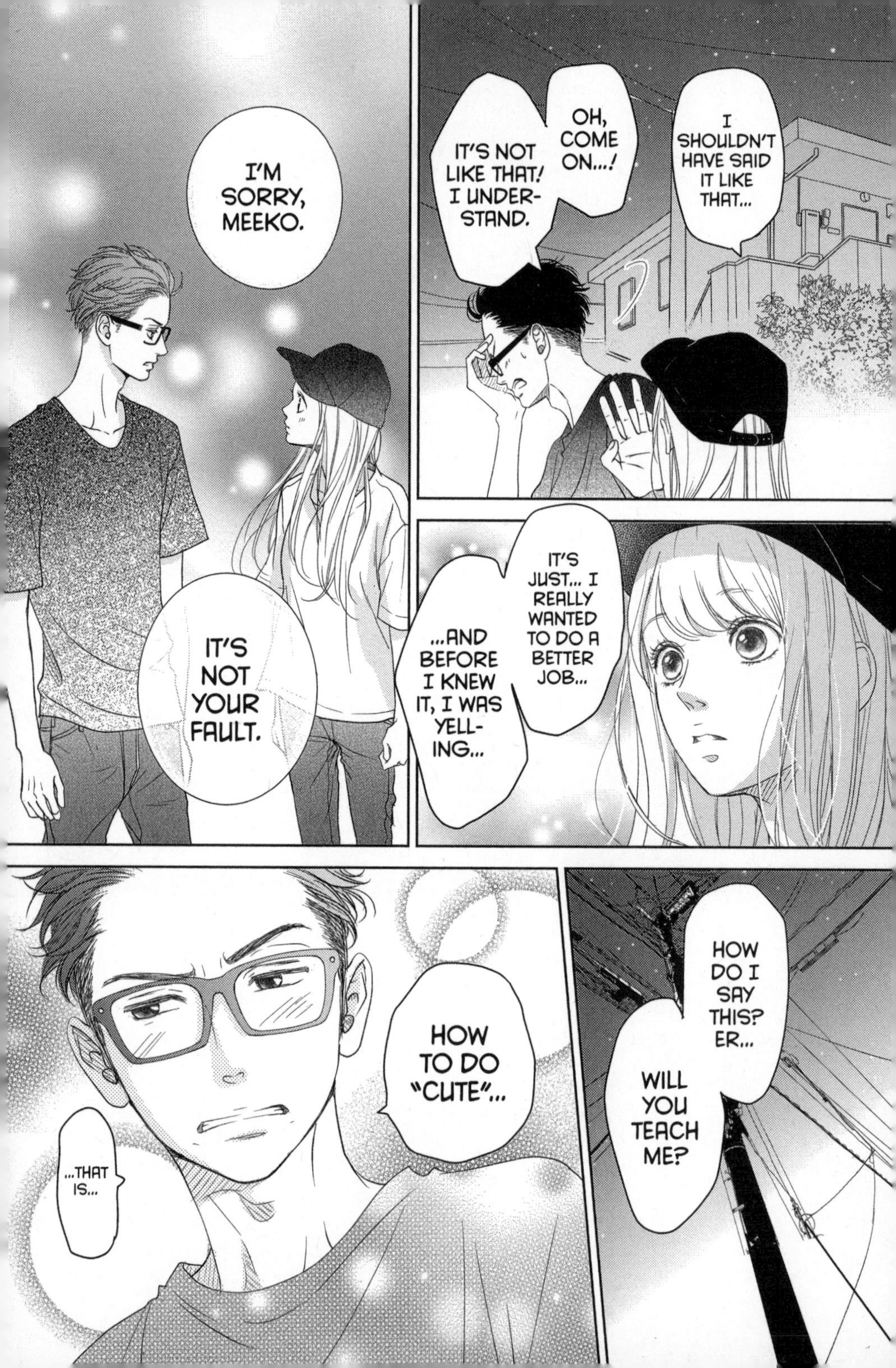
I SHOULDN'T HAVE SAID IT LIKE THAT...
OH, COME ON...!
IT'S NOT LIKE THAT! I UNDER-STAND.
IT'S JUST... I REALLY WANTED TO DO A BETTER JOB...
...AND BEFORE I KNEW IT, I WAS YELL-ING...
I'M SORRY, MEEKO.
IT'S NOT YOUR FAULT.
HOW DO I SAY THIS? ER...
WILL YOU TEACH ME?
HOW TO DO "CUTE"...
...THAT IS...

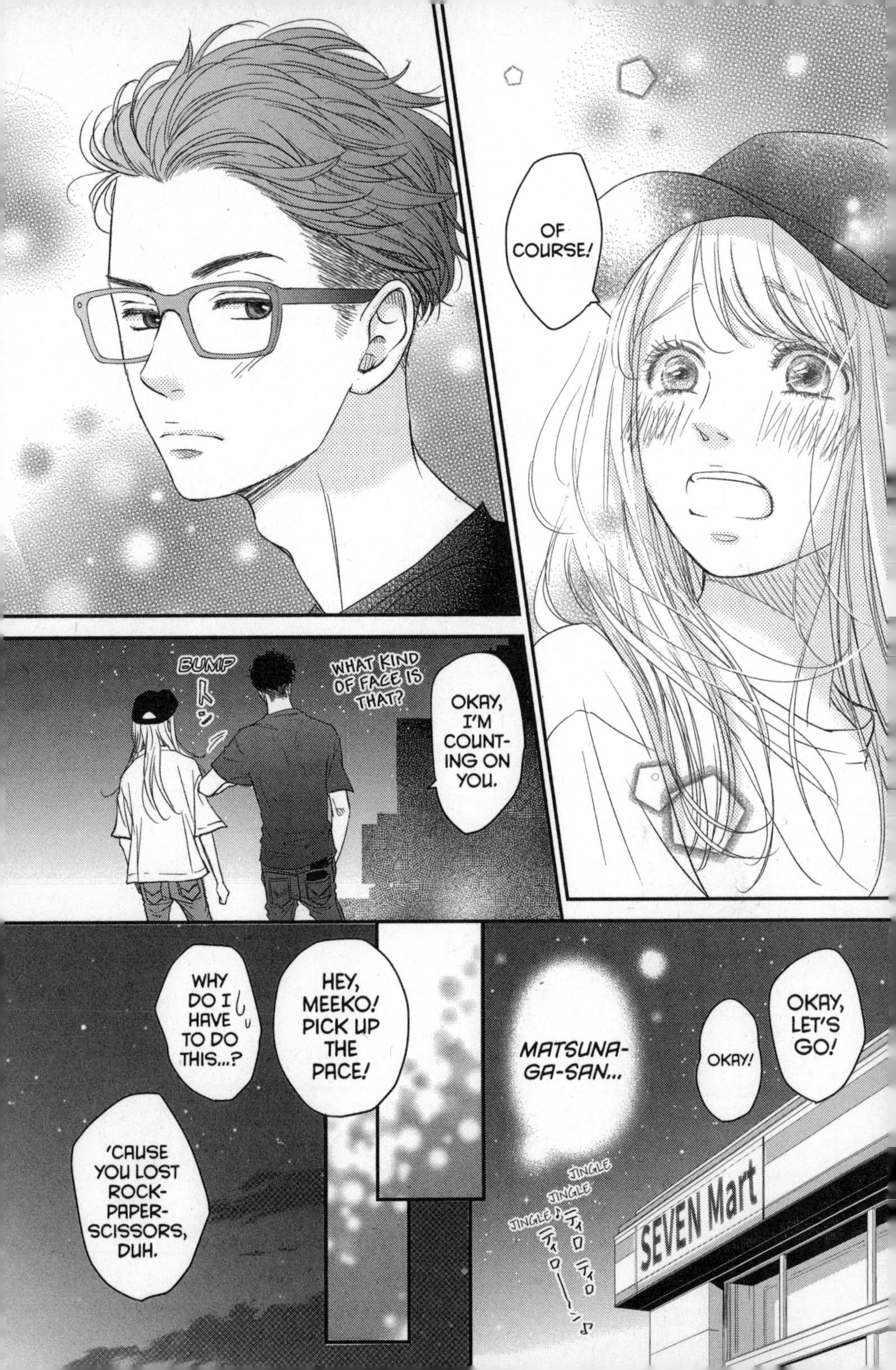
OF COURSE!
OKAY, I'M COUNTING ON YOU.
WHAT KIND OF FACE IS THAT?
BUMP
OKAY, LET'S GO!
OKAY!
MATSUNAGA-SAN...
JINGLE JINGLE JINGLE
SEVEN Mart
HEY, MEEKO! PICK UP THE PACE!
WHY DO I HAVE TO DO THIS...?
'CAUSE YOU LOST ROCK-PAPER-SCISSORS, DUH.

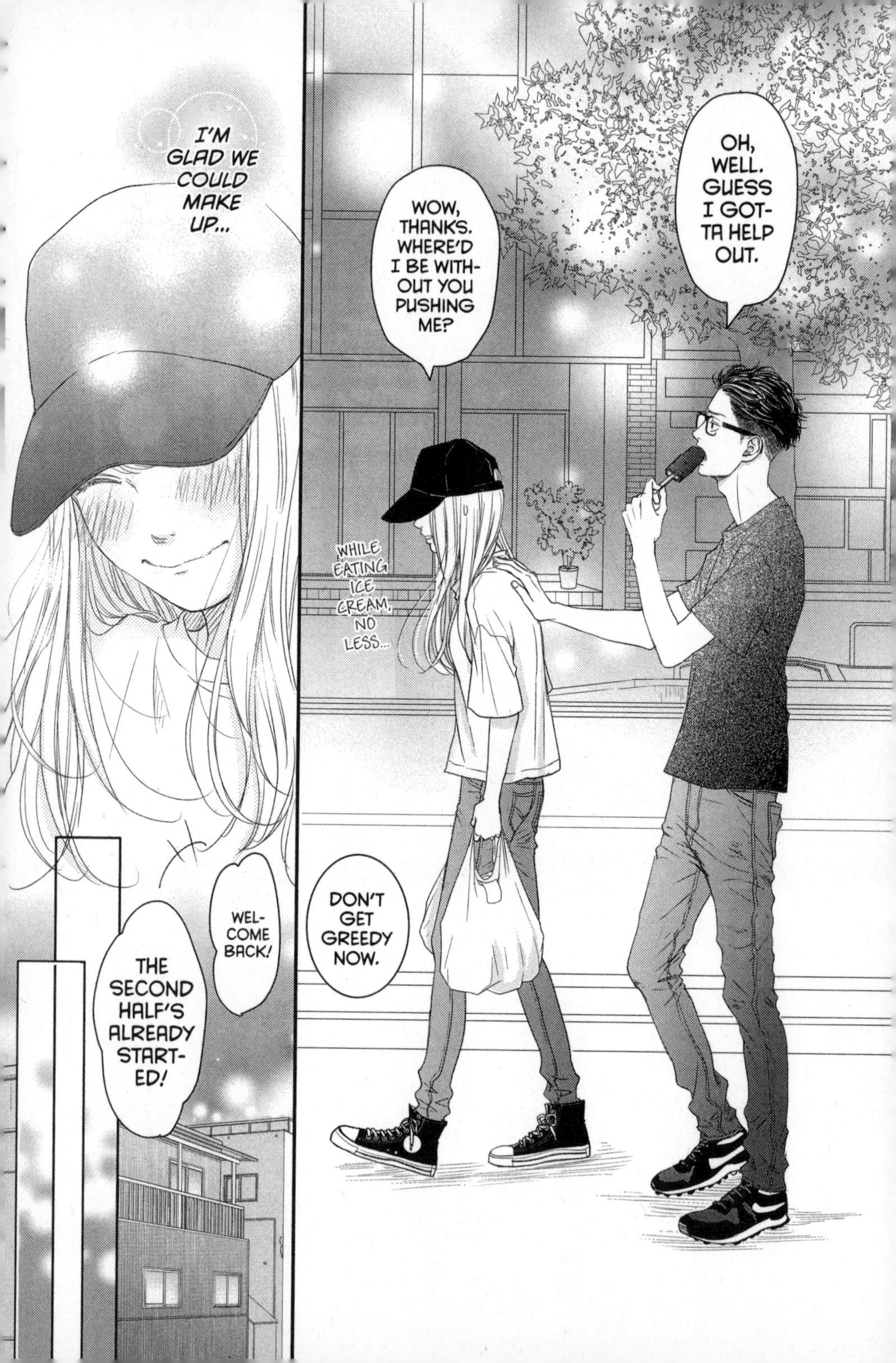
OH, WELL. GUESS I GOTTA HELP OUT.
WOW, THANKS. WHERE'D I BE WITHOUT YOU PUSHING ME?
WHILE EATING ICE CREAM, NO LESS...
DON'T GET GREEDY NOW.
I'M GLAD WE COULD MAKE UP...
WELCOME BACK!
THE SECOND HALF'S ALREADY STARTED!

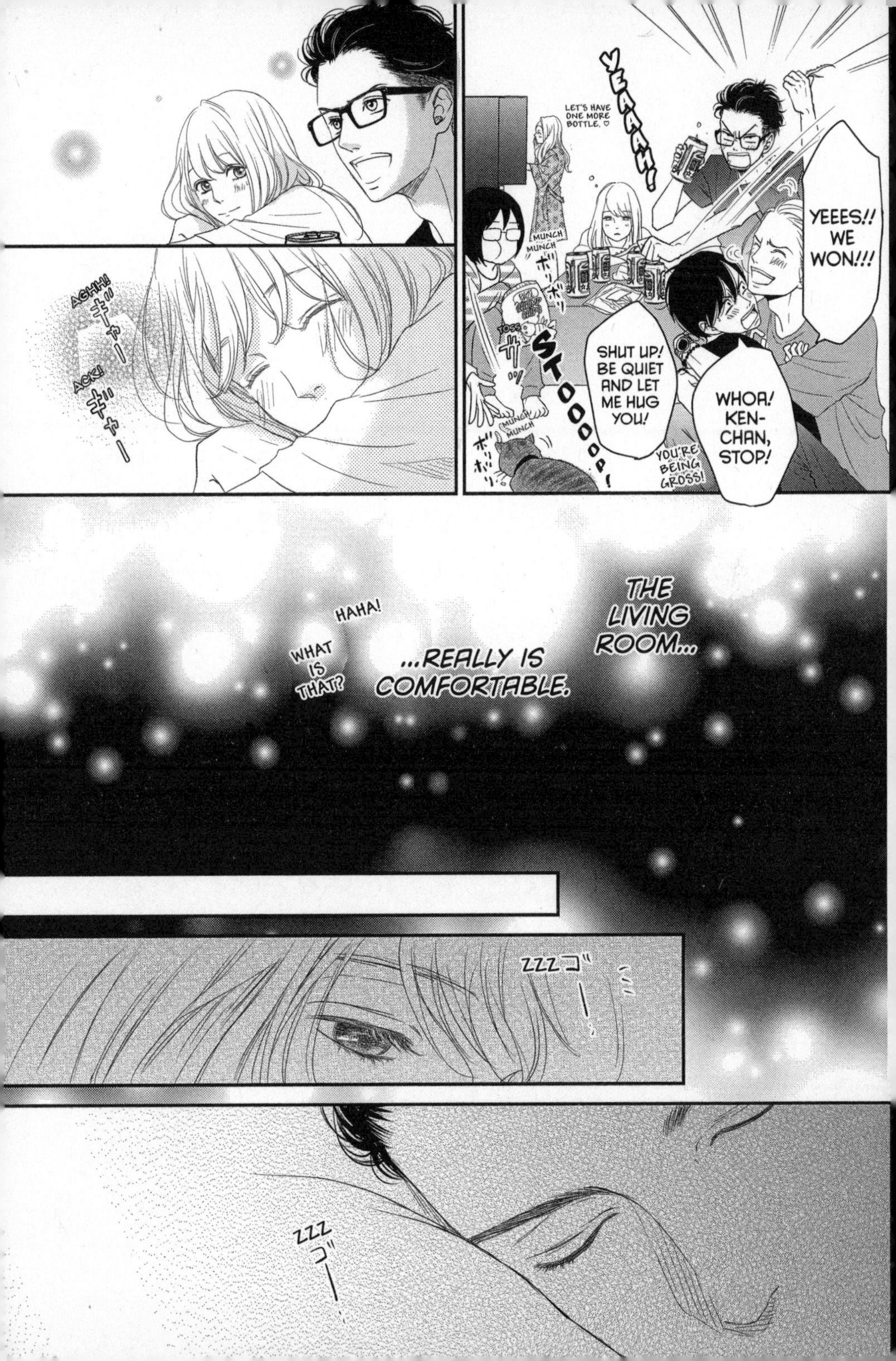
YEAAAH!
LET'S HAVE ONE MORE BOTTLE. ♡
YEEES!! WE WON!!!
WHOA! KEN-CHAN, STOP!
SHUT UP! BE QUIET AND LET ME HUG YOU!
YOU'RE BEING GROSS!
MUNCH MUNCH ボリボリ
TOSS サッ
STOOOOOP!
MUNCH MUNCH ボリボリ
AGHH! ギャー
ACK! ギャー
THE LIVING ROOM...
...REALLY IS COMFORTABLE.
HAHA!
WHAT IS THAT?
ZZZ ゴー
ZZZ ゴー

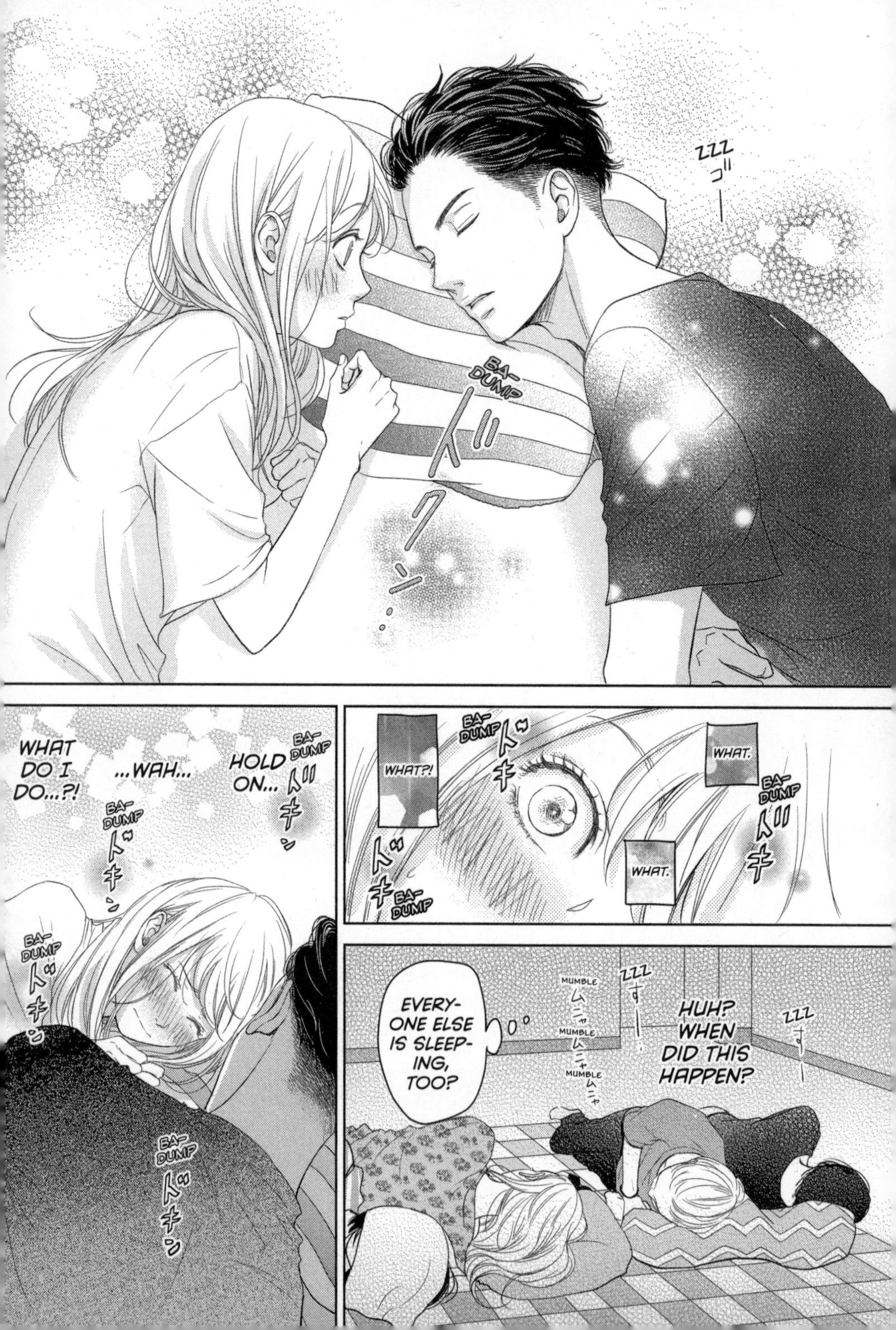
ZZZ
BA-DUMP
WHAT.
BA-DUMP
BA-DUMP
WHAT?!
WHAT.
BA-DUMP
ZZZ
HUH? WHEN DID THIS HAPPEN?
ZZZ
MUMBLE
MUMBLE
MUMBLE
EVERY-ONE ELSE IS SLEEP-ING, TOO?
HOLD ON...
BA-DUMP
...WAH...
WHAT DO I DO...?!
BA-DUMP
BA-DUMP
BA-DUMP

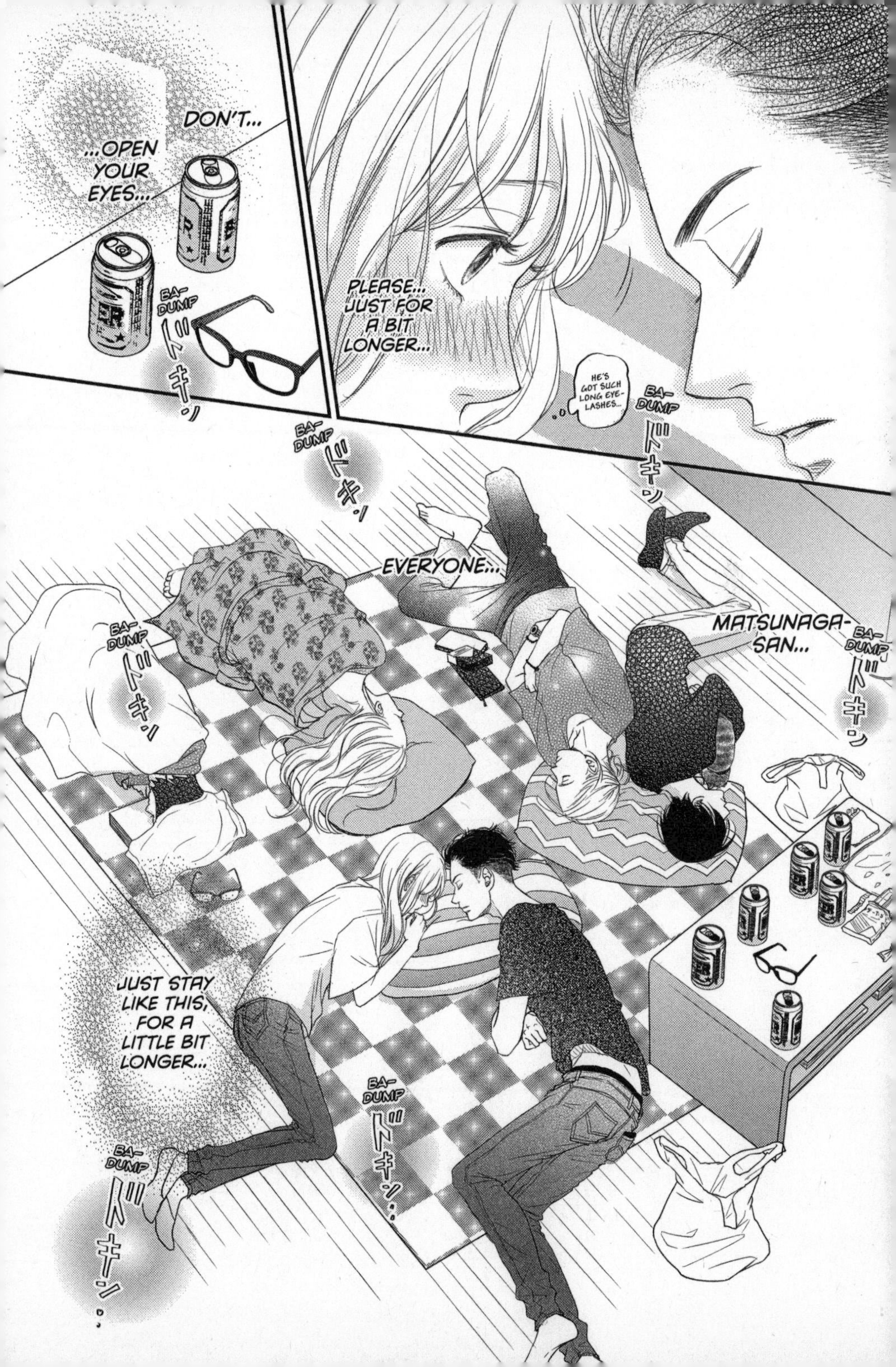
PLEASE... JUST FOR A BIT LONGER...
HE'S GOT SUCH LONG EYE-LASHES...
BA-DUMP
ドキッ
DON'T...
...OPEN YOUR EYES...
BA-DUMP
ドキッ
MATSUNAGA-SAN...
BA-DUMP
ドキッ
EVERYONE...
BA-DUMP
ドキッ
BA-DUMP
ドキッ
JUST STAY LIKE THIS, FOR A LITTLE BIT LONGER...
BA-DUMP
ドキッ
BA-DUMP
ドキーッ

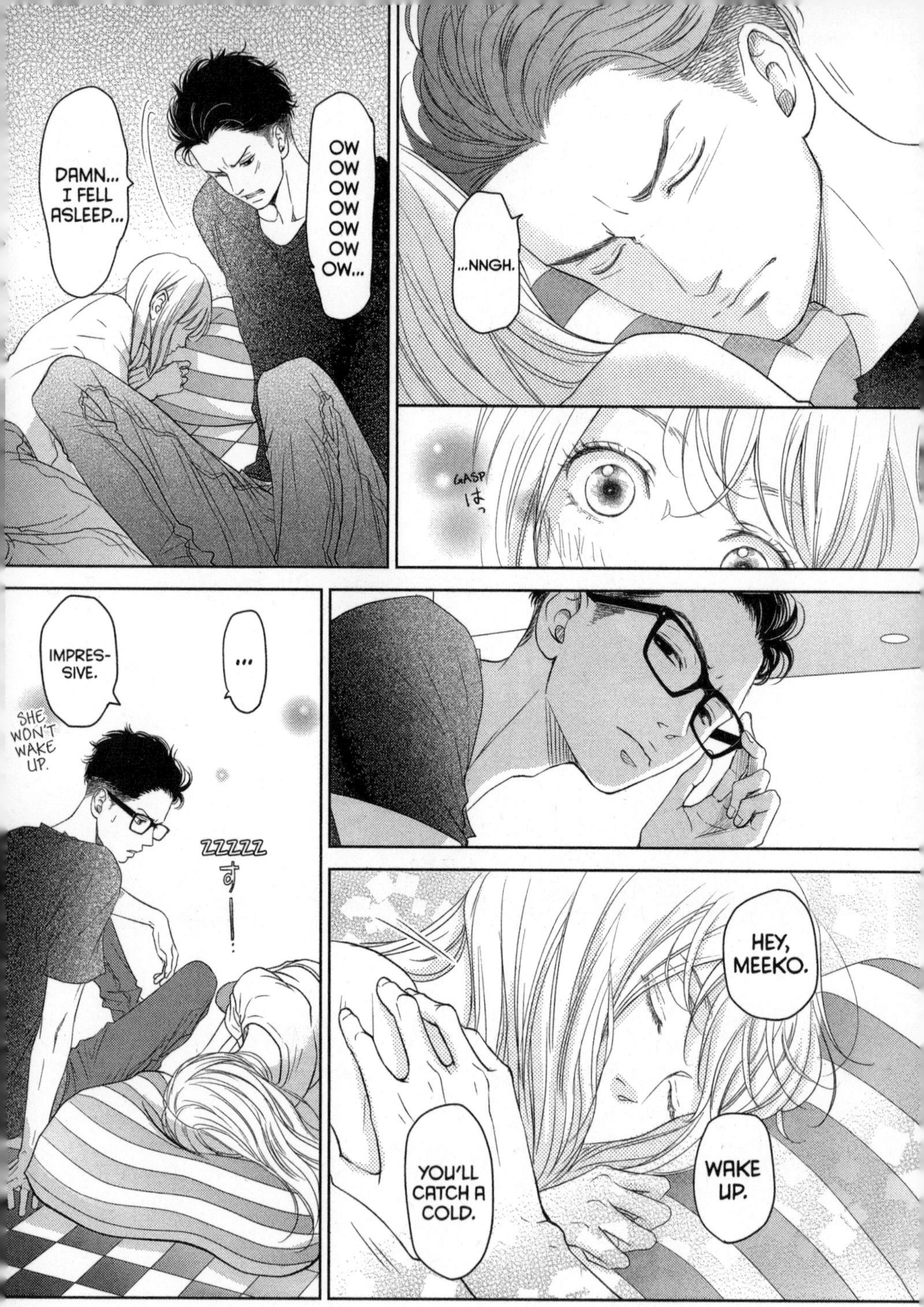
...NNGH.
GASP
はっ
OW OW OW OW OW OW OW...
DAMN... I FELL ASLEEP...
HEY, MEEKO.
WAKE UP.
YOU'LL CATCH A COLD.
...
IMPRES-SIVE.
SHE WON'T WAKE UP.
ZZZZZ
す—!

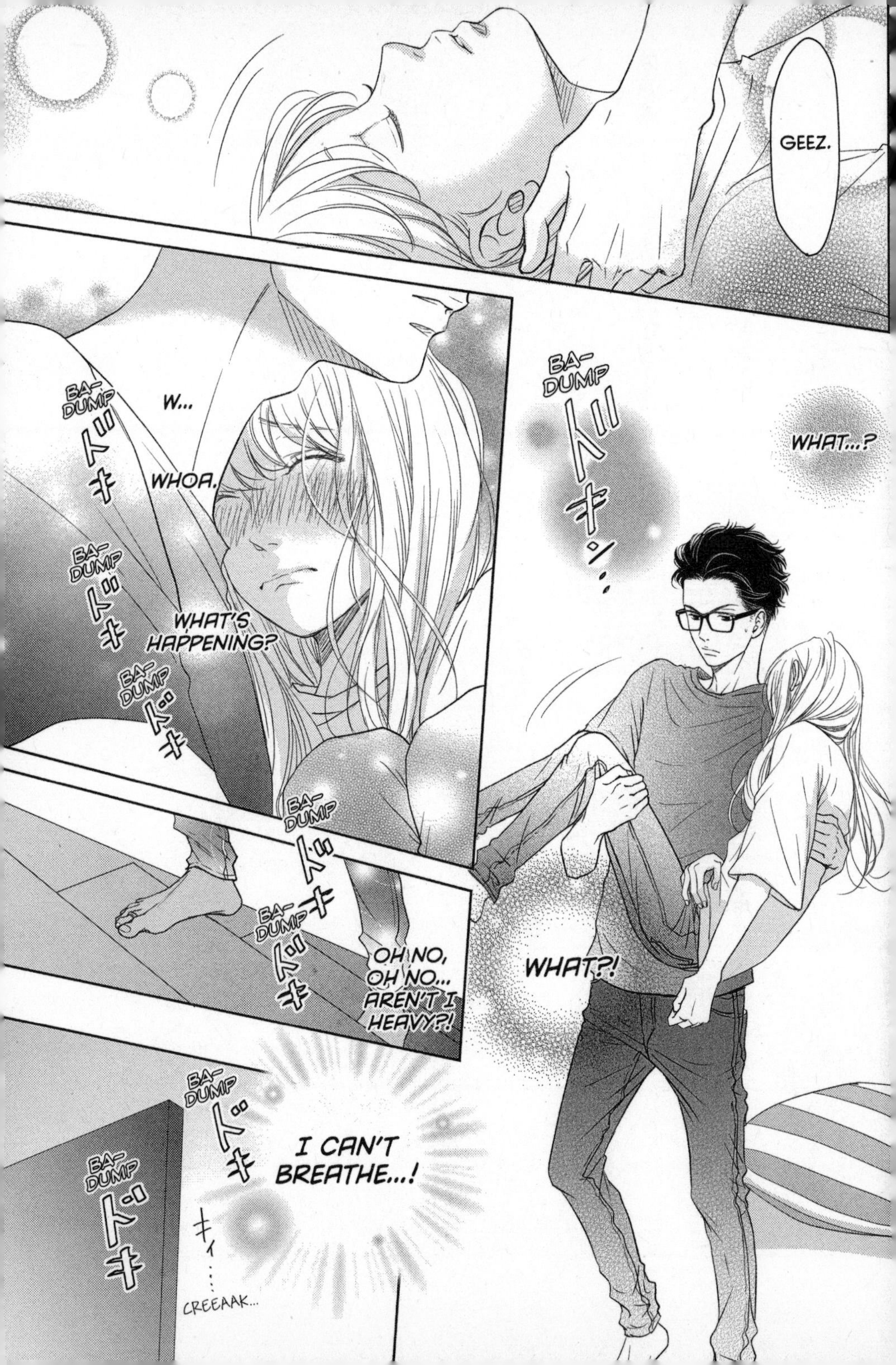
GEEZ.
BA-DUMP
ドキン..
WHAT...?
WHAT?!
BA-DUMP
ドキ
W...
WHOA.
BA-DUMP
ドキ
WHAT'S HAPPENING?
BA-DUMP
ドキ
BA-DUMP
ドキ
BA-DUMP
ドキ
OH NO, OH NO... AREN'T I HEAVY?!
BA-DUMP
ドキ
I CAN'T BREATHE...!
BA-DUMP
ドキ
キィ…
CREEAAK...

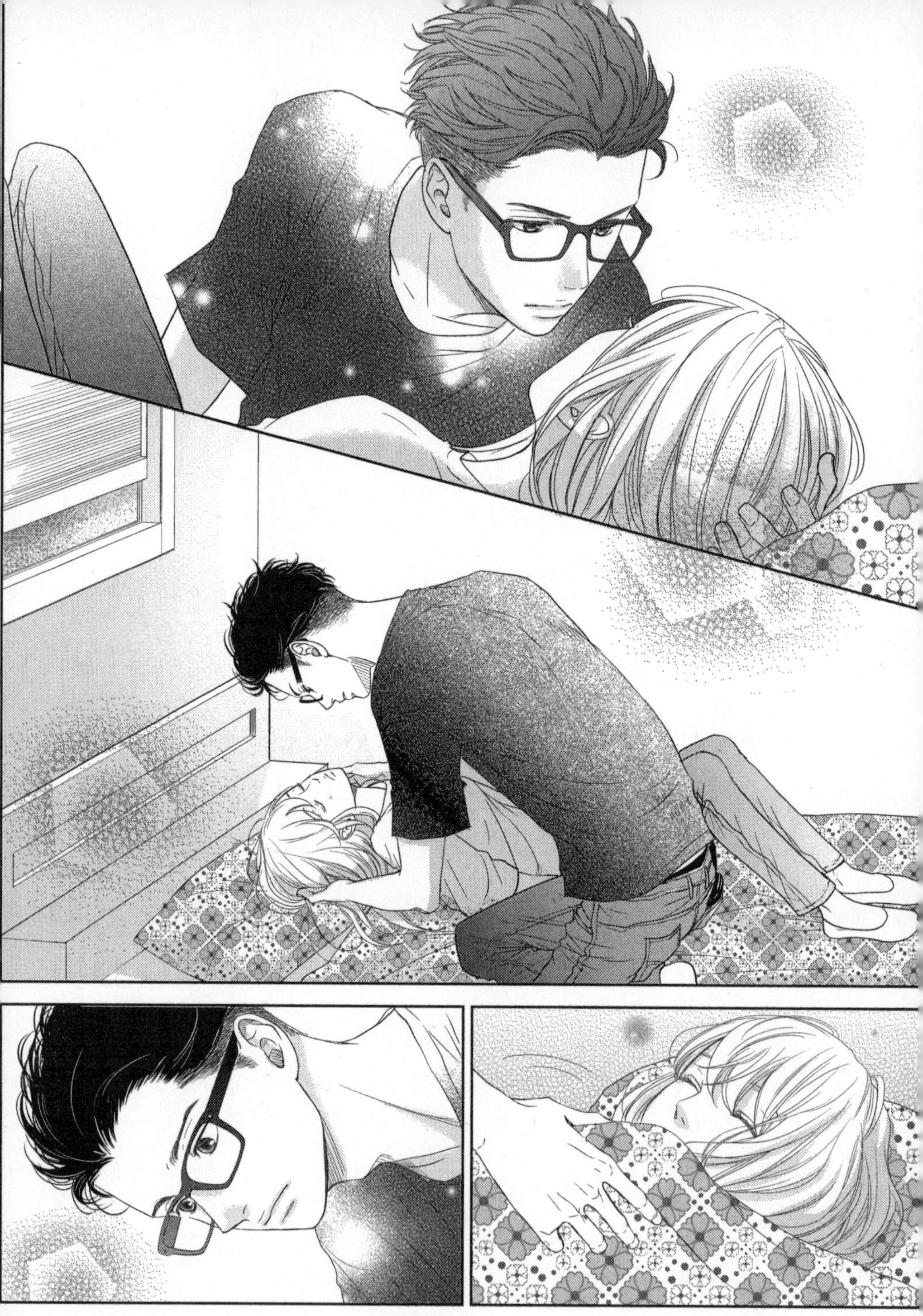

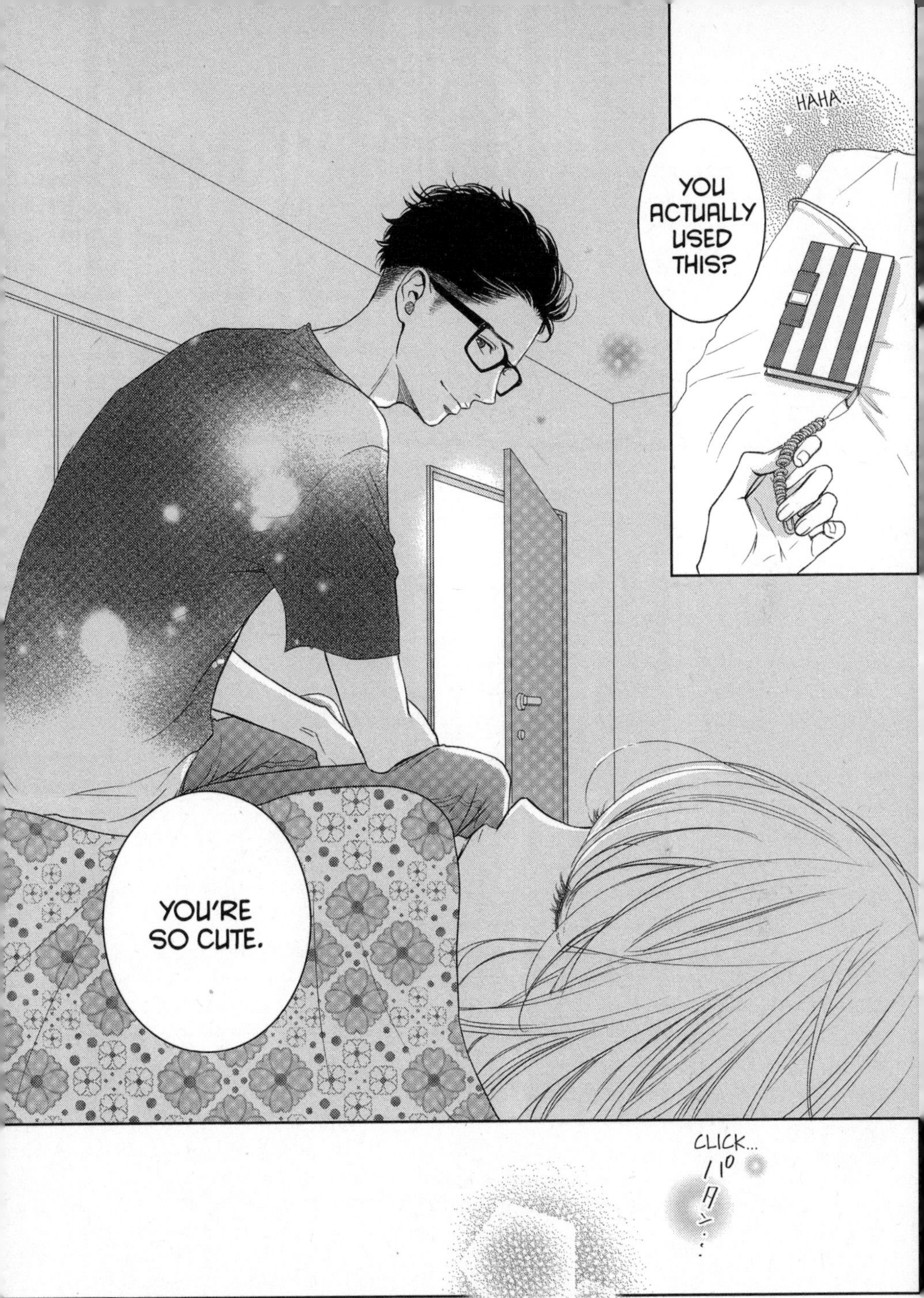
HAHA...
YOU ACTUALLY USED THIS?
YOU'RE SO CUTE.
CLICK...
パタン…

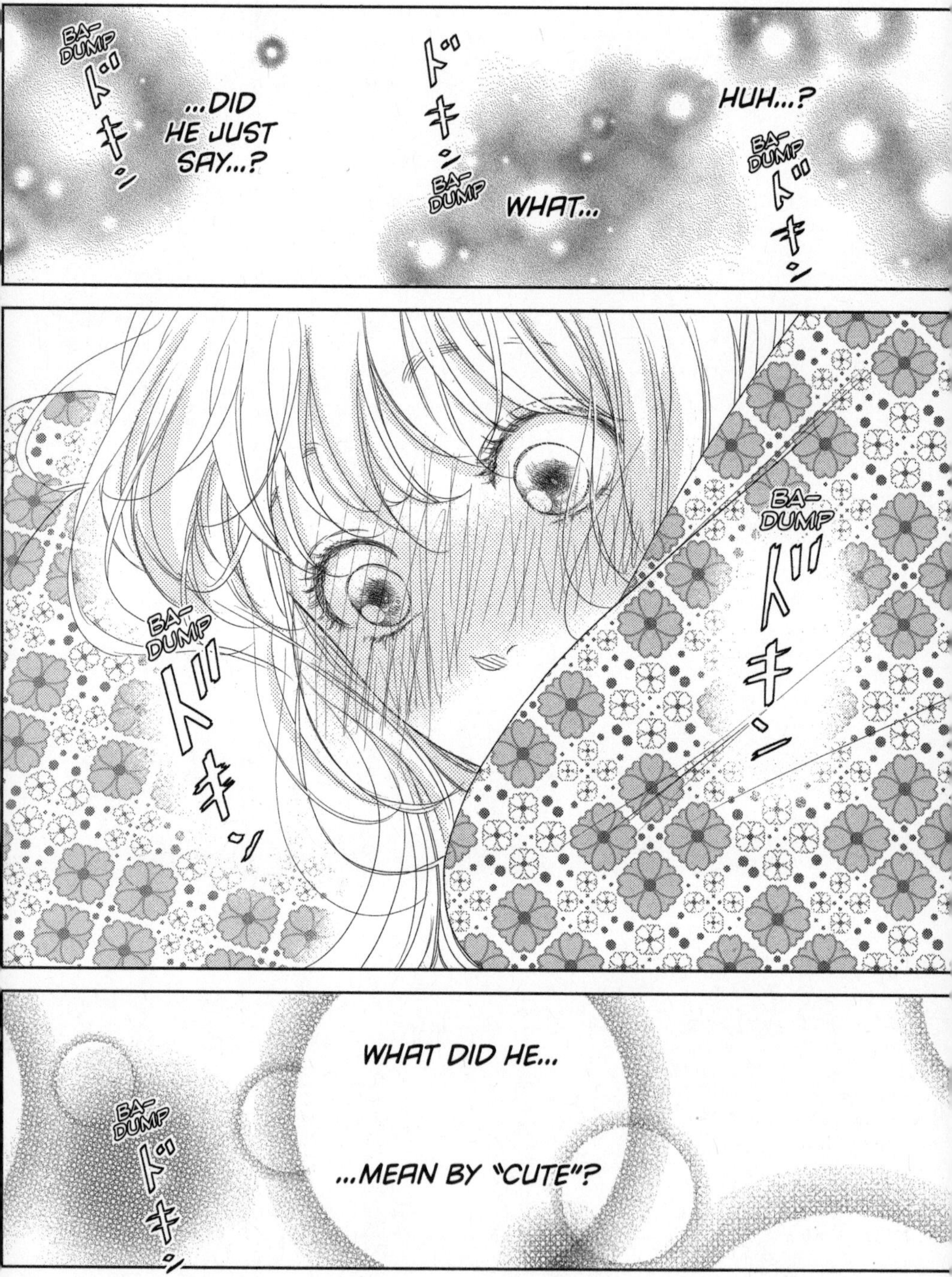
HUH...?
BA-DUMP
ドキッ
WHAT...
BA-DUMP
ドキッ
...DID HE JUST SAY...?
BA-DUMP
ドキッ
BA-DUMP
ドキッ
BA-DUMP
ドキッ
WHAT DID HE...
...MEAN BY "CUTE"?
BA-DUMP
ドキッ

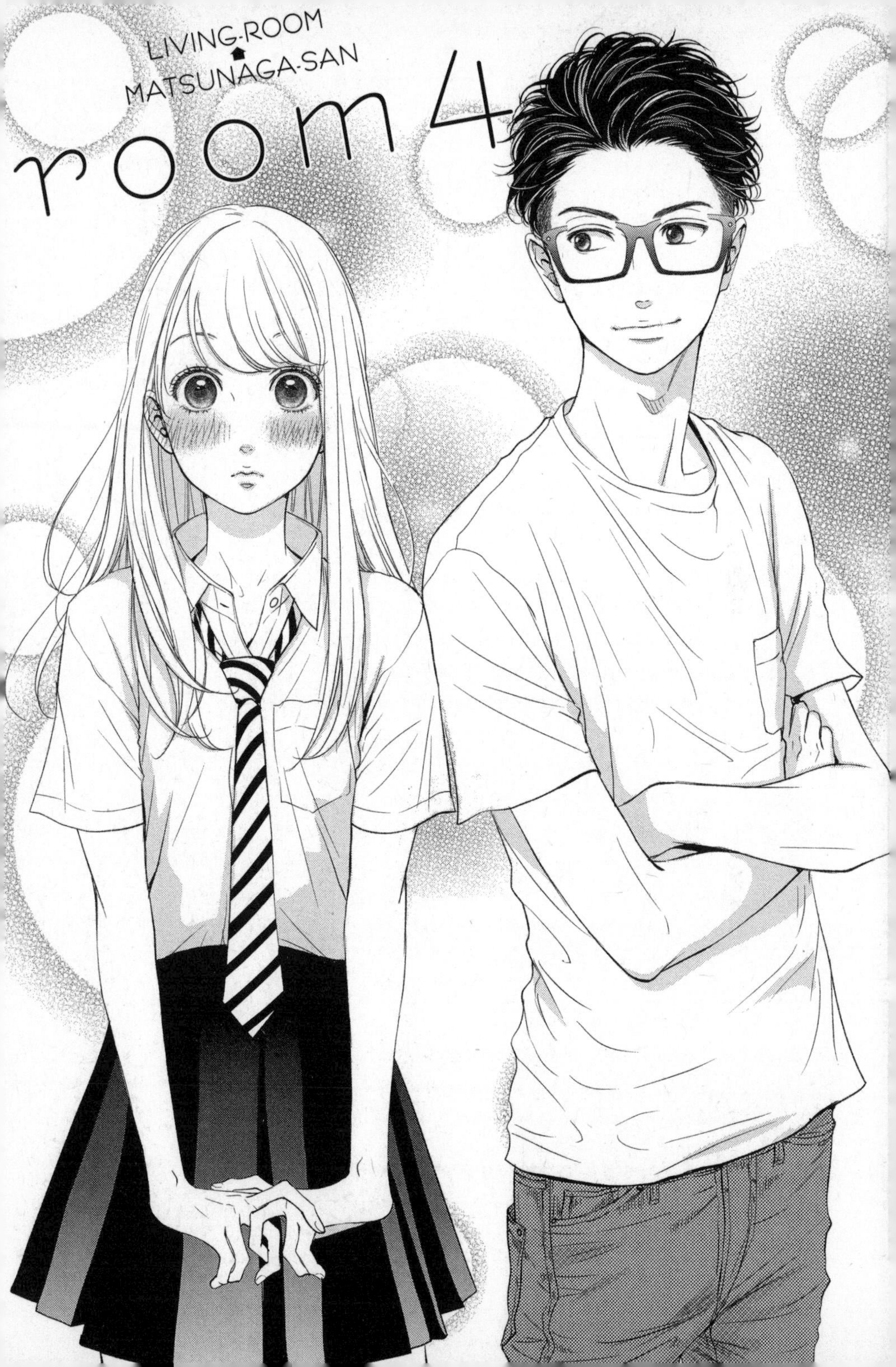
LIVING-ROOM
MATSUNAGA-SAN
room 4

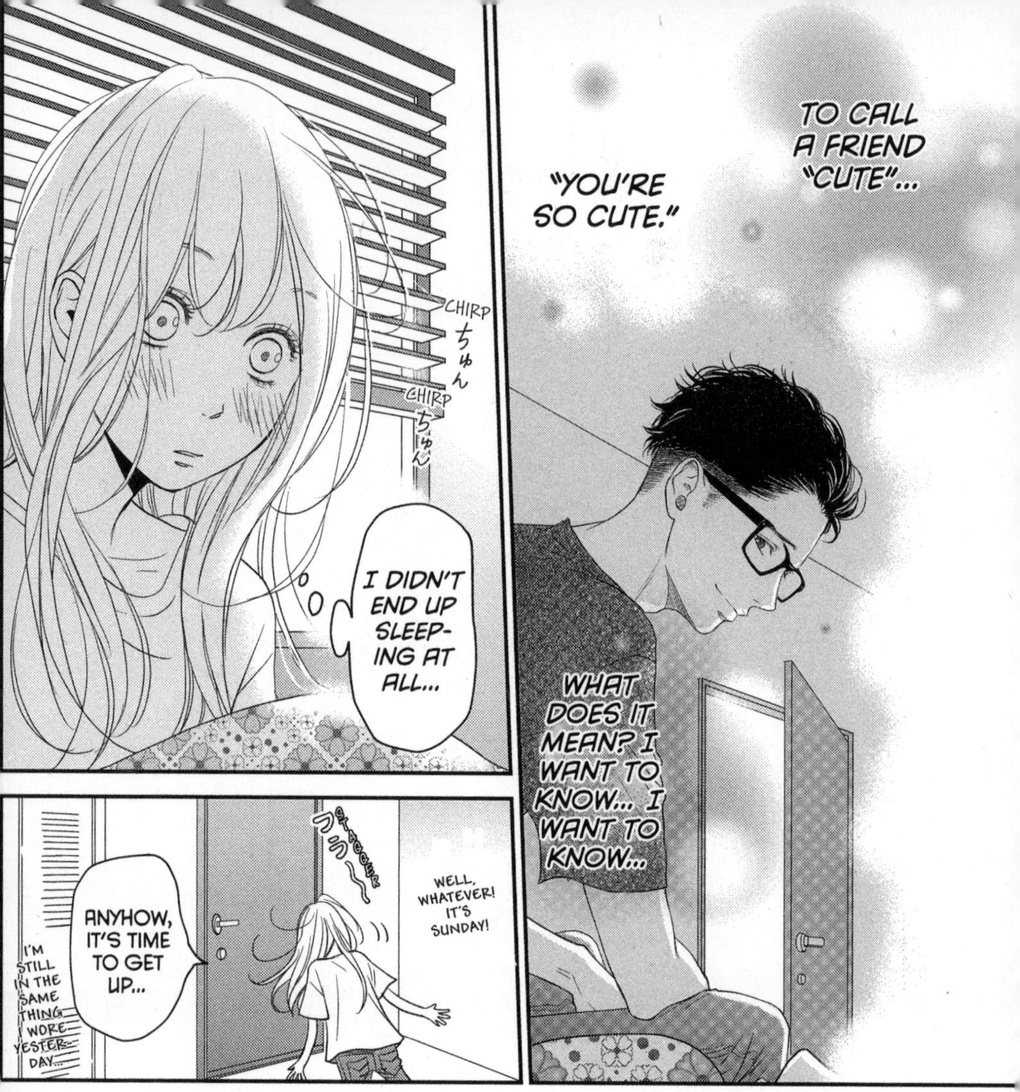
TO CALL A FRIEND "CUTE"...
"YOU'RE SO CUTE."
WHAT DOES IT MEAN? I WANT TO KNOW... I WANT TO KNOW...
CHIRP
ちゅん
CHIRP
ちゅん
I DIDN'T END UP SLEEPING AT ALL...
STAGGER
ふら~
WELL, WHATEVER! IT'S SUNDAY!
ANYHOW, IT'S TIME TO GET UP...
I'M STILL IN THE SAME THING I WORE YESTERDAY...

Boarding House Trivia

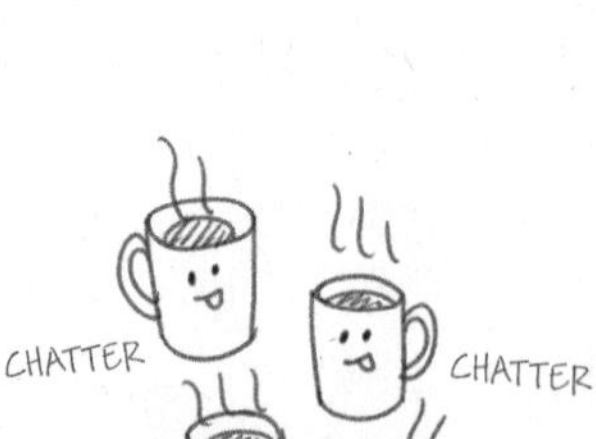
CHATTER
CHATTER

I listened to a lot of stories from people who live in boarding houses.

As a general rule, boarding houses tend to attract the sociable type, and everyone gets along regardless of gender!!

Ooh~ My boundaries have expanded!!

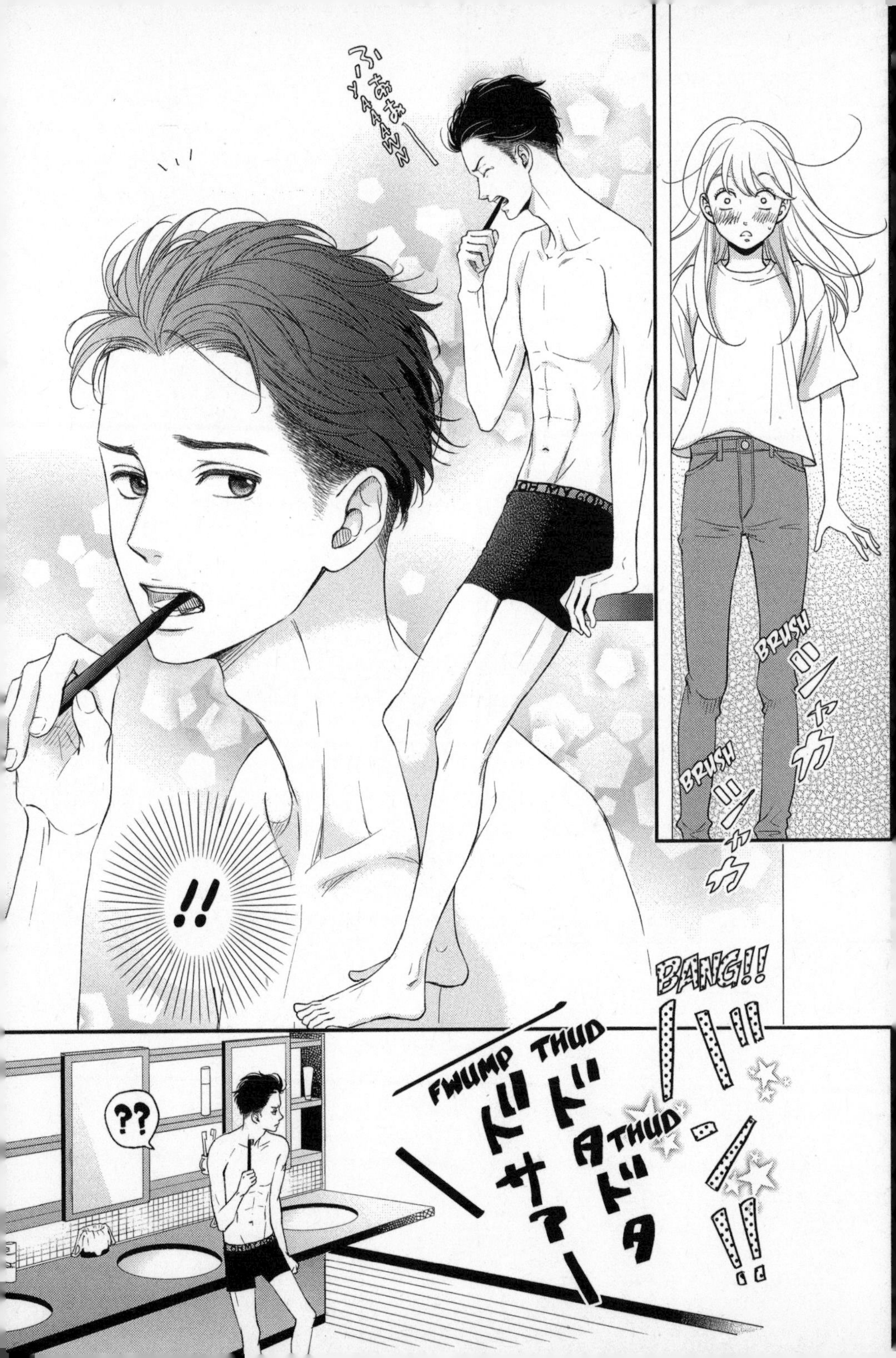

BRUSH
シャカ
BRUSH
シャカ
ふあぁぁ
YAAAAWN
!!
BANG!!
THUD
ドタ
THUD
ドド
FWUMP
ドサァー
??

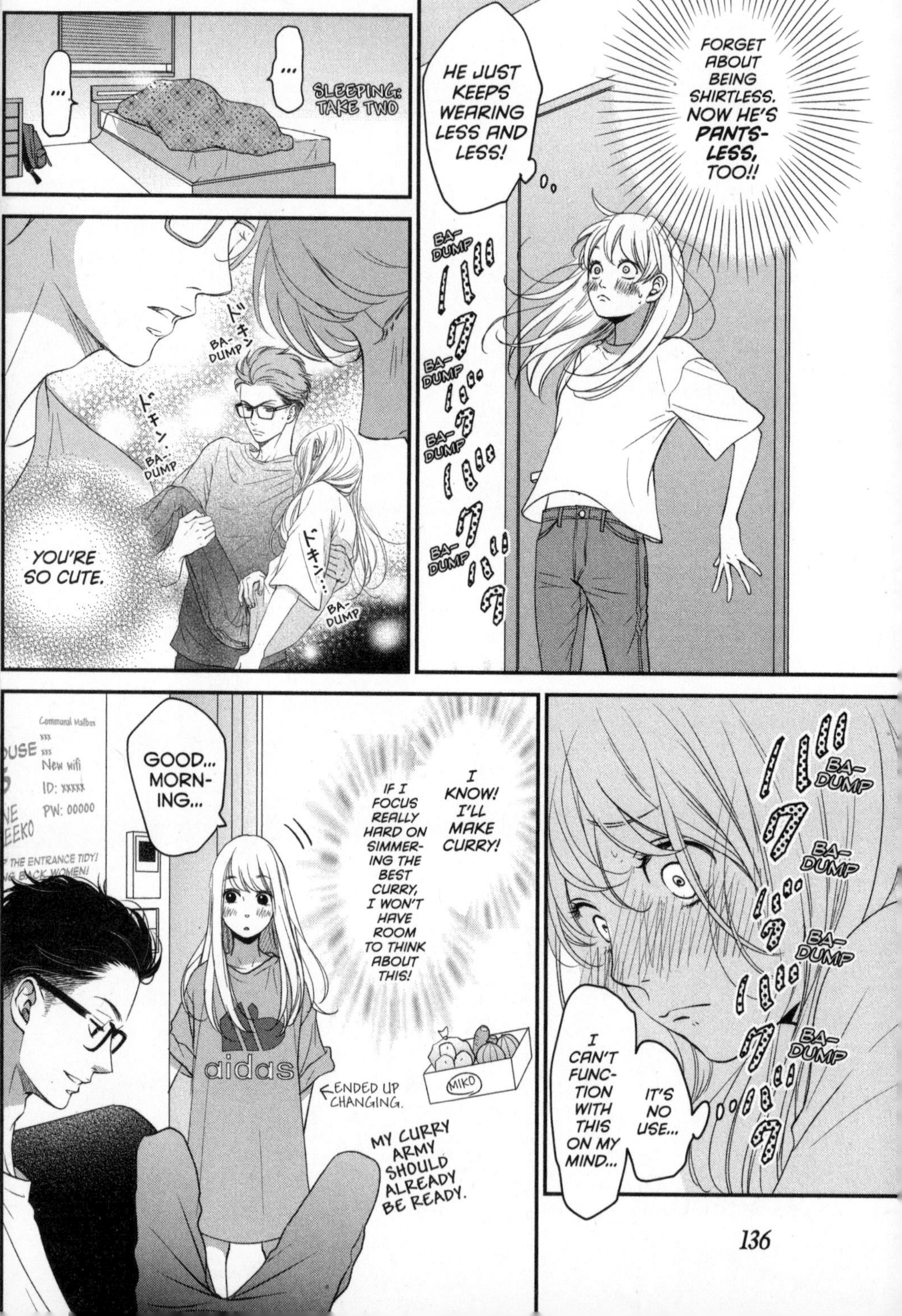

HE JUST KEEPS WEARING LESS AND LESS!
FORGET ABOUT BEING SHIRTLESS. NOW HE'S PANTS-LESS, TOO!!
BA-DUMP
BA-DUMP
BA-DUMP
BA-DUMP
...
...
SLEEPING: TAKE TWO
ドキン
BA-DUMP
ドキン
BA-DUMP
YOU'RE SO CUTE.
ドキン…
BA-DUMP
BA-DUMP
BA-DUMP
BA-DUMP
BA-DUMP
IT'S NO USE...
I CAN'T FUNCTION WITH THIS ON MY MIND...
Communal Mailbox
New wifi
ID: xxxxx
PW: 00000
GOOD... MORNING...
I KNOW! I'LL MAKE CURRY!
IF I FOCUS REALLY HARD ON SIMMERING THE BEST CURRY, I WON'T HAVE ROOM TO THINK ABOUT THIS!
aidas
ENDED UP CHANGING.
MIKO
MY CURRY ARMY SHOULD ALREADY BE READY.

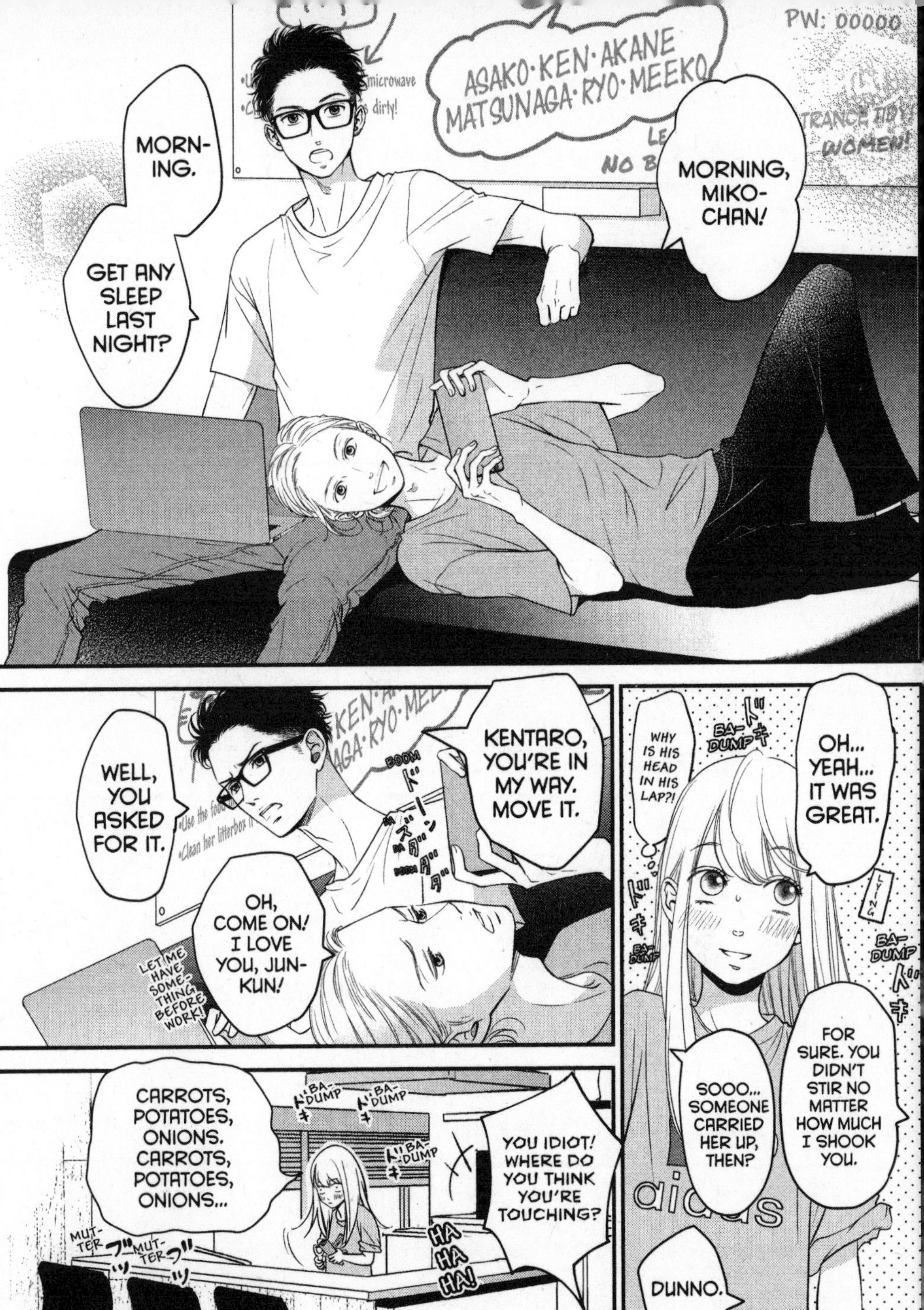
PW: 00000
ASAKO·KEN·AKANE MATSUNAGA·RYO·MEEKO
MORNING, MIKO-CHAN!
MORNING.
GET ANY SLEEP LAST NIGHT?
OH... YEAH... IT WAS GREAT.
BA-DUMP
WHY IS HIS HEAD IN HIS LAP?!
LYING
BA-DUMP
BA-DUMP
FOR SURE. YOU DIDN'T STIR NO MATTER HOW MUCH I SHOOK YOU.
SOOO... SOMEONE CARRIED HER UP, THEN?
DUNNO.
KENTARO, YOU'RE IN MY WAY. MOVE IT.
BOOM
WELL, YOU ASKED FOR IT.
OH, COME ON! I LOVE YOU, JUN-KUN!
LET ME HAVE SOMETHING BEFORE WORK!
YOU IDIOT! WHERE DO YOU THINK YOU'RE TOUCHING?
HA HA HA!
BA-DUMP
BA-DUMP
BA-DUMP
CARROTS, POTATOES, ONIONS. CARROTS, POTATOES, ONIONS...
MUTTER
MUTTER

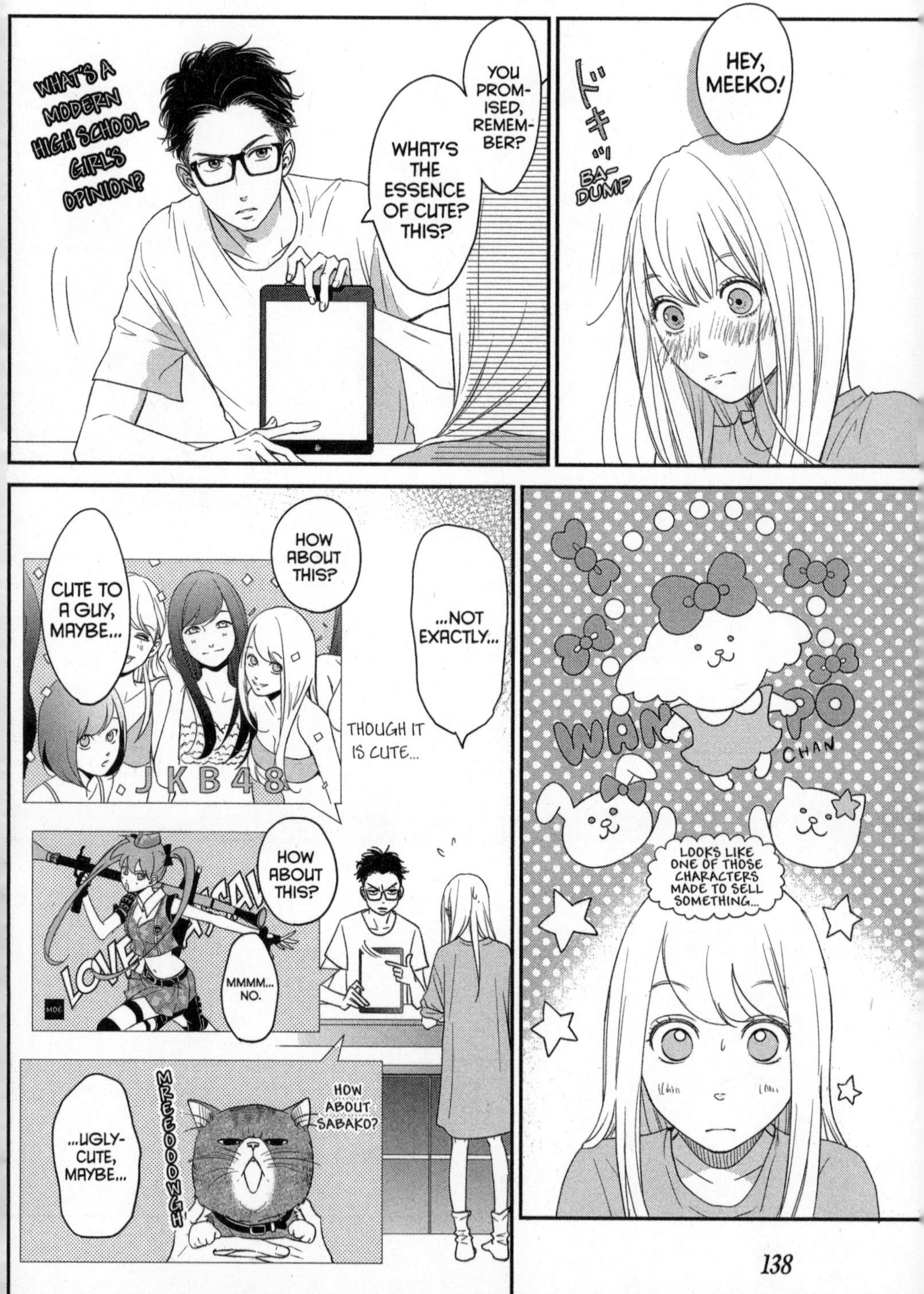
HEY, MEEKO!
ドキ
BA-DUMP
YOU PROMISED, REMEMBER?
WHAT'S THE ESSENCE OF CUTE? THIS?
WHAT'S A MODERN HIGH SCHOOL GIRL'S OPINION?
WAN PO
CHAN
LOOKS LIKE ONE OF THOSE CHARACTERS MADE TO SELL SOMETHING...
HOW ABOUT THIS?
...NOT EXACTLY...
THOUGH IT IS CUTE...
CUTE TO A GUY, MAYBE...
JKB48
HOW ABOUT THIS?
LOVE
MMMM... NO.
HOW ABOUT SABAKO?
MREEOOOWGH
...UGLY-CUTE, MAYBE...

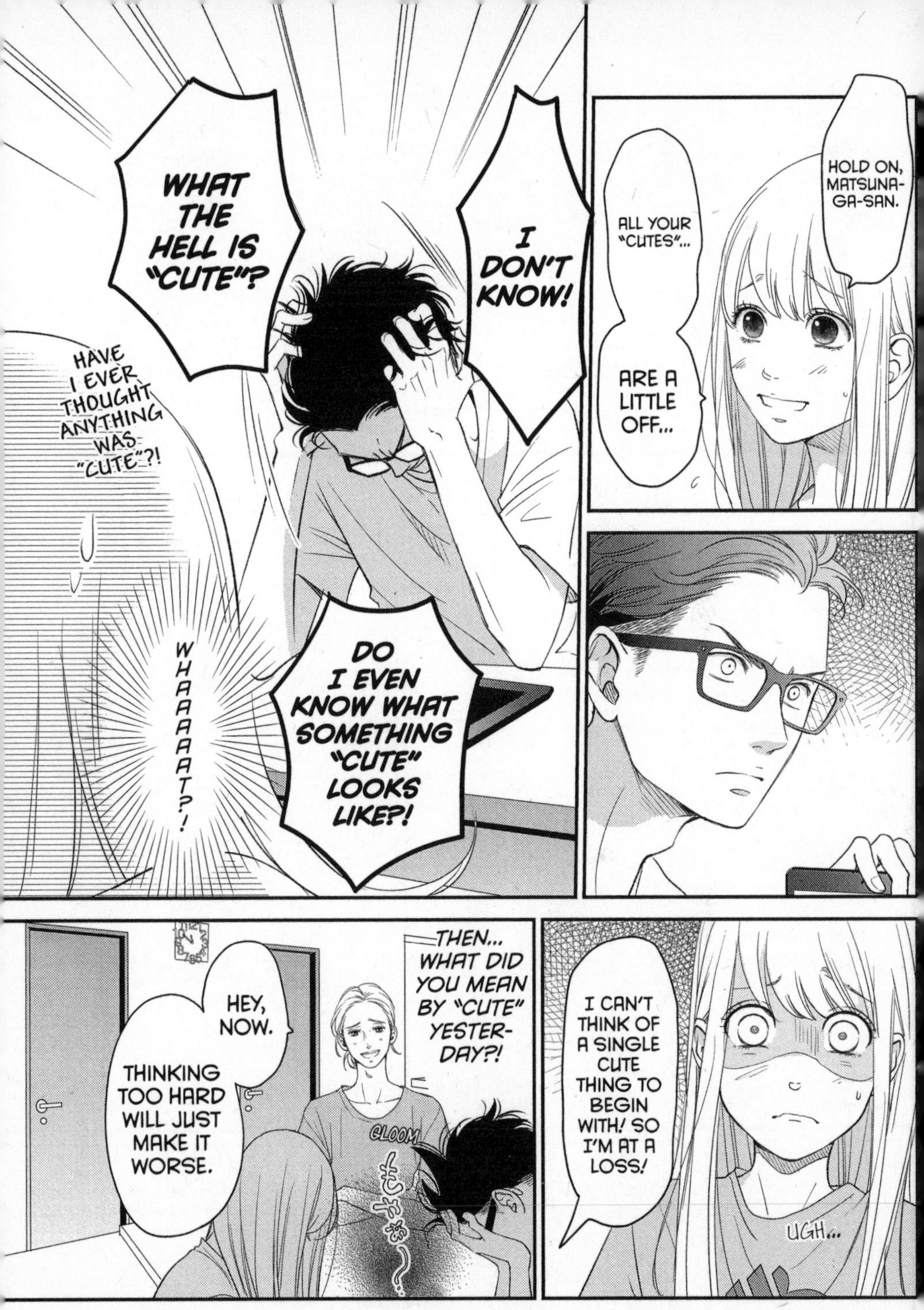
HOLD ON, MATSUNAGA-SAN.
ALL YOUR "CUTES"... ARE A LITTLE OFF...
I DON'T KNOW!
WHAT THE HELL IS "CUTE"?
HAVE I EVER THOUGHT ANYTHING WAS "CUTE"?!
DO I EVEN KNOW WHAT SOMETHING "CUTE" LOOKS LIKE?!
WHAAAAAAT?!
I CAN'T THINK OF A SINGLE CUTE THING TO BEGIN WITH! SO I'M AT A LOSS!
UGH...
THEN... WHAT DID YOU MEAN BY "CUTE" YESTERDAY?!
HEY, NOW.
THINKING TOO HARD WILL JUST MAKE IT WORSE.
GLOOM

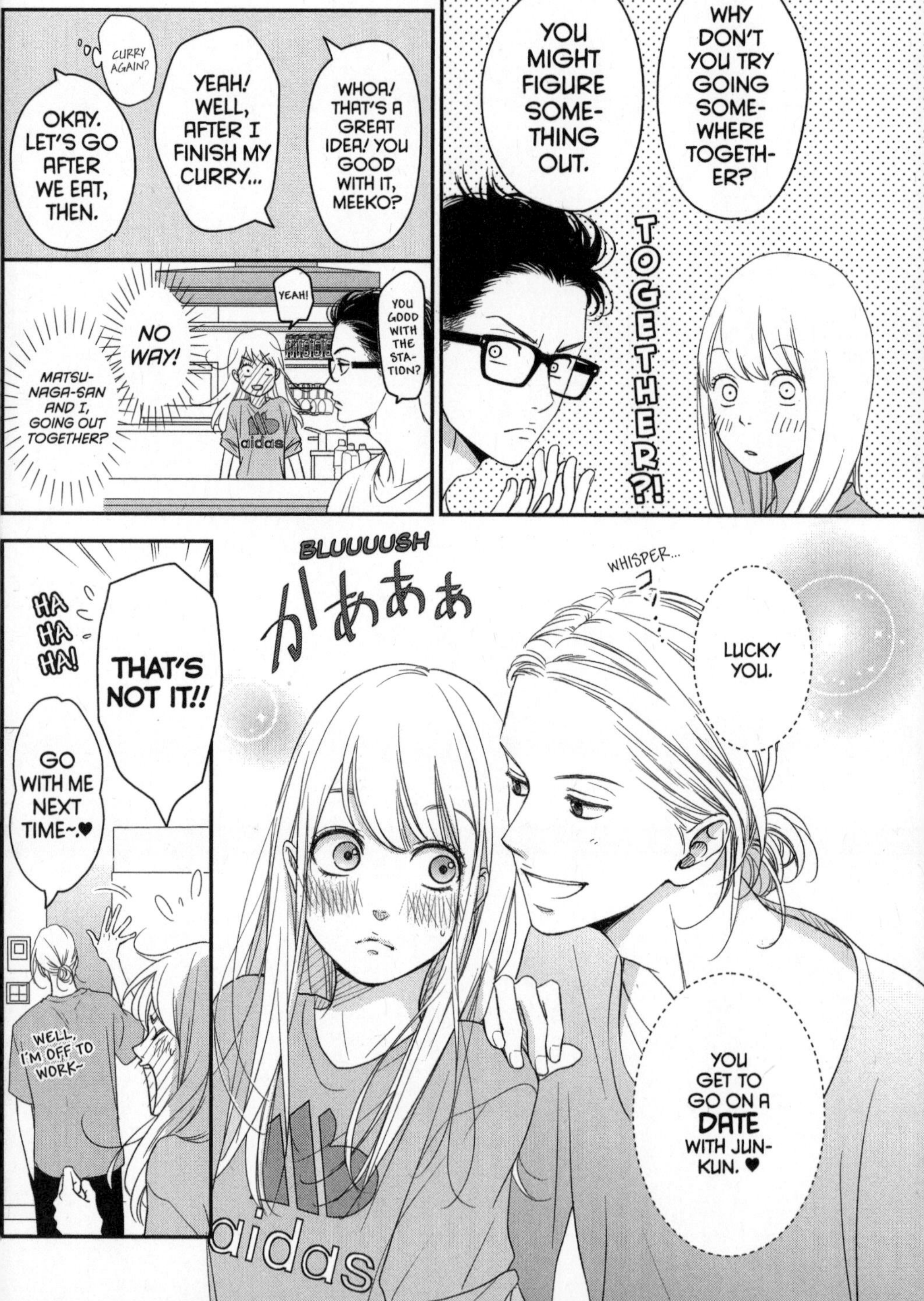
WHY DON'T YOU TRY GOING SOME-WHERE TOGETH-ER?
YOU MIGHT FIGURE SOME-THING OUT.
TOGETHER?!
WHOA! THAT'S A GREAT IDEA! YOU GOOD WITH IT, MEEKO?
YEAH! WELL, AFTER I FINISH MY CURRY...
CURRY AGAIN?
OKAY. LET'S GO AFTER WE EAT, THEN.
YOU GOOD WITH THE STA-TION?
YEAH!
NO WAY!
MATSU-NAGA-SAN AND I, GOING OUT TOGETHER?
BLUUUUSH
かあああ
WHISPER...
LUCKY YOU.
YOU GET TO GO ON A DATE WITH JUN-KUN. ♥
THAT'S NOT IT!!
HA HA HA!
GO WITH ME NEXT TIME~.♥
WELL, I'M OFF TO WORK~

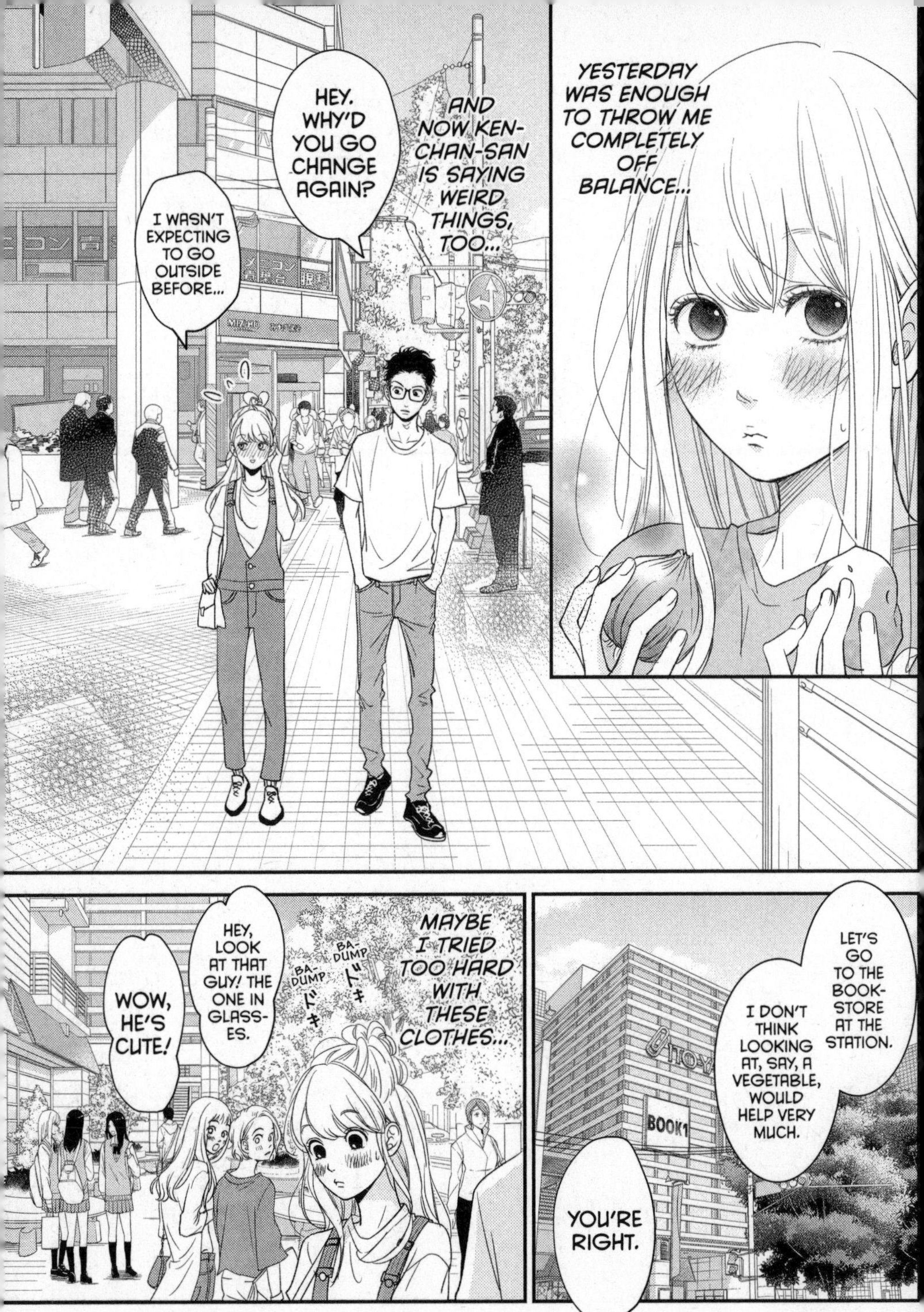
YESTERDAY WAS ENOUGH TO THROW ME COMPLETELY OFF BALANCE...
AND NOW KEN-CHAN-SAN IS SAYING WEIRD THINGS, TOO...
HEY. WHY'D YOU GO CHANGE AGAIN?
I WASN'T EXPECTING TO GO OUTSIDE BEFORE...
LET'S GO TO THE BOOK-STORE AT THE STATION.
I DON'T THINK LOOKING AT, SAY, A VEGETABLE, WOULD HELP VERY MUCH.
YOU'RE RIGHT.
MAYBE I TRIED TOO HARD WITH THESE CLOTHES...
BA-DUMP ドキ
BA-DUMP ドキ
HEY, LOOK AT THAT GUY! THE ONE IN GLASS-ES.
WOW, HE'S CUTE!

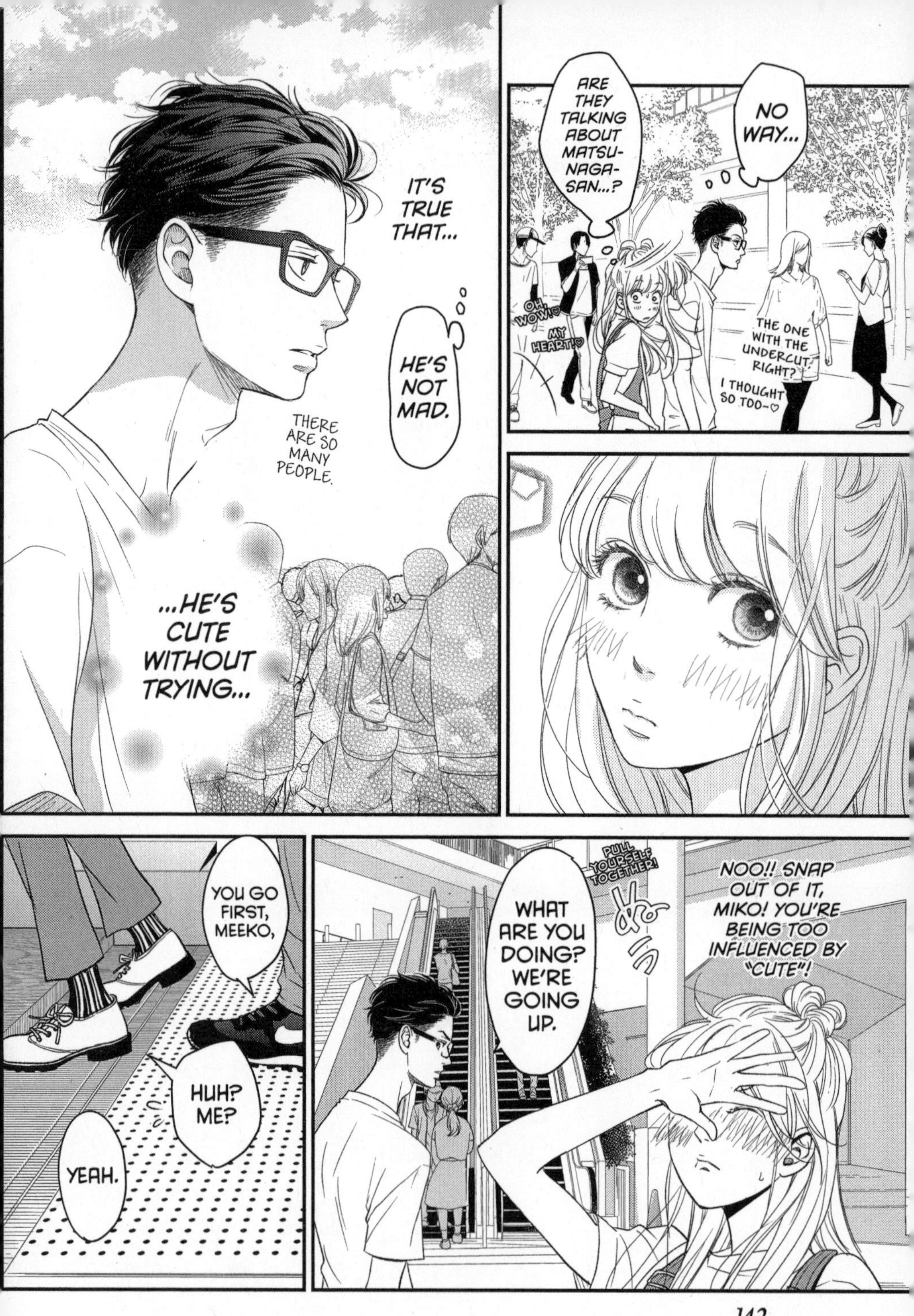
ARE THEY TALKING ABOUT MATSUNAGA-SAN...?
NO WAY...
THE ONE WITH THE UNDERCUT, RIGHT?
I THOUGHT SO TOO~♡
OH, WOW!♡
MY HEART!♡
IT'S TRUE THAT...
HE'S NOT MAD.
THERE ARE SO MANY PEOPLE.
...HE'S CUTE WITHOUT TRYING...
NOO!! SNAP OUT OF IT, MIKO! YOU'RE BEING TOO INFLUENCED BY "CUTE"!
PULL YOURSELF TOGETHER!
WHAT ARE YOU DOING? WE'RE GOING UP.
YOU GO FIRST, MEEKO,
HUH? ME?
YEAH.

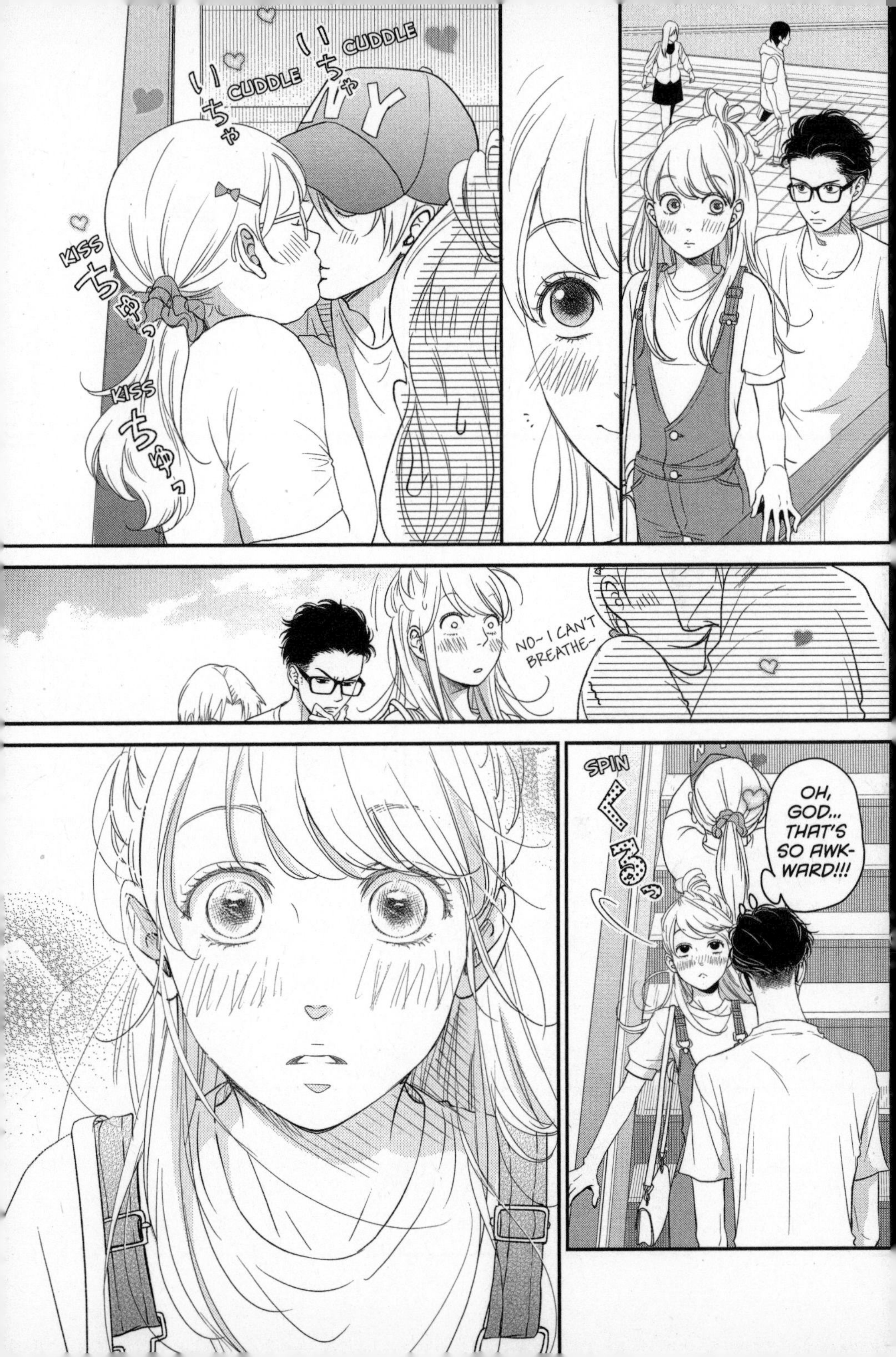

いちゃ CUDDLE
いちゃ CUDDLE
KISS ちゅっ
KISS ちゅっ
NO~ I CAN'T BREATHE~
SPIN くるっ
OH, GOD... THAT'S SO AWK-WARD!!!

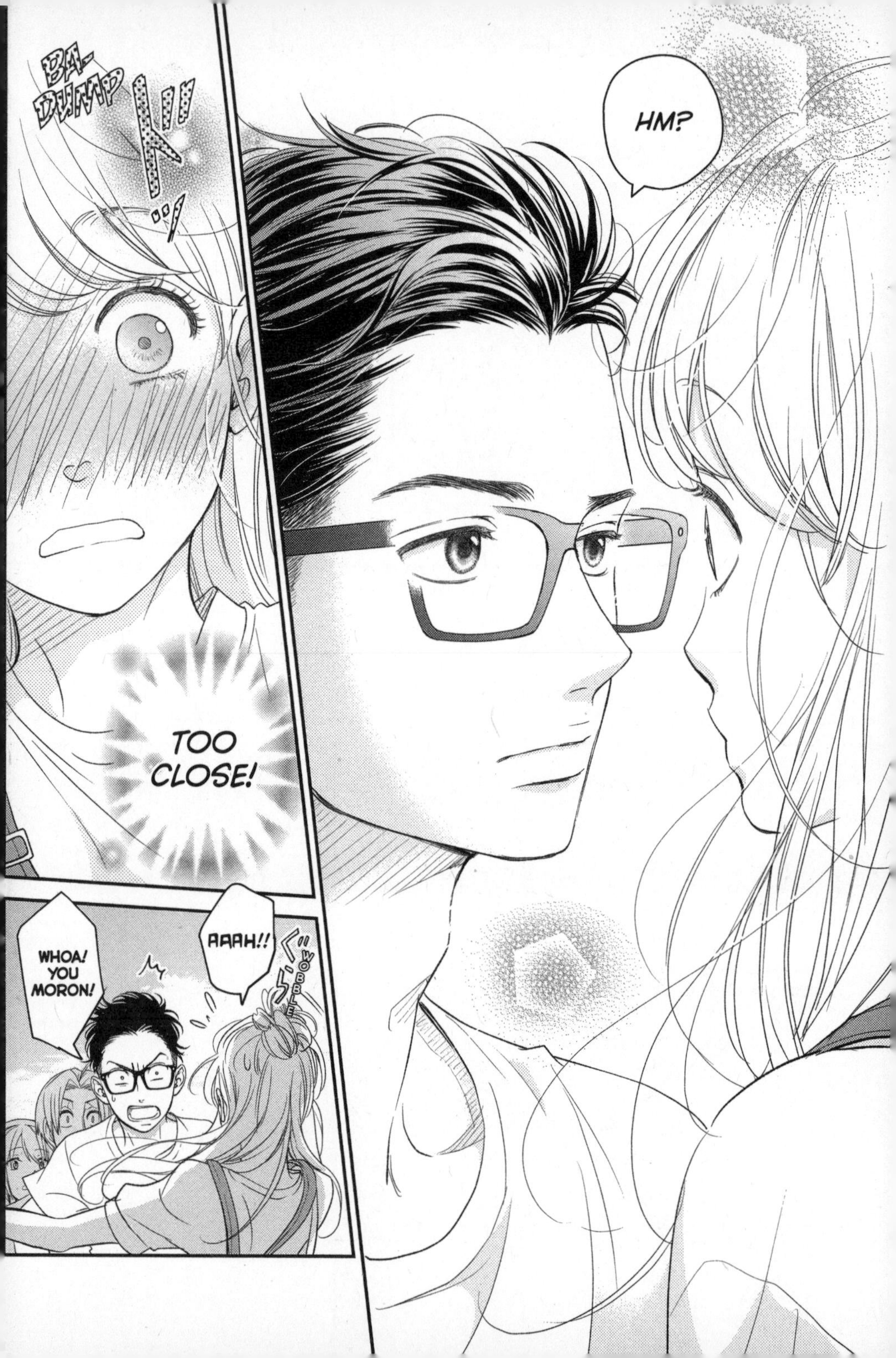
HM?
BA-DUMP
TOO CLOSE!
AAAH!!
WOBBLE
WHOA! YOU MORON!

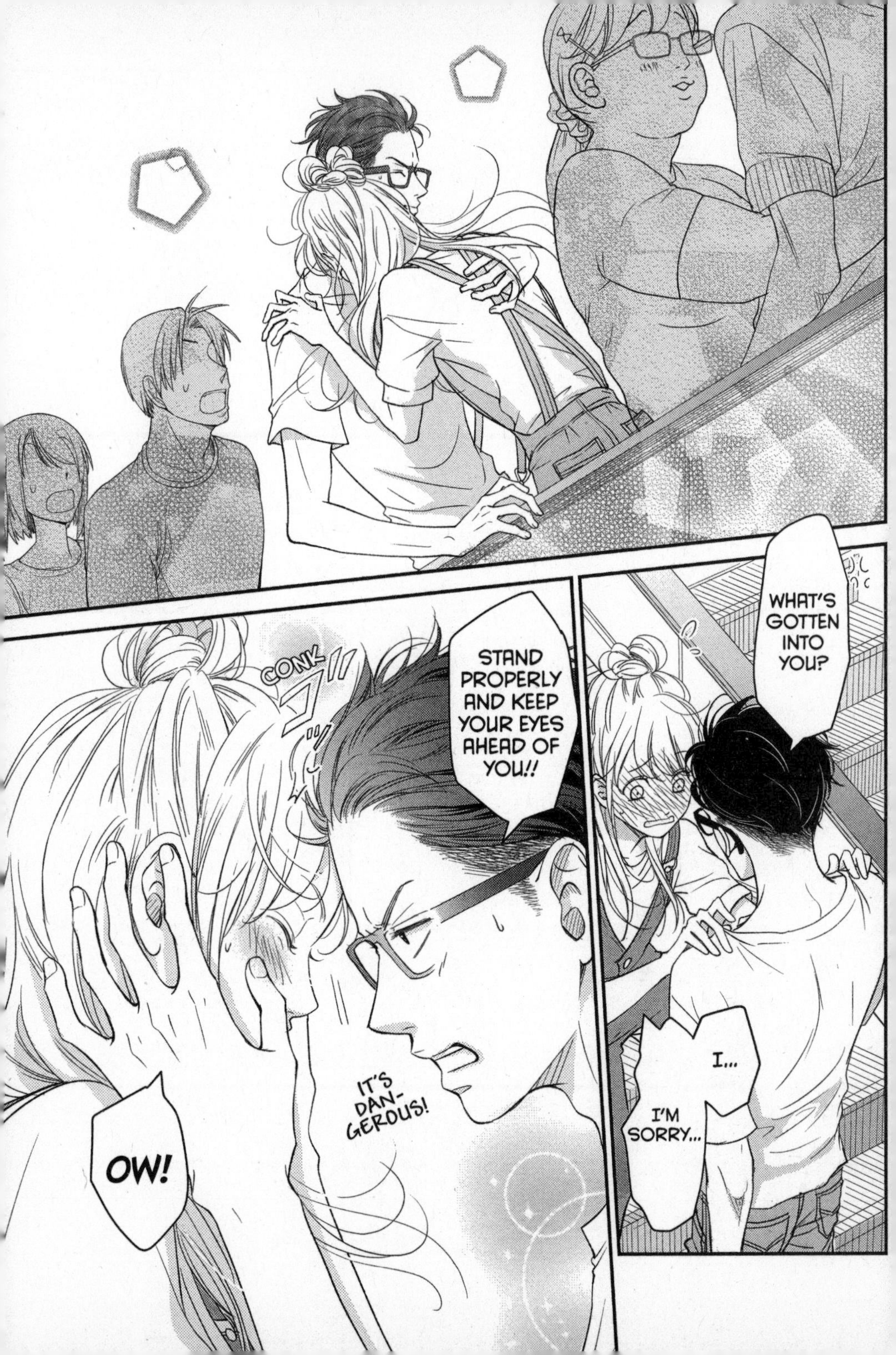
WHAT'S GOTTEN INTO YOU?
I...
I'M SORRY...
STAND PROPERLY AND KEEP YOUR EYES AHEAD OF YOU!!
CONK
IT'S DAN-GEROUS!
OW!

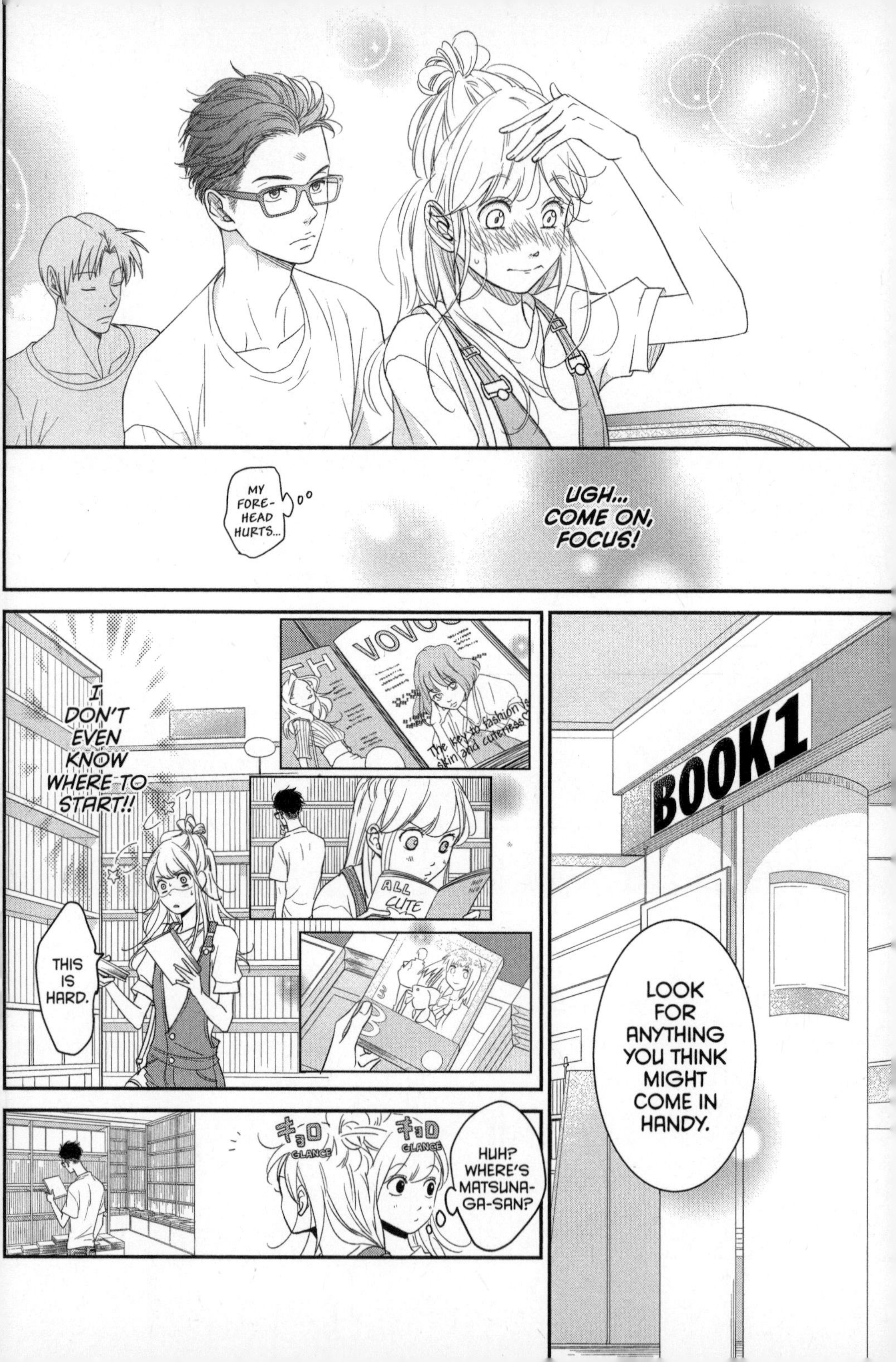
UGH... COME ON, FOCUS!
MY FORE-HEAD HURTS...
BOOK1
LOOK FOR ANYTHING YOU THINK MIGHT COME IN HANDY.
skin and cuteness
ALL CUTE
I DON'T EVEN KNOW WHERE TO START!!
THIS IS HARD.
キョロ GLANCE
キョロ GLANCE
HUH? WHERE'S MATSUNAGA-SAN?

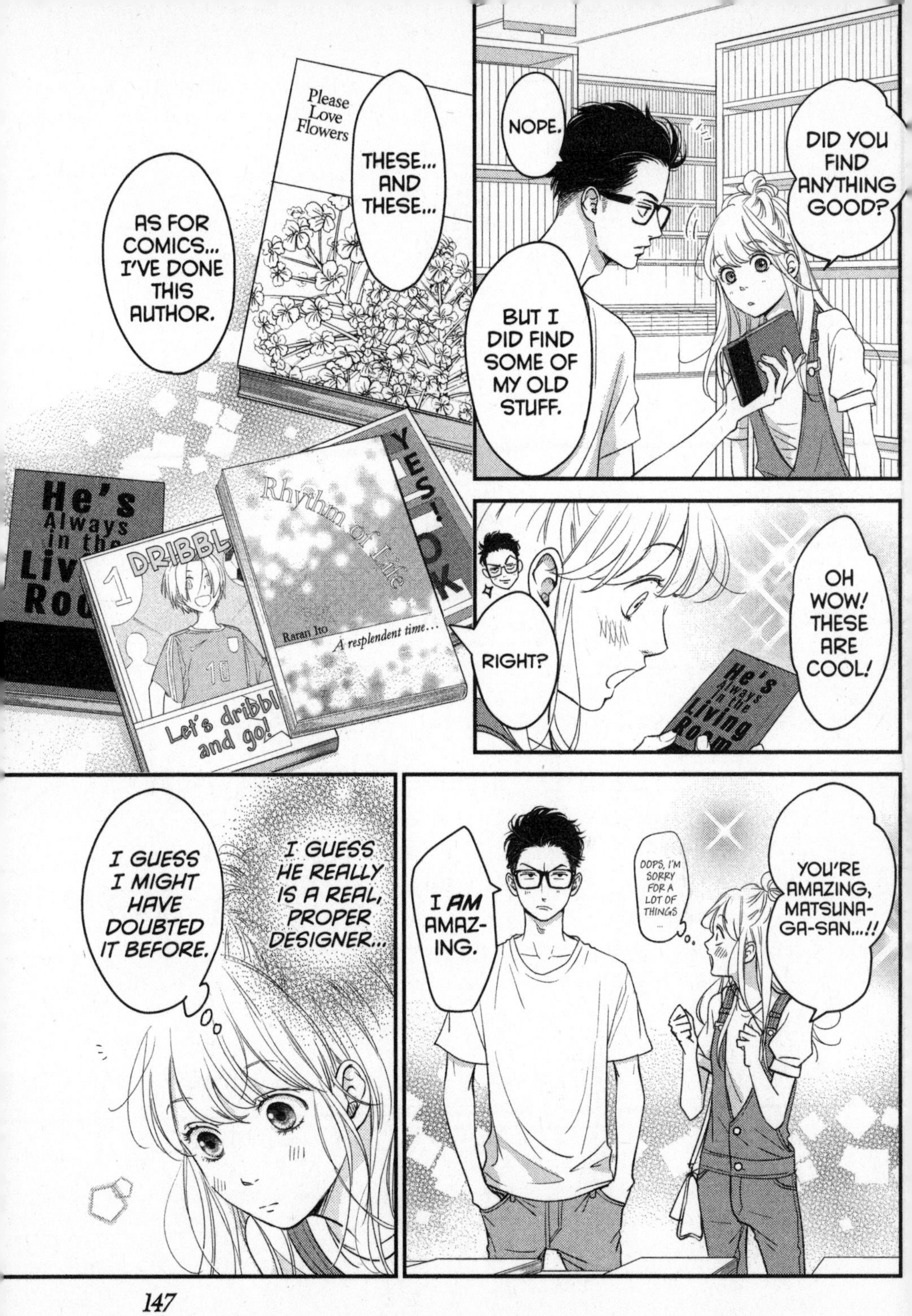
DID YOU FIND ANYTHING GOOD?
NOPE.
BUT I DID FIND SOME OF MY OLD STUFF.
OH WOW! THESE ARE COOL!
He's Always in the Living Room
RIGHT?
Please Love Flowers
THESE... AND THESE...
AS FOR COMICS... I'VE DONE THIS AUTHOR.
Rhythm of Life
Raran Ito
A resplendent time...
YOU'RE AMAZING, MATSUNAGA-SAN...!!
OOPS, I'M SORRY FOR A LOT OF THINGS...
I AM AMAZING.
I GUESS HE REALLY IS A REAL, PROPER DESIGNER...
I GUESS I MIGHT HAVE DOUBTED IT BEFORE.

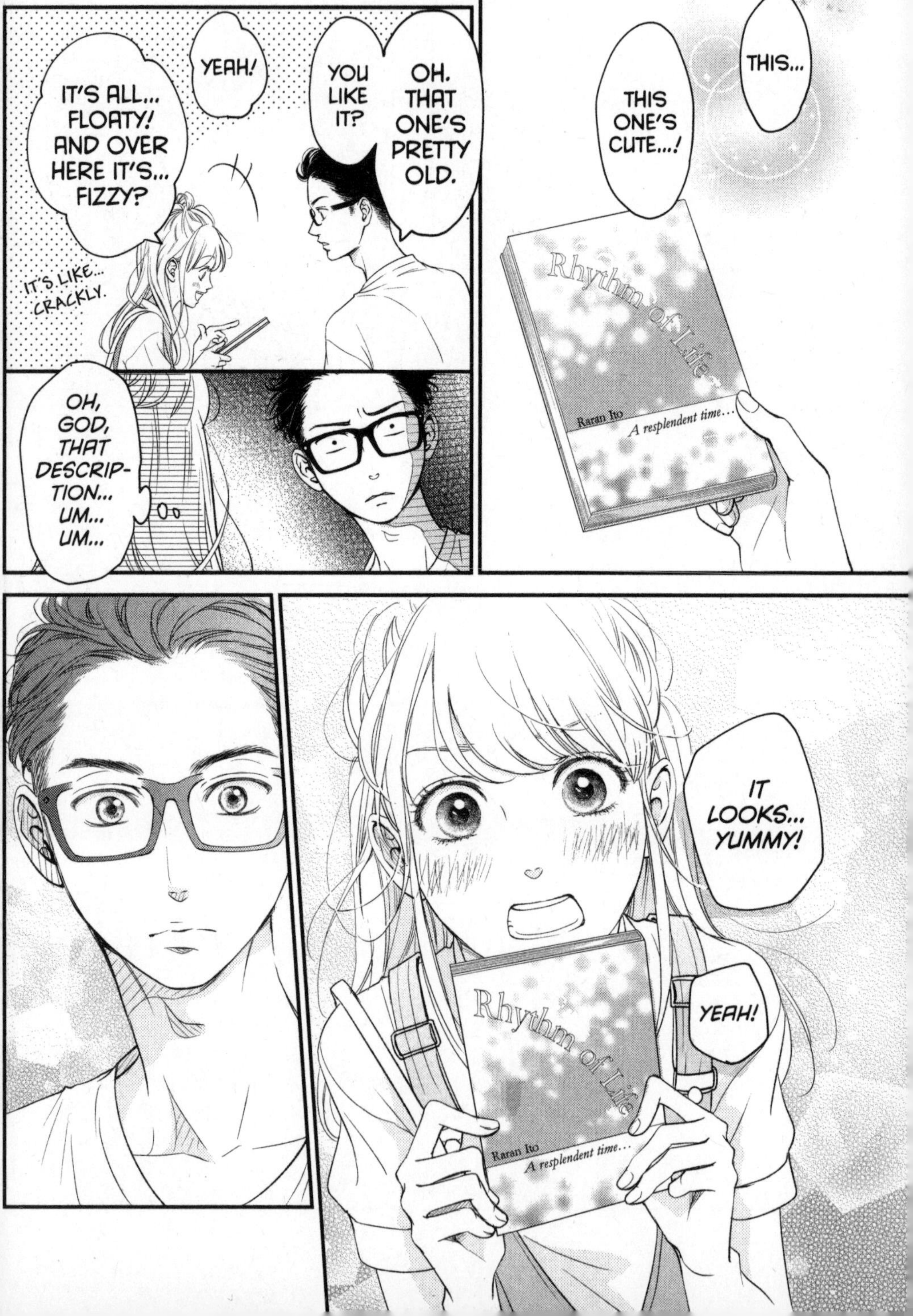
THIS...
THIS ONE'S CUTE...!
Rhythm of Life
Raran Ito
A resplendent time...
OH. THAT ONE'S PRETTY OLD.
YOU LIKE IT?
YEAH!
IT'S ALL... FLOATY! AND OVER HERE IT'S... FIZZY?
IT'S LIKE... CRACKLY.
OH, GOD, THAT DESCRIPTION... UM... UM...
IT LOOKS... YUMMY!
YEAH!
Rhythm of Life
Raran Ito
A resplendent time...

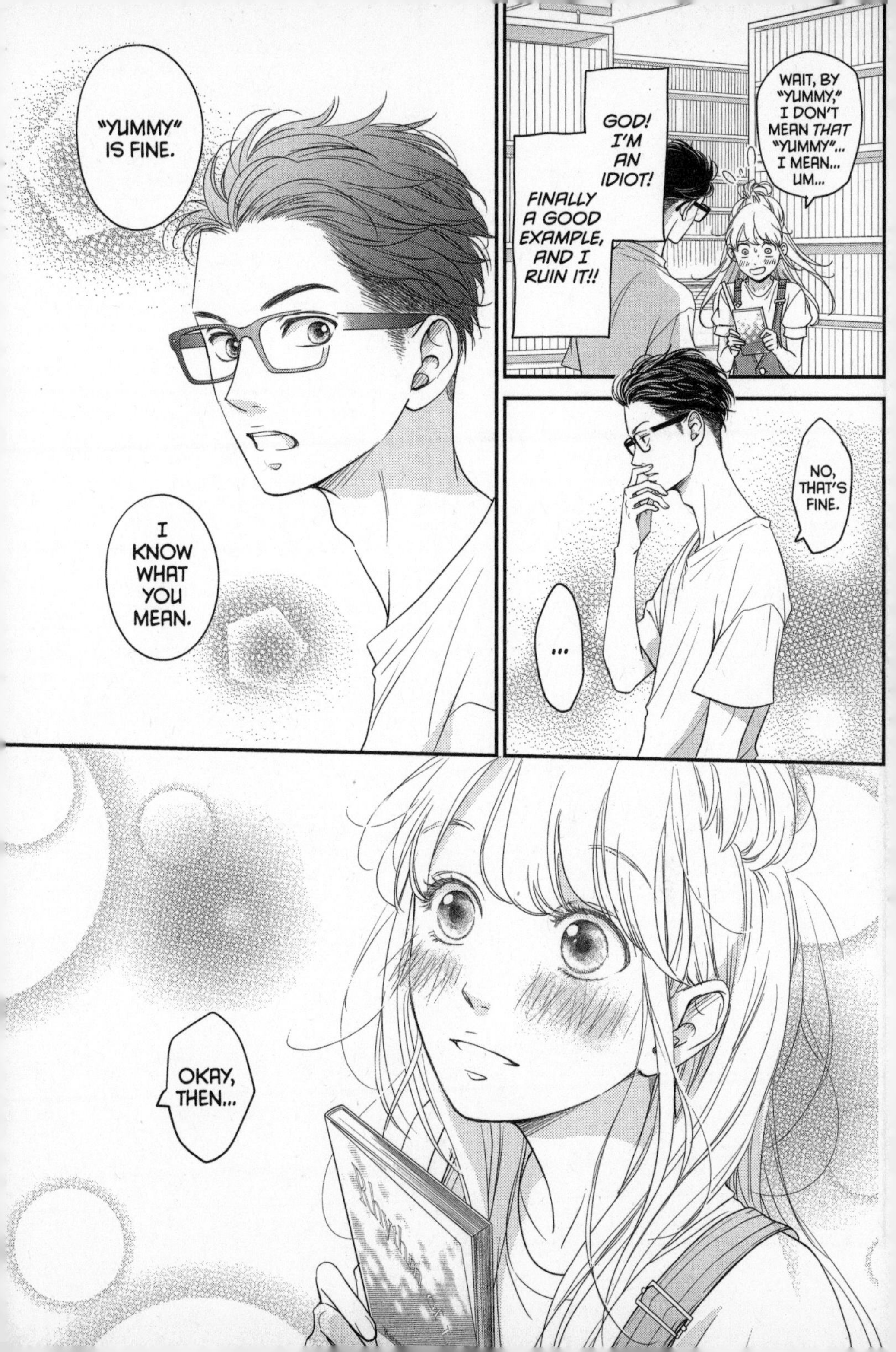
WAIT, BY "YUMMY," I DON'T MEAN *THAT* "YUMMY"... I MEAN... UM...
GOD! I'M AN IDIOT!
FINALLY A GOOD EXAMPLE, AND I RUIN IT!!
NO, THAT'S FINE.
...
"YUMMY" IS FINE.
I KNOW WHAT YOU MEAN.
OKAY, THEN...

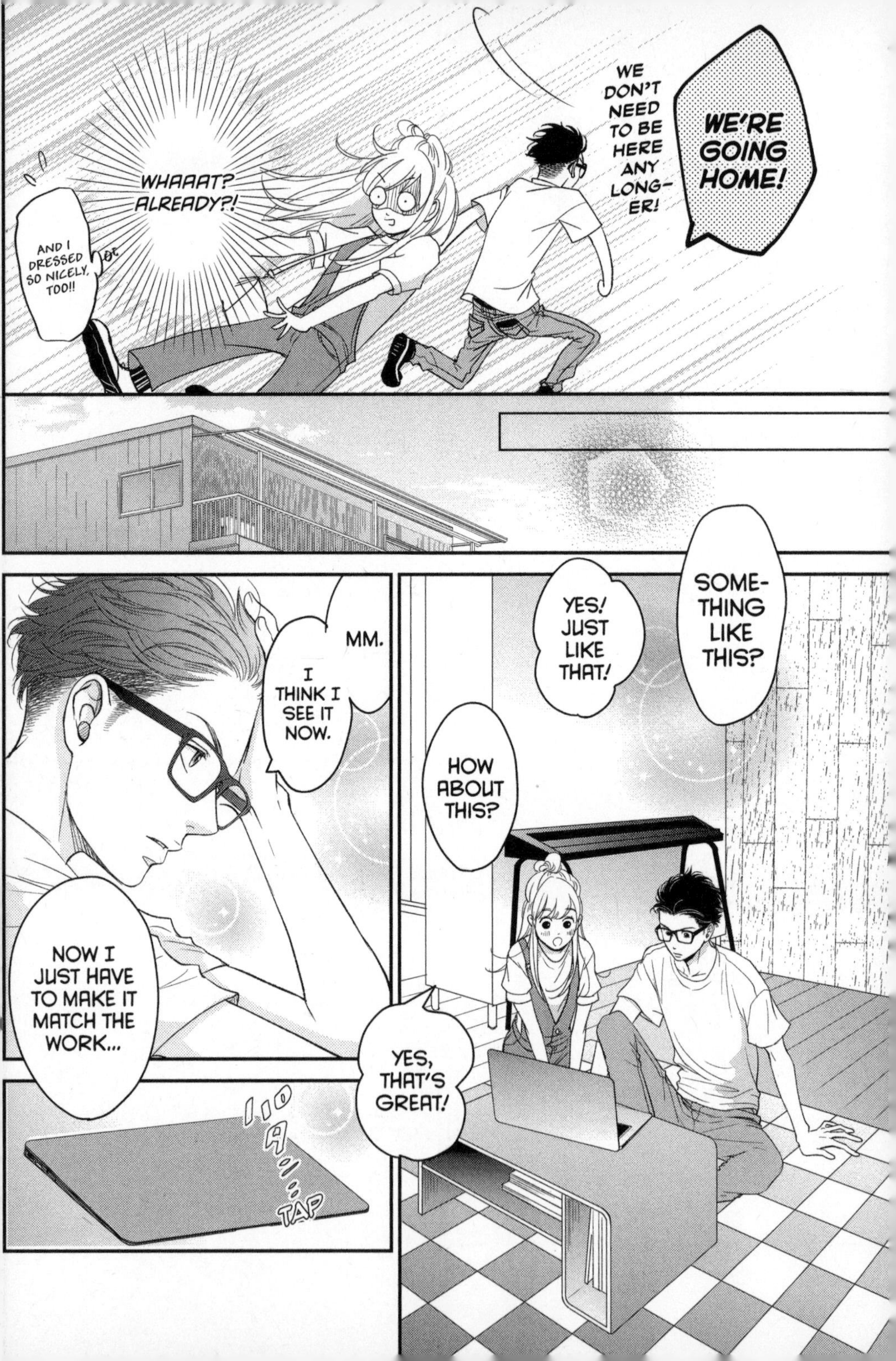
WE'RE GOING HOME!
WE DON'T NEED TO BE HERE ANY LONGER!
WHAAAT? ALREADY?!
AND I DRESSED SO NICELY, TOO!!
SOMETHING LIKE THIS?
YES! JUST LIKE THAT!
HOW ABOUT THIS?
YES, THAT'S GREAT!
MM.
I THINK I SEE IT NOW.
NOW I JUST HAVE TO MAKE IT MATCH THE WORK...
TAP

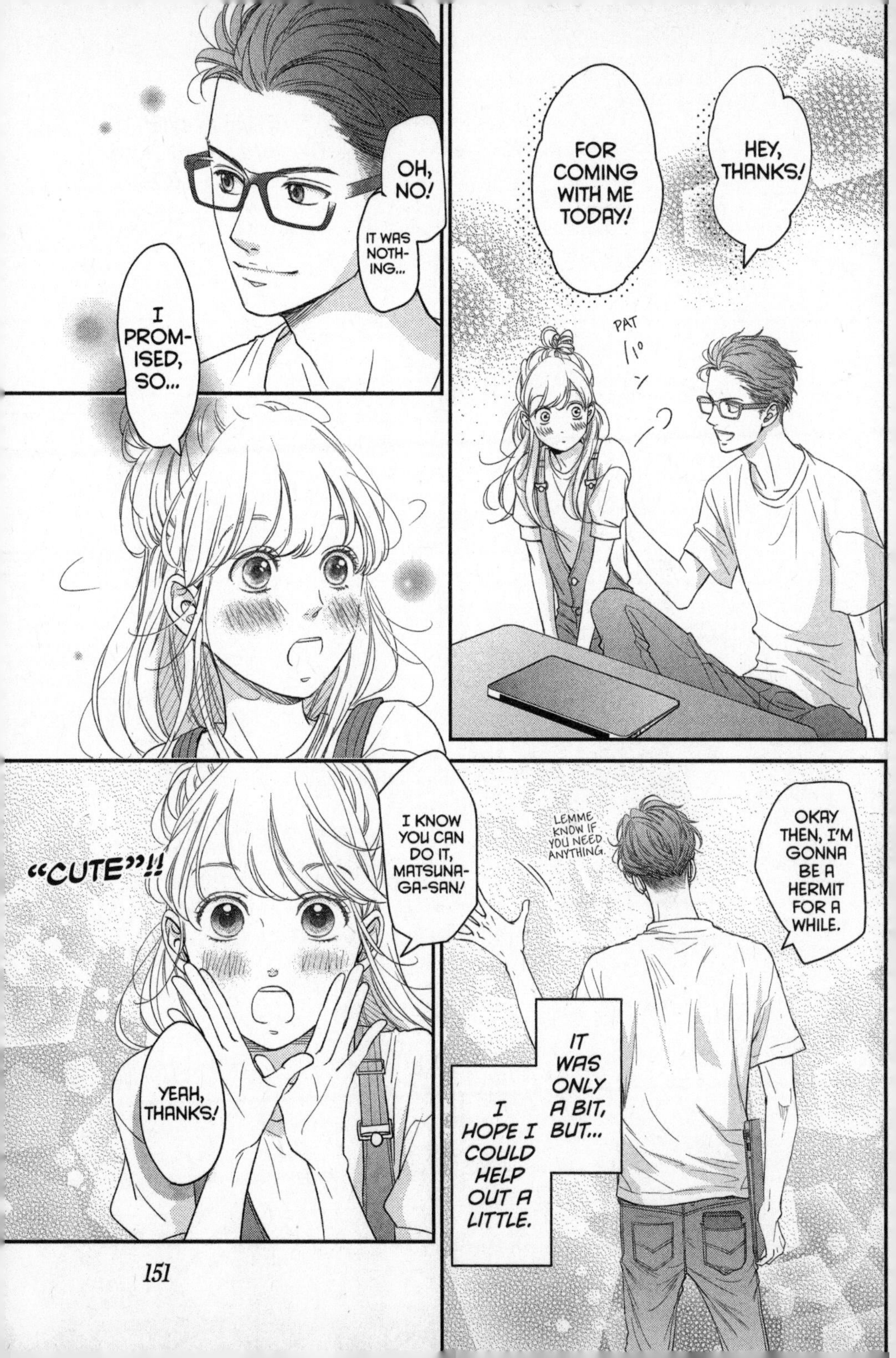
HEY, THANKS!
FOR COMING WITH ME TODAY!
PAT
OH, NO!
IT WAS NOTHING...
I PROMISED, SO...
OKAY THEN, I'M GONNA BE A HERMIT FOR A WHILE.
LEMME KNOW IF YOU NEED ANYTHING.
IT WAS ONLY A BIT, BUT...
I HOPE I COULD HELP OUT A LITTLE.
I KNOW YOU CAN DO IT, MATSUNAGA-SAN!
“CUTE”!!
YEAH, THANKS!

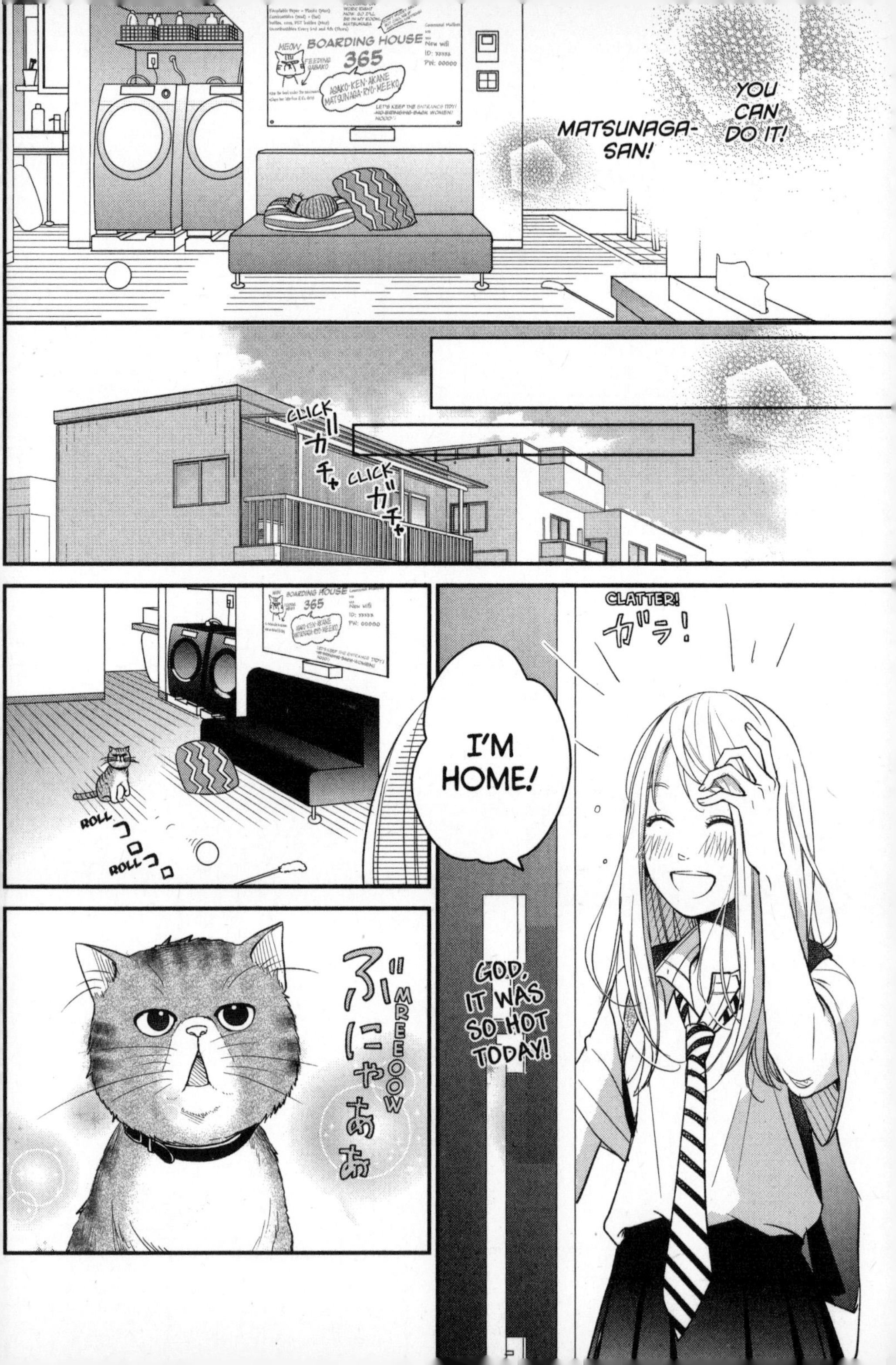
BOARDING HOUSE 365
MEOW
FEEDING GABAKO
AGAKO·KEN·AKANE MATSUNAGA·RYO·MEEKO
New wifi
ID: xxxxx
PW: 00000
LET'S KEEP THE ENTRANCE TIDY!
NO BRINGING BACK WOMEN!
NOOO!
YOU CAN DO IT!
MATSUNAGA-SAN!
CLICK ガチャ
CLICK ガチャ
CLATTER! ガラ!
I'M HOME!
GOD, IT WAS SO HOT TODAY!
ROLL コロ
ROLL コロ
MREEOOW ぶにゃあぁ

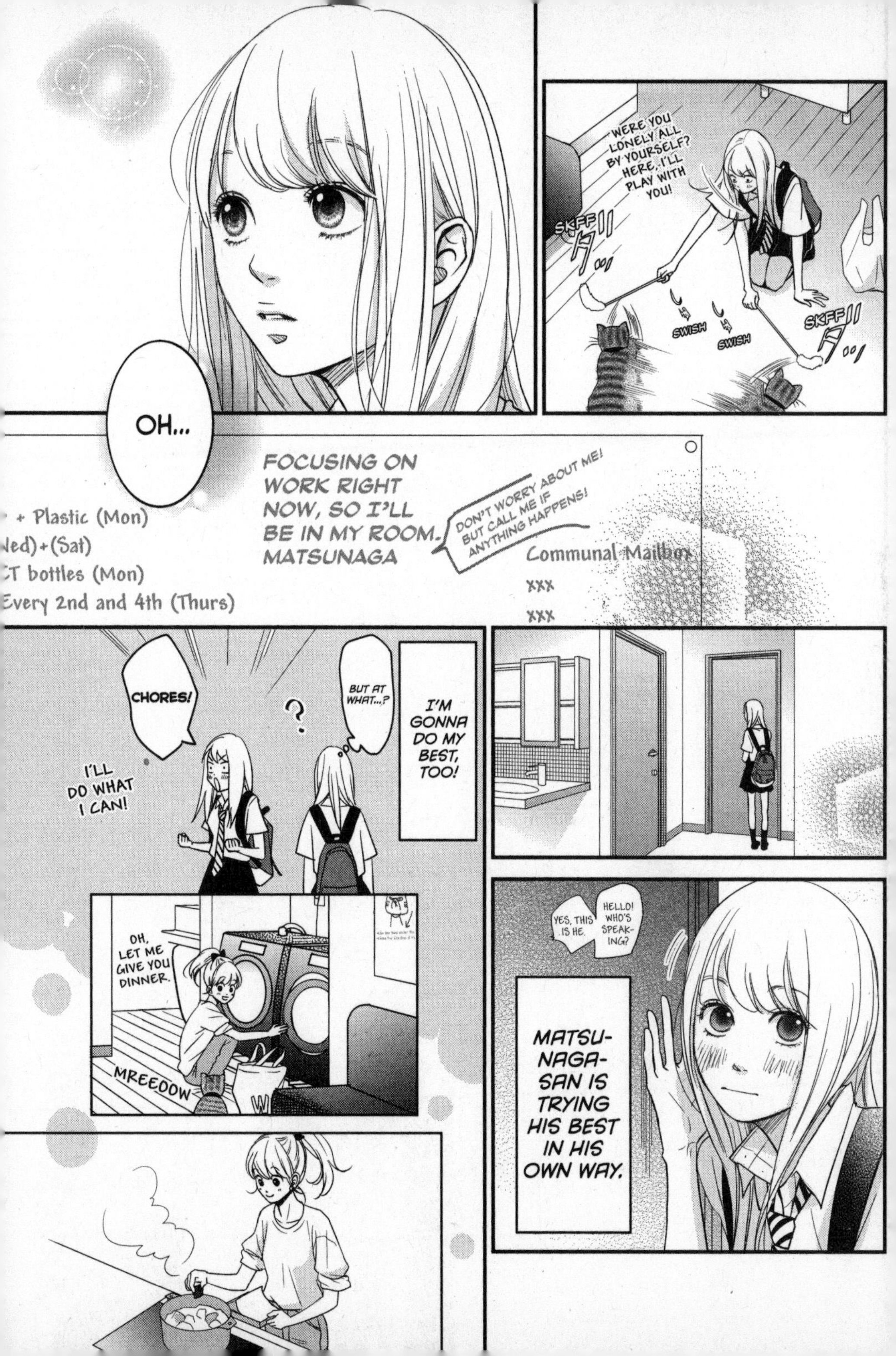
WERE YOU LONELY ALL BY YOURSELF? HERE, I'LL PLAY WITH YOU!
SKFF
SKFF
SWISH
SWISH
OH...
Communal Mailbox
xxx
xxx
DON'T WORRY ABOUT ME! BUT CALL ME IF ANYTHING HAPPENS!
FOCUSING ON WORK RIGHT NOW, SO I'LL BE IN MY ROOM. MATSUNAGA
+ Plastic (Mon)
Ved)+(Sat)
T bottles (Mon)
Every 2nd and 4th (Thurs)
HELLO! WHO'S SPEAK-ING?
YES, THIS IS HE.
MATSU-NAGA-SAN IS TRYING HIS BEST IN HIS OWN WAY.
I'M GONNA DO MY BEST, TOO!
BUT AT WHAT...?
?
CHORES!
I'LL DO WHAT I CAN!
OH, LET ME GIVE YOU DINNER.
MREEOOW

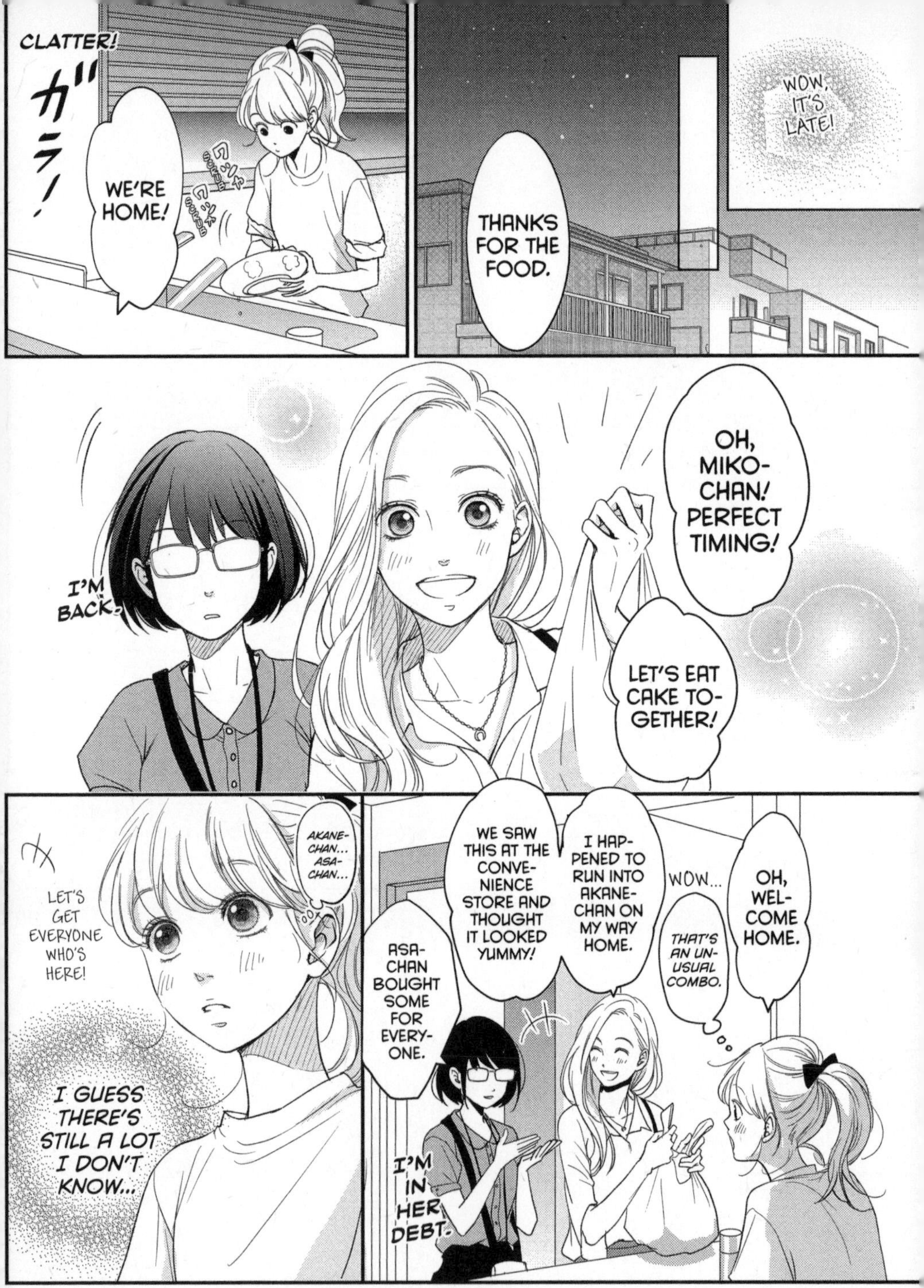
WOW, IT'S LATE!
THANKS FOR THE FOOD.
CLATTER!
ガラ!
WE'RE HOME!
OH, MIKO-CHAN! PERFECT TIMING!
LET'S EAT CAKE TO-GETHER!
I'M BACK.
OH, WEL-COME HOME.
WOW...
THAT'S AN UN-USUAL COMBO.
I HAP-PENED TO RUN INTO AKANE-CHAN ON MY WAY HOME.
WE SAW THIS AT THE CONVE-NIENCE STORE AND THOUGHT IT LOOKED YUMMY!
ASA-CHAN BOUGHT SOME FOR EVERY-ONE.
I'M IN HER DEBT.
AKANE-CHAN... ASA-CHAN...
LET'S GET EVERYONE WHO'S HERE!
I GUESS THERE'S STILL A LOT I DON'T KNOW...

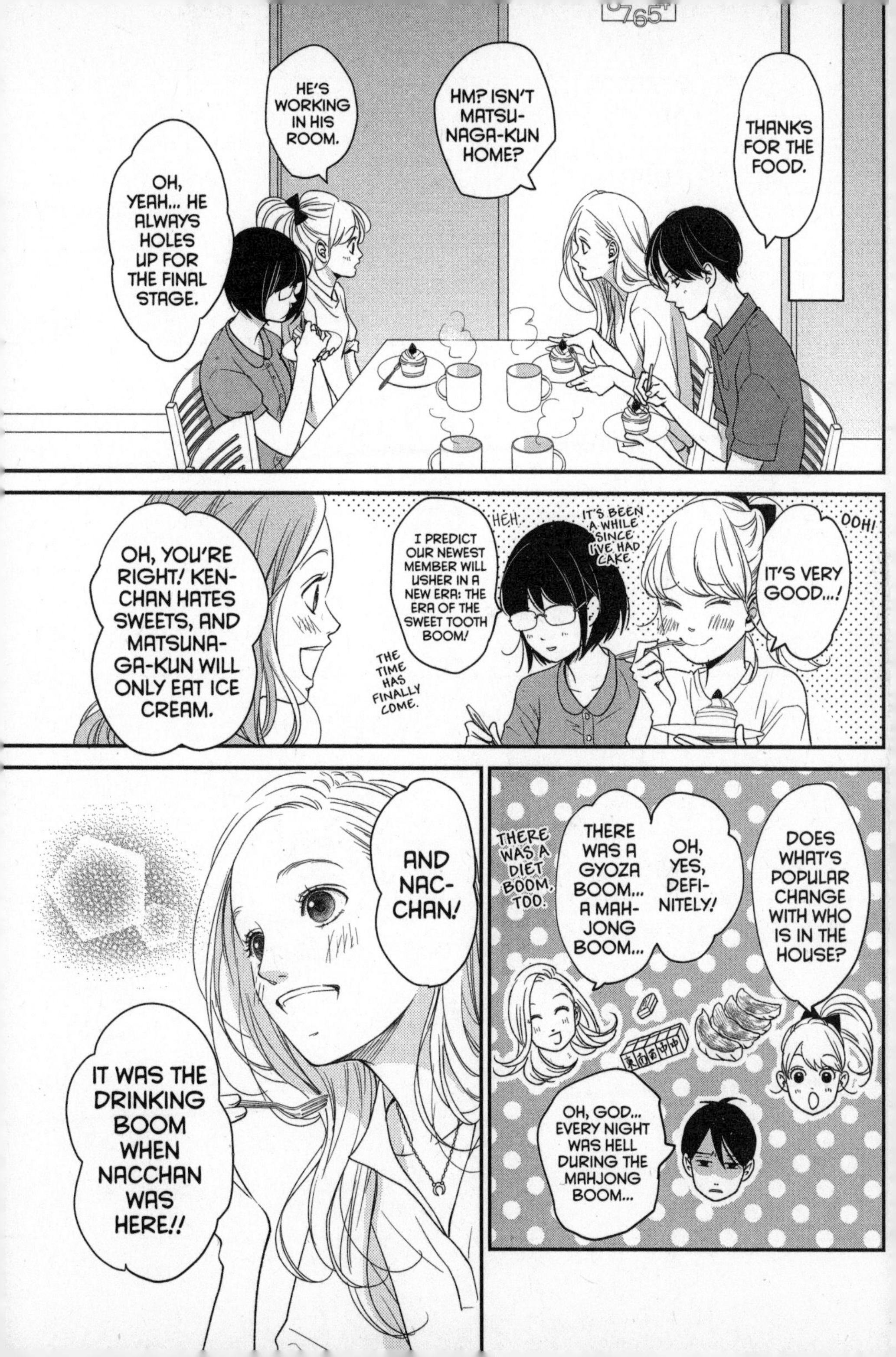
THANKS FOR THE FOOD.
HM? ISN'T MATSU-NAGA-KUN HOME?
HE'S WORKING IN HIS ROOM.
OH, YEAH... HE ALWAYS HOLES UP FOR THE FINAL STAGE.
OOH!
IT'S VERY GOOD...!
IT'S BEEN A WHILE SINCE I'VE HAD CAKE.
HEH.
I PREDICT OUR NEWEST MEMBER WILL USHER IN A NEW ERA: THE ERA OF THE SWEET TOOTH BOOM!
THE TIME HAS FINALLY COME.
OH, YOU'RE RIGHT! KEN-CHAN HATES SWEETS, AND MATSUNA-GA-KUN WILL ONLY EAT ICE CREAM.
DOES WHAT'S POPULAR CHANGE WITH WHO IS IN THE HOUSE?
OH, YES, DEFI-NITELY!
THERE WAS A GYOZA BOOM... A MAH-JONG BOOM...
THERE WAS A DIET BOOM, TOO.
OH, GOD... EVERY NIGHT WAS HELL DURING THE MAHJONG BOOM...
AND NAC-CHAN!
IT WAS THE DRINKING BOOM WHEN NACCHAN WAS HERE!!

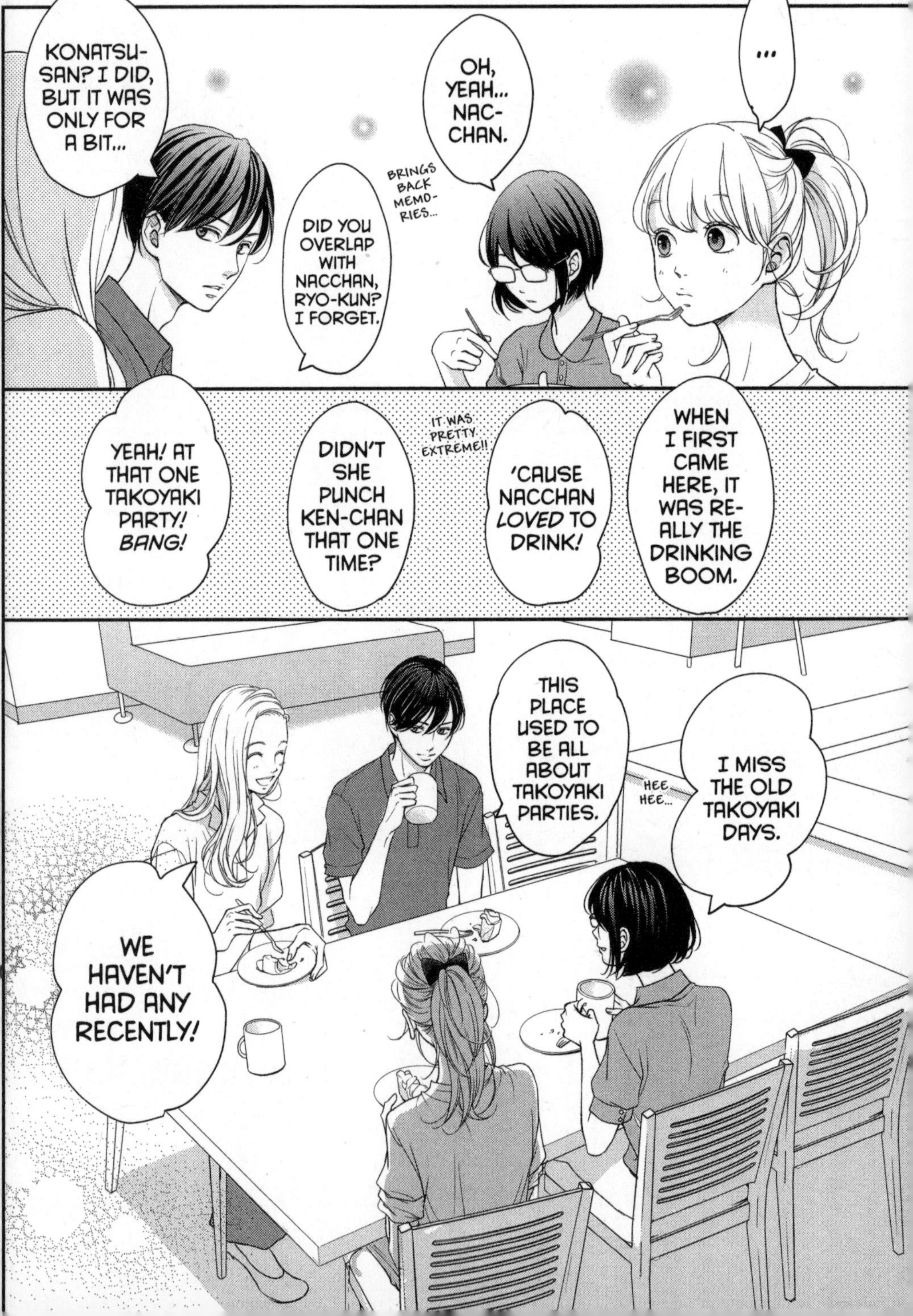
...
OH, YEAH... NACCHAN.
BRINGS BACK MEMORIES...
DID YOU OVERLAP WITH NACCHAN, RYO-KUN? I FORGET.
KONATSU-SAN? I DID, BUT IT WAS ONLY FOR A BIT...
WHEN I FIRST CAME HERE, IT WAS REALLY THE DRINKING BOOM.
'CAUSE NACCHAN *LOVED* TO DRINK!
IT WAS PRETTY EXTREME!!
DIDN'T SHE PUNCH KEN-CHAN THAT ONE TIME?
YEAH! AT THAT ONE TAKOYAKI PARTY! *BANG!*
I MISS THE OLD TAKOYAKI DAYS.
HEE HEE...
THIS PLACE USED TO BE ALL ABOUT TAKOYAKI PARTIES.
WE HAVEN'T HAD ANY RECENTLY!

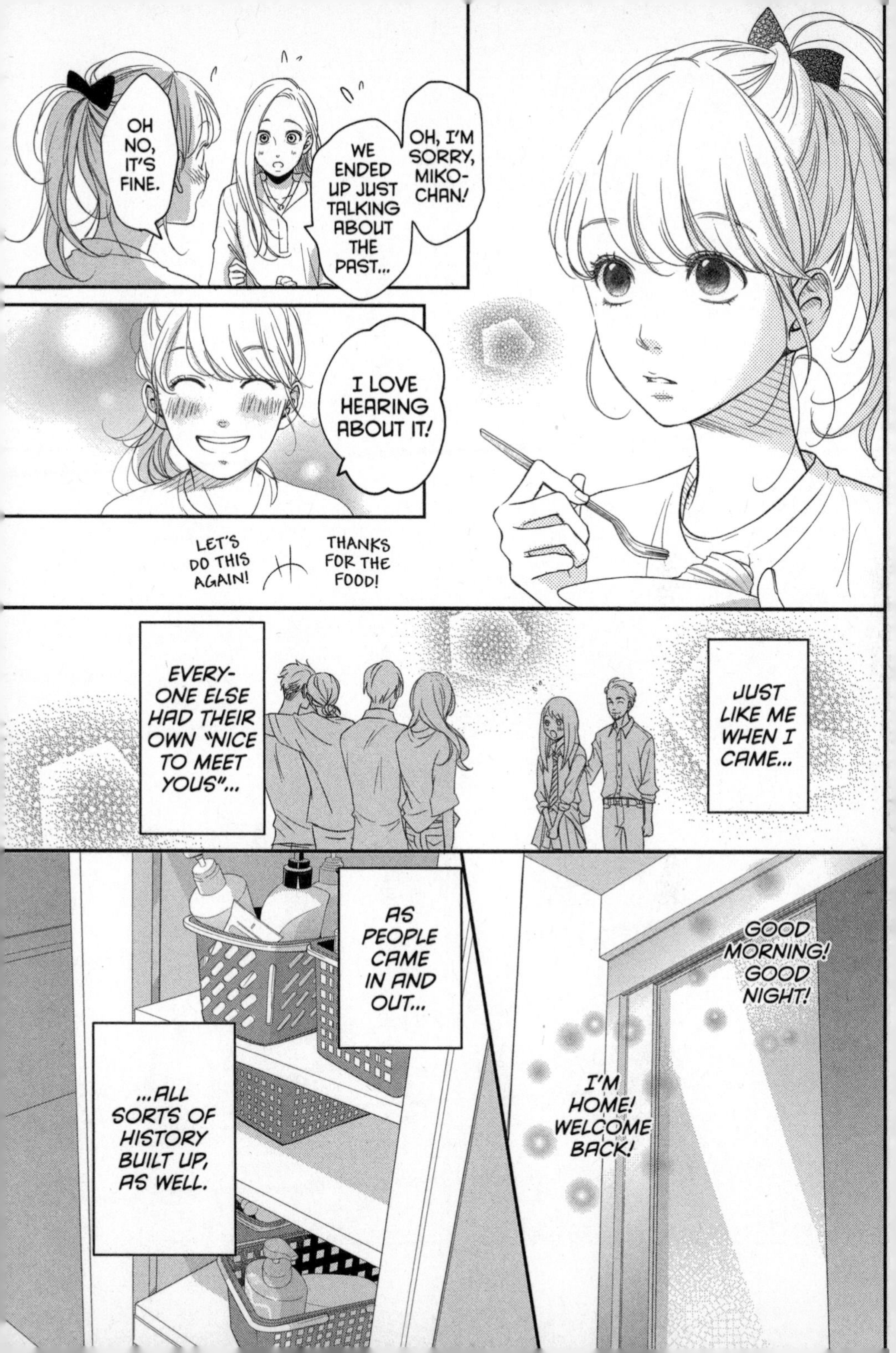
OH, I'M SORRY, MIKO-CHAN!
WE ENDED UP JUST TALKING ABOUT THE PAST...
OH NO, IT'S FINE.
I LOVE HEARING ABOUT IT!
THANKS FOR THE FOOD!
LET'S DO THIS AGAIN!
JUST LIKE ME WHEN I CAME...
EVERYONE ELSE HAD THEIR OWN "NICE TO MEET YOUS"...
GOOD MORNING! GOOD NIGHT!
I'M HOME! WELCOME BACK!
AS PEOPLE CAME IN AND OUT...
...ALL SORTS OF HISTORY BUILT UP, AS WELL.

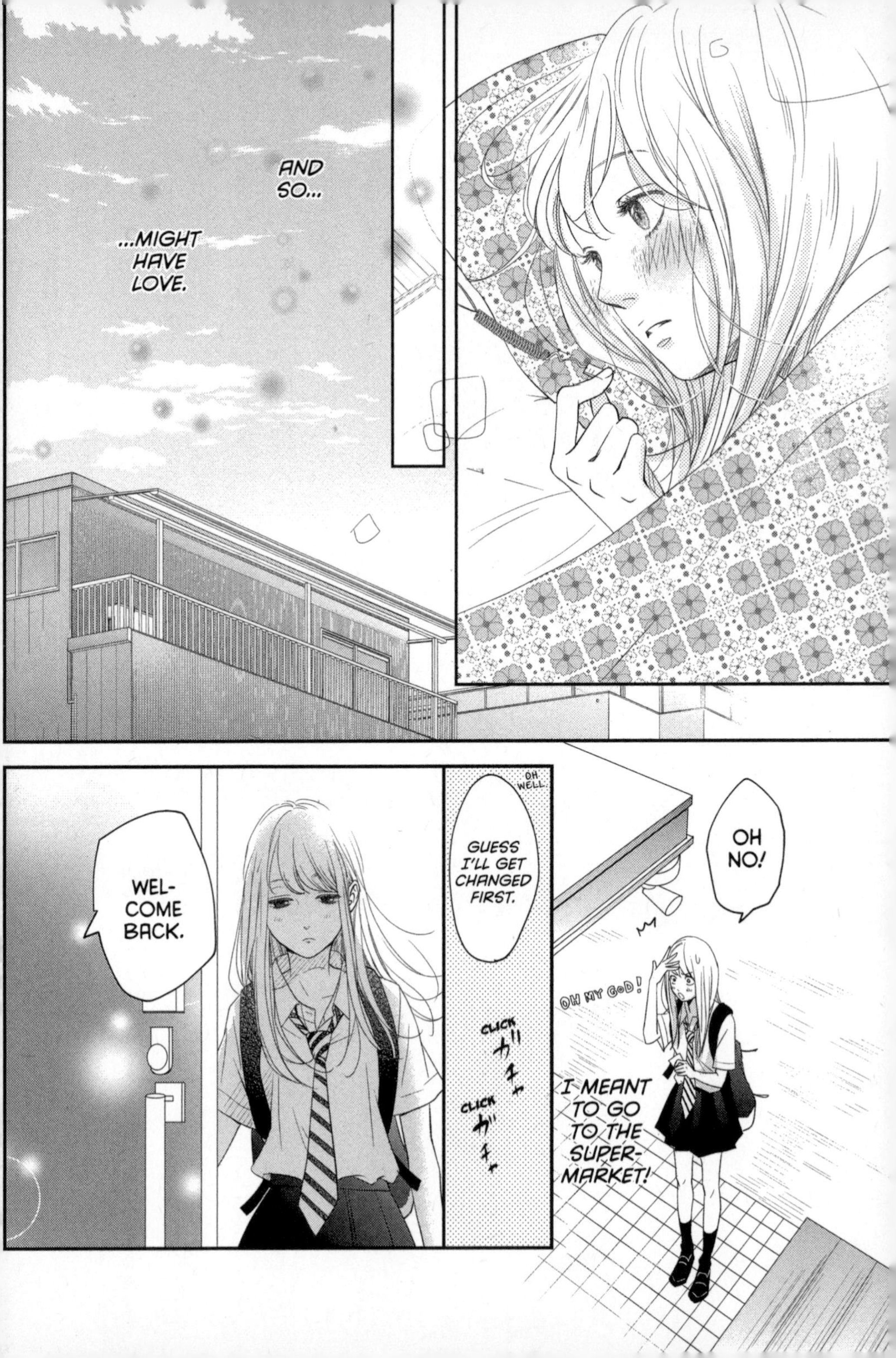
AND SO...
...MIGHT HAVE LOVE.
OH NO!
OH MY GOD!
I MEANT TO GO TO THE SUPER-MARKET!
OH WELL.
GUESS I'LL GET CHANGED FIRST.
CLICK ガチャ
CLICK ガチャ
WEL-COME BACK.

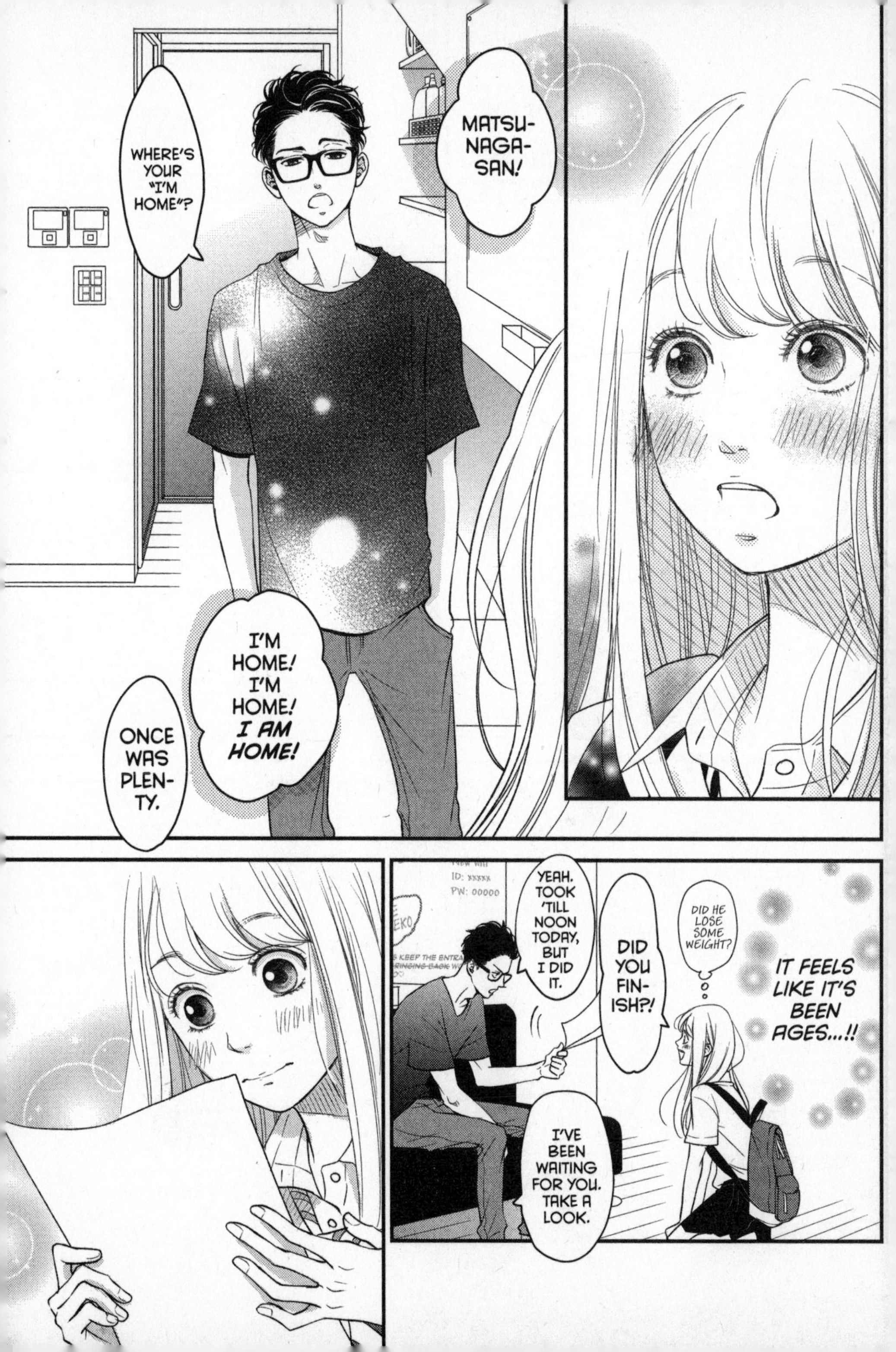
MATSU-NAGA-SAN!
WHERE'S YOUR "I'M HOME"?
I'M HOME! I'M HOME! *I AM HOME!*
ONCE WAS PLENTY.
IT FEELS LIKE IT'S BEEN AGES...!!
DID HE LOSE SOME WEIGHT?
DID YOU FIN-ISH?!
ID: xxxxx
PW: 00000
YEAH. TOOK 'TILL NOON TODAY, BUT I DID IT.
I'VE BEEN WAITING FOR YOU. TAKE A LOOK.

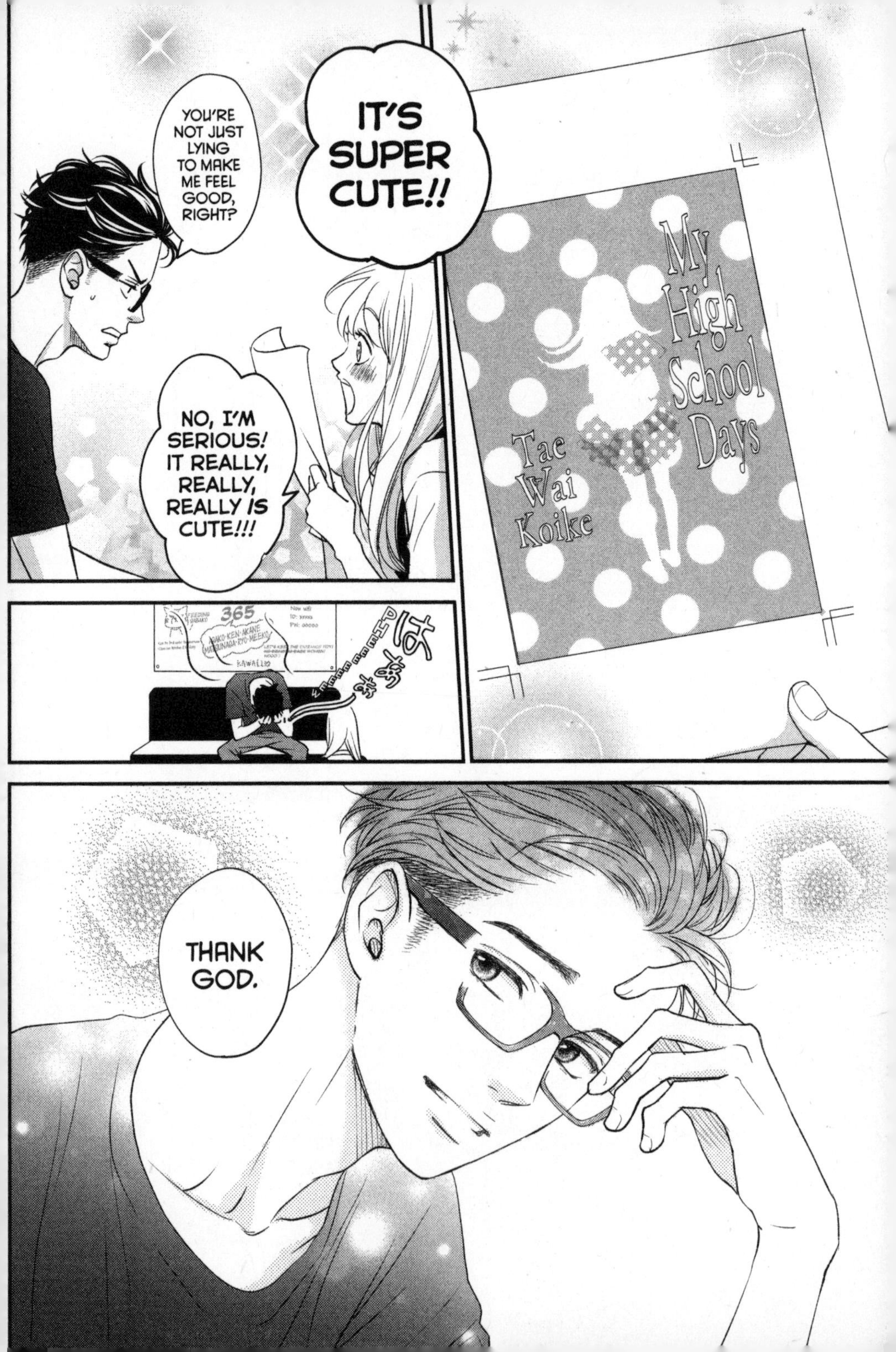
My High School Days
Tae Wai Koike
IT'S SUPER CUTE!!
YOU'RE NOT JUST LYING TO MAKE ME FEEL GOOD, RIGHT?
NO, I'M SERIOUS! IT REALLY, REALLY, REALLY IS CUTE!!!
365
THANK GOD.

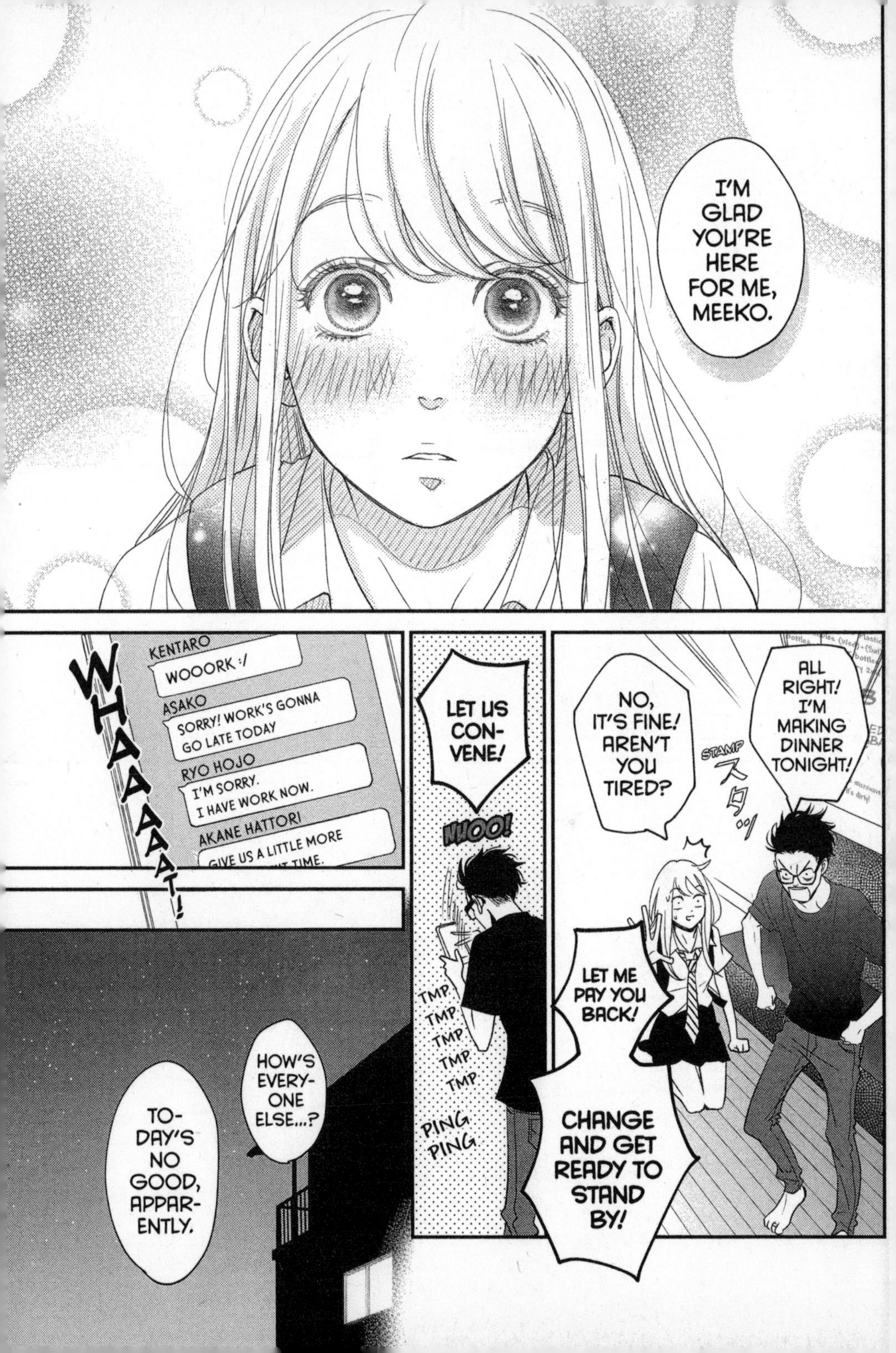
I'M GLAD YOU'RE HERE FOR ME, MEEKO.
ALL RIGHT! I'M MAKING DINNER TONIGHT!
STAMP
NO, IT'S FINE! AREN'T YOU TIRED?
LET ME PAY YOU BACK!
CHANGE AND GET READY TO STAND BY!
LET US CON-VENE!
WHOO!
TMP TMP TMP TMP TMP
PING PING
WHAAAAAT!
KENTARO
WOOORK :/
ASAKO
SORRY! WORK'S GONNA GO LATE TODAY
RYO HOJO
I'M SORRY. I HAVE WORK NOW.
AKANE HATTORI
HOW'S EVERY-ONE ELSE...?
TO-DAY'S NO GOOD, APPAR-ENTLY.

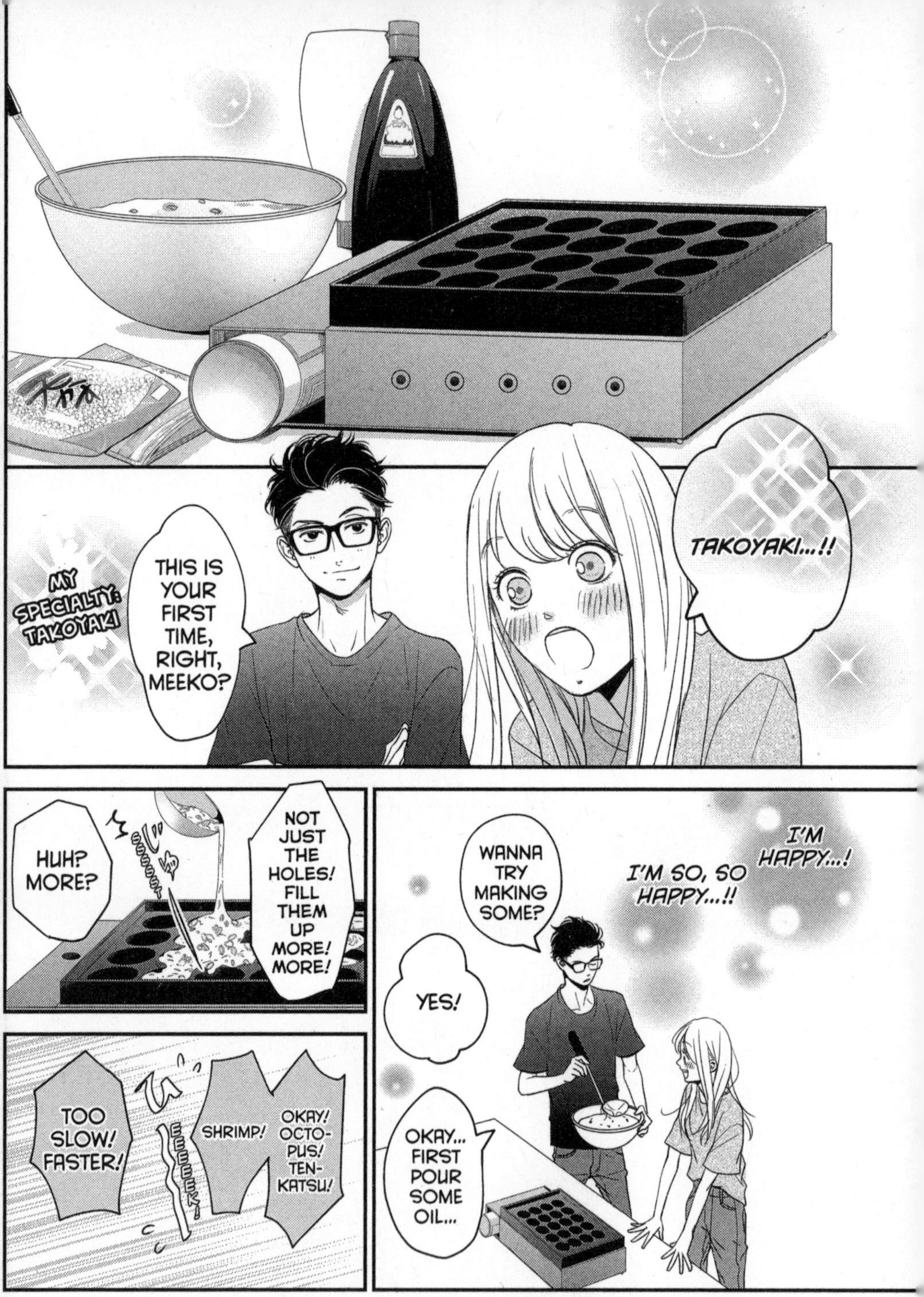
TAKOYAKI...!!
THIS IS YOUR FIRST TIME, RIGHT, MEEKO?
MY SPECIALTY: TAKOYAKI
I'M HAPPY...!
I'M SO, SO HAPPY...!!
WANNA TRY MAKING SOME?
YES!
OKAY... FIRST POUR SOME OIL...
NOT JUST THE HOLES! FILL THEM UP MORE! MORE!
SSSSST
HUH? MORE?
OKAY! OCTO-PUS! TEN-KATSU!
SHRIMP!
EEEEEEK!
TOO SLOW! FASTER!

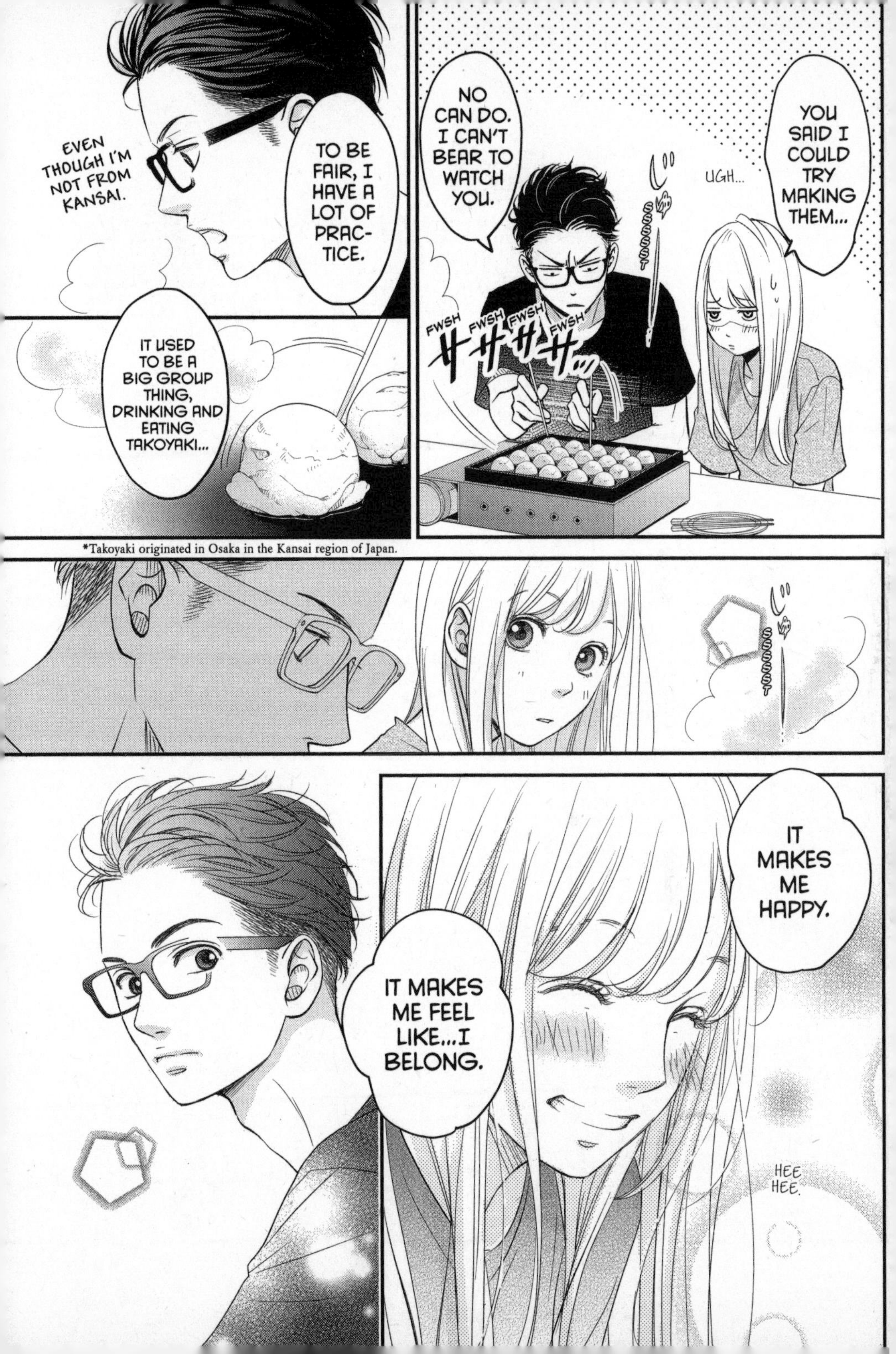
YOU SAID I COULD TRY MAKING THEM...
UGH...
NO CAN DO. I CAN'T BEAR TO WATCH YOU.
SSSSST
FWSH FWSH FWSH FWSH
TO BE FAIR, I HAVE A LOT OF PRAC-TICE.
EVEN THOUGH I'M NOT FROM KANSAI.
IT USED TO BE A BIG GROUP THING, DRINKING AND EATING TAKOYAKI...
SSSSST
IT MAKES ME HAPPY.
HEE HEE.
IT MAKES ME FEEL LIKE...I BELONG.

*Takoyaki originated in Osaka in the Kansai region of Japan.

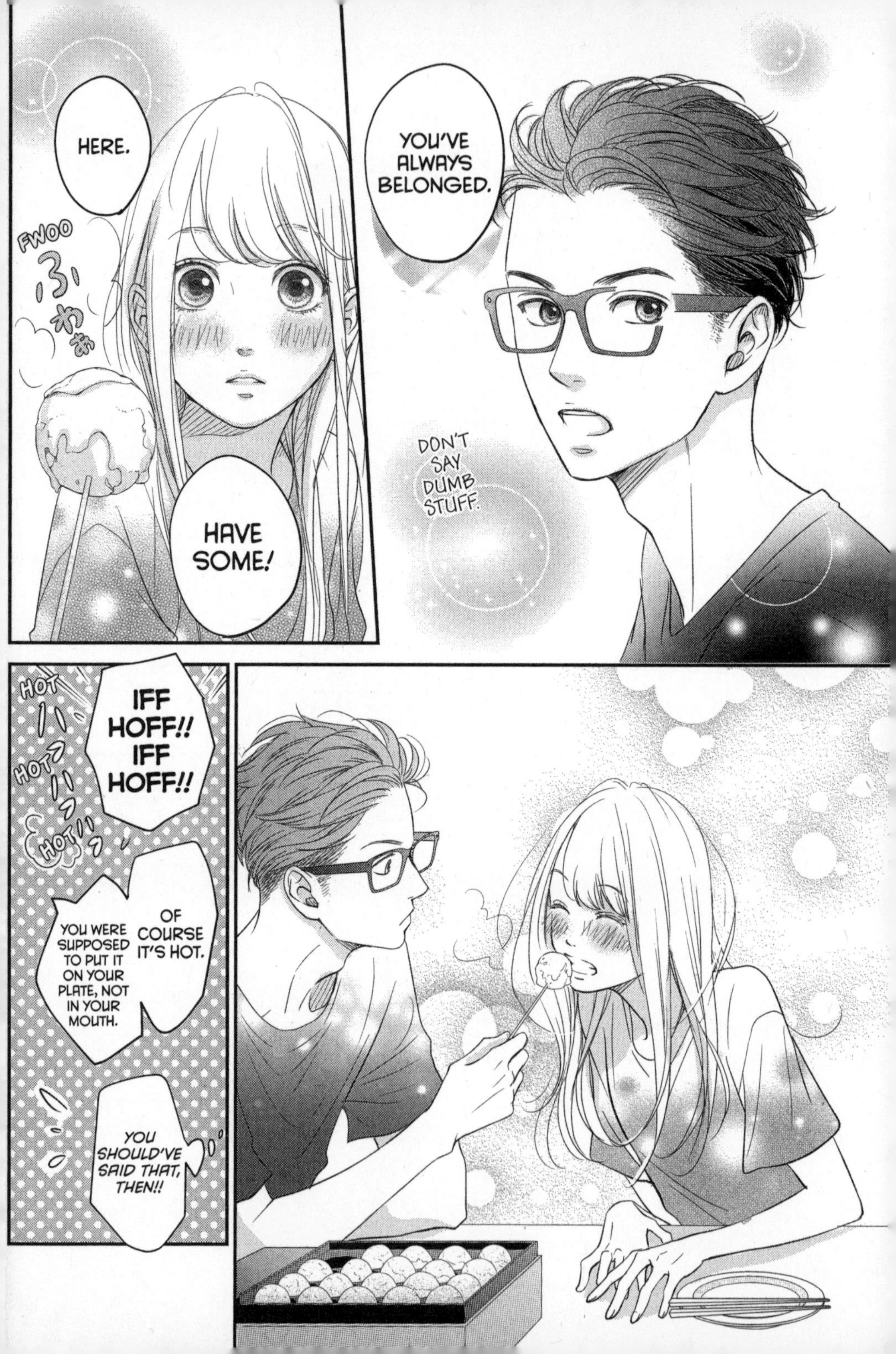
YOU'VE ALWAYS BELONGED.
DON'T SAY DUMB STUFF.
HERE.
FWOO
HAVE SOME!
HOT
HOT
HOT
IFF HOFF!! IFF HOFF!!
OF COURSE IT'S HOT.
YOU WERE SUPPOSED TO PUT IT ON YOUR PLATE, NOT IN YOUR MOUTH.
YOU SHOULD'VE SAID THAT, THEN!!

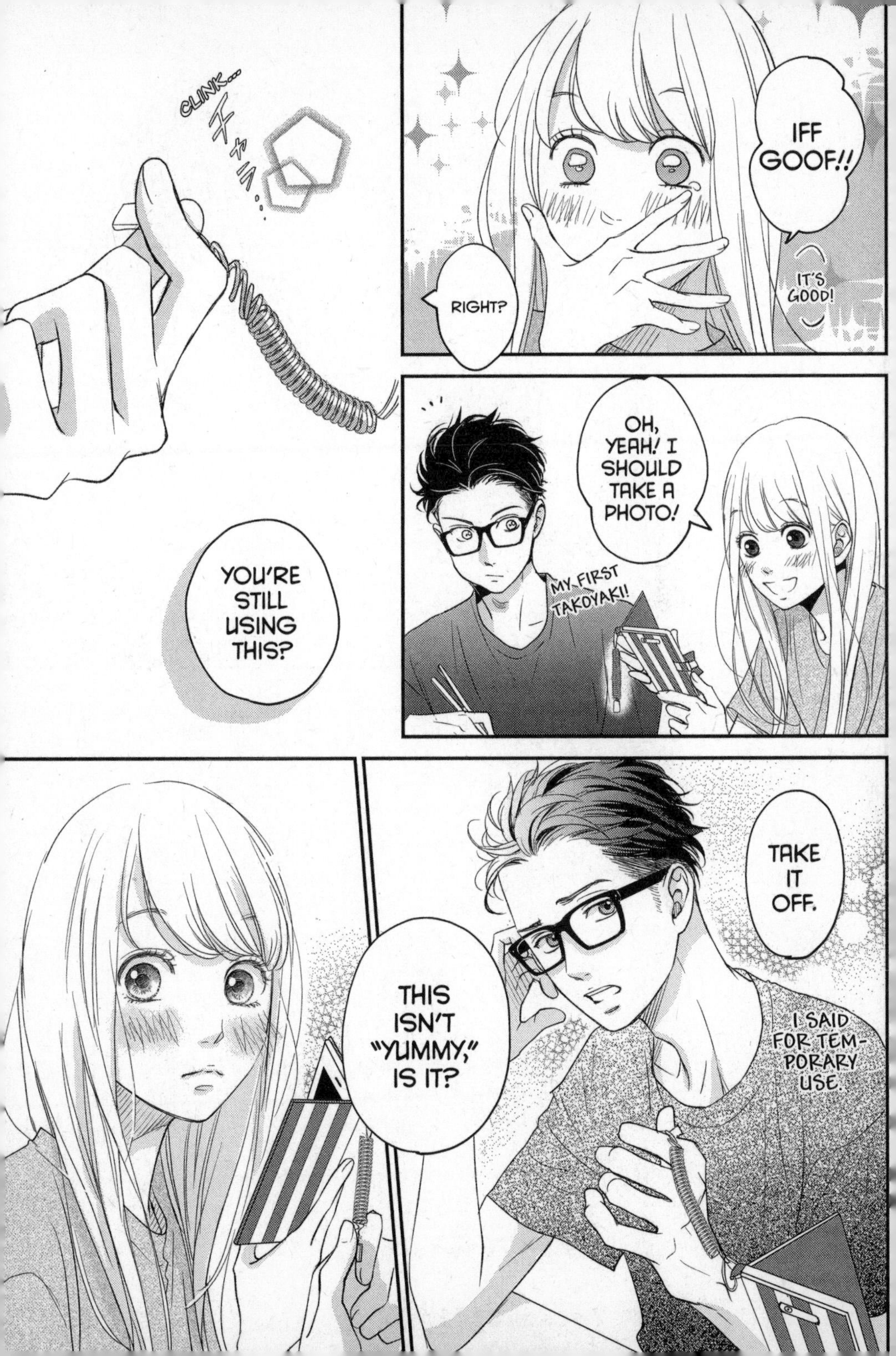
IFF GOOF!!
IT'S GOOD!
RIGHT?
OH, YEAH! I SHOULD TAKE A PHOTO!
MY FIRST TAKOYAKI!
CLINK...
チャラ…
YOU'RE STILL USING THIS?
TAKE IT OFF.
I SAID FOR TEMPORARY USE.
THIS ISN'T "YUMMY," IS IT?

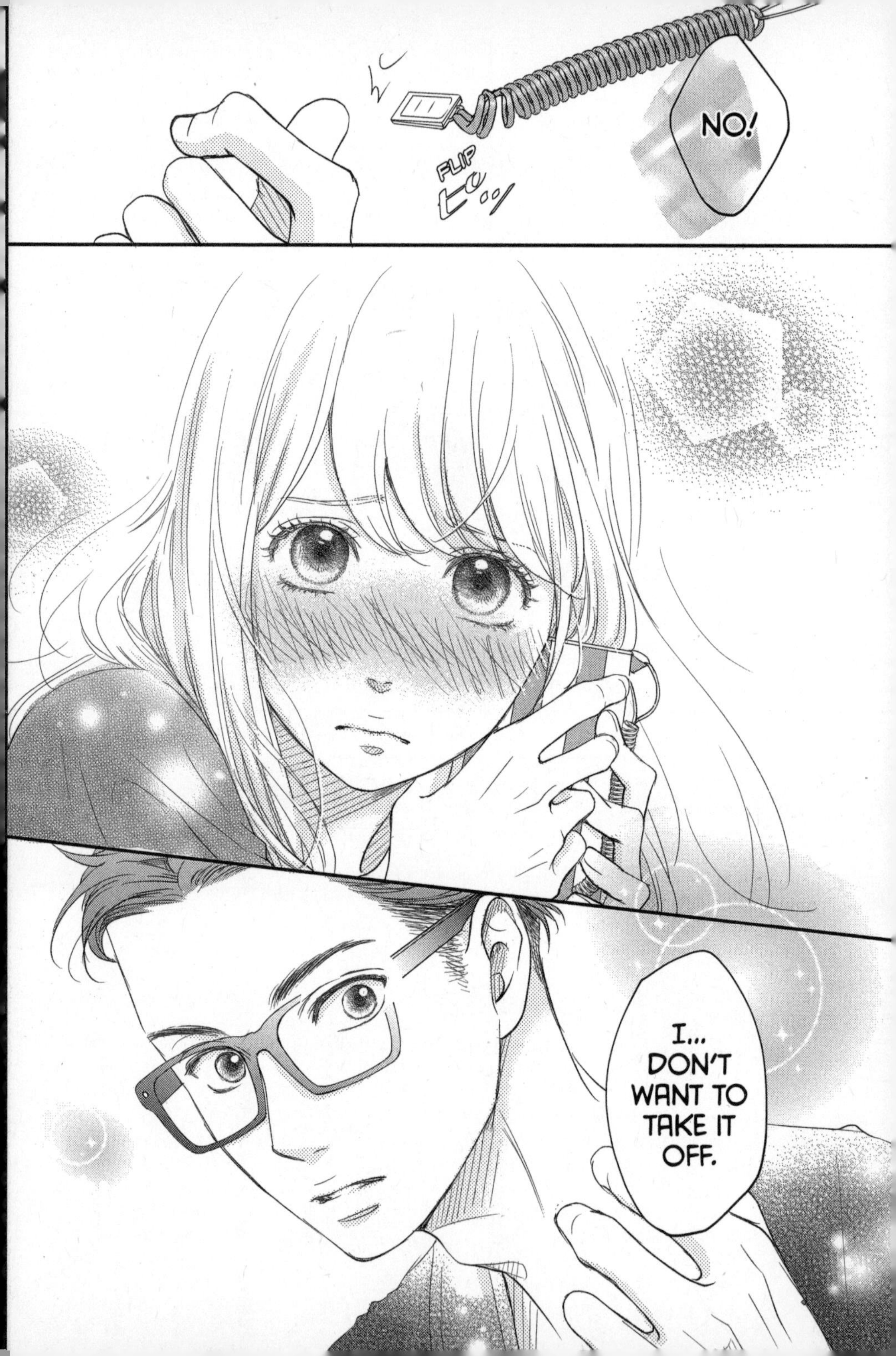
NO!
FLIP
I... DON'T WANT TO TAKE IT OFF.

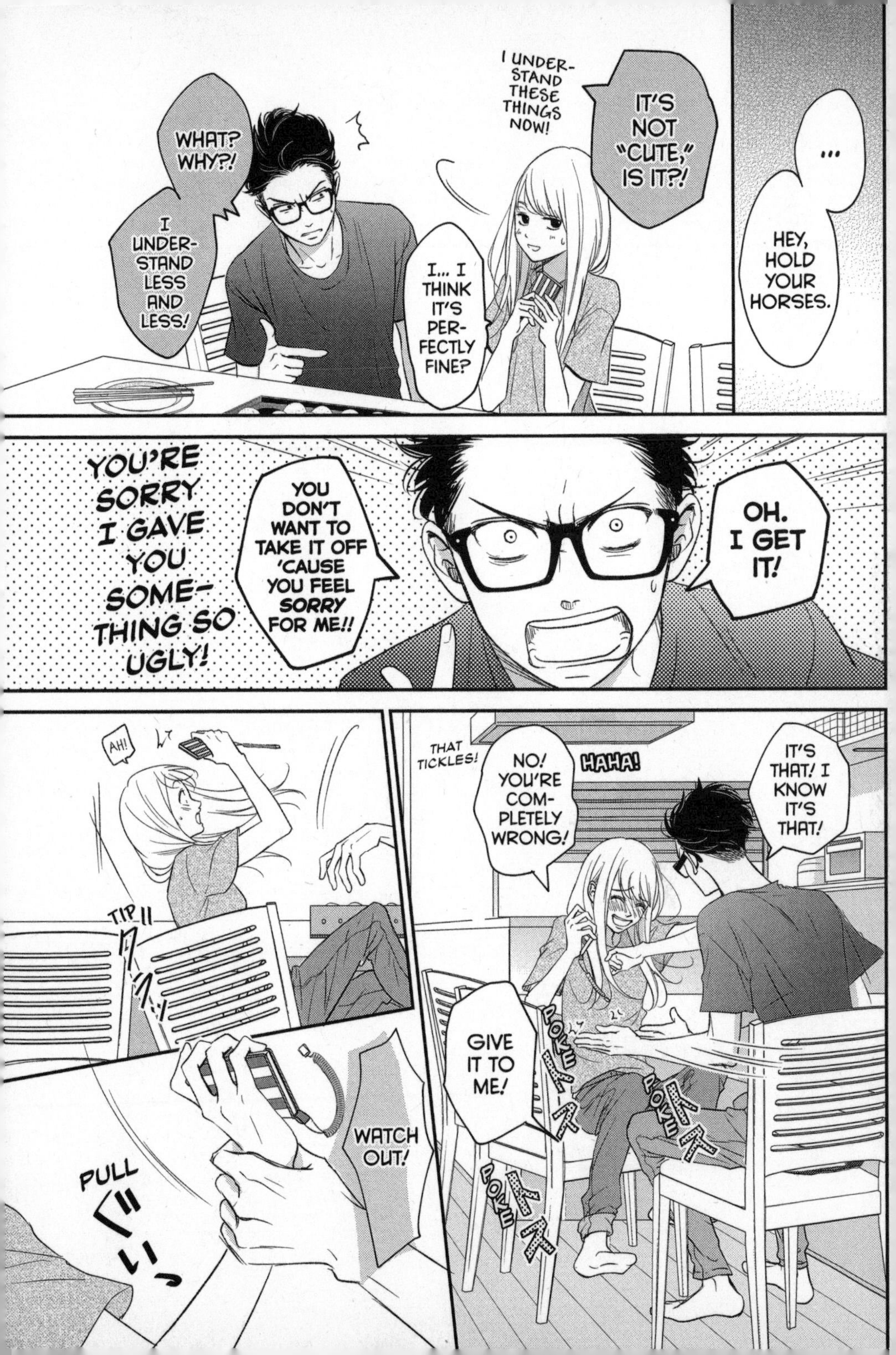
...
HEY, HOLD YOUR HORSES.
IT'S NOT "CUTE," IS IT?!
I UNDERSTAND THESE THINGS NOW!
I... I THINK IT'S PERFECTLY FINE?
WHAT? WHY?!
I UNDERSTAND LESS AND LESS!
OH. I GET IT!
YOU DON'T WANT TO TAKE IT OFF 'CAUSE YOU FEEL SORRY FOR ME!!
YOU'RE SORRY I GAVE YOU SOMETHING SO UGLY!
IT'S THAT! I KNOW IT'S THAT!
HAHA!
NO! YOU'RE COMPLETELY WRONG!
THAT TICKLES!
GIVE IT TO ME!
POKE
POKE
POKE
AH!
TIP!!
WATCH OUT!
PULL

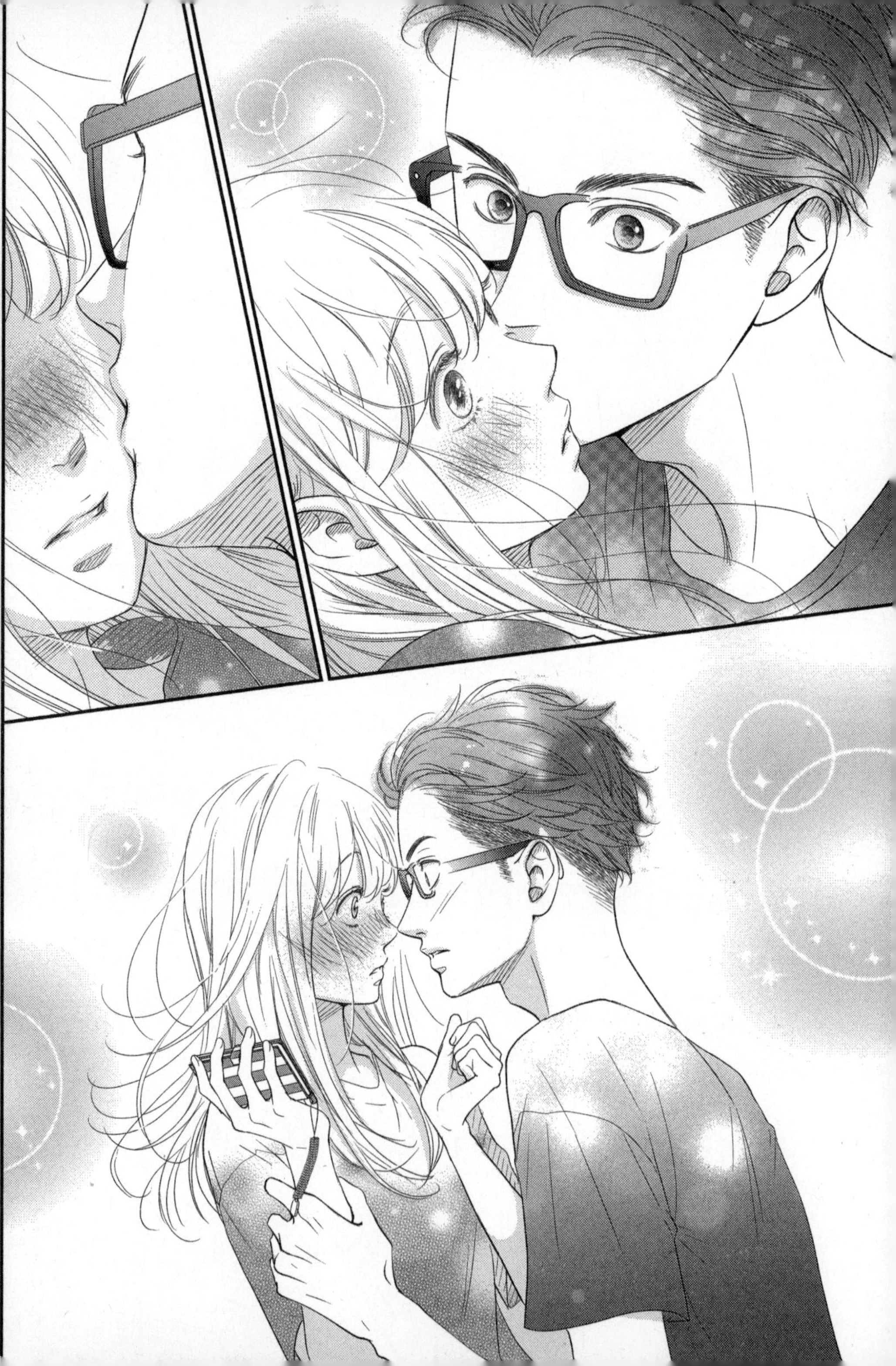

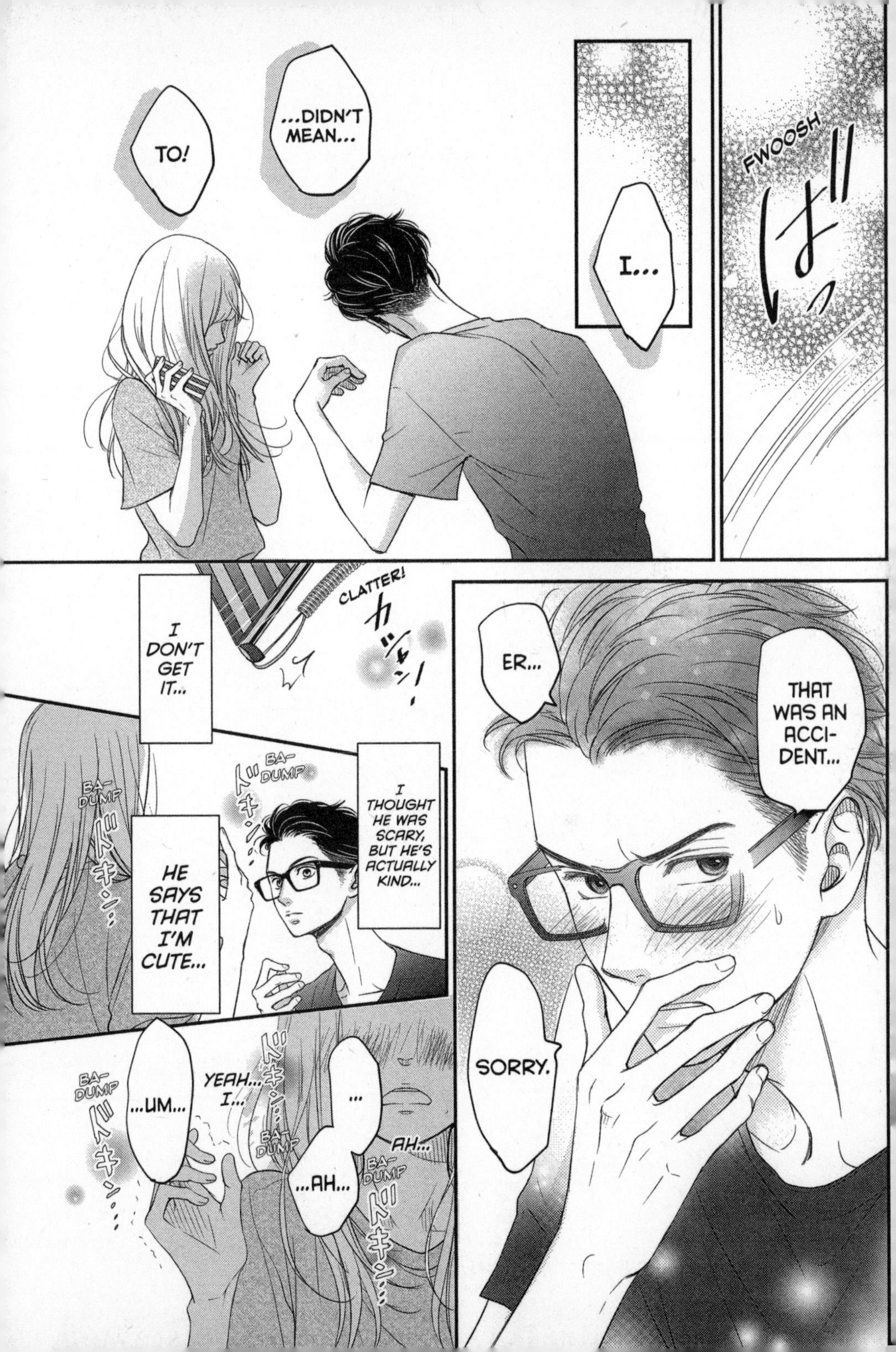
FWOOSH
ばっ
I...
...DIDN'T MEAN...
TO!
ER...
THAT WAS AN ACCI-DENT...
SORRY.
CLATTER!
カシャン!
I DON'T GET IT...
BA-DUMP
ドキン
I THOUGHT HE WAS SCARY, BUT HE'S ACTUALLY KIND...
HE SAYS THAT I'M CUTE...
BA-DUMP
ドキン
...
AH...
BA-DUMP
ドキン
...AH...
BA-DUMP
ドキン
YEAH... I...
...UM...
BA-DUMP
ドキン

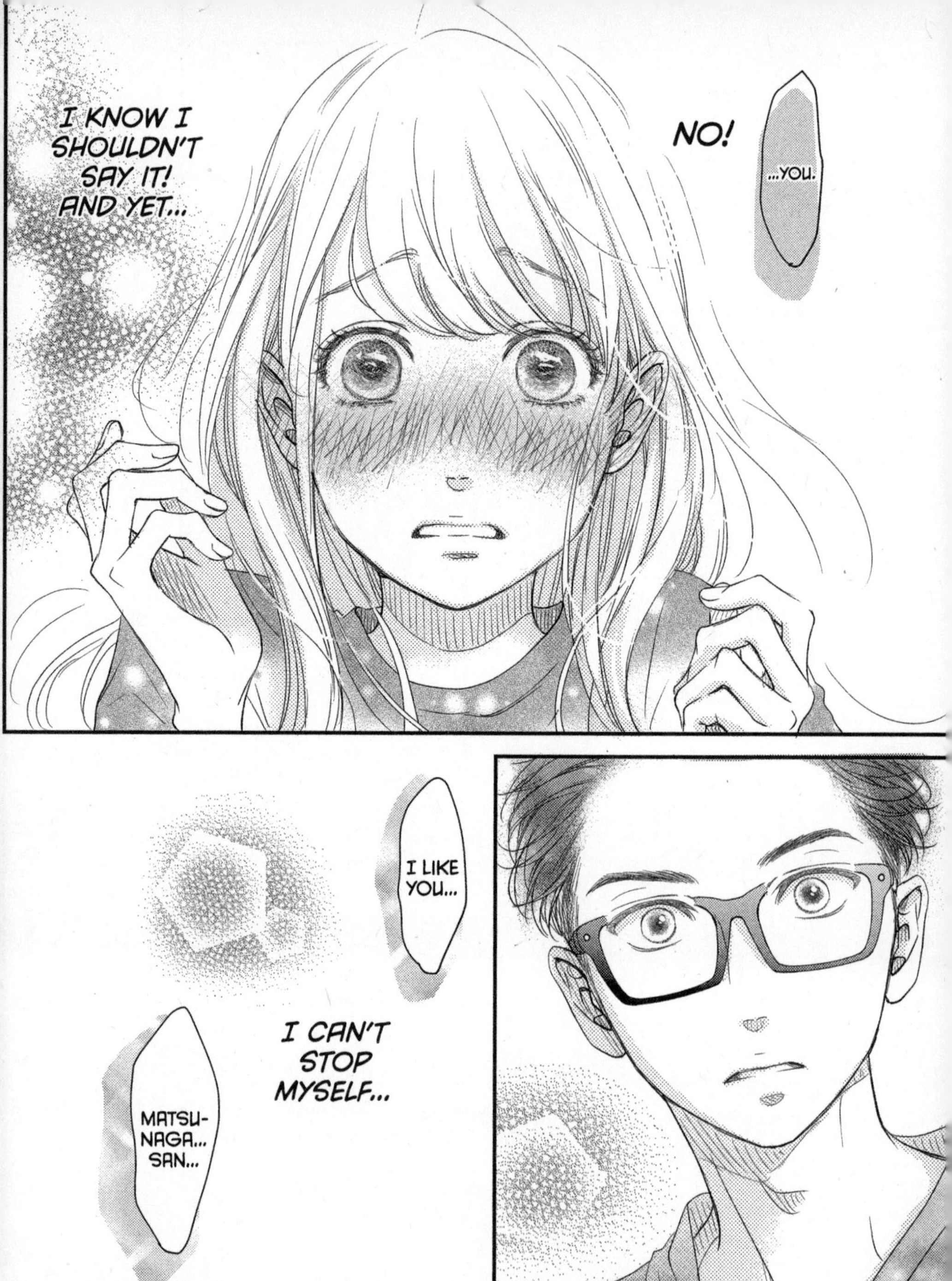
...YOU.
NO!
I KNOW I SHOULDN'T SAY IT! AND YET...
I LIKE YOU...
I CAN'T STOP MYSELF...
MATSU-NAGA... SAN...

TO BE CONTINUED IN VOLUME 2

LIVING-ROOM♦MATSUNAGA-SAN

THANK YOU FOR BUYING VOLUME 1 OF *LIVING-ROOM MATSUNAGA-SAN!*

THIS IS MY FIRST NEW PUBLICATION IN ABOUT A YEAR! WERE YOU EXCITED? PLEASE HAVE FUN WITH THESE NEW CHARACTERS.♡

♡SPECIAL THANKS♡

COLLABORATORS

NOBUAKI NAKAJIMA
EVERYONE AT UNITE

ASSISTANTS
EI
--CHIMI

THANK YOU SO MUCH FOR ALWAYS MAKING AMAZING BACKGROUNDS!

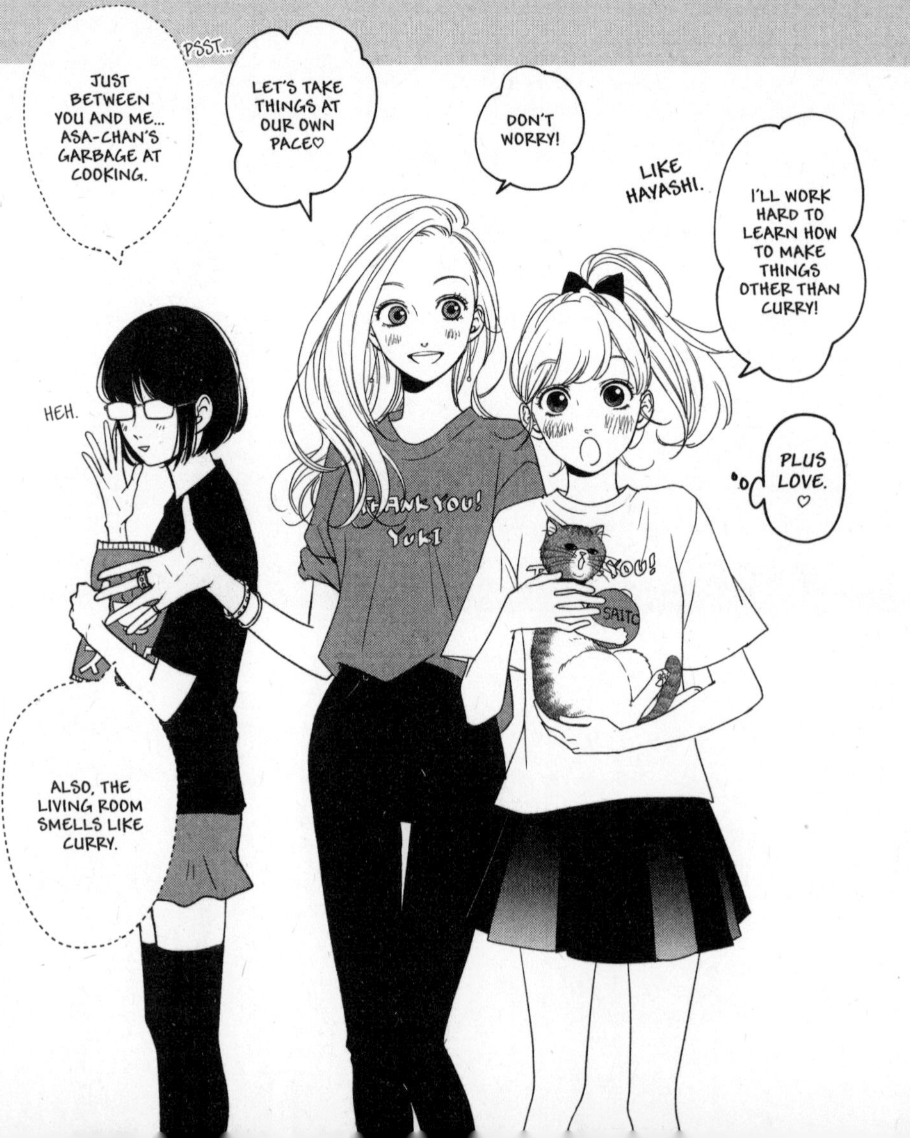
I'LL WORK HARD TO LEARN HOW TO MAKE THINGS OTHER THAN CURRY!
LIKE HAYASHI.
PLUS LOVE. ♡
DON'T WORRY!
LET'S TAKE THINGS AT OUR OWN PACE♡
PSST...
JUST BETWEEN YOU AND ME... ASA-CHAN'S GARBAGE AT COOKING.
HEH.
ALSO, THE LIVING ROOM SMELLS LIKE CURRY.

KEIKO
IWASHITA

2017.5.12

EDITOR KITAHARA
EVERYONE IN THE DESSERT EDITORIAL DEPARTMENT
THE DESIGNERS
EVERYONE AT THE PRINTER

MY FRIENDS AND FAMILY

AND
ALL MY READERS

THANK YOU, FROM THE BOTTOM OF MY HEART.

LET'S MEET AGAIN IN VOLUME 2!!

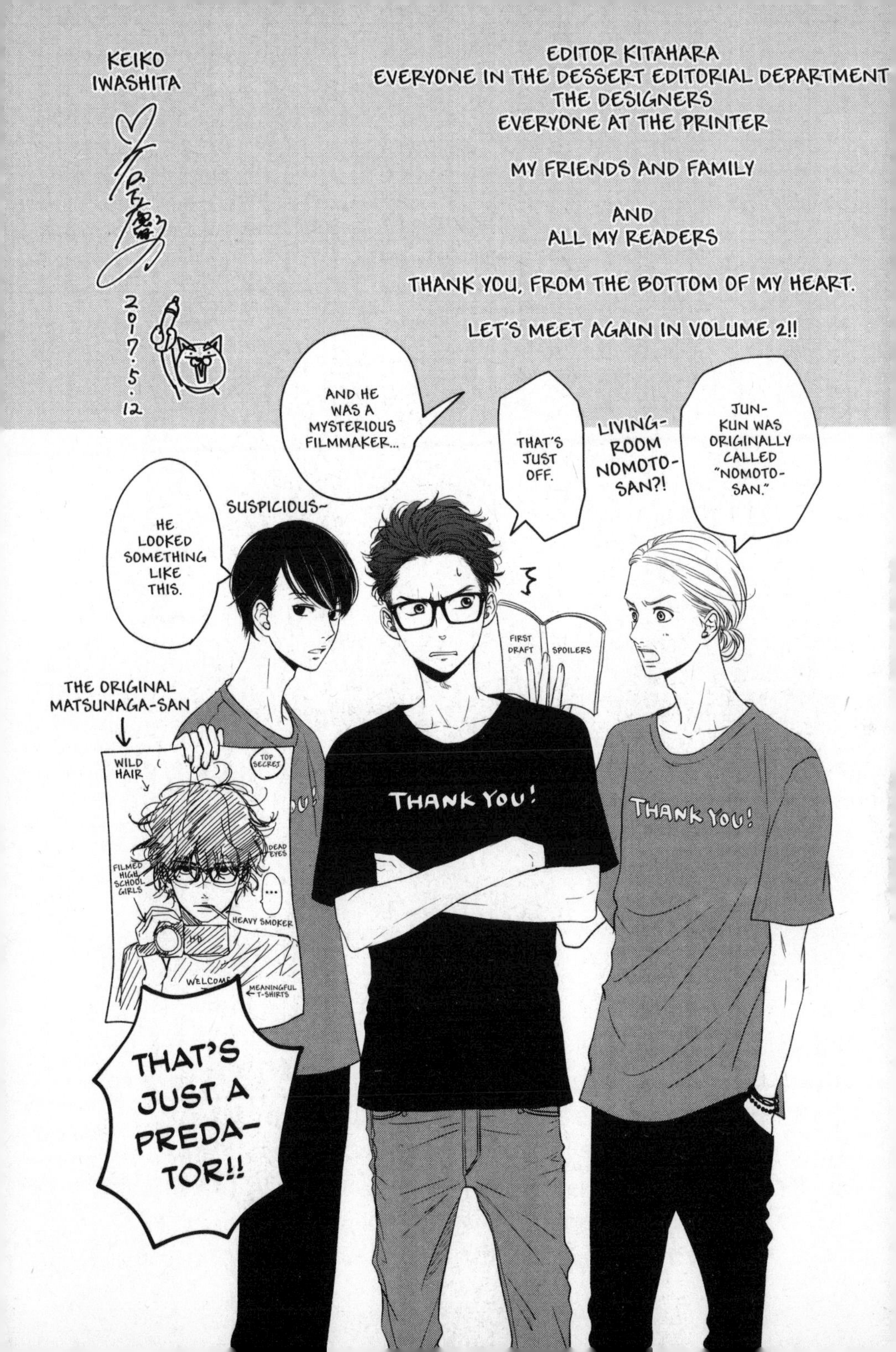

JUN-KUN WAS ORIGINALLY CALLED "NOMOTO-SAN."
LIVING-ROOM NOMOTO-SAN?!
THAT'S JUST OFF.
AND HE WAS A MYSTERIOUS FILMMAKER...
SUSPICIOUS~
HE LOOKED SOMETHING LIKE THIS.
FIRST DRAFT
SPOILERS
THANK YOU!
THANK YOU!
THE ORIGINAL MATSUNAGA-SAN
TOP SECRET
WILD HAIR
DEAD EYES
FILMED HIGH SCHOOL GIRLS
...
HEAVY SMOKER
WELCOME
MEANINGFUL T-SHIRTS
THAT'S JUST A PREDATOR!!

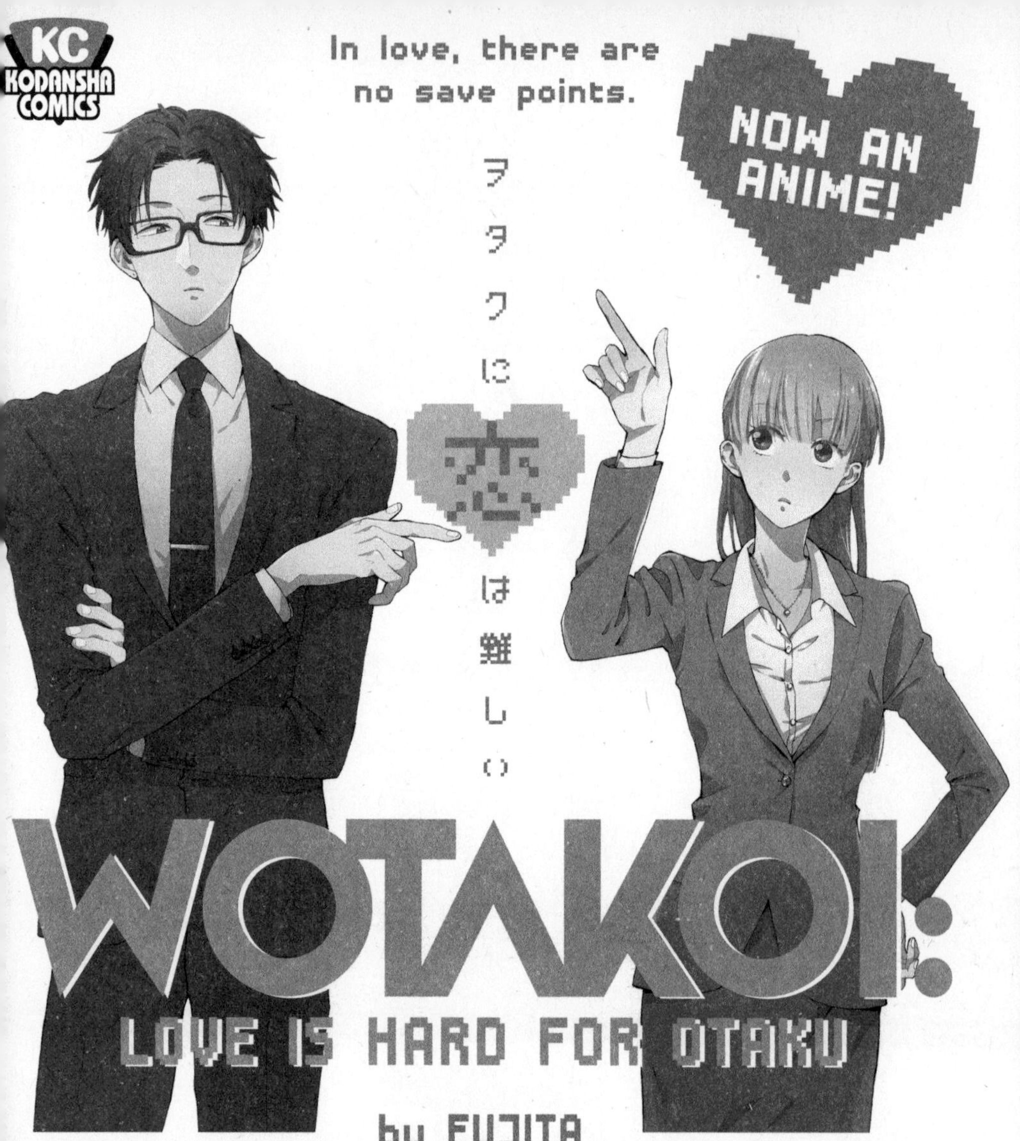
KC
KODANSHA COMICS
In love, there are no save points.
NOW AN ANIME!
ヲタクに恋は難しい
WOTAKOI:
LOVE IS HARD FOR OTAKU
by FUJITA

Narumi has had it rough: Every boyfriend she's had dumped her once they found out she was an otaku, so she's gone to great lengths to hide it. At her new job, she bumps into Hirotaka, her childhood friend and fellow otaku. When Hirotaka almost gets her secret outed at work, she comes up with a plan to keep him quiet. But he comes up with a counter-proposal: Why doesn't she just date him instead?

A Kodansha Comics Trade Paperback Original
Living-Room Matsunaga-san 1 copyright © 2017 Keiko Iwashita
English translation copyright © 2020 Keiko Iwashita

All rights reserved.

Published in the United States by Kodansha Comics, an imprint of Kodansha USA Publishing, LLC, New York.

Publication rights for this English edition arranged through Kodansha Ltd., Tokyo.

First published in Japan in 2017 by Kodansha Ltd., Tokyo as *Living no Matsunaga-san*, volume 1.

ISBN 978-1-63236-813-3

Original cover design by Tomohiro Kusume and Yuu Ikeda (arcoinc)

Printed in the United States of America.

www.kodanshacomics.com

9 8 7 6 5 4 3 2 1
Translation: Ursula Ku
Lettering: Dawne Law
Additional Lettering: Mike Martin
Editing: Ean Scrale and Tiff Ferentini
Kodansha Comics edition cover design by Phil Balsman

Publisher: Kiichiro Sugawara
Managing editor: Maya Rosewood
Vice president of marketing & publicity: Naho Yamada

Director of publishing services: Ben Applegate
Associate director of operations: Stephen Pakula
Publishing services managing editor: Noelle Webster
Assistant production manager: Emi Lotto